Also by Tom Mann

Desert Sorrow: asylum seekers at Woomera
Flawed Forensics: the Splatt case and Stewart Cockburn
Jericho Man (with Kent Lines)
Body in the Freezer: the case of David Szach
Two Fine Ladies

Launching out from
Scotland

Journeys, challenges and encounters

Tom Mann

BALBOA.
PRESS
A DIVISION OF HAY HOUSE

Balboa Press books may be ordered through booksellers or by contacting:

Balboa Press
A Division of Hay House
1663 Liberty Drive
Bloomington, IN 47403
www.balboapress.com.au
1 (877) 407-4847

Print information available on the last page.

ISBN: 978-1-5043-0384-2 (sc)
ISBN: 978-1-5043-0383-5 (e)

Balboa Press rev. date: 08/16/2016

For Liz, Rachel, Linda and families

Contents

Preface

I WROTE MY MEMOIRS PRINCIPALLY to pass on to family, friends, and for anyone with a passion for adventure. I also wrote to discover meaning in life's journey.

Life, I have found, is an adventure, of learning, being open, sharing and finding oneself in an ongoing journey that never ceases. *Launching out from Scotland: journeys, challenges and encounters* shares that passion. I hope my story is an absorbing and inspirational read.

A special thanks to family, friends and to those who have helped in shaping my career and journey through life. I am indebted to editorial comments and suggestions from Jan McInerney. I especially appreciate the support of my wife, Liz.

Introduction

BORN INTO THE ARENA OF war, I spend my first years in Norfolk, England, before growing up as a young lad in Elgin, a city in the north-east of Scotland. I do not think of travelling to distant lands. Later, in my early twenties, it dawns on me that a world outside Scotland is waiting. After brief forays to England, France and Israel, I migrate to Australia, possibly to stay two years but, I stay instead, fifty-two, and still counting.

While settling down in Australia, my agricultural career takes off with opportunities to work in Algeria, Pakistan, Bangladesh and China; to visit an orphanage in India; and to carry out a village study in West Timor.

I confront issues that include the cruelty and effects of war, the plight of refugees, homeless children, the growing of poppies for opium, agricultural and village development, land degradation, mental health, suicide, and miscarriages of justice. With a light-hearted approach, I try to make each situation as real as possible with anecdotes and short accounts relating to those challenges and personal encounters.

As well as focusing on journeys, challenges and encounters in these countries, I portray vistas of the wonders of parts of Australia, New Zealand and the Scottish Highlands. I bring everything back to my home turf with challenges I face in South Australia.

Chapter 1

War beginnings

I WAS BORN ON 30 April 1941 when the German Army conquered Greece with the capture of 7,000 British forces. At Tobruk, on the same day, the Germans and Italians launched an attack against the Australians but were defeated. And from the Habbaniya airbase outside Baghdad, the British attacked the Iraqis who had supported Nazi anti-Semitism.

What a strange phenomenon to born into! But, of course, for me nothing would register about the war for some years. Even stranger, when I look back, was the reticence of most to talk about the follies of war and the effects on those who had survived. Was it for our protection? Perhaps children of my era were too young to understand? Or was it something deep within our psyche to enable us to go on living? I still wonder.

I have been fortunate in not engaging in war or to have trained as a conscript. I feel, however, that I have walked in the shadows of war for the latter half of the 20th century and the first part of the 21st.

My first brush with war was about one month after my birth, in May 1941. Mum had put me in a pram at her home in Aylsham, Norfolk. She wheeled the pram to the far side of a tennis court and placed it under a weeping ash tree. She left me to sleep. A short time later she heard the air raid sirens and looked up to see a German plane with a Swastika on it, skimming over the top of the cedar tree

1

in front of my grandfather's house. Machine gun bullets rattled on the leaves. She tried to rush across the tennis court but her legs felt leaden. It was as though she were in a dream. She reached the pram and moved me to a shelter near the house.

A few weeks later bombs fell nearby and everyone crouched together in the hall until they heard the 'all clear'. The German planes targeted the Norfolk airfields, but they were not averse to unleashing their bombs on non-military targets.

We were lucky not to be hit, but tragedy of a different kind *did* strike our Norfolk home. My twin cousins, Anthony and Warren, were born the day after me to my mother's brother, Tom, and his American wife, Elinor. A few months later Elinor committed suicide. Compassionate leave was granted to Tom, grandfather's first son. He was due to accompany his regiment out to Singapore to fight against the Japanese who had invaded Malaya. Two days after the Norfolk regiment arrived in Singapore, they were overrun by the Japanese army and interned. A great number of them died on the infamous Burma Railway. Tom was saved because of a personal tragedy. Several months later, he met Peggy Cotterell, who had lost her husband in a car crash. They married and had three children, Jane, Jonathan and Peter. In 2001 they celebrated their diamond wedding, just before Peggy died. I realised that the tragedy of war often weaved its own kind of fortune.

Mum's sister Dorothy and brother John also became embroiled in the Second World War. Dorothy loved horse riding but hated school. When she made friends she kept them for life. She joined the Red Cross and, at the outbreak of the war, she was told to report to a small unit in West Norfolk. When she arrived, she asked a young woman, 'Who should I report to?'

'No one,' was the reply.

'Well, who is in charge?' asked Dorothy.

'You are,' the woman replied. Dorothy then moved to a hospital in Kent and became quite used to taking cover when the doodle bugs, or flying bombs, came over.

Later, Dorothy was posted to a general hospital at Nocera, south of Naples in Italy. It was not long before she became desperately ill with jaundice and was put on the danger list. She recovered, and, at the end of the war, accompanied the Army through north-east Italy into Austria. On one occasion Russian forces stopped to pull the ambulance, in which she was travelling, out of a ditch. On returning to England, Dorothy passed her exams to become a registered nurse.

Doffy, as we called her, was my ideal aunt — gentle, loving and considerate. Later, Dorothy cared for my grandfather and grandmother at their home in Aylsham. After the death of my grandparents — grandmother in 1958, and grandfather in 1960 — she lived in a bungalow built for her in Foulsham. She lived happily until 1989 when her heart gradually began to fail. Mum's brother Tom recalls, when visiting her in the evening at the West Norwich Hospital, that her face was a picture of serene contentment. She died the following morning.

Uncle John joined the West African Division in Nigeria at the outbreak of war and went as part of a reconnaissance regiment into Burma — often behind Japanese lines. His batman saved his life when he spotted a sniper sitting in a tree waiting for them to pass.

John's regiment was fed by air drop, but the parachute with the officers' mess stores did not open so the whisky bottles were always broken. However, when one lot fell on very soft ground, the bottles were intact, but they contained cold tea. What a letdown! John was convinced that it was the experience of walking over jungle-clad Burmese hills carrying a laden pack that led to his needing no fewer than five hip replacements in later life.

After the war, John became a colonial administrator in Northern Nigeria. In the summer of 1953 the region was in turmoil with inter-tribal and inter-religious conflict. In Kano, one of the major cities, tensions gave way to mob violence. John, as district officer, often moved by foot through the city, armed only with a walking stick. With disregard for his safety, he intervened several times to prevent deaths of individuals, including the rescue of a beaten man from a well. He helped quell the angry mobs by appealing to reason. His actions were recognised by an Order of the British Empire (OBE) award.

While in Northern Nigeria, John treated everyone with courtesy and respect, and many of the leaders became personal friends. As part of the collapse of the British Empire, he participated in the transfer of power to local leaders and in Nigeria's independence. On his retirement the new premier of Northern Nigeria nominated John for a Companion of the Order of St Michael and St George (CMG).

Back home John took up an appointment as bursar to Gresham's school in Holt, Norfolk. He married Elizabeth Sharp and they had three children, Robert, Andrew and Susanna. I admired John greatly and attended their wedding ceremony when I was sixteen.

War brought Mum and Dad together. It was soon after the outbreak of war, when the Seaforth Highlanders were stationed near Aylsham, and word came around that they were having a party on St Andrew's night, 30 November 1939. Three Voluntary Aid Detachment (VAD) members were invited and they drew lots as to who should go. That morning, Mum was cooking the lunch, and Paddy, an Irish batman assigned to help in the cleaning, said, 'You are to meet someone in a navy blue uniform and fall in love with him.' That was before she heard that she had won a place to go to the party. Dad saw Anne Purdy that night from the far end of the table and decided that she was the girl he was going to marry. They met a few days later ... and the mess kit of the Seaforth Highlanders *was* navy blue.

But Mum recounts a different story of their first meeting in London:

> I was studying at the Slade Art School, doing my diploma in art, which I must have completed a year or two before the war. I must have had an appointment near the city and took a number 73 bus which goes down Tottenham Court Road, crosses Oxford Street

and continues down Charing Cross Road. It's a very busy intersection and in those days there were no lights and there would be a policeman on duty, directing the traffic. I was sitting on top of the bus and we were held up as usual at the crossroads. As we moved on, I glanced at the tall policeman directing the traffic, and an inside voice said to me, as clear as anything, 'That is the man you are going to marry.' So I turned around to a have a good look at him. All I could see was a huge bobby's helmet and a round face underneath it. Then I forgot all about it, saying to myself, 'How silly can you be?' It wasn't until after we were married that I realised that Tom, being in the Metropolitan Police, in the Tottenham Court Road Branch, might very likely have been directing the traffic at that intersection.

On my Scots side, Dad excelled at sport at Elgin Academy, the main school in Elgin, Morayshire, north-east Scotland. His sporting prowess, however, did not transfer to the classroom. He drove his maths teacher to distraction as she tried her hardest to get him through lower maths. On the sports side, though, he led the Elgin Academy athletic team to win the North of Scotland schools' trophy at Inverness. He also played for Moray Rugby Club. In his last year at the academy he led the Scottish contingent of scouts to the World Scout Jamboree in Hungary in 1933.

Having left Elgin Academy, Dad joined the metropolitan police and was stationed at Tottenham Court Road — an elite station in the heart of busy London and 'a little bewildering for an Elgin loon' as he described it. In the first week on the beat, and having directed folk to places like Golders Green, he wandered around a few blocks and got completely lost. In the end he had to ask another policeman the way back to the section house. He found the training at Peel House hard with everything done 'at the double'.

Dad had studied German at school and corresponded with a German pen pal, whom he visited just prior to Neville Chamberlain's war announcement. 'Can you believe it?' he said later. 'I had to go and fight against my German friend.'

Dad fought briefly in France as a platoon commander. He had left Elgin with the 6th Battalion of the Seaforth Highlanders. The adjutant, a regular soldier, according to my father, was a bully of the worst possible kind and took very good care never to set foot in Elgin again, where there was a posse waiting for him.

In France, Dad's battalion very early on received a devastating blow when two of his battalion were gunned down by the Manchester machine gun battalion, who had been told that the next troops coming around the bend in the road were Germans. Both men fortunately recovered and were invalided out of the army.

Dad was the next to be wounded, this time by unfriendly shell fire from the Germans near Arras. At Dunkirk beach a medic grimaced on examining him and shook his head. Ignoring the odds, and with German fighter planes strafing the beach, Dad rallied to be evacuated by boat across the English Channel.

Many years later, while living in Australia, Dad said that it was akin to treason, no doubt, to voice any derogatory remarks of the local battalion in his home town of Elgin. But he was far enough away to say that they were a 'pretty poor lot, bearing little resemblance to the highly regarded and well-decorated battalion of the 1914 war.' According to Dad, the lack of ability of the commanding officer and adjutant had a lot to do with it.

After returning from France, and still recovering from his injuries, Dad in his kilt, and Mum looking radiant, married on 23 July 1940 at the Davyhulme hospital in Manchester with a guard of honour from the hospital sisters.

Although Dad was not fully fit, medically, he was appointed adjutant of Inverness Home Guard under the command of Lord Gough. Their main aim was to prepare against a German airborne attack. For this, the main weapons were huge petrol drums dug into the side of the road and ready to explode on passing enemy forces. Dad's guess was that, if operational, the explosions would have killed more of his own men than the Germans. He imagined them sitting at the roadside with their fuses ready to light, but with the Germans advancing across the fields in open formation, instead of marching up the road in fours. 'How stupid we would look,' he said.

Mum grew up in Aylsham in Norfolk and in her early years she developed a passion for poetry and painting. She attended the Slade School of Art at London University where she gained the Diploma of Fine Art. She continued with her interest in poems and painting as an art teacher in a school in Norfolk.

Mum was called up as a mobile volunteer at the outbreak of war, but she didn't have time for her fortnight's training in London. She had no knowledge of working in a ward so she asked her family doctor for a few hints on taking a pulse, temperature and respiration. The doctor told her to grasp the patient's hand firmly, to steady it, and place two fingers on the pulse, but not to use her thumb. On her first day in the ward she followed his advice. Her first patient looked surprised but made no comment when his hand was grasped firmly. The next one grinned from ear to ear and the third one squeezed her hand. Embarrassed, she went around the whole ward, each time her hand held firmly by the patient. She never made that mistake again, but being raw to the regime all the volunteers made mistakes. Her group had actually been assigned as a gas decontaminating squad but, as there was no gas, they were absorbed into the general working of the hospital as the wards began to fill. I don't think Mum was cut out for nursing duties. She was relieved when they asked for a volunteer to cook for the twelve VADs.

Dad spent part of his recovery at my grandfather's place in Aylsham. My grandfather Tom Purdy was lucky to be alive considering he survived the Gallipoli campaign. He had joined the Volunteers which became the Territorial Army. At the outbreak of the First World War in August 1914 he was second-in-command of the 5th Battalion Norfolk regiment. In 1915 the regiment sailed on the *Aquitania* for Gallipoli in Turkey and landed at Suvla Bay where the Australian and New Zealand forces should have landed.

They had been swept south by the strong tide. He was one of three surviving officers from the battalion going into battle on 12 August 1915 against the Turks on the Gallipoli peninsula.

The commander-in-chief, Sir Ian Hamilton, had decided to take Anafarta Ridge overlooking Suvla Bay. Colonel Horace Beauchamp, a self-confident officer, led the battalion into battle. As the men advanced into terrain wooded with stunted oaks, the fighting grew fierce with machine gun and sniper fire. Many were wounded, including my grandfather and two other officers. A sniper had hit Grandad in the side and also shattered a bone in his arm. He and others, who were wounded early on in the engagement, were the lucky ones; they were taken back to the camp during the night. But Colonel Beauchamp, with 16 officers and 250 men, kept pushing on — and then they disappeared in a 'strange cloud', which Ian Hamilton described as 'a very mysterious thing'.

To add to the mystery, two Gallipoli soldiers described later how they had seen the cloud which hid them from sight, and when it had lifted, the men had 'disappeared'. The account became a legend with a book *The vanished battalion* by Nigel McCrery. The book led to a BBC-TV documentary drama production *All the King's men*. A number of the soldiers were volunteers and had been employed at the royal residence of Sandringham Estate.

What had happened was that the Turks took no prisoners. After the war 180 bodies were recovered. Many had been killed behind the Turkish line and in a farm area, according to a local Turk who owned the place. He had returned to his farm after the fighting and found the whole area covered with decomposing bodies of British soldiers. He threw the bodies into a small ravine.

After the Gallipoli campaign my grandfather recovered to rejoin the regiment which was sent to Egypt. They marched through the Sinai Desert on one pint of water per man per day. Eventually they engaged the Turks in the Second Battle of Gaza and had to attack over open country to the east of the town. The Turks were well-prepared with machine guns and the regiment was again decimated, every company commander being a casualty. Wounded again, but not seriously, my grandfather was put in charge of a prisoner-of-war camp in Egypt.

Grandad never talked about the war, and I was too young anyway to appreciate what he had gone through. My cousin Jane recalled his ability to talk to all kinds of people: princes, paupers, privates, generals, laymen and archbishops, because he knew such a lot about a wide range of subjects. He was able to express genuine interest in what they had to say and to make everyone feel that they were the most important person. He was a generous man, freely giving of his time to all. And he made sure his guests were looked after with a bottle of wine appearing from his cellar before dinner, and, if more than four guests had joined him, another bottle was brought out.

Grandad loved his garden and so did the rabbits. He picked them off from his dressing room window with his 'garden gun'. When anyone else tried to use the gun the rabbit was in luck and escaped. 'Oh yes,' he would say, 'you have to aim a little high and two feet to the right.' On one occasion, I accompanied Grandad, a shotgun under his armpit, up the dirt driveway leading away from the house. A rabbit shot out from underneath a rhododendron bush. Grandad swung the gun around and took aim, but the rabbit raced to the other side of the road passing close to Grandad's legs. He thought better of taking the shot and the rabbit disappeared into the bushes.

Grandmother Nona Purdy had a vivacious personality and was an excellent horsewoman. She was commandant of the Red Cross Voluntary Aid Detachment at Aylsham in Norfolk. As war clouds gathered, my grandmother had to go to the local school at Aylsham to receive a batch of schoolboys from Bethnal Green, London. They were to stay at their home, called Woodgate House, a large red-bricked two-storey home with an attic and a facade of nine bays.

Fearing an invasion of a different kind, Mum and sister Dorothy worked non-stop on a hot summer's day to clean the attic of all the mattresses and the front drawing-room of ornaments and china. They rolled the mattresses down the attic stairs and down the hall staircase into the drawing room. A call came through to say that 27 boys and three masters were on their way. With an urgent plea from my grandmother, Mum and Dorothy raced around to have everything ready.

In the excitement, Esse, their ever hot cooker, was forgotten. Fuel-less, it went out that night. The next morning, my grandmother didn't panic and cooked breakfast on two primus cookers for the whole lot. They stayed a fortnight and my mum remembered standing in the front dining room with the boys and their masters when they heard Neville Chamberlain announce, *We are now at war with Germany.* 'A solemn moment for us all,' she told me later.

My grandfather was on Home Guard duty during the war while my grandmother helped drive the ambulance, frequently having to take soldiers on duty to hospital when they were injured. On the coast near Mundesley, the Home Guard had to keep continuous watch for fear of a beach invasion. They had first aid equipment and large stone bottles of rum, carefully stopped up and sealed as part of the emergency provisions. On being returned at the end of the war, the rum bottles, with stoppers still intact, were empty and with no visible sign of leakage. The guards, they found out, had methodically drained the rum off with hypodermic syringes.

On one occasion, my grandmother was out one dark and wet night in an ambulance with two untrained helpers. They had gone to pick up a soldier who was in great pain with acute appendicitis. They put him onto a stretcher, but the volunteers had not carried anyone before and twice ditched the man into a muddy field. They eventually arrived at the hospital in Cromer. My grandmother made sure later on that the soldier had recovered from his appendicitis and from other discomforts he would have had on the way.

One of grandmother's brothers, Gerald, and my great-uncle, also fought at Gallipoli and was said to be the last soldier evacuated in the withdrawal.

Another of grandmother's brothers, John, had specialised in chemistry and researched tanning methods. He set up a factory in Smyrna, an ancient Greek city on the Aegean coast of Anatolia, and known today as Izmir. After the end of the First World War, Greece occupied Smyrna from May 1919, but the Turkish army of Kemal Ataturk regained control of the city on 9 September 1922. Four days later the Great Fire of Smyrna resulted in a massacre of thousands of Greeks and Armenians. Somehow, John was able to evacuate all the Greeks from his factory and escape under the cover of darkness in a boat with muffled oars.

* * *

While staying at Inverness with Mum and Dad, my brother Frank was born in 1944. He was named after great-uncle Frank who had been a rector of a church in Toddington, Bedfordshire. Mum was in a private ward in a nursing home at the time. Two nurses were making the beds when the mail arrived. They chatted about something they had heard on the news, about a Norfolk woman dreaming of a German parachuting down near where she lived and ringing up the police station to report on the dream about the landing. While they were chatting, Mum read a letter from my grandmother describing how a friend of hers, Monica Buckingham, had had a dream about a German pilot whose plane was about to crash, and the pilot parachuting to a place which Monica could recognise in her dream. So, of course, Mum read out the letter to the nurses, who could scarcely believe they were getting a first-hand account.

After the war, we all moved back to my mother's home in Aylsham. Frank and I often went fishing in a pond on the farm, but, although we saw those magnificent pike and perch, we never caught them. I remember once Frank falling into the pond and coming out soaked. Another time, I could not open the bathroom door with the key so I threw it out of the window in the hope that someone might retrieve it and rescue me. But the key fell into a water tank and was lost. Eventually, after an hour, someone did come to my rescue.

In 1948 we moved to our new home in Swannington, a small village nearby and about 14 kilometres north of Norwich. I remember walking to the village school, about two kilometres away from our home. What I learnt at school was precious little.

Dad appeared to suffer more from emotional trauma than physical injury from the after effects of war. It was termed 'shell shock' but became more defined as 'war-related stress or post-traumatic stress disorder'. For the First and Second World War victims there was no counselling or help to cope with settling back into civilian life. It was more or less expected that stress-related disorders would subside with time.

Despite post-war effects on Dad's mental state, he managed to find a job as a salesman with Norfolk Canneries. In 1948, when I had just turned seven, he decided I would be better off with a Scottish education and sent me to his home town, Elgin, in north-east Scotland to stay with my grandmother. I would keep her company as she had been a widow living on her own for over twelve years after the loss of my paternal grandfather in 1936. My grandmother struggled to survive with a meagre income from one or two boarders.

I missed Mum and Dad, and my brother Frank, but I don't remember being bitter or resentful or even pining with being sent away from the family home. My grandmother was strict, like most Scottish grandmothers in those days; if something were not to her liking, I would not get away with it. She was fair; I could always go out to play if I had done my homework. And a shilling a week pocket money kept me content with a trip to the local sweet shop for a bag of humbugs. I had to do my fair share of household chores like chop wood and fetch coal from the cellar for lighting the fire. After school, she dished up toast and dripping. I scoffed the lot down while listening to Scottish music, especially liking the skirl of the bagpipes, on grandmother's croaky wireless.

I collected spare money for Guy Fawkes Night. One year, I could not resist lighting a sparkler in my grandmother's back garden, a few days before the night. The sparks flew over to my box of sparklers, squibs, Catherine wheels and rockets. I watched, powerless to do anything, as everything that I had cherished for that special night disappeared in two minutes of chaotic explosion — more like a fire-and-brimstone display. I was disgusted with myself. If only I had been patient enough to wait for the night and do things properly.

On one occasion a female boarder slapped me across the face. She probably had good reason. Grandmother came to my rescue and told her off in no uncertain terms. Shortly after, the boarder left. My grandmother said, 'Good riddance.'

My paternal grandfather, Thomas Mann, was born in Banff in 1885 and started his florist business in Elgin in 1912. He became an expert in floral design, which attracted business from many in Scotland and England, including royalty. During the First World War he grew food for the forces. He became very active in business and civic affairs; he was a town councillor and responsible for the resuscitation of the Elgin Horticultural Society. In sport he became president of the Morayshire Junior Football Club and an official with Elgin City Football Club. He won many trophies as a member of the Elgin Bowling Club. As a staunch freemason, he was an office bearer of Lodge Moray and a member of the Moray Royal Arch Charter. He was also an elder of Holy Trinity Church, Elgin. He died from a heart attack in 1936, five years before I was born, at the age of 51.

Dad, an only child, said, 'He was a good father, but was always so occupied with business and civic affairs that I never got as close as I should have. He never did me harm and never uttered an angry word to me, although there must have been many justifiable occasions. For my part, I always held him in very high respect.' How true those words would echo for me.

My great-grandfather Adam Mann, a head gardener in Banff, had, according to my father, nine brothers and one sister, but that was not the story we gleaned from family records which showed that Adam had 17 children, some of whom died at a young age. Dad had conveniently missed them out or didn't know about them.

One of Adam's sons, Thomas, married my grandmother, Jeannie Brockie, in 1911 and like the majority of married women of the time, her life centred on the running of the household. But she also helped to run the florist shop and nursery. On my grandfather's death, she took over the shop, and, armed with courage and sacrifice, but with no real business experience, kept it going during the Second World War. Cut flowers came from Covent Garden in London. After the war her health gave out and she had to sell the shop and eke out an existence by taking in boarders. She became a very important person to me in my growing-up years in Elgin.

Both my Scottish and English forebears had taken part in military campaigns overseas or served as district officers in Britain's colonial empire. The Highland Scots, having emerged from the highland clearances, and with little choice of farming except near the coast, struggled to earn a living. Only a few could inherit farming or fishing occupations. The rest migrated further south or overseas, or joined Scottish regiments. My English forebears saw the army, though, in a different way — they trained to become high-ranking officers. They served in India, Ceylon (now Sri Lanka), South Africa, Persia (now Iran) and the Far East.

I wonder, though, why war has been alongside us from the dawn of human existence; we have yet to progress beyond war. Perhaps war or the potential for war is wired into our genetic make-up. War affects us all in different ways. Some experience the horrors of war first-hand. Others suffer from the effects of war. Feelings of animosity pass down from generation to generation. Descendants share the chains of forebears. Suspicion and mistrust hover near the surface ready to uproot in fresh conflict. Ethnic, religious, cultural and family differences add to the tensions. On a global front, the scramble for resources, the economic divide between rich and poor, population increase and the impoverishment of the environment, all threaten the tenuous threads of peace and harmony among us. Must war and its aftermath be a part of our existence? At a young age I hardly ever thought about war and its consequences, but that took a turnaround later.

Chapter 2

Schooling days

I COMPLETED MY PRIMARY SCHOOLING at Springfield, the primary school attached to Elgin Academy. When I first arrived I displaced the lad at the bottom of the class. He was elated, and I realised that I couldn't add, spell, write or read. I never knew that I lacked so many skills. What had happened in the English classroom? Anyhow, our teacher, Ms Stewart, must have recognised a glimmer of hope and, wherever possible, encouraged me to catch up to the rest of the class. It worked. By the end of the second year at Springfield, I had moved in overall performance to the middle of the class. Ms Stewart was delighted and instituted a special end-of-year progress prize for students like me. She presented me with a book about the story of a spy in France during the Second World War, which I cherished. I kept in touch with Ms Stewart over the years until she passed away at the age of 96. Her enthusiasm for learning was infectious — I caught the bug, and this never waned with the passage of time.

When I was eleven, I took the Control Exam for entry into the appropriate class at Elgin Academy. The kids from different primary schools in Elgin were streamed into 1A, 1B, 1C and other classes. I ended up in 1B, but by the middle of the year I had come top of the class, and Duncan Davidson, a friend of mine, came second. They promoted us to 1A.

Elgin Academy was regarded as one of the premier schools in the country. The school won the prized BBC Top of the Form radio national schools quiz in 1949 and again in 1972. Elgin's school beginnings date back to 1224 with the foundation of Elgin Cathedral.

In our class I valued the friendship of Alan Macartney who seemed to breeze through his subjects with an impish smile on his face. With his quips and repartee he was a real live wire. He managed to come top of the class without too much effort. I recall our French teacher, Mrs Sinclair, correcting his exercises while Alan stood alongside her desk. Alan had hooked a white rubber skeleton to his back with a tube leading from the back of the skeleton to a bulb hidden in his hand. While the teacher discussed his work, he pressed the bulb and the skeleton extended its arms and legs in full view of the class. The class responded in laughter, much to the bewilderment of Mrs Sinclair. This went on repeatedly with Mrs Sinclair becoming more and more perplexed with the sudden outbursts of laughter. Eventually, Alan had to walk backwards to his seat to avoid revealing the source of the merriment. That was Alan. No malice to his humour — just good fun. We kept in touch over the years while he became a highly respected deputy leader of the Scottish National Party and rector of Aberdeen University. He also represented north-east Scotland in the European Parliament. Allan died at the age of 57 from a heart attack, but his life had touched many with his wise advice and gentle humour. He was a passionate advocate for Scottish independence, which materialised in the establishment of a Scottish parliament but not to the full extent of independence that Allan would have wished. He believed that nationalism expressed people's approach of self-determination which was tolerant and inclusive of all kinds of people. I valued Alan's friendship over the years.

The Scottish teachers were strict and kept us all in tow with lesson work. If we caused trouble, the teachers had no hesitation in using the strap. On one occasion our geography teacher threw a duster at me when I had been talking in class. It flew past my head, and he said, 'Sorry, I missed you.'

I replied — under my breath, I thought — 'I'm not sorry.'

He heard me and said, 'Come out here!' Everyone feared the strap and I was no exception. The teacher pulled it out from a drawer and wielded it high in the air as he beckoned me forward. I walked to the front of the class and held out a trembling hand. The teacher stretched his arm right back and I knew it would be a solid whack. As his arm came down, something snapped inside me — self-preservation, I expect. At the last moment before impact I pulled my hand away. The strap crashed down onto the floor. Needless to say he gave me six of the best following that embarrassment. I hid the red wheals on my hand from my grandmother who would have wanted to know why I had been so disobedient.

The headmaster, Harry Humble — his name a misnomer, I am sure — used to storm into our classrooms unexpectedly. Like Pavlov's dogs we stood up to say out loud, 'Good morning, Mr Humble.' We remained standing while he scrutinised every one of us, and then, if nothing untoward, such as a sloppily dressed student, he said, 'Be seated!'

I did not come anywhere close to Dad's sporting prowess; he had excelled in all sports at Elgin Academy, 25 years before me. I loved cricket, though, and the game opened an unexpected door later in life. I kept in touch with Duncan Davidson, a keen cricketer, over the years. Duncan had an uncanny ability to bowl fast leg breaks, putting batsmen on the defensive. I also enjoyed swimming, stamp collecting, and putting with another friend, Alastair Bissett, at Cooper Park.

Alastair and I once lit a fire in the entrance to a warehouse of a grocery store, Gordon & Macphail, next to my grandmother's house. Embers from the fire carried over to straw in nearby cardboard cartons and the flames roared up to set more boxes alight. We were in trouble, but nearby workmen managed to put it out. What we did not know was that some years before, my grandmother had spotted a fire in the warehouse and had called the fire brigade. The store owners rewarded her with a gold watch for saving the premises. And here we were, it seemed, trying to burn the place down.

In later life, Alastair became a journalist and an editor for the *Press and Journal*, one of Scotland's leading daily newspapers.

I palled up with two other lads. Iain Gordon came with his family from Inverness during the school holidays. Dad had known the family, and Iain's mother would invite Alastair and me to their seaside shack at Lossiemouth. Another school friend, Stewart Binnie, regularly invited me to his home. We kept in close touch over the years.

In the subjects I studied, I seemed to do the best at Latin. Mr Gillan, our Latin teacher, made Latin learning a breeze. In his fun class he cracked jokes at our expense and kept us moving from seat to seat. Whoever answered correctly would move higher up in the seat-pecking order. He reminded us from time to time of our school motto: *Sic itur ad astra* — such is the way to the stars. For me the whole motto was 'by striving — *per ardua* — to be well-educated, such is the way to the stars'; it stayed with me as an incentive to learn.

Mr Gillan accompanied us on weekend stays in the Grampians where we camped at Glenmore Lodge by Loch Morlich. Our memorable day-long hikes into the Cairngorm National Park toughened us up and gave us an appreciation of the Scottish Highland's natural beauty. Once, we climbed Cairngorm as mist swept down on top of us — a surreal experience. Hiking stayed with me as a lifelong outdoor venture, but I ran into trouble at times, as I describe later.

Every two years I had an opportunity to visit Mum and Dad in their home in Norfolk, and, later, in Leeds where Dad continued to work for Norfolk Canneries as a salesman. In 1953, I caught the steam train to Aberdeen, and then the overnight train to York, where Dad picked me up in his Austin A40. Miranda, my sister, was three years old and Frank had grown a lot taller than the last time I had seen him in 1950. Frank often laughed, I thought, for no particular reason. During the six weeks of school holidays we visited the seasides of Bridlington, Whitby and St Anne. We swam a lot in the open-air baths and went for family walks on the moors. A picnic on the moors or by the seaside was Mum's speciality.

On one occasion, we journeyed over to Aylsham in Norfolk, and I met up with my grandmother's sister, Gertrude. Living in a bungalow in Aylsham, she welcomed me like a lost child; she had never married to have children of her own. Gertrude had an acute social conscience and supported many charities. Her interest in people and things going on in the world never waned and her mind kept razor sharp right to the end of her 95 years. Seeing her at home was like stepping into a small piece of heaven where you felt at peace, rejuvenated and encouraged to go on with whatever you had decided in life. Her friendly and inquisitive eyes flashed all over the place. From time to time she sent me books on spiritual guides like *Man seen afar*. She was a deeply spiritual person but perhaps not in the conventional sense. She believed we were not alone — guides were here to help us along our way and steer us away from harm. On reflection in my seventies I often think about what she had said — it could explain some of the events in my life.

Aunt Gertrude was the first person to talk to me earnestly about spiritual matters. She wrote to me later about prayer:

> It is so difficult to pray. I believe it would help children as well as grown-ups to tell them this. When you first wake up in the morning, be still and think of 'New every morning', then wait quietly till you feel Jesus with you, and when you do, talk to Him. It doesn't matter what you talk about. All the things that matter to you, anything you are keen on, and anything you are frightened about. Ask Him that you may remember that He will be with you to help you all the time. Then kneel down, kneel very low in His presence, and wait, wait till you feel His hand upon your head. Then you can go ahead hard for the rest of the day. Don't forget to know Him better

and better. Mind you must read the Bible some time every day. Perhaps during that first morning time when your mind is fresh to see things and understand. But He will help you anytime you forget it. You can't love Him without knowing Him and you can't know Him without being loved by Him. And He said 'No man cometh to the Father, but by me.' When we find we can hear what Jesus says and have Him help to obey, aren't we becoming 'Those who are led by the Spirit of God?' It is sometimes very hard to obey, and when we do, we seem to have to tear out a part of ourselves. We do have to, and it makes room for our Lord to come in, and He wants lots of room in us. He wants all the room.

Aunt Gertrude's wise words and advice kept coming back to me in the years ahead.

While at Aylsham, I spent time with my cousins, David, Anthony and Warren. I remember climbing a big tree outside their home at Saxthorpe Hall. When I returned to Elgin, I started writing letters to them. David replied to say that he had fallen off the tree we had climbed. Not long after his fall, cancer developed in his leg which had to be removed. We continued writing to each other. The cancer, however, was aggressive and spread, and a few months later, he died. Because of our friendship I felt his loss deeply.

By the time I reached 3A at Elgin Academy I was in the top third of the class and felt at home with the Scottish way of teaching and with my classmates. But by the middle of the year my comfort zone was about to break up. My grandmother suffered from acute abdominal pains. She found it more difficult to look after boarders and soon had to ask them to leave because of her condition. Dad made arrangements to pick us up in his car and take us to Leeds. We wondered if Grandmother could cope with the journey, but she never complained although we knew she suffered a lot.

I felt sad to leave Elgin, my home for eight years, and I had no idea how I would adapt to an English school. I welcomed the family reunion though. On looking back I was very thankful that my Scottish education had lifted me out of the doldrums.

Shortly after, Grandmother died. She had been like a mother to me and I missed her dearly.

Frank and I felt strange being together again. He was twelve, and three years younger than I; he would not have remembered our time in Norfolk eight years before. My sister Mandy was ten years younger so I did not know her at all. Even with Mum and Dad it seemed like we were beginning afresh in a new relationship. We all needed time to readjust as a family. I soon realised, however, that the formative years under my grandmother had given me a sense of independence. Although I was not ready to be thrust out into the world, I felt the family bonding had weakened because of our separation. Frank and I gradually picked up the threads of being brothers again. But even with living in the same house, it seemed that our different backgrounds, schools, friends and interests, did not make it easy.

Frank went to a secondary modern school and did not study much, but he loved woodwork. Much to Mum and Dad's concern, he began mixing with a group of lads who caused mischief in the neighbourhood, like taking aim at the street lights with catapults. The police called around to let Mum and Dad know about Frank's escapades. Dad reacted strongly to Frank with verbal attacks. If Dad had free time, which was rare with his time-demanding sales job, he spent it with Mandy rather than with Frank. Perhaps, if he had spent more time with Frank it would have been different. Mum tried to be as understanding as possible, but at times her exasperation reached boiling point and the strain showed on her face with tears welling up.

I had enrolled at Roundhay School, an all-boys grammar school, but, because the English syllabus was different from the Scottish one, I had to repeat the third year. I adjusted slowly to the new environment. Being a foreigner from north of the border did not help. Learning was often by rote with heaps to digest. Surprisingly, one of the classes I really enjoyed was the Latin class where we constantly swapped places on answering questions. I vied with a Jewish student for the top position in the class. Gee Gee, we called our Latin teacher because of his prominent horse-like teeth and jaw to match, had that rare gift of making a potentially dull subject one of the most interesting for the class. I passed eight General Certificate of Education (GCE) subjects at O-Level, and Gee Gee commented that I had excelled in the north of England GCE Latin.

About 20 per cent of the students were Jewish. It was the first time I had associated with Jewish boys, and, although I did not make any close friendships, I felt that I got on well with most of them. Later on, I would appreciate even more that first introduction to people with a Jewish background. At that time I had little understanding of Jewish history and of how much they had been persecuted during the Second World War. No one talked about the Holocaust. We were barely a decade out of a world war that had impacted on millions of lives, especially Jews. Our history teacher preferred to dwell on characters like Oliver Cromwell and Charles II rather than the ruthless regimes of Hitler and Stalin.

The headmaster addressed about 1,000 boys in the assembly each morning. He glowered at us with never a smile to soften his stern-looking face. On one morning I had forgotten to wear my tie and must have thought that I would be invisible in the middle of a vast assembly. But no! The headmaster eyed me and bellowed, 'You, boy!' I looked behind. 'No! You, boy! See me after in my room.' For the first and last time I came face to face with my ogre. He said, 'Why do you dare to come to school improperly dressed?' I had no answer. He took out a cane, swung it in the air and said, 'Bend down.' He gave me six of the best — English style.

I did not enjoy playing rugby, so with a number of other students who thought the sport too aggressive, we switched to cross-country running. From that time running became a natural part of my life. I kept up with cricket and, in the school colts team, I usually opened the bowling as a medium-paced bowler, out-swinging the ball to make it more difficult for the batsman; my batting average for one season was thirty. Yorkshire was the home of well-known test cricketers Len Hutton and Maurice Leyland, and, luckily, I joined in with one of their weekend training camps. A veteran of some 40 tests, Maurice Leyland checked the way I held the bat, while a local news reporter flashed away with his camera. The cricket highlight of my time in Leeds was to watch bowlers like Ray Lindwall and Richie Benaud play for Australia against England in the Third Test at Headingley Stadium in 1956.

As part of a scout team, we camped in the Yorkshire Dales and climbed the three peaks of Ingleborough, Whernside and Pen-y-ghent. Our scoutmaster led us into a cave which was full of water and said, 'There is an opening at the other end. You will find it.' At first we nimbly jumped from rock to rock so as to avoid getting our feet wet. Then, to our surprise we were up to our knees in water. We shrieked and howled. Worse was to come. We had to crawl along the bottom, trying to avoid stalactites piercing us from above and stalagmites stabbing us from below. These hazardous obstacles prevented us from appreciating the full beauty of this magical wonderland. We continued to crawl on our stomachs in icy water but never found the exit. Amid a fresh outburst of yelling and shrieking we retreated to the entrance. At the camp fire which restored our joie de vivre, the scoutmaster said, 'Sometimes life is like that cave — full of obstacles with no short cuts, but still you must get your feet wet.' Years on, I remembered and realised the value of what he had said. In another scouting adventure, we hiked around the Isle of Man during the annual Tourist Trophy (TT) motorcycle race. At various vantage points, we watched riders top speeds of over 200 kilometres an hour through the mountainside, towns and fields.

At Roundhay School we had to choose between science and arts for the Advanced GCE Level (A-Level). The science course concentrated on mathematics, physics and chemistry, to the exclusion of English language and literature, foreign languages and other subjects. Hardly a balanced education! And with a career course that was most likely decided at the tender age of fifteen or sixteen. I felt deprived of Latin, French and English studies. Why did I choose the science pathway? Truthfully, I cannot give a sound reason. Perhaps most of the students I knew chose the science option. Perhaps it seemed the better way to go for a job in the workforce. Anyway, I felt as though I had parted with friends — my better subjects went overboard. The Scottish system of higher education was far more desirable, I would find out, with its broader coverage, higher standard of English and less emphasis on rote learning.

I completed the first of two years of force-fed science study for the A-Level GCE. Teachers crammed into you as much as they could. Our chemistry teacher, Mr Geeves, strutted up and down the aisle with a large swimming gala watch hanging from his waistcoat, while he dictated everything we had to write down. We rapidly devoured equations on the blackboard. With an eye on his watch he kept the pace up until the bell sounded. He was a natural choice as a timekeeper for the school swimming galas.

Dad meanwhile seemed to excel as a salesman and travelled all over England selling produce from Norfolk Canneries. He was often depressed or moody, and this we attributed to his war experiences. Mum never complained but showed the strain in her face at times. A kind, patient and godly soul, she was always ready to encourage us. Frank, my brother, showed great promise in woodwork and metalwork, and had joined the RAF cadets. He seemed to be cheerful on the whole but could be glum, especially when Dad picked on him for losing his belongings or for not doing his homework. Dad frequently called Frank a 'fool' or 'stupid'. That played on Frank's mind and affected his mood.

Then in 1958, after I had completed the first of two years for the Advanced GCE, Baxters of Speyside in north-east Scotland, known for their speciality soups and jams, offered Dad a job as a sales manager.

He bought a house in Garmouth, a village in Morayshire close to the mouth of the River Spey, where King Charles had come ashore on piggyback in 1650 to sign the Solemn League and Covenant to endorse Scots Presbyterianism. Garmouth was about half an hour's drive away from Elgin so Dad and I felt at home again, while for Mum, Frank and Mandy it was a whole new experience. Mum never argued with fate. She adjusted to her new surroundings with self-assurance, while taking an active interest in the village folk and in Maggie Fair, an annual event with stalls, sideshows, a flower show, fancy dress and a wide range of entertainment. She formed a close friendship with Mrs Sievewright from England who had also married a local Scot. And I started to take an interest in Mrs Sievewright's daughter, Sheila. We met up and walked around the Speyside area and along the beach near Kingston.

I caught the steam train into Elgin daily to go back to Elgin Academy for the sixth year — really an extra year to consolidate our Scottish education for university. On the train I met up with Norman McKinlay, a draughtsman with a firm in Elgin. Like me, Norman was a keen cricketer and we played for Fochabers, home town to Baxters of Speyside. Norman had mentioned in casual conversation that his brother was working in Melbourne and he might go to Australia one day.

Most of my former classmates at Elgin Academy had either left school for employment or further study. The Scottish Higher exams were usually taken in the fifth year with Higher English a prerequisite for entrance into a Scottish university. Aberdeen University would not accept a mixture of GCE Ordinary Level passes from England — considered a lower standard than Scottish Lowers — and Scottish Highers. What could I do? The only solution was to study at Elgin Academy for GCE Advanced Level in maths, physics and chemistry, and return to Leeds to sit for the exams. This was not easy as the two syllabi did not match up. But I persevered and managed to arrange for past English exam papers to be sent up so that the Scottish teachers could spend time going over them with me.

Feeling uncomfortable about the whole exercise and not having a clear conviction in what I should study if I did end up going to university, I journeyed down to Leeds at the end of the year to sit for the A-Levels. I felt I did poorly as the questions covered unfamiliar ground. Back in Scotland I waited for the results while I took on a job as a village postman for the Speyside area. The results came through: I had managed to scrape a pass in all three exams — maths, physics and chemistry. Aberdeen University accepted me for a science course, and thanks to a grant from the Morayshire County I was able to pay for my expenses while studying.

I boarded with Mr and Mrs Fraser in Westburn Park near Foresterhill Hospital. Mrs Fraser, an agricultural science graduate of Aberdeen University, looked after six to eight students in her three-storey house. She was like my grandmother — strict, down to earth and suffered no nonsense, but we felt part of her extended family. Two corgis licked our plates clean if we left any scraps. I hoped Mrs Fraser washed the plates, but never found out for sure what happened to those licked ones. At times the plates banked up and dinner took second place as Mrs Fraser followed the Dons play soccer on TV with an unremitting passion. Her daughter Eileen had married the captain of the Dons team, Archie Glen. So, whether we liked it or not, soccer became a natural part of our conversation and education at meal times.

Allan Carmichael, one of my classmates at Elgin Academy, happened to board next door. We joined the university Hares and Hounds for cross country running. We ran against other Scottish university running clubs in all kinds of weather, including snow and sleet. Once, while racing against Edinburgh University, the tail end runners, including us, got lost. We had followed the footprints in the snow of faster runners, but these quickly covered over with the heavy snowfall. We eventually found our way back in the dark. For each race, Allan and I had found the pace set by the leading runners too fast so we were content to finish towards the end. We had joined in more for the social occasion.

On Sunday we usually attended the university chapel service. We sometimes went to the evening service at West Church of St Andrews to hear the inspiring messages of George Reid urging us to have a vision and speak up on a whole range of issues, such as what's important in life, the need to hold communities together in turbulent times, and war and peace.

Allan and I rode our bikes everywhere. No motorcycles or cars in those days. On Saturday evenings we ended up going to jazz dives or dancing in the university hall at Marischal College — a towering granite building in the centre of Aberdeen.

Because we had covered a substantial amount of the material in the sixth year at Elgin Academy, I breezed through the first year subjects of chemistry, physics, mathematics and zoology with a moderate amount of effort. The breeze was my undoing. I would learn in the second year that life was not a coaster.

One of our lecturers, Reginald Jones, a professor of physics, would invite students, once a term, from all courses to an entertaining display of physics in action. Nothing prepared me for the circus which unfolded. I recall Professor Jones walking into the lecture theatre to a medley of catcalls, cheering and chants. Paper projectiles flew through the air and a flour bomb landed near the front bench. None of this exceptional behaviour perturbed Professor Jones, who with dignified aplomb proceeded to carry out his first experiment to demonstrate the force of an expanding liquid. He filled a model of a tall chimney on the front bench with water. The chimney, about two metres in height, had been carefully constructed to simulate a coal-fired chimney which needed demolishing. With appropriate showmanship, Professor Jones took aim at the base of the chimney with a rifle and fired. The bullet entered the chimney and, with the sudden expansion of water, shattered the chimney into small pieces. Professor Jones acknowledged the applause which followed and explained the physical principles before proceeding with the next demonstration.

Professor Jones wrote up about his war time experiences of British Intelligence in *Most secret war*. On a more subdued note some of the freshers were invited to an evening gathering to meet the staff. I was fortunate to meet with Professor Jones and ask him about his war exploits. He said that he had been attached to Air Intelligence branch of MI6, and in 1940 he had discovered that the Germans had an intersecting radio beam system for bombing cities and strategic targets in England. He had explained the beam threat to the prime minister, Winston Churchill, who gave him the go-ahead to develop ways to counter the guidance system used by the German bombers. With the aid of a handkerchief he described how they were able to steer the German planes away from the beam. I did not take it all in but realised he must have played an important role in the Second World War. He regretted that the German bombers had succeeded in bombing the city of Coventry with a large loss of life.

I travelled home by bus every now and then for a weekend in Garmouth. Frank and I would often spend time together fishing for salmon in the River Spey or mackerel off the coast near Kingston. We took our 12-gauge shotguns and shot duck as they came in at dusk to settle on the river. For the first time in our lives I believe we felt like brothers. But it was short-lived as his condition deteriorated, and he had to go into a mental hospital in Elgin for shock therapy. While there, he smashed windows of the hospital, so he had to be restrained. No one really knew how to treat him. On release from the hospital sessions he appeared in a drugged and lethargic state.

In the second year at university I studied biochemistry, physiology and chemistry, but I slipped into the doldrums with no real dedication or purpose in study. I failed the end of year exams. It was a rude awakening, and for the first time I had to really take stock of myself and ask what I wanted to do in life. I thought of switching to medicine, but that would have taken me at least five more years. Engineering did not attract me. An arts course did not seem to lead in any practical direction. Finally, after serious study during the summer break, I sat and passed the supplementary exams. I worried, though, that I lacked ambition and direction in life.

In the meantime I had subscribed to a newsletter which gave details of numerous volunteer projects for students during the vacation period in Britain, European countries and even as far away as the Middle East. The projects were sponsored by government or non-government organisations. As long as we paid for our fares, everything else would be paid for, but, of course, there would be no payment for work. I started to spread my wings with a two-week visit to London followed by participating in a volunteer project to lay the foundation of a car park for Tunbridge Wells Hospital in Kent. I joined in with mostly English students and we completed the task to everyone's satisfaction.

On another vacation I ventured further afield with my first visit abroad to Vallon Pont d'Arc, a tourist town in the Ardèche region of southern France. The gorges of the Ardèche were the Grand Canyon of Europe. About thirty of us as volunteers, mostly from France, England, Germany and Algeria, helped build a canoeing centre from scratch.

Our reward was the use of the canoes. We paired off, and our instructor made sure we could paddle in unison and steer our way through the rapids. The steep-sided limestone cliffs of unforgettable beauty dwarfed us as we paddled along the river. Most of our canoes overturned at some stage, especially as we negotiated the rapids. Heiko, my canoeing partner from Berlin, and I worked well together without a spill. At one stage we arrived at the famous Pont d'Arc, a natural arch of more than thirty metres in height, the largest they said in Europe, and carved out by the Ardèche River.

With the help of an instructor we descended into nearby caves, using aluminium ladders, and acetylene lamps attached to our foreheads. We marvelled at the architectural wonders of limestone formation. Sometimes we encountered a subterranean river which had us sailing along in inflatable dinghies.

I felt sorrow for one chap from England who was too fat to crawl through a small opening and had to stay behind. At one stage he had wedged himself so hard against the sides of the opening we despaired whether he could go forward or back. With someone pulling on his legs he eventually came out the way he had gone in.

The French government ran the project and it gave me my first encounter with Algerians — six of whom had joined our group.

They introduced me to the savagery of the French–Algerian war which ended with Algeria's independence. Amar, a tall, gangly and good-natured Algerian, described the terrible human cost to both sides. We corresponded for about ten years after our time together at Vallon Pont d'Arc and then we lost touch. My Algerian experience, however, had only just begun.

I still correspond with Heiko, my canoeing partner, to this day. I also wrote to several pen pals. One was a Burmese girl, Esmeralda Chan Htoon, whose English writing was impeccable and expressive. After two years she stopped writing, maybe because conditions in Burma had deteriorated. A chap by the name of Eddie Tan of Singapore also wrote to me, but after two years he handed me on to a New Zealand girl, Alison. She came from Timaru, a town on the east coast of South Island. We corresponded for about a year before she told me she had become engaged, but her sister Judy was keen to write to me. There is nothing like being handed on, so Judy, a speech therapist, and I started writing to each other. That was the beginning of a lifelong friendship.

After landing back in London from France in August 1961, I discovered to my horror that I had spent all my money and still had to make my way back to Aberdeen. I had a florin left for an underground train ride to the outskirts of London where I would link up with the A6 motorway. I walked along the side of the motorway for two hours trying to thumb a lift. No one stopped. In despair I lay down in a field near the motorway and fell asleep. When I woke up I found a truck had stopped in a nearby lay-by. The driver opened the cab door when he saw me approaching, and said, 'You won't find anyone stopping for you. Don't you know what's happened?'

'No,' I said, 'I've just come from France.'

'You haven't heard about the A6 murders, then?'

'No.'

'Well, a man forced a couple at gunpoint to drive along the road until he pulled them over in a lay-by. He shot them both. There's talk he raped the girl first before shooting her.'

He paused for that to sink in while I shook my head in disbelief. Then he said, 'Okay, you look genuine enough. Where do you want to go?'

'Aberdeen,' I replied.

'Take you as far as Luton, if that's any good.'

I thanked him, and he let me off at a truck stop on the outskirts of Luton. From Luton I managed to get another lift to Newcastle. On reaching Newcastle it was dark so I lay down on a park bench to sleep. At about midnight a policeman shook me and said, 'Come with me!' I ended up in a police cell for the rest of the night. I thanked the policeman for his hospitality, although he did not give me breakfast. And I *was* hungry. However, the next driver, who picked me up for a trip to Perth, had too many sandwiches prepared by his wife and was happy to share them. The journey from Perth to Aberdeen went smoothly with another driver.

Later, I learned that James Hanratty, a petty criminal, was found guilty of the A6 murders and hanged.

For the next two years I knuckled down to study zoology, soil science, chemistry and biochemistry. I rekindled an interest in learning, especially in soil science. In the long summer period I worked as a relief postman or helped a local farmer, Graham Reid, in the harvesting of his wheat crop or took part in a volunteer project. In summer I played cricket for Fochabers. Norman and I opened the bowling; we vied with each other to see how many wickets we could take. We played teams all over the north-east of Scotland and came home late on the bus singing songs and bothy ballads. Some of us were a wee bit 'fou' which helped in the singing but increased the number of pit stops.

We played against Aberdeen when their team included Rohan Kanhai, the West Indian test cricketer, arguably the best batsman in the world at that time. Usually, the test cricketers played with English county sides in the off season, so it was surprising for one to go as far north as Aberdeen — a big boost for Scottish cricket though. As a bowler, Kanhai varied the pace and flight of the ball, which took me by surprise when I faced him. No one had told me he could bowl as well. As a batsman he moved nimbly on his feet to strike the ball for four or six which he did to my first two balls. Then he hit me for several more runs. I noticed he had no trouble in dispatching a shorter pitched ball to the boundary. And he knew how to cope with good length balls, so I decided to slightly overpitch the ball. He took one almighty swing at it. Everyone looked up to see where the ball had gone. For certain it was a four or six. But he had completely mistimed his stroke, and the ball went straight through to the middle wicket. I could not believe it. Nor could he! He looked down in disgust and headed slowly towards the pavilion. Everyone else on the field came over to congratulate me.

I graduated with a Bachelor of Science degree in 1962 and then went on, courtesy of the biological chemistry department, to study another year of biochemistry. Professor Kermack, who had been appointed as the first professor of biochemistry, tested my resolve to complete that year by calling me in for an interview. He was a worldwide authority on Vitamin A, so I swotted up on his subject until I felt like an up-and-coming authority — well, enough to convince Professor Kermack that I could continue with biochemistry. Fortunately, he asked questions on Vitamin A and nothing else.

One of our lecturers in biochemistry, Derek Burke, inspired us with his talks at meetings of the Student Christian Movement. He described life as a pilgrimage. We were the pilgrims and we could choose to walk by faith. We won't know where we are going and we probably won't be planning the path, which could involve issues we could never imagine. His words did not fully resonate with me until much later. Derek wrote about spending a life in science and faith in *Real scientists: real faith.*

News came from Aylsham in Norfolk that Anthony, my cousin, had taken his life. I could not understand why. He was the more outgoing and cheerful of the twins and seemed to have had a promising future ahead of him with being a student at Cambridge University. No one had the answer.

Frank meantime was sent for further treatment to a mental hospital, close to Westburn Park where I was staying, so I would walk over to visit him and try to offer what comfort I could given his condition. He kept saying that he knew the problem but the doctors would not operate. He wanted a lobotomy. I worried for him but felt powerless to help.

Chapter 3
Israel

AFTER SUCCESSFULLY COMPLETING ANOTHER YEAR of study, I decided to test out employment opportunities. But first I would go on another overseas project — this time to Israel to join a group of 25 Jewish and non-Jewish volunteers to work on a kibbutz for three months in a semi-desert area of Israel known as the Negev.

We seemed a motley lot as we assembled at Victoria Station in London. Richard introduced himself as the leader of our party. I felt a bit out of place with my shirt, tie, sports jacket and flannels. Everyone else wore an open-necked shirt or top, a sweater or jerkin, and jeans.

'Where's Johnny?' Richard shouted. About five minutes before our train was due to leave for Dover, Johnny arrived, broadly smiling as he produced our tickets.

'Wasn't there someone else from Aberdeen?' I asked Johnny.

'Yes, there was. But she backed out at the last moment. Her father was a policeman and had evidently objected to her going. Some other guy from Aberdeen filled her place.'

'That's me,' I said.

'Oh, yes. You are from Aberdeen as well, so we thought it would be best if you took her place. You are the only one from Scotland.'

When we reached Dover, we staggered up the gangplank after coping with the formalities. We said goodbye to England. Someone responded from the crowd, 'See you in three months' time.'

On the boat from Dover to Ostend we started to get acquainted.
A small Jewish girl introduced herself as Ann. We talked for some
time before she dived into her bag and brought out bread and cheese.
'I'm a vegetarian,' she said as she munched away.

At Ostend we boarded the train for Munich. On arrival we had
six hours to spare before catching the next train. First, at a street
stall, we devoured a Bockwurst sausage. Then we made our way to
the town hall to see Munich Cathedral with its striking twin towers
and onion-shaped domes.

We then descended into the busy thoroughfares and walked into
a packed shop that resembled Marks and Spencer. German guttural
sounds rang out as demonstrators proclaimed the worth of their
products to eager-listening housewives.

We trooped into a restaurant for more tucker and then made our
way back to the station. I met Maurice, a hyperactive Londoner, who
pranced around like a dog off a leash but eventually settled down on
a suitcase to read the latest on the Profumo affair.

The train rolled in and half of our group, including me, boarded
the front of the train, while the other half boarded a carriage to the
rear. Greeks and Yugoslavs sat on our reserved seats so we politely
asked them to leave. When they wouldn't budge, we called an
official who ordered them out into the corridor, which then became
packed with people and suitcases. Just as the train was about to
leave we heard a commotion from further down the platform. We
looked out to see the other half of our group being hauled out by
burly policemen. The train started to move out. Flabbergasted, we
looked on as some of our group on the platform turned towards us
and waved.

We discussed what to do as we settled into our compartments.
Barbara, a vocal Londoner, thought we should carry on as far as we
could, while Ann suggested we get off at the next station, Salzburg.
As we neared Salzburg, Ann took matters into hand when she let the
ticket collector know what had happened and that we did not have
tickets. The ticket collector ordered us off.

Pandemonium set in as we tried to retrieve our luggage. The Greeks and Slavs in the corridor would not budge so we passed the luggage out through the windows. The train started up again, but a woman had the presence of mind to pull the communication cord and the train shuddered to a halt. We scrambled onto the platform while the Greeks and Yugoslavs laughed at our predicament.

The next train from Munich would arrive at 2 am, six hours later. We expected the other half of the group to be on it. I talked to Arthur, a well-educated 20-year-old with a polished English accent, on education and science. Several of the group, including Arthur, then fell asleep. I chose to look around Salzburg, birthplace of Mozart and set off towards the Salzach River. A well-lit fortress, one of the largest medieval castles in central Europe I learned later, sat atop a hill overlooking the city. I walked for a while along the bank of the river, drinking in the cool night air and the comforting stillness of the waters. I crossed a bridge to the other side where I gazed for some time at a church with a bright-shining cross.

Back at the station, I was ready to sleep, but Maurice coaxed me into going to a nearby night club. We entered to see people jiving on a dance floor. Maurice ordered gin cocktails. He spotted a 'fair bit of stuff', as he called her, and approached her for a dance, but she refused. He shrugged his shoulders and returned to our table. 'All the girls are partnered,' Maurice said in a flat tone. Then he went up to the band and asked for one of his favourites — a Charleston. The band leader obliged which lifted Maurice's spirits.

We returned to the station and the train from Munich rumbled in with the rest of our group on board. Johnny had sorted out the problem with the tickets. We dozed for about two hours before arriving at Jesenice on the Yugoslavian border. A smart Yugoslavian official entered our compartment and asked for our visas.

All through the day, the train rumbled its way through Yugoslavia. At first, the mountains, thinly-clad with trees, rose steeply on either side. Then we reached the plains with the land divided into strips for farming. Later, as we journeyed through

Greece, we passed through rough mountainous countryside with Greeks coaxing their horses along isolated roads.

At Piraeus, after soaking up the impressive Acropolis and the bright-shining Parthenon in Athens, we boarded a boat for Israel. As we approached Israel's coastline we could make out the city of Haifa, built above the harbour on the slopes of Mount Carmel, and with the golden dome of the Bahai temple gleaming in full sun.

Yehuda Bauer, our leader for our three-month stay at Kibbutz Shoval, greeted us as we disembarked. We journeyed by bus to the kibbutz, and on arrival a green oasis in the middle of a semi-desert area lay before us. Already a Jewish contingent of young students from the city had arrived and settled in. Another Jewish group from Argentina would arrive in two weeks' time. The kibbutz residents including children numbered over 250. To me, it was amazing how a farm in the middle of barren land could thrive and support so many people. The kibbutz was not poor by any means; in fact, it boasted a 25-metre swimming pool, an open-air theatre, well-established housing and lawns, a dairy herd and fruit orchards.

We rose in the morning at 5.15 am — not one of the strongest points for a number of us. Joshua took most of us to the orchard where we picked fruit for two hours before breakfast, and then for another session until lunch at the communal dining room. After lunch we cleaned up and rested before assembling for Yehuda Bauer's afternoon session to learn Hebrew, followed by a discussion on an Israeli topic of interest. The topics covered Zionism, settlement in Israel, Arab–Israeli war in 1948, anti-Semitism, the Holocaust, kibbutz life and ideology, life outside the kibbutz, and Arab–Israeli relations. These topics fascinated me, and I threw myself into learning Hebrew.

'Everything in the kibbutz is shared,' Yehuda said. 'Everyone helps everyone else. No one is paid anything for their work. All necessary expenses are met though. And that includes holiday expenses but, of course, these must be approved.'

'What if you don't want to work?' someone asked.

'No one can make you work. If you wish you can idle your time, but you will be ostracised. Moral pressure is powerful on the kibbutz,' replied Yehuda. The whole kibbutz would talk and circumstances would force you to prove your worth, or else clear out.'

'What about people joining the kibbutz from the city?' someone else asked.

'Although groups of young people from outside regularly experience the kibbutz way of life, few stay to make it their home. But members of the kibbutz, or kibbutzniks as we call them, feel at home and rarely leave; and they play an important part in Israeli society.'

We soon found out in our group who were the workers and who tended to slacken. In the orchards, Joshua took command. Everyone knew Joshua. Somehow he symbolised the ethos of the kibbutz way of life. His small, well-built frame bounced along as though a pair of concealed springs gave him added power. Most of the time we could not tell what Joshua was thinking; he wore that innocent boyish look. Since he was in charge of the fruit picking, everyone in the group tapped into his peculiar but friendly way of overseeing our work in the orchards. 'People,' he said at the beginning of each day, 'you will begin to start here.'

The girls in our group were more intent on talking over their previous night's activities. As a result, their rate of picking dropped off to a lackadaisical pace. They left apples on the trees and failed to pick up those that had fallen to the ground. This would perturb Joshua, but he let out no scathing remark or fiery words, just a wry look of peevishness that spoke volumes. One of his favourite expressions was: 'Please, people, I must remind you, don't forget to pick the apples off the ground.' Towards the end of our four-week picking on the kibbutz we had heard Joshua repeat that line so many times that he would only get as far as 'please people' and everyone else in the vicinity would chime in with the rest of the chorus.

Joshua was worried at our late morning efforts of rising. Usually the lame excuse was that the alarm hadn't gone off. Most of us rose at 4.55 am and it was a mad dash to the *khoder ochel* — the dining room — for a cup of coffee before racing to the tractor and leaping onto the trailer. Joshua's wide-eyed expression hastened the last few latecomers. After the tractor moved off, there was always a shout of *rega, rega* — wait, wait — from one or two pickers who had left it too late. Joshua slowed the tractor down until they had clambered aboard or were hauled up over the tailboard by fellow pickers. Joshua always sat upright as he drove, and he wore the same golfer's cap and close-fitting T-shirt. Maurice aptly described him as a 'dinky driver'.

My admiration for Joshua grew as we drew him into conversation. Joshua went to great pains to explain the Sinai Peninsula campaign and the Jewish refugee problem. Despite his muddling of the English language, we began to respect him as a person who had suffered a lot. His outward relaxed appearance belied his inner thoughts. If Joshua had gained a peace of mind it was most remarkable since we discovered that he had spent most of the Second World War in a concentration camp. The stamp mark on his forearm was clearly visible.

Joshua told us that he couldn't help his feelings towards Germans. Later in our stay, two young German travellers happened to spend a couple of days at the kibbutz. Despite knowing they were German, Joshua talked to them with no indication of an anti-German feeling. Unlike some Jews, he didn't mind speaking German. We were surprised after what he had said but realised later that his feelings would not affect his civility. I remember Joshua with admiration and respect.

On one occasion I was elected as work organiser for our group. My role was to collect the list of various jobs that were assigned to us from Rubeck, the kibbutz work organiser, and to allocate them to everyone in our group. Several of us requested to work with Gerry, an American Jew, in the cow pens. I knocked them all back in favour of myself. One way to solve the problem of who should work there, I thought. I chose Albert, who had a sore back, to work with me.

We marched down to the cow pens and met Gerry, the dairy manager, who explained that he wanted all the bulls herded into one pen. After that, five at a time would be shoved into a raceway ready for weighing. 'If you want to move a bull that won't budge, you do this.' Gerry then twisted the tail of a bull to urge it forward. 'Don't be afraid of them. Let 'em know you're boss,' Gerry said in his American drawl. 'They are more afraid of you.'

The three of us managed to get all the bulls into one pen without too much trouble. Gerry shouted, 'Yahoo! Yah!' And we shouted, too, to give ourselves courage. We rounded up the first five bulls into a raceway and then shut the gate. After coaxing the first one onto the weighing scales, we recorded its weight. 'Carry on,' Gerry said. 'I have to leave you to feed some calves.'

Left on our own, we weighed the first five bulls. Then I opened the gate to push the next five into the raceway. They seemed more difficult to round up. One of the bulls took a few steps towards me. I sensed danger. The bull lowered its head and charged. I turned to run, but his head caught me on the backside. He threw me against the railings. I struggled to my feet as he pawed the ground ready to charge again. This time I managed to dodge the full impact and took a glancing blow on the side. With adrenaline running high, I clambered over the railings into the next pen. I lay there winded for several minutes. Albert came over and helped me to my feet.

Hearing the commotion another kibbutz worker came over to assist. We still had ten bulls to put through the raceway and weigh. But it happened all over again. The bull hit our new assistant in the buttocks and threw him about two metres along the ground. The bull kept charging while the man tried desperately to get to his feet. We managed to grab the man and haul him to safety. He was taken to hospital where it was found he had a broken rib.

That night in the communal dining room conversation buzzed with the Shoval bull fight. Gerry was most apologetic saying it had never happened before. When it was time to leave, the kibbutz held a farewell party, and Gerry presented me with a medal in the form of a bull's head, made by his wife.

During the weekends Yehuda usually organised visits to cities, villages and historic sites all over Israel. He took us on one weekend to Jerusalem where we visited the Israel Museum to view the Dead Sea Scrolls — ancient manuscripts discovered in caves near Khirbet Qumran on the north-west shore of the Dead Sea. Most of the scrolls were written on parchment in Hebrew about two thousand years ago.

We visited Yad Vashem, the world centre for documentation, research and commemoration of the Holocaust. For me, it was a sombre moment to try and grasp the enormity of what had happened to the Jews during the Second World War. Wherever we went Yehuda opened our eyes to a piece of Jewish history. Later I discovered, however, there was much more to the ongoing conflict between Jews and Arabs than revealed by Yehuda.

On some weekends we were free to go where we wished. Geoff, who came from Leeds, and I were keen to explore the northern part of Israel and visit Montfort, a Crusader castle. We hitchhiked up north to the mixed Jewish–Arabic town of Akko, on the shores of the Bay of Haifa. We explored this ancient port, the largest natural port in Israel and one of the main Crusader fortifications. From Akko we hiked our way to the ruined castle of Montfort in Upper Galilee. We explored the ruins that stood on a rocky ridge overlooking a river and wooded hills. We found out later that the site was originally an agricultural farm owned by an aristocratic French family who bought the land in the 11th century. At the beginning of the 13th century the farm was sold to the German Teutonic Knights who built the fortress.

As the afternoon shadows lengthened, we decided to hike back to the main road from where we had come. But we lost the path in the fading light and blundered off our route down a steep-sided mountain. And finally in the darkness we stumbled and fell among rocks and bushes. We were lost. What worried us most was that we might be close to the Lebanese border, a very sensitive area where we could be shot. Eventually we spotted lights of a settlement.

We made our way cautiously to the outskirts of the settlement and approached the first house. I peered through the window to see a woman at a stove, cooking the evening meal. She turned towards the window and yelled, and within seconds several men rushed to the house. One of them pointed a gun at us. We froze waiting for the next move. I heard one of them speak in French so I spoke in my schoolboy French to explain that we were from England and staying at Kibbutz Shoval, and that we had lost our way after visiting Montfort. The man seemed to accept my story, lowered his gun, and ushered us towards an open area. He indicated we could sleep on benches and continue on our way in the morning. I thanked him. Later, he came out with two bowls of food.

The next morning, after an uncomfortable night, Geoff and I continued on our way after thanking the man who had been so hospitable. We exchanged addresses and I corresponded with him in French for several years after.

We learned that we had stumbled upon a French–Jewish *moshav*, a privately run farming settlement — in contrast to the communally-run kibbutz.

The next day we visited Safed, an artist colony, which overlooked the Sea of Galilee. We slept on the mountainside that night before hiking down to the lake for a swim the next day. Later in the day we arrived back at Kibbutz Shoval.

On another trip north, this time going along with a group of 14 Jewish Argentinians who had arrived for their stay at Kibbutz Shoval, we were packed into the back of a truck. We soon broke out into song, the Argentinians rivalling their lusty Spanish songs with our English ballads.

At about 9 pm the truck passed Nazareth; the lights of the town dotted the hillsides and valley, and fired my imagination of the stories about Jesus with his humble beginnings.

At about 11 pm we reached Lahavot HaBashan, a kibbutz in northern Israel, located in the Hula Valley. A kibbutznik showed us to a hall where we unrolled our blankets. The sounds of Israeli folk dance music attracted us to a nearby hall. A few of our group joined in; the rest were content to watch the lively performance.

As we trickled back to our sleeping places the Argentinians decided it was time to perform their acts — monkey ones. Someone stole Barbara's sleeping bag. She stormed around to the Argentinian side. Meanwhile someone else had turned the lights off so she tripped over someone who yelped. She struggled to turn on the lights, but the fans came on instead at high velocity. She retrieved her sleeping bag but had no joy in turning off the lights, just the fans at a slower or faster pace. Finally, an Argentinian turned off the lights. Blackout again but no peace. Yells and screams. Lights on. Argentinians everywhere. Geoff cursed. Someone had trodden on his face in the dark. Maurice was also in full verbal flight. After a lot more talking we all dozed.

Early next morning, after three hours sleep, we made our way north to Dan and stopped at a kibbutz. After breakfast, the truck climbed a mountain path to arrive at Tel Hai where Trumpeldour and his friends had held out against the Arabs in 1948. They were all killed and a memorial shaped in the form of a lion commemorated them.

Eventually, we reached the highest point in Israel near Metulla and we took in the breathtaking view of the valley below with toy-like villages and fishponds.

We descended again and for a time we travelled close to the Lebanese border where we sighted Arab villages that seemed deserted. Then the Sea of Galilee shone in the distance. We stopped at Tabgha, a town that bordered the lake, and stayed the night at a youth hostel. After dinner we went down to the shores of the Sea of Galilee where we slipped silently into the calm waters for a refreshing swim.

On the bunk next to me a chap from London was hitchhiking around Israel on his own. He had already been in Israel a fortnight and told me he had just about seen everything. I found it odd that anyone could say that about Israel. I asked him if he felt lonely travelling by himself. He stroked his goatee beard thoughtfully and said he was always meeting people wherever he went, especially other hitchhikers and people at youth hostels. As dawn approached I invited him to go for a swim with us in the Sea of Galilee. The lake was very calm with water gently lapping the edge. Geoff, Valerie and Jonathan joined us and we swam out into the lake. The sun rose over the Syrian hills with golden rays dappling the water. I looked towards a hill overlooking Tabgha and wondered whether it was the Mount of Beatitudes where Jesus gave the Sermon on the Mount. Then we all joined hands and attempted to dance the Horah but without much success.

The road out of Tiberias zigzagged up a hill that overlooked the Sea of Galilee. Eventually we reached Cana where Jesus performed the miracle with the wine.

Our next stop was at the packed church of St Joseph in Nazareth, an Arab town. Jennifer and Barbara were obliged to put on skirts. And the same skirts were necessary for boys with shorts too short. Arthur shouted, 'This is ridiculous.' I managed to pass the length test, but Arthur was not so lucky and was given a skirt. We laughed at the odd figure which presented itself. Even the tourists regarded him as an oddity. If he had worn a veil to cover his face it would have been better; he could have passed as an Arab woman.

Our guide took us down a flight of steps below the Church of St Joseph. He explained that the church was built on the site of Joseph's carpenter shop. We descended another flight of steps and entered a small grotto where Jesus and his family were supposed to have lived.

Then we visited the Church of Annunciation where we viewed the remains of Byzantine mosaics. The Crusaders were the last people to rebuild the church. Below the church was a crypt where we admired a beautiful alcove and a bench made of marble with a statue of the Virgin Mary on it. A Roman Catholic priest eyed us nearby.

Everywhere in Nazareth, tourist shops sold bags of holy earth, Jordan water, silver crosses, olive crosses, necklaces, Jesus Christ mementoes, such as small wooden plaques with pictures of Joseph and Jesus Christ — everything you could imagine. Price tags meant nothing. You bartered until finding common ground for a sale. The Argentinians had all bought Arab headdresses, and some of us bought flutes and drums; our trip back to our kibbutz was both colourful and deafening.

Although our group did not fraternise much with the Jewish group that had come from Tel Aviv, I began to chat to a vivacious Jewish girl, Malka. She had migrated to Israel with her family from her home town Kiustendil in Bulgaria. She said her entrance to the troubled world of 1943 was healthy, among plum and apple groves, and being bathed in hot mineral water. She spoke excellent English and had an infectious sense of humour. With impish mischief she imitated the mannerisms of one of our more eccentric characters, Peter.

Malka helped look after the young children in the nursery. It was common practice for mothers to leave their children from about six months onwards in the care of the nursery while they worked on the kibbutz. She was studying to become an English teacher but would have to complete her army training first.

We journeyed by bus one weekend to Rehovot, a city to the south of Tel Aviv, to meet her family and do some local sightseeing. We also visited the Volcani Agricultural Research Institute where a research staff member spoke about the prospects of working with the institute. I had started to think about what I would do for a living and a career. Could working in an agricultural research institute open up a pathway?

Meanwhile, back at Kibbutz Shoval, an alarm sounded one evening and every member knew exactly what to do and where to go. The rest of us had to take shelter in the nearest home if we were outside or to stay in our quarters. I happened to be chatting to Malka near her room which housed two other Israeli girls, so for the next three hours I stayed there until about midnight when the all clear was given. Having enjoyed the company of three Israeli girls,

I returned back to my room which I shared with Peter and Arthur. Arthur and Peter were sound asleep, but the next morning Arthur ribbed me about staying away most of the night with Malka. 'I came back about midnight,' I protested.

'I don't believe you,' he said.

When the time finally came for Malka and me to say goodbye in September 1963 we promised to write to each other. And we did for the next two years.

My time in Israel had opened up a new world to me, one in which I was keen to explore further. I thought about a revisit to Israel, perhaps, even work there. The ongoing violence between Israelis and the Palestinians concerned me, but it did not dampen my keenness. A fuller picture of the conflict emerged later on — a much more complex one than I had first realised.

Chapter 4

Australia bound

BACK IN LONDON I DECIDED not to hitchhike — one A6 murder was enough. I went by train to Aberdeen and Garmouth. Mum welcomed me with her favourite dinner — roast beef and Yorkshire pudding. Judy, my 'handed on' penfriend, had arrived from New Zealand to find work. Within a week, a bright-eyed and outgoing Judy felt right at home with our quirks, jokes and foibles. Mum and Judy clicked straightaway to become lifelong friends.

In Aberdeen Judy found work as a speech therapist while I found employment with Torry Fisheries Research Laboratory as a laboratory research assistant. I carried out quality tests on fish caught by the Aberdeen trawling vessels in the North Sea.

Judy joined us for the New Year celebrations for 1964. We watched Andy Stewart's show before first footing — the Scottish custom of visiting friends and family after midnight. We visited Dr Struthers' family in Garmouth. In ebullient form, Dr Struthers asked Judy, 'What do you find interesting in New Zealand?' And before Judy could reply, Dr Struthers quipped, 'Sheep.'

Later in the day, Frank appeared with a pheasant for our lunch, but two farmers had spotted him with his shotgun and taken his car number. We tucked in despite the dampener for Frank who might have to appear in court. Feeling a touch sorry for him I brought him a cup of tea while he lay on his bed after lunch. 'Not a New Year's resolution,' I said, 'just a novelty act.'

Frank blinked his eyes and said, 'What's the matter with you? Is it poisoned?'

'Now, there's gratitude,' I replied.

We talked about the trip to Israel and Malka, the girl I had met. Then I mentioned that I was thinking of going to Australia for two years under the assisted migration scheme. Norman, with whom I had played cricket, had already gone and settled in Melbourne.

'I think you should go to Israel instead of Australia,' Frank said. 'It's a long way to Australia, but not to Israel.'

It was tempting to try and settle in Israel. Maybe I could work at the Volcani Institute or somewhere similar. Kibbutz life was fine for a short period, but it did not appeal to me as a long-term proposition. Malka helped to make up my mind when she wrote, 'Two years is just like two dreams if you know how to dream them.' If we felt strongly about each other after two years I would go back to Israel.

I really didn't know much about Australia except for the test cricket team. And apart from Norman, I knew no one. Mum and Dad knew of a family in Sydney — the Cullis-Hills — whom they had met in Norfolk during the war.

I could have gone to Canada or New Zealand, countries also accepting new migrants, but Australia won out, almost, it seemed, with the flip of a coin. Something innate stirred within me — perhaps, the Scots wanderlust for a sense of adventure and discovery.

Judy and I returned to Aberdeen by bus to recommence work. At the first opportunity we saw *Lawrence of Arabia*. The stunning desert scenes brought back memories of the Negev and a trip our kibbutz group had made by truck through the desert to Eilat at the northern tip of the Red Sea. After the movie, we met up with one of my university friends, Jim Hardy. Jim, an accountant with a firm in Aberdeen, took an immediate liking to Judy and made no bones about it. He was looking for someone to marry. 'Something to do, somewhere to go and someone to love,' he said openly to Judy as the most important things in life.

We ended up at Judy's apartment and tucked into her dish of curried prawns and rice. Jim never stopped praising her and gave her a wee peck and hug. 'Auntie Judy,' he said, 'you are the best.' I am not sure Judy appreciated the endearment tag, but she smiled. I did not think they were a match. Jim was bold with the ladies but lacked subtlety. On one occasion, after speaking with a prospective blonde, he said, 'It's a pleasure speaking to an older woman.' That ended any hope of an alliance.

Back in Garmouth, a letter had come to say I had been accepted for Australia as a migrant. I would have to stay at least two years; otherwise, I would have to pay the full cost of the fare.

Malka sent a box of oranges from Tel Aviv. 'Yeah,' said Frank, 'it's a long way to Australia but not so long to Israel. You can still change your mind.'

'No, Frank. I will go to Australia,' I said.

I didn't know when, but it would be within three months from the time of confirmation. I looked up the boat sailing times. The *Flavia* left on 14 February, the *Fair Sky* on 28 February and the *Southern Cross* on 3 March.

On Sunday, Mum ushered us along to church, as was her custom, and we heard the minister, Douglas MacKay, talk about unity with folks around us before there was unity with God. 'How can you be at one with God,' he said, 'when you are not at one with your neighbour?' Mum always extended herself to neighbours and strangers. She never spoke too much about her faith, but lived it. She did let us know, however, that we were to spend our lives like stories to be told.

We drove back from church a different route, and Mum said, 'You get a lovely view this way.' And the next moment she broke down and cried, 'I'm going to miss you.' I did not know what to say. Her tears touched me deeply. Finally, I said, 'Mum, you could come out to Australia.' She looked at me with wondering eyes, and I realised that I had sowed a seed that might germinate.

I wrote a poem for Malka:

> The surging crests are in mixed emotion,
> Meeting shore and wave like true devotion.
> And as the sea wrinkles her brow upon the rocks,
> Like some calm summer's day on Sea of Galilee,
> The beauty of it all, the mind unlocks,
> And gives an air of serenity.

Malka wrote back:

> Tom, sometimes I am so sorry that we can't sit down and discuss things, or dream them or just think about them. What a pleasure it would be to try to see the other side of the moon, or to dry all the seas or just to water the deserts. I am lucky that I can write these things once a week and they are read by you ... And you must come back just as the sun must shine every morning (in Israel), just as the poet must write his poems, just as I must write to you ... But don't feel so sorry (if you are sorry) for going to Australia. Don't you remember, when you told me about it in Israel, I did not prevent you. I even told you to try Australia. As a matter of fact I am a little bit sorry about that. If you only were brave enough to be irrational and even crazy you would change your course and come to Israel just to see the almond buds blooming and the blue 'sea wrinkles her brow upon the rocks', just to look upon the starry sky, just to see the ocean of snowy flowers on the orange trees ... Excuse me if I sound too romantic, but I just feel that way while writing you these lines.
>
> I understand that a belief in God would never be explained. It is true that God is in every human heart, and that is just because he created us in his image. But it is not our conscience only. It is the ability to see the cosmos, to see his creation, to see ourselves. Tom, I understand nothing about the laws of nature, nor can

I explain the wonders by physical proofs. My eyes
are open, my ears and my heart too. I can only judge
the things I see and feel, and surely they couldn't be
explained. They could only be understood.

No wonder I looked forward to each letter.

Our workplace put on a Burns night for 24 January 1964. Our
laboratory scientist, Johnnie, and I attended to the soup, tatties, neeps
and haggis. A piper welcomed us, and Mrs Hay paraded into the room
with the haggis on a silver platter. The address to the Great Chieftain
o' the pudding-race followed. Jim Burt, our senior research scientist,
gave the immortal memory and praised Burns for his humanity, his
love o' his fellow men, his love o' the countryside, and especially his
love for the lassies. Nine illegitimate children — well, that was by the
way. One of our engineers reeled off *Tam O' Shanter*. He kept running
dry and had wee stops for the water of life — *usquebaugh*. Singing and
highland dancing followed. Later, I breathed in the fresh night air,
walking along the banks of the River Don, entranced by the city glow
and glittering patterns from beacon lights on the waters of Aberdeen
harbour. They would remind me of 'the northern lights of Aberdeen
mean home sweet home to me'. I would miss them.

Judy could not come to the Burns night as she was recovering from
the flu, so I called by to give my own rendition of *Tam O' Shanter*.

Malka's letter arrived also telling of her love for Burns' poetry,
especially, 'My love is like a red, red rose.' She said I was like Burns.
The postman was her sweetheart.

'The wisdom teeth have to come out,' said my dentist. 'You will
pay the earth over in Australia.' They came out, and later I wrote:

> Trembling like a leaf,
> And I canna keep still,
> O what mortal grief,
> The dentist maun hae his will.
> In the dentist's chair
> And that I canna bear

When yer knees start knockin'
And yer heart goes trottin'
But the teeth come out
And you begin to doubt
If all those fears and faces
Couldna be left for better places.

I went back once again to Garmouth for the weekend, each one being precious. Mum looked washed out. She did not know how to cope with Frank's behaviour which had worsened. He was still on drugs for depression, but he had become snappy and irritable. 'His table manners are atrocious and his room is a rubbish dump,' Mum said. We had a long talk by the fireside, and I said that I would look into things the next day.

The following day Frank was spotted poaching again. He did not have a licence and fished on private land. It was not even the fishing season. Despite this latest escapade Frank brightened up after we had a talk. He seemed to realise that he needed to pull his weight.

Back in Aberdeen, a blizzard greeted me as I walked to work on Monday, 17 February 1964.

When I arrived at work, Johnnie, my immediate boss, was in a stew. He had lost his treasured pipe. Never had I seen him without a pipe. 'Have you taken it?' he said. 'If I think you have, I will tell all your girlfriends that you are married.'

So I wrote the following for Johnnie and his pipe:

Ane pipe have I left, ane pipe to see me through,
No sign, no mark of theft, this is a sad to do,
Lookit I in every cranny, lookit I in every nook,
Cast an eye at every mannie, case he was a wanton crook
(including me)
But no sign of my lost love,
This is a time to shed a tear,
Surely you must reappear.

Johnnie's pipe did turn up a little later, and I continued in peace to measure glycogen and lactic acid levels in fish.

Norman wrote and said he was looking forward to seeing me in Melbourne. Then on 11 March 1964, Mum rang to say the flying date — not a sailing date — was 30 March.

Jim and I met at Judy's place to celebrate the occasion with a curried meal, beer and soft music. Judy tried to remain calm as Jim hugged her in thanks for the evening. We walked into another blizzard as we left.

Then in the next few days I said goodbye to everyone in Aberdeen. Judy, however, would meet me again at the Aberdeen railway station on my trip down to London. We had grown fond of each other. She wrote out a special word of encouragement:

You go to new surroundings, thought, way of life
Not to force acceptance of present ideas
But rather, to accept the new
So that, in the knowledge of two worlds
You can live with the best of both
And in that living you can find the way —
To give your utmost to life
To make best use of your talents
To come to terms with yourself and fellow man

You go to stay — who knows — two years or twenty
Time may not be certain but the heart is
Of the inseparable bond with the homeland
Which saw your birth, childhood and rise to manhood ...

And in the heart of those who love you
And who perforce must stay behind
There is a wish which all hold for you
For Good Luck
For Friendships
For Happiness, and peace of mind
GOD SPEED

Back home Mum and I had a quiet talk together. She wanted to see me off at London airport so we would travel down together. And she had written to her friends, the Cullis-Hills, who lived in Sydney. She said: 'Don't shut your mind to anything. Don't accept anyone else's views. Always weigh up in your mind what you really think.' I realised later how wise her words were.

The goodbyes took some time because, as a relief postman, I knew everyone in the villages of Garmouth and Kingston. People offered advice as well as good wishes. I called around to say goodbye to Mr and Mrs Seivewright, Sheila and her sister, Moira. Sheila and I had been close friends, but I knew we would go our separate paths. Mrs Seivewright advised me to watch my companions. The local minister Rev Douglas Mackay said, 'Ask yourself each day what God wants of you and not so much what you want for yourself. If this is done, there will be new horizons, new opportunities and new challenges. The battles we fight may not be the battles God wants us to win.' He advised me to see the rector of an English church, not a Scottish church.

'What does it matter?' I said. That put the wind up him, and he ordered me to join the English church. I succumbed.

A lady in her eighties, Mrs Cassie, whom I used to see in Kingston while delivering the mail, grasped my hand to say goodbye and wept. Then she kissed me as though I were her son. I felt sad at that moment, realising that I would probably not see Mrs Cassie and others again.

Close by Mrs Cassie was Miss Alexander, a woman also in her eighties, who was a geography teacher in her younger days. She had always welcomed me in for tea and cakes. On my first round as a postman her pet dog had grabbed hold of the letter I was going to deliver and shredded it. With no ill will she had invited me in for a cup of tea, and that became a regular feature of my postman's round. With a tear welling up in her eye she said her goodbye.

I walked Peter, our Collie, for the last time.

Dad, Frank and Mandy wished me the best and hoped to see me again soon.

Mum and I hopped on the steam train for Aberdeen, and there I met Judy, who said that she intended to go back to New Zealand within two years, so perhaps we would meet again soon.

Chapter 5

Sydney

AT FIRST, I COULD NOT see Mum when I walked to the plane, then I spotted her waving. As the plane taxied down the runway I lost sight of her in a milling throng of wavers. Overcast clouds hovered over London to add a sombre tone to our parting. The plane then soared into bright rays of sunshine to break through the bleakness and herald a new beginning.

We introduced ourselves. Jim, nearest the aisle, was not qualified in anything but had tried a number of jobs. He was going out 'on spec' like me. Ted, in the middle, had a job lined up, having trained in hotel management. As we passed over Cyprus we sighted the Troodos Mountains. Referring to the fighting on Cyprus, Ted said, 'Glad they didn't use ack-ack on us.' We touched down at Beirut and then at Karachi before crossing over the Bay of Bengal to Singapore.

Later, as we passed over Timor, the captain said it was not a good place to ditch the plane. 'Head hunters,' he said. At Darwin airport, I met my first Australian — a native-born Scotsman who offered me a wee dram.

On our way to Sydney, the dense tropical foliage surrounding Darwin gave way to drier open woodland. Water holes and brownish-coloured rivers appeared, meandering their way through a scorched red and sandy-coloured landscape. Then the reddened face of land stood out, and here and there I spotted a few dwelling places, which seemed like frontier posts swallowed up in a vast expanse of aridness.

Later, we crossed over mountains — the Great Dividing Range — with farm settlements closer together and on greener patches. We caught glimpses of Sydney's suburban areas of mostly bungalow-type homes, and, finally, before landing, a breathtaking view of Sydney's harbour.

At the airport, Ted and Jim discovered that their luggage had not accompanied them. On that sour note we wished each other the best.

In the fading light and after clearing customs, Mr Cullis-Hill and his daughter Caroline welcomed me to Australia. We drove over the Sydney Harbour Bridge and down to the water's edge for a memorable view of the harbour and city lights. As Caroline drove through the northern suburbs, Mr Cullis-Hill kept up a running commentary on all the notable buildings, including his 'pride and joy' — a tall office building. 'Quite impressive, isn't it?' he said. He had been the main architect, and Caroline had assisted in the design. A family of architects, I was soon to discover, with Eleanor, Cullis' wife, and three daughters, Caroline, Jo and Mary, all architects. Young David, their fourth child, was still at school and had not yet decided on a career.

'It's a real bomb of a place,' Jo said, as we met at their home in the suburb of Warrawee. They showed me to my room at the back of the house with a view of the shrubbery and a tennis court. Eleanor had kindly prepared a welcome dinner with prime steak and vegetables, topped off with red wine. Caroline, Jo and Mary talked non-stop while Cullis, as Eleanor called him, chipped in every now and then with a wry remark like 'he must be a drongo if he said that'. After dinner, as I prepared to go to my room, Cullis said, 'Don't be worried about noises during the night. If you hear a growling noise, it's a possum.' What he did not tell me was the noise of a nearby refrigerator, a plover and cicadas during the night, and a laughing kookaburra at sunrise. I didn't hear the growling possum.

In a laid back manner at breakfast, Cullis said, 'We'll see what the score is today.'

What score was he talking about? I thought.

He caught my puzzled look and smiled, 'Don't worry. You won't take long to get used to the Aussie way of speaking.'

Cullis and I went for a walk to the local shopping area and stopped on the way to chat to a road worker lopping a tree. 'Shame to cut the tree down,' he said. 'But that one over there is an awful looking tree — it wouldn't matter if it came down.'

The workman didn't seem to mind being told how he should go about his job and said, 'And you take those beaut trees. You have to keep those.'

'You can go up to any person and start a conversation,' Cullis said. 'Most people you'll find are friendly. And you can call people by their first name, even your boss.'

On Sunday, Caroline, Jo, Mary and I trooped off to a polo match between Australia and Argentina. When the match was in full swing and the star of the Argentinian side, Carlos, was in hot pursuit, the commentator, in an understatement, remarked, 'Yes, the match is warming up now.' One of the Australians galloped off thinking it was the end of a chukka, and the commentator promptly called out, 'Come back, Sid. We need you badly.' Meanwhile a poodle ran out and panicked the horses.

Richard, Jo's boyfriend, joined us, and, after we had talked a while, he kept recharging my glass with beer. Was he trying to get me drunk? He took great lengths to explain what 'bullshit' meant and gave me plenty of examples like a man who got bald chasing girls against the wind. On the way back to Warrawee, Richard suggested, because of the presence of the girls in the car, that, if I needed to go somewhere in a hurry, I was to shout 'kookaburra'. The driver would stop the car while I rushed out to see this imaginary kookaburra in the bush. Anyhow, my bladder held out without the need for a 'kookaburra'.

At the polo match I also met Tony, Mary's boyfriend, a sheep grazier from Binalong, about 100 kilometres from Canberra. 'Come to our property whenever you have the opportunity,' Tony said.

'I'd like that,' I replied.

And Mary said, 'That's beaut.' A new word, I thought, for my Aussie vocab.

Through friends of the Cullis-Hills I met Professor Geddes who had carried out research on farm dams to hold water during drought. He suggested I meet with Dr Walker, a research scientist in the field of animal nutrition at Sydney University. We met, and Dr Don Walker advised me of a vacancy as a research assistant in his department. I applied.

I was successful and, 20 days after arriving in Australia, I started work as a research assistant in Dr Walker's laboratory at the department of animal nutrition of Sydney University. He explained the nature of the work — studies on the nutrition of the milk-fed lamb, the main purpose of which, according to Dr Walker, was to apply the results to children suffering from malnutrition in developing countries. I would be assisting four PhD students and eventually enrol in a master's course.

The PhD students included Karl Jagusch from New Zealand who was studying body composition under different nutritional regimes. Barry Norton from Brisbane was well into his nitrogen balance studies. Farouk, from Pakistan, had not long arrived and was carrying out digestibility analyses. Len Cook was writing up his PhD study. Denis Bogsanyi, from Hungary, was the laboratory technician. And Hilton Sinclair, a technical handyman, welcomed me with a mischievous twinkle in his eye.

At lunchtime Karl asked, 'Are you interested in girls? Plenty of 'em round here.' Karl had told me he was married so I said for fun, 'Don't you wish you weren't married?'

'You're damned right,' he replied. Karl never minced words.

Two weeks later, I moved from the Cullis-Hills to a boarding house at Neutral Bay. Mr and Mrs Auer looked after about ten of us in their weatherboard house. I had a poky room at one side of the house. From the window I looked out on to Sydney Harbour Bridge. Otherwise, the boarding house lacked appeal with its cracked walls, drab decor and cobwebbed rooms. Mrs Auer was friendly, though, which softened the forbidding ambience. She invited me to one of her weekly meetings on theosophy which focused on philosophical and religious thought. The meeting left me bewildered with a mystical approach to the divine nature. At the meeting I met John Shaw, a solicitor, who invited me to his home in Edgecliff. A generous and outgoing person, John and I became firm friends. As for theosophy, I kept that at bay and preferred a more conventional approach.

I attended St Augustine's Anglican Church in Neutral Bay, fearing Rev Douglas MacKay's wrath if I didn't. I joined in with a singles group run by Rev John Lousada and his wife Isobel who had been missionaries in Malaya.

One of the boarders, Alex Tommerup, also invited me to Dr John Hercus' home for meetings to discuss spiritual matters. Dr Hercus, an eye surgeon, had written *Pages from God's casebook* and *David*, thoughtful studies on biblical truth from a scientific perspective. He was in popular demand as a speaker to university students. A group of us played tennis on his court which fronted the harbour at Neutral Bay, and then in a relaxed atmosphere in his lounge, he encouraged us to ask questions. The way he handled those questions with an open and independent mind struck a chord with me.

He impressed on us that we should distinguish clearly between faith and belief. 'Faith implies response and action,' he said, 'while belief, resulting from careful thought and reasoning, contributes only a small part to faith — perhaps, less than 5 per cent.'

Dr Hercus pointed to the steps we could take. 'We have to try, like riding a bicycle for the first time,' he said. 'Unless we try and fall off we will never learn. The secret of walking by faith is staying in tune with God. Each day, hand over the day to God by thought, word and action. Allow the stillness of God to empower you. Later, review and close the day with God. Slowly we learn to walk with the mind of God.'

He emphasised that we can become the person we are meant to be — in harmony with God and in harmony with ourselves and at peace with our station in life. In a way I found that this step into the unknown was liberating like a journey to a foreign land. Nothing is prescribed, or falls into categories, or is certain. The uncertain takes over, as we venture out, and becomes a reality with a fresh infusion of life and energy.

The idea of reaching out came also with the words of George MacLeod, founder of the Iona Community in Scotland:

'For Christ is a person to be trusted, not a principle to be tested. The Church is a movement, not a meeting house. Faith is an experience, not an exposition. Christians are explorers, not mapmakers.'

After a short walk each morning I caught the ferry at Neutral Bay to Circular Quay, and, from there, took a bus or train to the university. The harbour views always captivated me with chugging ferries, pleasure craft, hydrofoils and larger vessels, all sharing the large expanse of the harbour and inlets. At nighttime lights twinkled on the Sydney Harbour Bridge and along the bays, where boats moored and houses nestled at the waterfront.

Once, as I waited on a bench for the ferry, a sunburnt Aussie sat down alongside and started talking about his time in the bush — 21 years. He was brown, lean and healthy-looking, and youngish despite his grey hair. The housing problem, according to him, was the only thing wrong with Australia. 'It's a good life,' he said, 'if you buy a car and a house before you get married. Don't spend money on the poker machines, card games and horses. O my word, they're the worst. Once you start chasing money you play right into the hands of bookies.' I thanked him for his advice and we parted on a friendly note.

Regular ferry travellers at that time had a prime view of the Opera House going up, its sails unfurling skywards.

Usually, each weekend I took the train back to Warrawee to visit the Cullis-Hills and join in with their activities. When I arrived at their house, Cullis would always greet me in his Australian twang, 'How yer goin'?' His favourite expressions included 'mad as a galah' and 'that was a crook deal'. If someone had said something ridiculous he would say, 'shut up, will yer' or 'give it a fair go' or 'that's a load of bull'. But if he agreed with you he said, 'that's fer sure'.

On one occasion we watched the regatta on the Nepean River. The most exciting race — the Mens Eight — drew us all in with wild cheering. On another occasion we visited Bobbin Head, a favourite picnic spot with a marina in Ku-ring-gai Chase National Park. On the way back we bumped into mud-caked boys, who could have been mistaken for Aborigines, battling in a river bed. We avoided the mud fight, but the pelting rain soaked us to the skin.

Tony de Mestre, Mary's boyfriend, encouraged me to take an interest in sheep. He rang up one day, inviting me to meet him at the Australia Hotel in Castlereagh Street. Just as I arrived at Wynyard Station by train, a fellow stopped me and asked where Castlereagh Street was. 'That's where I'm heading for,' I said. We both found it, and Tony, in an Irish tweed suit, was already there. Mary, in a stunning blue outfit, joined us and we headed off to a sheep show.

At the show, Tony examined each sheep with a trained eye, carefully parting the wool and checking its quality. 'Look at this one,' he said. 'See the distinct pattern. That's character for you.' My introduction to the finer qualities of wool had begun.

In June, I spent a weekend on Tony's sheep and cattle property at Binalong. He showed me over his paddocks and explained his rotational scheme for grazing lucerne and phalaris. We fed the Herefords, but I kept well away from the bull, remembering my previous encounter in Israel where I ended up with two cracked ribs. In the afternoon we journeyed to Yass to meet up with Tony's mates in a pub. The beer flowed freely, accompanied by strong points of view on politics and other pressing issues. At one point, Tony said of a politician that 'he goes round like a headless chook'. Later, Tony drove like Stirling Moss to Canberra to meet up with more friends, and I viewed the well laid out city with its tree-lined avenues and bridges spanning Lake Burley Griffin. I just survived a great weekend of hospitality with my first look at a grazing property.

After two months the routine laboratory tests had become monotonous — maybe this wasn't my line after all. I asked for a week off when Gordon Baxter, of Baxters of Speyside, the firm for which Dad worked, jetted in for a food exhibition at the Sydney Showground. Gordon had asked for my help with a display of Scottish soups, preserves, condiments, beetroot, chutneys and a wide range of fine quality food products — all prepared by Baxters.

I dished out samples of soup to a never-ending stream of samplers. One young girl helped herself to sample after sample and her comments ranged from 'not bad' to 'very good'. The Scotch Broth, Royal Game, Cock-a-leekie and Highlanders Broth all sold fast. And so did the jams. Pamela, a buxom lass, assisted and put on the airs of a refined demonstrator: 'Come on now, ladies — try the Scottish jam. It's wonderful. Jam from the Scottish Highlands. It's a treat. Don't go away without your soup, ladies.'

Gordon Baxter arrived on the scene and so did the tins of haggis his company had produced. I had some misgiving, as I had never heard of haggis being sold in tins. Anyhow, we went to work and sold tins of haggis to customers who for one reason or other were willing to have a 'bash', as one sampler said. Gordon displayed the largest haggis ever produced in the world to draw in the crowd and reporters. And I wrote a few lines for the unfortunate haggis:

> Help, let me get oot
> This is nae a place for me
> I canna run aboot
> Nor jump wi' joy and glee
> Just nae fun at a'
> Locked up like this,
> I canna run awa
> Like ony other haggis
> It's a disgrace
> To be in sic a place
> Dinna tell a soul
> In case of ridicule

But if ye've a min'
To be thoughtful and kin'
Ye just tak a bite
And I'd squeal with delight.

Gordon Baxter read the poem but was not impressed — I could tell — after all, it would do nothing for the sale of tinned haggis.

Once, on the way back from the showground at nighttime, I met a Scot who seemed half-canned. He looked distressed so I stopped to give him a word of encouragement. Five minutes later he burst out crying and said, 'Folk looked me up and down and couldna care a docken.' I realised how wrong we can be in judging other people's letdowns.

Everything ran out before the end of the food exhibition — the jams, soups, pheasant, and even the haggis. 'What a shame!' said Lorna, one of the demonstrators, 'the public are going to be so disappointed.' The tinned haggis eventually died a natural death, but Gordon was pleased with the publicity he had secured for Baxters. For me, I welcomed the change from the growing monotony of laboratory routine.

At work, I took the Melbourne Cup as another horse event. Len Cook, in our laboratory, was busy with the sweepstake and drew Polo Prince for me. At the all-important race time I had gone to the library. Another horse race I had thought. I had not realised that this was *the* most important horse race event of the year. How shameful! When I returned from the library, Len hollered, 'You've won.'

'Here he is,' someone else shouted.

'You're a hard case,' said Karl, as Len forked out my winnings.

Shortly after the Melbourne Cup, I took up an invitation by friends of Mum — Harry and Jean Craig — to visit their cattle property in Queensland's mulga country.

As the train rumbled up to Moree, an Aboriginal — well tanned, or perhaps his normal colour, and wearing a broad-brimmed hat — came in from the next carriage. 'Three drunks in my carriage,' he said. 'Where you from?'

'Sydney, and going to a cattle property near Goondiwindi,' I said. We chatted for a while.

'I love station life, but it is quite lonely for me,' he said. At times his eyes showed sadness, but then he would smile warm-heartedly. We parted at his station.

The train stopped at Moree, and I made my way to the hot baths, which seemed to be full of old fogies with rheumatism and other complaints. I wandered over to the swimming pool and met another Aboriginal who talked about his experience as a jackaroo and then as a railway worker.

Harry Craig greeted me with his 7-year-old daughter, Polly. When we arrived at his property, Harry explained about his solar trapping device, his diesel engine which supplied the power, and his reticulated water system with tanks. From then on Polly took charge. She even questioned the possibility of marrying me. I took that as a proposal, my only one as it turned out to be, so I treasured it.

Out on the property we stopped at water tanks and turkey nest dams, and gazed at emus and kangaroos. We spotted plovers, galahs, a crane bird, and goannas that scuttled across the road tracks. We listened to one of the jackaroos explain how his trousers had come off when a wild boar chased him. And Polly chatted non-stop. 'Next time you come,' she said, 'you'll have an emu egg.'

In the evening she dressed up as Santa — a little early for Christmas, though. And she sang 'The dying stockman'. Outside, a full moon lit up the ghost gums with ethereal beauty, their white trunks shimmering in the light breeze. The next day, Polly and I went horse riding together. 'You can't ride,' she said. 'I can ride.' She could, too, and taught me the basics.

Later as I watched Harry change a tyre on his tractor, I stepped back and almost trod on a curled up brown snake. 'Yeah,' Harry said, as he killed it with a blow from an iron bar, 'they're common out here.' We then toured the mulga scrub to check on the cattle and the watering points. At nighttime I read bedtime stories to Polly, and she listened to me for a change.

The following day was party day with jackeroos, jillaroos, governesses, a physiotherapist, and others who could be anybody from university students to drifters. We danced in the light of the full moon. Then, just when I was getting to know a brunette who had sidled up to me with a beer and asked about my Scottish background, Polly grabbed my hand and said, 'We're going.' So that was that. With fleeting farewells we went back to the homestead.

I returned to Sydney invigorated and keen to explore more of Australia's outback. A letter had arrived from Mum asking what the heat was like. Was she concerned about me? Or—?

Back at work, Hilton had not lost his form. 'You know,' he said, 'the Chinese made the bagpipes and passed them on to the Irish, and the Irish passed them on to the Scots as a joke, but the Scots did not quite wake up to the joke and kept them.'

'And I wish I could play them,' I replied.

Karl, a strong Catholic and with strong views, battled it out with Len and Barry, both of whom were non-believers. 'I am an intelligent Catholic,' he said. 'People who spend all their money on cars, television sets, a good home, should be having kids instead. The more kids you have the more children there will be to bring into God's fold.' That kind of statement and 'I don't believe in contraception' drew up the battle lines.

'Would you marry to have kids, Karl?' Barry asked, wading into the debate. 'If everyone thought like you, we would have a very narrow outlook on life. What about the population problem worldwide? Shouldn't every couple be responsible in having fewer kids these days?' Karl fought back, defending his convictions.

I expected some day to go back to Israel, but did not know when. My Hebrew lessons went well with my teacher, Ester Udovich, who lived with her husband and son Eytan in North Sydney. She was full of praise as I began to master the language.

Ester invited me to Eytan's Bar Mitzvah, the Jewish coming-of-age ceremony. I sat in the front row, wearing a Jewish kippah, a skullcap. Few people took interest in the Jewish prayers and readings. A number of young Jewish boys chattered and fidgeted. But there was a hush when Eytan read from the Haftorah, a short selection from the prophets. Then he sang a passage about David's love for Jonathan, his closest friend. This he did superbly without any faltering. When he came down from the pulpit there was excitement as everyone shook his hand. From an alcove covered by a curtain the teacher read from a parchment roll and sang for ages, it seemed. Then singing by the whole congregation reminded me of the haunting melodies from a concert at Kibbutz Shoval.

The next day, I attended Eytan's Bar Mitzvah party — a lavish affair with champagne and a spread fit for royalty. Even though I was a stranger, everyone made me feel quite at home. A feeling of Jewish togetherness, strengthening of ties and reliving their tradition, all bonded them in their heritage. Eytan, in an immaculate suit, gave his first speech as a man. Later, a Jewish woman sang in Yiddish and Hebrew, and all joined in with the singing of *Hava Nagilah* and *Hevenu Shalom Aleichem*.

I spent the first Christmas in Australia with the Cullis-Hills, but I had to pass on the Christmas turkey and plum pudding because of an upset stomach. For New Year's Eve, a few of us listened to Andy Stewart and then ended up at Kings Cross. The chock-a-block traffic vied with masses of young, festive-crazed people, screaming and loudmouthing. Young lads doused each other with water from Kings Cross fountain. Then 12 o'clock struck —

Frank, my brother, sent a letter from the Aberdeen Royal Mental Hospital wishing me well for the New Year and asking whether I got drunk for Hogmanay, the last day of the year. I worried for him, though, despite his light-hearted jokes. I knew he would be having electric shock treatment again.

I often walked from North Sydney station to my boarding place in Neutral Bay. On the way I stopped off at Gerhard's café. Gerhard and his wife Susi were Jewish and we often talked about what was happening in Israel and their Jewish background. As I sipped my espresso coffee on one occasion, Gerhard whispered, 'You know,

Tom, Sydney has nothing for me and Susi. Our sons will turn into men but will have lost their Jewish identity. I don't want to make money. I have lived here for eight years and still I feel a stranger. Look here, I must tell you something. Can you keep a secret? We're going back to Israel.' I felt happy for them, as this seemed the right way for them, to make something new and meaningful in their lives as Jews.

Not long after, Judy arrived from Scotland on her way back to her home in New Zealand. She looked great in a red frock as we hugged each other. With a short en route visit we lost no time in hiring a car and headed for the Blue Mountains where we walked to Echo Point, the Three Sisters and along the rim of Jamieson Valley. Later we partied at a friend of Judy's where everyone talked about their travels. All too soon, the next day, Judy left for New Zealand.

A long silence from Malka, but then she wrote to say that she was going to marry an Israeli captain of a passenger ship. She said, 'I don't want to be a bit sentimental now, so I don't want to tell you how I really feel ... I'm going to marry very soon. I believe that time and faith will help you to understand my cruelty.'

I felt numb and empty. I should have realised that something like this would happen. Two years apart was too long. We had grown very fond of each other, I was sure, and the bond between us had strengthened with our letter writing. Oddly enough, I was still keen to try my luck as an agricultural scientist in Israel if the opportunity arose.

In a confused state, I continued as a research assistant, but my resolve to start my master's degree waned as time went on. Dr Walker poured cold water on my ideas to implement a study of milk-fed lambs. I had outlined a method of putting the lambs on various restricted diets and then re-feeding them, with measurements of elements and metabolites to follow their progress. The plan, according to Dr Walker, was not detailed enough, hastily contrived and had restricted the analyses. Later, I discussed it over beers with Karl, Barry and Len, and they let me know that I had to tell Dr

Walker in no uncertain terms what I would like to do and pressure him. It was easy enough for them to say that.

Another problem worried me, though, as time went on. I felt that the laboratory routine was stifling my own development. I had spent over a year being a research assistant, and, while I had helped others in their work, mine had faltered. It seemed to drift into no man's land with no enthusiasm to continue. I tried, nevertheless, to restart the motivation button.

One night after a game of squash, I caught the ferry back to Cremorne Point and was walking back to the boarding house when I noticed the wobbly gait of a man just in front of me. He looked as though he was drunk. I tried to sidestep him, but he stopped in his tracks and faced me. The man's right eye was missing and the right side of his face showed hideous scars. I stayed rooted to the spot not knowing what to do. He pointed to his face and in broken English explained that he had been in a car accident. He had come from a Russian ship that had anchored in the harbour, and he did not want to go back to it. He fumbled around for a cigarette and allowed me to light it. And then he asked for some money to visit his friend in Mosman. I obliged. He held out his hand and grasped the money with some hesitation. At that moment he mentioned something about Jesus Christ and that a woman had given him a cross. 'I don't want war,' he said. 'Why do we have to fight each other?' I agreed, and as we parted, he mumbled, 'Bok bless you'. Realising what he meant to say, I said, 'God bless.' Although a small incident it left an impression that this man was crying from the depths of his heart, seeking a measure of peace for himself and for the world.

Meanwhile, Gerhard let me know that his family were sailing for Israel in two days' time on Sunday, 6 June 1965. On that day I joined a crowd of people milling around the barrier to the Greek ship *Piraeus*. Everyone, it seemed, shouted in Greek. Gerhard and I greeted each other like long-lost friends and we said our goodbyes with a promise that I would make it to Israel one day. We parted with Gerhard, Susi, and their son Micky, all crying. David, their other son was too young to understand. We kept waving until the ship slowly moved away from the quayside.

A little later, I attended Jo and Richard's wedding on 24 July 1965; the church was packed. Polly, the sweet little girl I had met in Queensland, headed the bridal procession, smart and proud in her role. Several hundred guests gathered in a marquee afterwards; they spilled over into the tennis courts. With champagne glasses held aloft Cullis made the first toast to the Queen.

By August I had made up my mind to leave my position as research assistant. I knew I was living on borrowed time with the way I felt about the whole research project. I squared my feelings with Dr Walker, and we agreed I leave at the end of October. Then about the same time Mum wrote to let me know that Dad had had enough of his job at Baxters and that she sought relief from cold winters. I realised then why she had asked about the heat here in summer. They had made up their minds to come to Australia for a new life. Australia House had accepted their application and they would most likely sail in October.

I rang up home to say how happy I was with their decision. But I had reservations. 'Dad,' I said, 'you will be 49 in two months' time. You will find it difficult to work here, despite having been an export sales manager with Baxters.'

'I will take my chances,' he said. 'Your mum also needs a change. She can't stand the cold wintry weather; she needs a warmer climate.'

I worried, too, about Frank adjusting to a new environment, especially with his mental health situation. I was surprised that Australia House had accepted Frank as a migrant.

They boarded the *Australis* in the second week of October.

On 19 October 1965, I received the worst possible news by telegram from the ship. Frank had disappeared from the ship somewhere in the Mediterranean Sea. They had searched the whole ship to find no sign of him.

I could not imagine how Mum, Dad and Mandy felt having lost Frank and having to endure three more weeks on board. Had

Frank felt that everything was too much and taken his own life? I did not know what to believe. I had lost a brother, aged 21, who had been deeply troubled. He would have loved the wide open spaces of Australia.

Not long after leaving the Sydney University, and having said goodbye to everyone, I watched the *Australis* dock near Circular Quay in Sydney at midnight of 12 November 1965. I saw Dad first, then Mum and Mandy. We all kept waving until the ship had anchored. In their cabin we talked for hours before snatching some sleep. Dad and Mum looked in good health despite the strain of the journey.

Mr and Mrs Cullis-Hill arrived in the morning and drove us to their home in Warrawee. A new beginning in our lives.

With my father, mother and grandmother (1941)

Frank, my brother, with a fish caught from the River Spey

Student boarders, Simon, Graham, Robin, Annabel
and Tom, at Mrs Fraser's in Aberdeen

Joshua directing work in the apple orchard of Kibbutz Shoval

Malka minding children on Kibbutz Shoval in Israel

Judy, a penfriend, with my mother, Anne

Taking in the wonder of Lake Marian, South Island, New Zealand

Courting days with Liz

Wedding day, 28 October 1967

Rachel and Linda setting off for school

Chapter 6

Adelaide

AFTER A TRIP TO MELBOURNE to meet with people who might be able to help Dad in finding employment, we journeyed to Adelaide. Adelaide seemed a more sedate city, with the River Torrens meandering from the Adelaide Hills through the city parklands to the sea. We moved into a rented flat while Dad found a sales job with SAFCOL, the South Australian Sea Foods Cooperative.

I had a promising interview with Harold Chamberlain who supervised the running of the field research centres of the Department of Agriculture. A vacancy for a livestock research officer opened up and I applied for it. While waiting for a response, I decided to take a three-week holiday in New Zealand. Judy encouraged me to come over and tour the South Island. Her friend Jan from Sydney would join us.

Close to New Year's Day, Jan and I arrived at Judy's home in Timaru. We watched the New Year come in while standing on a cliff edge overlooking Caroline Bay. Red flares and a bonfire on the beach set the sky aglow for the start of 1966. A party at a friend of Judy's followed. I ended up with a roomful of about 20 girls to myself — not that I planned it, but the boys had drifted into an adjacent room for men's business. A Kiwi custom, I thought.

Later in the day, Judy, Jan and I set off in a packed Viva to explore the South Island. Our first stop heralded Lake Tekapo with its milky-turquoise colour and surrounding snow-capped peaks.

Mt Cook towered over its companion peaks. We caught sight of the Tasman Glacier before moving on to Lake Wanaka with a silvery, bluish-green sheen to its surface, and mountains as a backdrop rising gently from its shores.

Then we pitched our tents for a night at Lake Wakatipu, with an eye-catching view of a range of mountains — The Remarkables — rising sharply from the south-eastern edge of the lake. A quaint hotel nearby closed at six o'clock in the evening, but an unofficial drinking den attached to the hotel opened up, and the patrons simply shuffled to their new venue and business continued as usual far into the night. We joined them for a while.

The next day we took the Skippers Canyon Road, one of the most dangerous roads in the world the locals said. With room only for one car, and with a 100-metre drop to the river, Judy negotiated the winding road with extreme care while Jan and I took in the spectacular views of the Shotover River and the surrounding hills of the Otago region.

That night I had a strange dream about Frank. I entered a room and Frank was there, so I shouted with joy. Dad and Mum were there too and told me that Frank had changed his name and had jumped onto another ship. I awoke and felt awful.

The next day, we motored on to Lake Te Anau, a peaceful lake, nestled in the south-western corner of the South Island. Further on towards Milford Sound each snow-capped peak held its own wonder. Tree-clad slopes lay beneath the sharp serrated heights. Waterfalls cascaded down steep-sided cliff faces, the fresh crystal clear water foaming over rocks into the depths below.

We took a trip up the Milford Sound in a fishing boat, the spray catching us by surprise. With not a cloud in the sky, our guide let us know that we had come on one of the very few rain-free days in the year. The Sound was carved out by glaciers during the ice age and Rudyard Kipling had described it as 'the eighth wonder of the world'.

One of the most secluded and prettiest lakes still lay in store for us. We were the only ones to take in the magical beauty of Lake

Marian with its snow-capped peak towering above its southern end. We braved the green, icy cold water for a swim, but not for too long.

We spent the night at Dunedin at a motor camp and then continued back to Timaru the next day. South Island's spectacular scenery surpassed all my expectations — a memorable experience.

Judy and I parted the best of friends. She would visit the family one day when we had settled down in Adelaide.

Back in Adelaide I dreamt about Frank again. This time he was drying dishes. A long corridor separated the kitchen and the room Mum was in. I tried to force Frank to come and see Mum. He refused, and, as I tugged his arm in the corridor, he disappeared.

Dad was upset with the lack of progress in his work. He had accepted a new job as a sales demonstrator with Murray Riverland, quite a climb down from his position as sales export manager with Baxters. Trouble arose with problems over mouldy pears. At one point, Dad said, 'We are going back to Scotland.' That cast a spell of gloom over the dining table.

'I am not going back,' Mum said.

'Me too,' said Mandy.

Fortunately, the next day Dad had simmered down and there was no more talk of going back.

Mandy attended Adelaide High School and studied hard in her final year of schooling; she was thinking about becoming a nurse.

Harold Chamberlain, superintendent of the research centres, and Cec Mulhearn, head of the livestock division of the Department of Agriculture, interviewed me. At the end of two hours, which included a rundown of the activities of the extension, regulatory and research activities of the department, Harold said, 'We think you are the bloke for the livestock research position.' I welcomed his offer.

Although I had not completed my master's degree with Sydney University, Harold did not hold that against me. I had accepted the University of Sydney as my break-in time. It was a valuable learning experience of becoming attuned to the Australian way of life. I had studied courses in animal nutrition, animal husbandry and statistics, all of which might assist me in a new job. I looked forward to a change from laboratory to field work.

On my first day with the department, 21 February 1966, Cec introduced me to the other livestock research officers. Then we drove to Wanbi research centre, passing from the high rainfall ranges on Adelaide's eastern flank to the Murray plains.

The River Murray, the longest river in Australia, offered irrigation to nearby paddocks as well as supply water for domestic use. The Murray Mallee, a vast grain growing and sheep farming area of South Australia, had been largely cleared of native Mallee vegetation — trees characterised by the growth of multiple stems.

We met Paul Guerin, the manager of Wanbi research centre, who had worked there for seven years and had achieved a lot in combating erosion on the sandy soils by sowing pastures which had adapted to the drought prone region. Paul condemned the government policies giving little support to providing amenities for people living in Wanbi town and the local farming areas.

The following day we attended a local agricultural bureau meeting with about 80 farmers coming to listen to talks by the department officers on aspects of pig, poultry and sheep husbandry. I learned that the agricultural bureau was run by the farmers themselves and had been in existence since about 1890 with more than 100 branches forming throughout the State. The groups met regularly to exchange ideas and discuss farming practices. Officers from the department of agriculture were invited to speak on specialist topics. The department's extension officers worked in with the bureau groups to provide speakers at meetings and special field days, where demonstrations of farming practices were carried out. The bureau, it seemed, was a great way of linking farmers and department officers together.

Cec Mulhearn then called me into his office, and, in an easy-going manner over a cup of coffee, he detailed my first project. 'Farmers are telling us,' he said, 'about their heavy lamb losses at lambing time, particularly with Merinos. Up to 30 per cent of lambs born are lost in the first few days of life. Sheep farmers attribute this loss mainly to the weather and to predators — foxes, and, to a lesser extent, crows, ravens and wedge-tailed eagles. But we don't really know how important the fox is as a predator in our flocks. We need to observe foxes at lambing time to find out what is really going on.'

'Observe the foxes?' I queried.

'Yes, we are constructing hides at three different lambing sites on the Minnipa research farm on Eyre Peninsula. At each site we will have an enclosure protected from foxes and an unprotected one. These enclosures are close to native scrub which harbours foxes. From the hides you will be able to record the activities of foxes at lambing time in the unprotected enclosure and what impact they have on ewes and their lambs.'

'I gather we will be observing the foxes throughout the night,' I queried.

'Sure, we have tried to make night observations easier by arranging the peak of lambing to coincide with full moon in May. With night binoculars and clear skies, hopefully, you should be able to follow the activities of foxes and lambing ewes. We use vasectomised or 'teaser' rams on the ewes to help concentrate lambing.'

'Has any work at all been done on foxes and their activities?' I asked.

'Well, they have looked at the diet of foxes in the Canberra area and it seems the fox is an opportunistic scavenger and will eat just about anything, even a Granny Smith apple, and the leather wrist band of a watch was found in the stomach of one fox. And we have already discovered at last year's lambing at Minnipa Research Centre from examination of dead lamb carcasses that the fox was responsible for deaths due to primary predation. But no one has carried out direct observations on a lambing ewe flock exposed to foxes. We would like you to take charge of the project and to write up your research findings for the *Australian Journal of Experimental Agriculture and Animal Husbandry* as well as present the results at the next conference of the Australian Society of Animal Production.

Nothing like being thrown in the deep end for the start of a new job, I thought.

'You will take responsibility for the project from now on,' Cec said. 'And there's already been keen interest shown by George Alexander, a research scientist with the CSIRO division of animal production in Sydney, and from Ian Rowley of the CSIRO wildlife division in Canberra. You'd better contact them to see what their plans are and how they can join the program. They and their assistants will help you in recording observations, I am sure.'

George Alexander had carried out a number of experiments to determine how wind, rain and temperature, influenced the behaviour of ewes and lambs at lambing time. A combination of cold, wet and windy weather was the worst to affect the mothering-up of lambs. If a lamb had not drunk from its mother in the first few hours, then there was little chance that the lamb would survive. They also found that a large percentage of lamb deaths was due to a 'mismothering complex' which took in a number of factors such as birth weight, vigour of the lambs at birth and mothering ability.

How would the presence of foxes in the lambing paddocks contribute to this mismothering of lambs? And how big a problem was predation of healthy lambs compared to other losses?

I contacted Ian Rowley, who was interested in the activities of crows and ravens in lambing flocks, and George Alexander, who would bring an assistant to help out with observations.

Next, Harold Chamberlain called me into his room to meet Jack Messenger, a sheep advisor, who had published a paper on fox predation as a cause of lamb mortality, based on his findings at Minnipa Research Centre in 1965. After chatting for a while about his work, another officer entered. 'Bunny Fennessy, meet Foxy Mann,' said Harold. I acknowledged Harold's sense of humour but thought it a bit premature to be calling me 'Foxy'.

Bunny, an acknowledged expert on rabbits and their control in Australia, discussed Jack's findings on lamb mortality. He did not like the term 'rogue fox' which the officers were using. 'The fox was in the dark for most people,' he said. 'We know little about its favourite pursuits, its social behaviour, its diet, habits and territories, so the whole question involving lambs becomes complicated.'

Jack brought up the likelihood of lambing practices, such as lambing at a different time to neighbouring flocks, which might affect the level of predation. Finally, Harold proposed a clearer definition of the problem and distribution of work to the various departments concerned. By the end of the two-hour meeting everyone was foxed out and it was time for lunch. Bunny, not his real name, was pleased we had invited him to discuss the problem.

I flew up to Minnipa on Eyre Peninsula, or the West Coast as they say, for my first visit to the research centre. From the air, as the plane approached the airport, I looked out on to granite outcrops and patches of cleared land surrounded by scrub.

Don Winn, the manager, greeted me, along with Bob Asser, the clerk, Ken Holden, the agronomy advisor, and Ian Bidstrup, the farm manager. We went to a bureau meeting where Ken gave a lively talk on managing weeds in cereal crops. I gathered from Ken that the annual rainfall of 350 millimetres for the Minnipa area was almost too sparse for cropping, but if it came at the right time the farmers usually harvested a reasonable crop of wheat, barley or oats.

The next day, Don and I visited the three lambing sites, which adjoined native scrub. We revisited them again at nighttime with spotlights and picked up several pairs of red eyes. 'There are plenty of them around,' Don said. 'We haven't shot any foxes for quite a while knowing we might run this trial.' We discussed the details of the trial the next day before I helped in yarding sheep ready for crutching.

I returned to my office in Adelaide to finalise arrangements with those coming from interstate and to make sure I had all the equipment I needed. I then set off again to Minnipa in a packed Land Rover. On the way I picked up a couple of hitchhikers from England. We lunched at Port Augusta before moving on to the birthplace of the steel industry at Iron Knob on the Eyre Highway.

We stopped at Kimba, a rural service town on the highway, before moving on to Wudinna and finally Minnipa.

At Minnipa I raced around to check all the paddocks and help put the finishing touches to one of the fox-proof enclosures with wire netting mesh 1.8 metres in height and extending 15 centimetres into the ground. An electrified wire connected to an Anders 6V fence unit extended around the enclosure, and was supported 15 centimetres outside the top of the fence. It seemed to me like overkill, but no one knew for certain how high a fox could jump or how deep a fox could burrow under a fence. Don had persuaded the neighbouring sheep producers not to shoot foxes for one month prior to lambing.

The roofed hides were located in the lanes which separated the protected and unprotected enclosures. The hide consisted of a four square metre room with sliding glass windows on each wall; window curtains could be drawn. The room itself was mounted on a moveable steel frame, four metres high, made from a disused hay stacking machine called a Jay Hawk. Fifty ewes were then placed in each paddock and fed a mixture of oats and wheat. They were identified by numbers 15 centimetres high, branded with Siromark on both sides.

George Alexander arrived from Sydney with an assistant, David Williams. Ian Rowley and a couple of officers from the Department of Agriculture also flew in. We organised ourselves into three shifts: midnight to 8 am, 8 am to 4 pm and 4 pm to midnight.

On my first shift from 4 pm to midnight, about an hour after sunset, I spotted my first fox emerging from the scrub and heading towards the unprotected lambing enclosure. It stopped in its tracks for a minute before moving into the enclosure where a ewe had just given birth. The fox approached the ewe and her lamb with caution. As the fox moved closer, the ewe pawed the ground and moved towards the fox in an attempt to butt it. The fox retreated and skirted around the ewe and finally feasted on discarded foetal membranes. The other ewes in the enclosure were only slightly agitated, which surprised me.

A little later another fox entered the enclosure and approached a stillbirth lamb in a circumspect manner. Twenty minutes passed before the fox had enough courage, it seemed, to pick up the dead lamb and carry it away. In my eagerness to see what was happening I knocked the tape recorder onto the floor. The fox dropped the lamb and scurried back into the bush.

The noise had not deterred other foxes from coming into the unprotected enclosure and before long I was busy recording the movements of three foxes moving amongst the ewes and newborn lambs. The ewes showed slight agitation but again no sign of panic. A protective ewe attempted to butt one of the foxes if it came too close. And on more than one occasion a healthy lamb moved towards a fox and the fox retreated. The foxes appeared to be more interested in afterbirth and dead or dying lambs than attacking healthy lambs.

The mild disturbance in the flocks contrasted markedly with that of a vagrant Border Collie dog that entered one of the enclosures. A group of ewes, not yet lambed, stood up, showed alarm, and, as a tight group, moved rapidly towards the dog which retreated. The dog circled the paddock and finally returned to pick up a moribund lamb which it carried away.

In a larger paddock of lambing ewes, which was not part of the trial, one of our watchers spotted a fox attacking a healthy lamb and killing it. But the normal pattern of activity was for the fox to be in the paddock as an opportunistic scavenger. And there was plenty of food for a number of foxes with afterbirth and dying or dead lambs without the need to prey on healthy ones. We found no evidence of foxes causing mismothering.

During the day we sighted large numbers of crows and ravens in the lambing paddocks, apparently attracted by the grain fed to the sheep. While on a day shift I noticed that the crows waddled like ducks, while the ravens seemed to bounce along like kangaroos. The ravens showed the greater interest in the lambs and spent considerable time probing the tail region of lambs from where they ate the fresh nutrient-rich faeces. I observed a vicious attack of one lamb by several ravens, but on examination of the lamb later there was no sign of damage to the lamb. On three occasions, a raven kept pace with a running lamb by holding the lamb's tail in its beak. The raven bounced along as though on a pair of water skis. Two ravens attacked a lamb that had been temporarily separated from its mother. The ravens pecked at the anus and the eyes of the lamb. One of the ravens then jumped up on top of the lamb's back and gripped the rump of the lamb with its claws and pecked at the lamb's eyes. The lamb ran for some 50 metres with this alien on its back, the whole performance appearing like a comical chariot ride. When I examined the lamb later no wounds could be found.

I carried out postmortem examinations on all the dead lambs in the enclosures and in the larger lambing paddocks that were not part of the trial. Three of the lamb carcasses showed evidence of being killed by a wedge-tailed eagle with talon marks penetrating the skull. In most dead lambs I was able to tell if the lamb had breathed, walked, sucked, and was healthy or not at the time of death. There was no difference between the two types of enclosure in the numbers of lambs dying. Primary predation by foxes, ravens and eagles, only accounted for a small percentage of lamb deaths.

We pooled all our observations. But would sheep farmers be happy with our findings? I was doubtful. Sheep farmers still claimed, as I found out later, that the fox was a costly predator.

We achieved our foxy outcome with a journal article of the first Australian behavioural study of the activities of foxes and crows in lambing paddocks, and I was able to present the findings at a conference in Sydney for the Proceedings of the Australian Society of Animal Production.

Back at the office in Adelaide, Cec greeted me, 'How are you, Foxy?'

'Fine, but I should be out chasing rabbits,' I replied.

We discussed further studies I could do in the field of improving ewe fertility. I would continue to carry out observations at Minnipa and assist with research work elsewhere in South Australia.

While living in Neutral Bay, Sydney, John Lousada of St Augustine's Church suggested I go to the Holy Trinity Church in the city centre of Adelaide. I started going to the evening services and joining in with a group that met for a game of squash during the week. Another Tom and I had made arrangements one night to pick up some players. But we missed picking up a nursing sister, Elizabeth Webb. She was left standing. How embarrassing when we found out! Each of us had thought the other person would pick her up. To make up for whoever made the error, I invited her to have dinner with our family.

Liz's warm, friendly, outgoing and fun-loving nature struck a chord with me. A ready smile on her face and sparkling eyes accompanied her tall, slim attractive presence. We seemed to be natural companions and started seeing each other.

Liz was born on Australia Day 1945 in Adelaide and grew up in Mitcham. Her mum, Jean Webb (née Williams) met her dad, Martin Webb, during the Second World War when he was a gunner in the Royal Australian Navy.

On returning to civilian life, Liz's father had become an alcoholic. Liz's mother could not cope with the violent episodes that accompanied his drinking binges. Looking after daughters, Christine, Margaret and Elizabeth, and son, Johnathan, proved too much. They were all made wards of the state and placed into Church of England Children's homes. Liz has fond memories of her sister Christine, who died at the age of fifteen from a brain haemorrhage. 'She was an inspiration to us all,' Liz said.

From the age of three to 17, Liz grew up in two Church of England homes. After completing her schooling at Unley Girls Technical High School, she trained at the Royal Adelaide Hospital to become a registered nurse in 1966. She was studying a midwifery course at the Queen Victoria Maternity Hospital when I met her. She stayed with a former missionary couple, Max and Marjorie Hart, who regarded Liz as a daughter. Their two sons fortunately had their own girlfriends.

After a whirlwind courtship of parties, tennis and squash, outings to the beach, parks and to the Adelaide Hills, family get-togethers, and joining in with a fellowship at Holy Trinity Church, I suggested we might get married. Her response was an ecstatic 'yes'. We had been to a live performance of the *Engel Family* and the timing seemed right. We were in love and felt right for each other.

We married on 28 October 1967 and went to Tasmania for our honeymoon. For Liz I wrote:

> Heart of my belonging
> Heart of my delight
> What treasure to behold
> In the soft fading light
>
> With warm loving eyes
> And laughter of life
> Such treasure to behold
> My adorable wife
>
> The flower of youth
> Passes by in the night
> But your bloom's forever
> Lizzies's sparkle of light
>
> The truth that awakens
> The dawn will come again
> And always you will be
> Such a sweet refrain
>
> Heart of my belonging
> Heart of my desire
> Eternally yours
> In a sunset of fire

Liz and I settled into a rented apartment in Malvern, Adelaide. She nursed at the Home for Incurables, and I continued to work with the

Department of Agriculture until the end of August 1968. During that time I carried out further studies on lamb losses, took part in field demonstrations and gave talks to farmers. I became absorbed in all aspects of agriculture and read widely — all the journals and fact sheets I could find. I attended field days, sheep shows, and visited farms in the high rainfall and cereal-sheep zones. I tried to grasp the intricate interplay of crop and pasture varieties, management for weeds, pests and diseases, and the interaction of crops and pastures with livestock for best management, which included type of livestock, stocking rate and movement of stock; and how to make provision for drought, which occurred every few years in the cereal-sheep zone. As officers of the Department of Agriculture, we helped improve the decision-making of farmers so they could run a viable and sustainable farming business. And like a farmer we weighed up the importance of weather and market prospects.

I made several visits to the Parndana Research Centre, on Kangaroo Island, where John Obst, a research officer, was also carrying out studies on factors influencing lamb mortality. But there were no foxes, fortunately, just cold, wet and windy weather when most farmers lambed down in the middle of winter. Most lambs, especially smaller lambs with fine birth coats, succumbed in the worst of those conditions. I spent a cold night in a hide observing about 20 ewes lamb in driving rain, accompanied by thunder and lightning. By the morning only one lamb had survived, and I think luck was on my side, too.

John had married Kate, a physical education teacher from Edinburgh, who had also studied at Aberdeen. John talked about his PhD studies and motivated me into thinking about recommencing a master's course, but I was unsure after my failed attempt at the University of Sydney.

By the middle of 1968, even though my position with the department was in one sense fulfilling and secure, I felt I had to test the waters elsewhere. I was still searching for my way in life, to express myself in perhaps more meaningful activity. Agriculture had opened the door with exciting challenges facing developed and developing countries. But how was I to find my way in this multi-avenue field?

Liz and I were keen to visit England and Scotland before having a family. We decided to resign from our positions and work in the United Kingdom for a year. Leaving a secure position, which most likely would have taken me right through to retirement, and flitting overseas all seemed illogical, but I felt it was the right thing to do.

Chapter 7
Overseas

WE SET SAIL FROM ADELAIDE for England on 3 September 1968 aboard the *Castel Felice* in a fanfare of music and blasting of steam. Hoots, cheering and intertwining streamers all added to the send-off.

The six-week voyage across the Pacific Ocean, through the Panama Canal and on to Southampton, however, became an ordeal for most passengers. The *Castel Felice* was on its last seaworthy legs, and didn't we know it with constant breakdowns, shabby state of the aged ship, blocked and overflowing toilets, and the lack of stabilisers to ease our stomachs.

We learned that the *Castel Felice* was first launched in 1930 and by the end of the Second World War was ready for the scrapyard, but was refitted with basic accommodation and facilities for the migrant trade. An Italian crew had run the immigrant ship to Australia and New Zealand since 1952.

Our port stops at Auckland, Tahiti, Cristobal, a port on the Atlantic side of the Panama Canal, Acapulco on the Mexican coast, and Lisbon were cut short because the *Castel Felice* had to make up for breakdown time. From a schedule of a day in these exotic places we had to be content with fleeting stops of two or three hours.

We should have taken more notice of the passengers disembarking in Adelaide and Melbourne. They were signing a petition to protest against the conditions and service for passengers on their way out from England. Little did we realise that the new influx of passengers would be drawing up a similar petition.

What a mixture of young and old, and of all nationalities on board. The hippies were a motley group, getting around in grubby jeans, bare feet and long hair.

On board we met our dining companions: Helen — a young and determined Aussie traveller, a young German couple, a disheartened English couple returning to London after finding life too hard in Australia, Kathleen — a nanny from Somerset, a dog-loving couple, and a mother with six kiddies. After our first dinner in our shining best, Liz and I sauntered onto the promenade deck and felt a chill as the wind curled around the sides of the ship.

We met Norman after docking in Melbourne. He said, 'I have no intentions of going back home to Scotland. I wish you the best, though.'

When we reached Sydney, memories flooded back of ferry rides from Neutral Bay to Circular Quay, and watching the many ocean liners, the Opera House, the Sydney Harbour Bridge, hydrofoils, and a host of seagoing vessels that plied the harbour waters.

Mrs Thompson, my landlady at Cremorne, met us, and, with Liz out of earshot, said, 'Liz is a wonderful girl.' I agreed. Liz's uncles, Harry and David, also arrived, along with the Cullis-Hills. We chatted in a coffee lounge, forgetting about the boarding time.

When we realised our time of departure, we rushed back to a streamer-covered ship. 'Help! They have taken away the gangplanks,' Liz shouted.

'Don't worry,' a crew member said, 'we'll carry you aboard.'

Ship life and stopovers

On our way to Auckland, the boat pitched and rolled in heavy seas across the Tasman Sea, which upset the weaker stomach passengers.

We lazed on the sundeck watching albatrosses swoop with wing tips caressing the waves.

We relished our stopover in Auckland with a tour of the city museum depicting the history of Maoris and South Sea Islanders.

Back on ship we joined the keep-fit classes before breakfast. Reading, writing letters and a quiet time filled the morning before we lazed on deckchairs. A juke box below the sun deck throbbed all day. I went to Italian classes in the afternoon. We swam in the pool when the weather became warmer and played deck tennis.

After a short stopover in Tahiti we sailed on to Acapulco, a port on the Pacific coast of Mexico. A hot steamy day greeted us at a picturesque bay, with a backdrop of hills overlooking its calm blue waters. I tried to picture the Spanish galleons with their booty entering this haven.

Liz and I escaped the hassling of souvenir vendors by boarding a bus to Puerto Marques. On the way, ultra modern homes with oblong swimming pools and tropical gardens dotted the hillsides, in contrast to shabby, squalid homes in the downtown area.

Puerto Marques surprised us with its bay fringed with tropical vegetation and golden coloured sands. Open wooden shelters would allow us to relax, so we thought. Once we sat down, small Mexican boys and girls presented their strings of shells; also, women with fruit, clothes and charms, and men who repeatedly asked us whether we'd like to go in their sailing boat or water ski.

To escape, we went for a swim in the warm waters, but one of the more persistent opportunists waded out to meet us. 'You like to go for a sail?' he said.

'In half an hour,' I replied, which was a mistake for he hung around like a foreman. At the end of half an hour he swam toward me, but I didn't let on I'd seen him and swam like an Olympic swimmer in the opposite direction. Back on shore, two guitarists serenaded us. After a while, we excused ourselves for another swim. The chap who had been waiting waded out once again to meet us. We were on a merry-go-round so we headed back to Acapulco.

Later, we watched the famous Acapulco divers perform with dives of about 35 metres from the cliffs of La Quebrada into the sea below. The depth of the water varied from two to four metres depending on the waves, so timing was crucial. A Mexican boy, with arms extended, readied himself and plunged. He performed a first class dive, and everyone clapped as he surfaced from the water.

We learned later that Acapulco was one of the most violent cities in Mexico with a murder rate about thirty times higher than in the United States. High-rise hotels and luxury hillside villas overlooking an enticing bay lulled us into a false sense of paradise. Coming face-to-face with the poverty of desperate people trying to survive brought us back to reality.

At our next stop, Bilboa, the ship went through the Panama Canal in the early hours of the morning. Four huge mule trains dragged the ship through the locks. Lateral ducts let water in at a terrific rate, and the ship rose 25 metres in a matter of minutes. Dark-skinned workers operated the massive gates and drove the mule trains. Three series of locks carried us to the level of the Gatun Lake and finally to the Atlantic Ocean. Dredges worked to deepen parts of the canal, and road gangs building a road waved to us. We waved back.

At the other end of the canal, Christobal, we disembarked. They warned us not to walk the streets of this shanty town in Panama. A passenger had been stabbed on a previous voyage. Instead, we took a bus tour through the densest jungle I'd ever seen. You couldn't see five metres inside for the vegetation was a thick mat of waist-high plants, tall grass, thin straggly trees, huge towering palm trees, and enveloping vines and creepers.

We arrived at a fortress that had been captured by Henry Morgan, a pirate who had invaded Panama in 1671. In 1672 the British government cracked down on piracy and arrested Morgan. Morgan, however, convinced the British government that his actions against the Spanish were justified. With wealth and the right connections,

Morgan was knighted and appointed governor of Jamaica. What a turnaround for a scoundrel of the high seas!

Back at Christobal we saw poverty and riches. Attractive tropical gardens, well-kept parks and white spotless dwellings lay beyond the city, but in the heart of Christobal, broken-down buildings needed a bulldozer. Dark-skinned people everywhere sauntered through the streets and alley ways, leaned over the railings of balconies, relaxed on rooftops and sat on doorsteps. They warned us about the pickpockets, and one old man stopped Kathleen in the street and told her not to wave her bag around, but rather to hold it tightly under her arm. Later, on the ship, we learned that four people had been robbed. Others had witnessed a stabbing and a fight. Life in Christobal was tough, and I was sad for the people who had to endure those living conditions.

What a difference Curacao turned out to be! We entered a harbour filled with vessels of all shapes and sizes — fishing boats, bulk carriers, huge oil tankers, cargo-carrying ships and passenger liners. And overlooking the harbour, many Dutch-styled homes. The city dwellers were mostly West Indian and spoke Dutch, Spanish, French and a conglomerate of all three called Papiamento. We chatted to friendly West Indians dressed in light clothing, their white shirts in marked contrast to their brown bodies.

Curacao hosted a large oil refinery, the oil coming from Venezuela. After refining, the oil was shipped all over the world but mostly to the United States. The night sky lit up with flames escaping from chimney stacks. A few West Indians came to see our ship off at 1 am. They cheered, waved and said 'Bon Voyage' and 'Come again. Don't forget to write.'

Tempers flared from time to time on ship as we sailed across the Atlantic Ocean. Our dog lover walked off to another table. We complained about the weevils in our breakfast cereals. One old Scottish woman asked me for a swear word in Italian — she wanted to get her own back at one of the Italian stewards.

We celebrated Kathleen's 21st birthday party. After we danced, a man in shorts flung her around the floor a few times. A passenger came over and kissed her after the band played 'Happy Birthday'.

On the transatlantic crossing to Lisbon I read true adventure stories of the South Pacific which included tales about whalers, pirates, cannibals, mutineers, shipwrecks and tests of endurance, such as having to last 40 days in a rowing boat with little food and water and little hope of land.

We cruised by night into Lisbon, up the broad River Tagus. The bridge over the Tagus and several monuments were lit up —Torre de Belem, St Georges Castle, Jeronimos Monastery and Monument to the Discoveries. Set amidst low-lying hills, Lisbon showcased most of its oldest buildings and monuments close to the River Tagus. It was from Torre de Belem — a tower built in the sixteenth century — that Vasco Da Gama set out on his great voyage of discovery around Africa's Cape of Good Hope to Asia.

We walked for three hours around the quaint shops and cobbled streets before turning in. Next morning we joined a bus tour and visited Jeronimos Monastery, a masterpiece of Manueline architecture erected in the 16th century in the reign of King Manuel to commemorate the voyages of the Portuguese navigators, especially Vasco Da Gama's voyage around the world. Liz was thrilled to see the cloisters.

While in Lisbon, a young man in his twenties, whom we had seen on deck, was run over by a car while crossing a street and killed. It seemed ironic that this unfortunate passenger had lost his life in a supposedly safe port when we had all survived Cristobal and Acapulco, the more hazardous of our stopovers.

Finally, with our sea legs battered and hardened for all future sea voyages, we landed at Southampton. We missed signing the petition, but we were sure that the *Castel Felice* was on the point of seizing up for good.

Land cruising

John Matthew, my cousin, along with his wife Jean, met us after we had disembarked. Liz and Jean took to each other like long-lost friends. John later showed us around Winchester College where he worked as a bursar. This was a real privilege as Winchester College, a full boarding public school for boys, claimed to be England's oldest school, established by the Bishop of Winchester in 1382.

After spending two days with John and Jean, we travelled up to Norfolk to introduce Liz to all Mum's relatives. They all took to her straightaway and included her as part of the family. After a few days at the family home of Woodgate in Aylsham, we journeyed north by train to Aberdeen and onwards to Elgin and Garmouth in Morayshire, where we met up with many friends I had grown up with.

Mrs Cassie welcomed us with a few emotional tears. We talked over the years and bonds that still united us all. Mr Cassie kept Liz busy with his political volleys. Mrs Mitchell, a friend of Mum's, welcomed me like the prodigal son. Mrs Sievewright prepared a homecoming meal that seemed more like a royal banquet, and then we listened to her singing melodious arias. With wee nips of whisky, port or sherry to fortify us, we continued on visiting old friends in Garmouth and Kingston and then on to Elgin for a fresh round of people to see.

At Fochabers, Douglas Mackay, the minister, spoke to a packed congregation on Remembrance Day: 'We have to remember or else we face hell. Hitler was one who didn't remember. The statistics reveal the cold slaughter of the Jews as a result of his amnesia.' Strong words, I thought.

Gordon Baxter of Baxters Fine Foods cornered us after the church service and insisted on us visiting his home, which displayed antique furnishings, paintings of sheep, and his Order of the British Empire (OBE) award.

From Garmouth we journeyed to Aviemore but hardly recognised the town with its new ski centre. At Glenmore we climbed the

Cairngorms and later walked to the Green Loch. We could have stayed the night in a bothy, a one-room hut with a platform bed, table, bench seat, sofa, sink and stove — enough Scottish comfort for someone to survive an icy change of weather. But the weather was fine so we headed to Inverness where we met Iain Gordon from school days. He bounded out to meet us, the same flamboyant and wild highlander I had known.

The next day we visited Culloden Moor not far from Inverness, the site of the Battle of Culloden where the Duke of Cumberland's superior artillery decimated the Jacobite lines, while Bonnie Prince Charlie moved out of sight for safety.

Following the Jacobite rebellion of 1745, the highlanders, especially in Sutherland, were forcefully evicted from their homes. The highland clearances, along with social unrest and hard times, then pushed highlanders out from Scotland to resettle in North America or in Australia.

I chatted to an officer of the Department of Agriculture who explained the hill farming and crofting situation. He said: 'The displacement of people led to the introduction of large numbers of sheep grazing the highlands and the formation of extensive hill farms replacing the croft, a small area of arable land with a crofter's dwelling. The hill farms today are run by managers, their owners being successful business men who know little about the management of sheep and cattle. The wilderness that you will pass through was largely man-made.'

'How important is crofting today?' I asked.

'About 25 percent of the land mass of the highlands and islands is under crofting tenure,' he said. 'With more than 17,000 crofts, it's still a unique social farming system for small-scale food production, and it takes care of the environment. Most of the crofters own the improvement but not the land, so there is a big upheaval when a crofter decides to leave and sell out. Most crofters have other jobs to supplement their meagre farm income.'

After thanking the officer for his explanation, we motored north into my beloved highlands and lochs, the sun shining radiantly on brown hillsides and ragged outcrops of rock. On Scotland's north coast we stopped at a cosy hotel in Durness where the friendly owner and his wife gave us cups of tea, sandwiches, and, best of all, an electric blanket.

Close to Durness we visited Smoo cave, a smugglers hideaway and linked to tales of the supernatural. The first chamber had been formed by the action of the sea, while two inner freshwater chambers had been formed from rainwater dissolving the limestone.

From Durness we drove to Kinlochbervie, a remote town on the north-west coast, its scattered houses on hill slopes overlooking fishing vessels in the pale blue waters of the harbour.

All along the west coast, lochs popped up, each one different in its setting, like a new play waiting to be read. The peacefulness of loch and mountainside, dotted with innumerable rocks and covered with a mantle of heather, belied its harsh and violent past.

We stopped at a guesthouse in Ullapool, a small town lying on the eastern shore of Loch Broom. The next day we drove around Loch Broom to Corrieshalloch Gorge, situated on the Droma River, where Liz gasped on viewing the sheer drop of the Falls of Measach. We drove on to Dundonnell, a village on the south side of Little Loch Broom, all within the mountain grandeur of An Teallach. Next, the rocky coves and golden sands of Gruinard Bay reminded us of faraway places.

Ben Slioch towered over beautiful Loch Maree on our way to Gairloch on the west coast. We strolled through Inverewe Gardens, where warmer climate plants grew, such as Tasmanian eucalypts and olearia from New Zealand, and flourished because of the warm currents of the Gulf Stream. The gardens overlooked a placid Loch Ewe.

The road from Inverewe Gardens to Inverness rewarded us with more spectacular vistas of mountains and lochs. From Inverness we drove alongside Loch Ness and stopped at Urquhart Castle, an impressive stronghold on the banks of the loch. The Loch Ness monster, affectionately know as Nessie, was nowhere to be seen. Something rippled in the water, but it was only dark shadows playing on my imagination. A guide cheerfully showed us the chapel, the dungeons and the dining area of the castle. 'If the enemy approached the gate,' he said, 'another gate descended and trapped them before boiling oil was poured over them.' That didn't bear thinking about.

With a snowfall threatening we made our way back to Aberdeen. We found a place to board, and, after two weeks of searching, Liz started work at Foresterhill Hospital as a nursing sister in the emergency ward. She did not mind the hectic pace of work but had difficulty with the Aberdeen brogue when answering the phone. In the meantime I found work as a temporary science, biology and mathematics teacher at Hatton Junior Secondary School in Peterhead. I travelled each day by bus to the school and arrived back in the dark.

We endured a bitterly cold winter with falls of snow that persisted right through to the end of February. On one occasion a blizzard — the worst I had experienced — forced me to stay at the school in Peterhead. Eventually, the weather calmed a little and the snow ploughs cleared the snowdrifts from the roads.

My first teaching experience was more a learning one. Knowing your subjects was one thing, I found, but motivating the students and imparting knowledge in an absorbing and challenging way was much harder. And, of course, there was always the problem of keeping the more unruly students in check. I should have undertaken a teachers training course instead of jumping into the fiery den. I survived — just.

During our stay in Aberdeen, Liz discovered she was pregnant. Great news! We decided to resign our jobs in April and see something of Europe and Israel before settling down again. Perhaps I could find a job in agricultural research in Israel. Liz put a dampener on the idea saying she would prefer to return to Australia where she could have the baby in home surroundings.

We caught the train from Newhaven and then a boat to Dieppe in France. The crossing was perfect with no rolling and pitching. We went by train to Paris and walked up the Champs-Élysées to the Arc de Triomphe which glowed in a darkening sky. The next day we made our way to the Eiffel Tower and stood underneath its giant basal arches, eating hot dogs and watching the lifts take holiday makers to the different platforms. Then we watched the barges on the Seine, before taking a bus to the Île de la Cité where we gazed in awe at the facade of the Notre Dame Cathedral with its rose-coloured stained glass window and gothic arches. The cathedral had stood as a symbol of French unity over the centuries of France's turbulent history.

While waiting for our train to Milan, we wandered through the Jardin des Plantes. Life away from the maddening crowds seemed easy again with women pushing prams, old men reading newspapers and children playing on the grass. We visited the zoo, the Menagerie du Jardin des Plantes, where Liz became captivated with the monkeys that pranced around their cage like excited kids.

Our train from the Gare de Lyon whistled on through many French towns. We slept a little but with a full carriage we could not shift or stretch out. A howling baby mercifully went to sleep. At first light we viewed the majestic Alpine scenery of the Swiss Alps, with white-capped peaks towering above the clouds.

Arriving in Rome station we met a trustworthy-looking chap who invited us to stay at a pension. We took a chance, although Liz was not happy at all about accepting his offer. Within quarter of an hour we had arrived at the pension's convenience and comfort — nothing flash, reasonably priced, and just fine for us. We must have broken the record for finding a place in a foreign country. After a comfortable night and a breakfast of rolls we set out to explore ancient Rome.

We wandered around the Roman Forum with its columns, temples and arches. We then made our way to the Colliseum and looked down on its amphitheatre and vast array of tunnels, arches and galleries, used for gladiatorial contests, public spectacles and dramas. Later, we opted for a guided tour of the catacombs with their underground burial places.

Liz felt nauseous and had to see an obstetrician. At the maternity hospital we struggled through 'no speak English' to a waiting room. After waiting half an hour a nurse said, 'Come back tomorrow.' Liz burst into tears, and a tall, fair-haired obstetrician with a kindly disposition came to the rescue. He treated Liz's ailment and we thanked him profusely for saving the day.

We sailed from Brindisi and landed at Patras in Greece. Our bus to Athens bumped, rocked and jarred its passengers as it sped along uneven roads to Corinth and Athens. 'Our poor baby!' Liz said. 'I hope that he or she suffers no irreparable harm.' Outside, orange groves dotted the landscape, donkeys rested peacefully, and women in black sat with young children on the doorsteps of homes.

The night lights of Athens twinkled as we arrived. We managed to find a place at Hotel Phoebus, and from our window an unexpected surprise greeted us — a view of the Acropolis — all lit up in the night sky.

The next day we explored the wonder of the Acropolis, admiring especially the design and structure of the Parthenon, a temple dedicated to the goddess Athena. Athens stretched out before us as far as the eye could see.

In the afternoon, Ted Edwards, an Australian guide and friend of the Cullis-Hills in Sydney, led us on a well-informed tour through the Archaeological Museum. The different stages of pottery development and the bronze statues especially appealed to us.

After arranging to meet again for dinner we wandered out into the street. Thirst overcame me — we were close to 40 degrees Celsius — and I went into what I thought was a café and asked for a glass of water. Men sat at tables, chatting and drinking a pale-looking beverage. The man behind the counter looked at me strangely — I was sure he could not understand a word of English — but came out with a glass of water which I downed in one swig. I spluttered and gasped. My throat exploded. He had given me a glass of ouzo, an anise-based spirit. Everyone in the café stopped what they were doing and stared at me in disbelief. I knew then what they had been sipping.

At nighttime the streets swelled again after siestas, and the Greeks seemed busy with trading or talking in small groups or just idling down the main streets. We walked to one of the main squares and listened to band music. Ted joined us for dinner at the Myrto Hotel where I tasted cannelloni and Liz enjoyed pizza. He kept us amused with all his adventures with Greeks and Italians. 'Greek hospitality,' he said, 'was the best yet.'

We hopped on a bus the next day to Voula beach and sunbathed too much — our faces and backs glowed — before swimming in a placid sea. Despite having to pay for our beach pleasure and having to put up with planes roaring overhead to Athens airport every five minutes, we relished our dip; we had not swum in the sea for nine months.

At 6 am the following morning I bounded down to the Olympic Stadium. A cheery runner greeted me as I entered its portals. I pounded around the field track three times, for every bit feeling like an Olympic athlete, and trying to sense the atmosphere of the first Olympic Games in 1896. My companion runner, a U.S. officer in charge of naval trainees on an exercise, had come for the same purpose.

At Piraeus, the shipping office was closed and we could not leave our luggage anywhere. A small, well-groomed wiry man came to our rescue and took us to a restaurant where we stored our luggage. 'A real provision,' Liz said.

To fill in time, we entered a local cinema that was full of sweaty men. Liz observed that she was the only female. With no air conditioning, we watched a cowboy film — not our film of choice. After surviving the intense odour and oppressive heat, we tasted the sweetest, purest, freshest air on earth as we left the cinema. We were ready to board our ship for Haifa.

Tony Druce, a distant relation on my mother's side, met us at our first port of call, Limassol, in Cyprus. Olive and carob trees studded hill slopes as we drove to Nicosia. On the plains grain crops were ripening. 'The biggest problem on the island,' Tony said, 'is lack of water.'

Tony had retired from his post as a district officer with the British government. He explained that the United Nations troops were everywhere trying to keep the peace between the Turks and the Greek-Cypriots. If I had been born one year earlier when conscription was compulsory I might have been posted there, too.

Tony's place in the foothills was luxurious by Cypriot standards and poles apart from the Turkish mud dwellings. With pride, Tony showed us his racing horses and his prize white Arab stallion. His extensive garden flourished with eucalypts, cypress trees, carob, olives and vines. Too late to become a district officer, I thought, with the British Empire shrinking. Tony guided us around Nicosia before taking us back to our ship.

We arrived at Haifa, six years after my first visit to Israel and almost two years after the Six-Day War. Golda Meir had become prime minister, two months prior in March 1969, after the death of Levi Eshkol, the previous prime minister. At about the same time, Yasser Arafat had been elected as chairman of the Palestinian Liberation Organisation — defined by Israel as a 'terror group'. Also in March, Gamal Nasser, Egypt's president, had launched the war of attrition to reclaim the Sinai Peninsula, which included the eastern bank of the Suez Canal. As well as the Sinai Peninsula, Israel had taken over the West Bank, an area west of the Jordan River, and East Jerusalem from Jordan, the Golan Heights overlooking the Sea of Galilee from Syria, and the Gaza Strip from Egypt. What a precarious time to set foot on Israeli soil!

We took a bus to the top of Mount Carmel where the city of Haifa and the coastline stretched out before us. We strolled through the gardens of the Bahai temple before catching a train to Jerusalem. Mountains loomed up on both sides of the track as we approached the biblical city. Gerhard from Sydney days warmly welcomed us at the station.

We first booked into St Andrews Scottish Guest House, set on a small hill with panoramic views of the walls of the Old City, and then enjoyed a special catch-up time with Gerhard and Susi. They had settled in well with Gerhard working for Egged, the largest bus company in Israel. 'Have you any regrets in leaving Sydney?' I asked. Their elder son Micky burst into tears when we mentioned Sydney, while David, their younger son, was too young to remember Sydney with any fondness.

'Of course, we miss everyone,' Susi said. 'We made a lot of friends while in Sydney, but we did not feel it to be our home. Our home is in Israel — we belong here whatever the difficulties we have with our neighbours. We have not come here just for ourselves. Our sons will feel more Jewish being in Israel and more appreciative of their history and culture. We are not very religious but we want our children to celebrate what it means to be Jewish. We are reaffirming an affinity for the land we had 2,000 years ago.'

'What about Micky and David? Will they be happy?' I asked.

'I am sure they will adopt Israel as their country.' Gerhard said. 'Already, they speak fluent Hebrew after four years. And they have made new friends.'

We talked about the tension of living under the threat of attack by Arabs and the conflict with Egypt in the Sinai Peninsula before arranging to meet again.

The next day we entered the Old City by the Jaffa Gate, the gate through which British general Edmund Allenby entered the city in 1917 on foot in a show of respect for the city.

We strolled through the narrow streets with Arab shops crammed together on either side displaying their wares. Oddly enough, no one — sellers, little boys or guides — hassled us, as expected. I wondered how they felt about being under tight control from the Israeli military.

Liz and I then wandered through Mea Shearim, literally meaning 100 gates, a community of mostly ultra orthodox Jews who adhered strictly to Jewish law, prayer and study of the Jewish texts. The long black-garbed men wearing fur hats took little notice of us — we were both properly dressed with Liz wearing a long skirt and me with long trousers and a long-sleeved shirt. Small boys, with ringlets of hair dangling down, played in the streets. Houses crowded on top of each other with small shops jutting out onto the pavement.

Then we stumbled on the Garden Tomb, a tranquil setting, where a guide explained that this was most likely the site of the tomb in which Jesus lay. Nearby we visited the Place of the Skull — Golgotha — where Jesus was crucified.

We visited the convent of the Sisters of Zion, at the eastern end of the Via Dolorosa, Jesus' walk to his crucifixion. We looked at the tower of Antonia, the traditional site where Pilate sentenced Jesus, and arches, cisterns and old Roman paving stones built about the time of Christ. The sister who showed us around seemed like a living saint with her eyes shining with love. Liz bought two candlesticks made of olive wood — for her, a wish come true.

At the Mount of Olives an Arab boy insisted that Liz stand in the acclaimed footprint of Jesus where he ascended. Liz put her foot down all right; she was having none of that nonsense. We walked down through the Garden of Gethsemane where Arab boys stationed at strategic Christian sites and tombs hailed us.

Our most memorable part of the day was a visit to the Sisters of Mary, who had courageously withheld their position on the Mount of Olives in a fierce battle for Jerusalem in 1967. They refreshed us with drinks and held a small service in which they attributed their survival to the Lord's care.

Later, with Liz resting at the hospice I went to the Pool of Siloam, where a French group of tourists were holding a service. A young boy handed me two lit candles and I waded into Hezekiah's tunnel. King Hezekiah had prepared the city for a siege by the Assyrians and built the tunnel to ensure a water supply to the Pool of Siloam from the Gihon Spring outside the city walls. Two teams had dug the 500-metre-tunnel from opposite ends, using sounds made by hammering on the solid rock above the tunnellers. I had to crouch and wade as fast as I could through the knee-deep water to avoid the candles burning out and plunging me into darkness. A glimmer of light appeared as my second candle flickered its last flame.

The next day Gerhard gave us a free bus pass to the Dead Sea. We stopped first at the Church of St Lazarus at Bethany, the town where Jesus raised Lazarus from the dead. At Bethlehem, the Church of the Nativity seemed like a commercial hotchpotch of religious enclaves all vying for Jesus' birthplace. I think Jesus himself would have taken pity on them and told them to close up shop.

At Hebron, we were warned about hostile Arabs. On the way up to the tomb of Abraham, an Arab boy confronted us with blankets, pipes, drums and fur hats — none of which appealed to Liz who took evasive action. For me the tombs were of passing interest. I was more interested in the activities of Arabs, who clustered around stalls, squatting and talking, and with some astride donkeys and camels. They ignored us with no hint of hostility.

We passed two abandoned army tanks before spotting several Bedouin tents on the hillslopes. We moved on through a desolate region where, it seemed, not a scrap of vegetation was visible and then finally we arrived at the Dead Sea with hazy heat rising up from its surface. I floated for a minute and that was enough with the blazing sun and oily feel from its waters. A priest seemed to be enjoying his float with a black umbrella shielding his rotund mid-portion.

At our next stop at Jericho, where the ruins of the oldest civilisation were 10,000 years old, refugees from the Arab–Israeli wars lived in a pitiful state in mud houses, eking out an existence.

The next day we hired a taxi and our Arab driver sped through the Judean Hills to our first stop, Jacob's Well, where Jesus had met the woman at the well. We passed by Shechem, the ancient capital, and arrived at Nablus where a family of Samaritans greeted us. But it was a pitiful sight with their genetic abnormalities evident from inbreeding.

Our Arab driver gave us our first account of what the Arabs had endured from the heavy fighting during the Six-Day War. We saw burnt-out tanks and bullet-scarred buildings, evidence of the bloody fighting. Many people had fled their homes and become refugees.

Further on, we admired the view of the Sea of Galilee from the Mount of Beatitudes near the village of Tabgha where Jesus preached the Sermon on the Mount. Later, at Nazareth, we declined to pay an entrance fee to enter what our guide said was Jesus' home and carpenter shop.

After a sad goodbye to Gerhard, Susi and others, we made our way by a train that rumbled through the hills onto the fertile plains and then on to Tel Aviv. We found a place to stay at an old French hospital in Jaffa. The sisters made us feel at home in this unusual hospital setting that had been opened to receive travellers. Outside, an enclosed garden of trees and flowers provided a haven for birds and a rest for Liz who was now in her sixth month of pregnancy. Later, she revived and we walked along the Jaffa seafront.

I was keen to find out if there were any employment opportunities, but Liz had set her mind on going home. She wanted to have her baby in Adelaide and not in a foreign place. At a post office she broke down in tears, so I realised how important it was to go back to Australia.

We visited Malka and her husband Giora. Malka appeared a little plumper than six years before but still the same with her infectious sense of humour. It seemed odd that we should meet like this with both of us married. Her daughter Livnat gave us a shy shalom and baby Itzhak smiled in her mother's arms. Giora chatted about his life as a captain of a cruise ship while in the kitchen Malka advised Liz about having babies. She tried to persuade Liz to stay in Israel, but we had already made up our minds. After a tasty meal we walked along Dizengoff Street, which seemed to be filled with the whole of Tel Aviv and more. Pregnant mothers, mothers wheeling little ones, small groups of girls and boys, courting couples, and older ones ambling along, all going somewhere or nowhere in particular.

After our walk in the cool night air — a refreshing change from the heat of the day — we parted the best of friends.

On our second to last day we visited Kibbutz Shoval, where I had stayed for three months in 1963. Gad, one of the kibbutzniks, recognised me and showed us over the kibbutz. Others joined, and we all ended up in the swimming pool, a welcome relief from the heat of the day. I felt as though I was part of the community again, but to live there would have been too difficult for us.

Yehuda Bauer, our group host in 1963, met us in the dining hall. He had not changed in the last six years. Nor had I, he said. He was continuing with his studies of the Holocaust at the Hebrew University, especially looking at anti-Semitism and the Jewish resistance movement during the Holocaust years. I said, 'I did not know there had been an active resistance movement from the Jews.'

'Most people *do* believe that Jews had gone to their deaths passively. But what is surprising is how much resistance there was, not how little,' Yehuda said.

'How could this genocide occur?' I asked.

He said, 'This genocide was the worst in all history and targeted the whole Jewish race. Hitler was the key figure who caused the Holocaust. There was no real evidence of a master plan prior to the war and nothing noted about genocide in Hitler's book *Mein Kampf* — lots of invective, of course, against the Jews. Himmler had written down in his notebook towards the end of 1941 "What to do with the Jews of Russia?" Hitler's response, according to the notebook, was "Exterminate them as partisans." His plan had evolved during the Second World War to exterminate Jews, and Hitler was solely responsible for that decision.'

I tried to comprehend the deadly combination of power and evil that Hitler had used to manipulate the German people to forge a new empire, an empire without Jews.

'Do you think that there is a possibility that genocide could reoccur if the Palestine people became stronger and regained Israel?' I asked.

'Yes, but the Jewish people would take extreme measures to prevent that happening again.'

With that sobering thought and more discussion on the problems of the Middle East, we wished each other well and hoped to meet again one day. Yehuda became one of the world's top authorities on the Holocaust; he wrote *A history of the Holocaust* in which he traced the roots of antisemitism and why the Holocaust occurred.

On our return to Australia, a young Israeli mother, Dahlia, sat beside us on the plane; she was on her way to rejoin her husband in Iran. We touched down in Tehran and wished her the best, not realising what her family would be facing in ten years time with the overthrow of the Shah of Iran by Ayatollah Khomeini and the installing of an Islamic republic. In 30 years time I would come face-to-face with people who had escaped from Khomeini's ruthless regime.

We flew over the ruggedness of Turkey, the arid vastness of India, the jungle-covered landscape of Burma and the rain-soaked countryside of Thailand with its elaborate system of rivers and canals. With the plane skimming over harbour waters, we held our breath as we touched down in Hong Kong. And finally, on 4 June 1969, we landed at Sydney to a welcome from Liz's uncles and aunts, before our final leg to Adelaide where Mum, Dad, Max Hart and Mandy, my sister, met us in a happy reunion.

Chapter 8

Return to Adelaide

HAVING SETTLED INTO A RENTAL unit in the suburb of Oaklands Park in Adelaide, Liz said, 'I would like a new washing machine with the baby arriving in six weeks.' That meant work, especially as we were low in finances. I met with the principal of Roseworthy Agricultural College, Bob Herriot, who practically offered me a job on a platter to assist in practical classes and tutoring while pursuing a master's degree. Even though I was keen enough to teach, I hesitated re-starting on a postgraduate research course because of my recent experience at Sydney University. A similar opportunity presented itself with Dr Adrian Egan offering a position as a research assistant at the Waite Agricultural Institute, but this was poorly paid.

Doubt about being a research assistant and lack of money influenced my decision. I started work with the Institute of Medical and Veterinary Science on 7 July 1969 as a technical officer, carrying out routine blood analyses — haemoglobin, haptoglobin, vitamin B12 and folic acid. For the first time in Australia I had a worthwhile paying job, and Liz had her washing machine.

By the end of July I had a measure of financial security, but a comment in *The Australian* struck me as thought-provoking: 'People try to find security in their lives and become prisoners of their own doing, but those who live bravely and creatively and chancing fate in the process find their true freedom.' Knowing that my last experience in a laboratory at Sydney University stifled my freedom I wondered how long I would last.

On 20 July, everyone stopped work to watch on TV the landing on the moon. Neil Armstrong, the first man on the moon, uttered the historic words, 'That's one small step for a man, one giant leap for mankind.'

In contrast to the giant leap, a backward step for mankind at that time was the continued use of Agent Orange by U.S. forces in Vietnam to defoliate large areas of land and cause untold suffering. Widespread opposition to the war was growing both in America and Australia because of the cost in human life. Many were waking up to the fact that the United States had led Australia into the war because of an irrational fear that communism would take over Vietnam and other Asian countries.

Rachel was due on Mum's birthday, 31 August 1969, but decided to be late — she always has been. Marjorie Hart, who had adopted Liz as her unofficial daughter, hoped the baby would arrive on her birthday, 3 September. Rachel waited until 7 September, Father's Day — what better timing! The Queen Victoria Hospital allowed me to be present at the birth, but the midwife on duty suggested I go home for a few hours as nothing really was happening despite early contractions. On the way back I developed stomach pains. Could this mean ...? I rushed back to the hospital to find Liz in the full throes of delivery. After a prolonged effort in which the doctor had to assist with forceps, Rachel appeared with, it seemed, a compressed forehead. 'Don't worry,' said the doctor. 'The pressure on the head has caused the compression. The baby will be fine.' We relaxed and relished the wonder of a new birth.

Rachel arrived as the Australian federal election build-up vied with the news of Ulster riots and the Russians going into space. Six weeks after her birth, the Liberal Party, under the leadership of John Gorton, won another term with the Coalition on 25 October 1969, despite public attitudes changing with the conflict in Vietnam and with conscription becoming unpopular.

Rachel meanwhile threw her arms and legs in all directions while lying in the bouncinette. I managed somehow to change her nappies, but once she wriggled so much that she fell off the changing table. After hitting the floor, she inhaled for a few moments before screaming. She suffered no damage, fortunately. I used her delay in screaming to good effect on another occasion when she fell off a pew in church at a vital point during the sermon. I picked her up and rushed outside. Rachel held her scream long enough for me to get out of earshot and not spoil the pastor's message.

After six months of routine laboratory blood assays, I welcomed a position as a technical officer with CSIRO Division of Animal Nutrition. John Lee, a research scientist investigating the importance of trace element nutrition at Glenthorne Field Station, interviewed me. An engaging man with a down-to-earth sense of humour, John offered me the job of supervising the experiments at Glenthorne Field Station on the outskirts of Adelaide. I told him that I saw the position as being two to three years, and then I would most likely move on to something else. Surprisingly, he did not hold that against me.

Liz and I settled into one of the homes built for those working at the field station, in the suburb of O'Halloran Hill. Ralph Jones, the manager, showed us around and introduced me to my field staff, Roy, Rick and Joe, who would feed and care for penned sheep on the research trials.

The main thrust of research work carried out by scientists, based at the CSIRO headquarters in the city, dealt with the sheep and cattle requirements of trace elements, cobalt, selenium and copper. In the less fertile soils of South Australia, particularly the lighter sandy soils, a shortage of these elements had a profound effect on the growth and fertility of sheep and cattle. On the other hand, too much of the element, especially copper and selenium, could cause toxicity. Offering a corrective dose by mouth, or drenching, as it was called, proved time-consuming and costly. A solid pellet or 'bullet' containing the trace element seemed the answer where the heaviness of the bullet would cause it to sit on the floor of the rumen and gradually release the element over the lifetime of the sheep. Before releasing the bullet to the farmer, we had to ensure its effectiveness and that the meat was safe to consume. The bullets were perfected during the time I was there, although sometimes it became coated and less effective. But that was solved by giving the sheep a grub screw which would rub up against the bullet and keep it clean.

We carried out routine sampling of blood, weighed the sheep, biopsied livers, and retrieved the bullets for examination. The research laboratories at Adelaide University performed more detailed analyses. John kept me well-informed and often invited me to take part in the research seminars.

Eric, the clerical officer in the main building, hobbled over to my office in an adjacent building to join me for morning tea-break. He had suffered a lot from his time as a prisoner in a Japanese war camp. I did not prompt him, but a few times he opened up to talk about the misfortunes of his mates, many of whom died or were killed by the Japanese. He could not forgive the Japanese for their cruelty. And he could not talk about the details of that cruelty — it was too painful — but he needed someone to listen and acknowledge what he and others had gone through. It seemed to me that the most powerful of nations in the Second World War, Germany and Japan, had aligned themselves to conquer and be cruel in the process. Eric suffered terribly with the painful memories of that internment. No one had counselled him, and he lived with the wounds which would never heal.

In a similar way, Liz's father, on HMAS *Australia* had fought against the Japanese Imperial Navy in the battle of the Coral Sea during 4–8 May 1942. He suffered traumatic stress from the fighting which affected his family life. Jean, Martin's wife, found it too difficult to manage four young children and a husband who had become dysfunctional. All four children, including Liz, had ended up in Church of England homes.

While we stayed at Glenthorne Field Station, Liz worked part-time as a midwife and sister-in-charge at the Blackwood Community

Hospital, and had one shift on Saturday at a nursing home in the suburb of Glenelg.

Towards the end of 1971, I realised that I had developed a routine which I could manage despite it being taxing at times with competing demands from the research scientists. But the spark had died — there was no challenge in the job itself. I had to move on and let John Lee know. He understood and wrote me a reference which praised my work ethic and team spirit — more than I deserved.

I decided, but not too wisely, to go to England for a month to follow up leads in agricultural development. Liz and Rachel meanwhile would stay with Max and Marjorie Hart until I returned. Liz was not happy about me leaving her but agreed reluctantly.

I flew to London and checked up on possible opportunities with various development companies and organisations — Ford Foundation, Food and Agriculture Organisation, Shell Chemicals, World Bank and the Overseas Development Institute. I talked to a number of professional agriculturists in the field, and, although there were a number of promising avenues, none opened up at the time. I decided at least to undertake further study in agricultural development by correspondence with Wye College of London University, a world-class centre for research and teaching in agricultural sciences.

On the way back to Australia I stopped in Israel for two weeks to investigate potential opportunities. On landing at Tel Aviv a taxi driver suggested I stay at a reasonably priced hotel, the Savoy Hotel. To me the hotel looked rundown and did not do justice to its billboard advertisement which stated: 'The Savoy is one of Tel Aviv's foremost orthodox hotels, well-known for its Friday evening programs and Sabbath atmosphere. The cuisine represents the best in Jewish cooking, and the public rooms and lounges are decorated with a rich collection of ceremonial art. Here you won't feel you're in a hotel lounge, but in a traditional Jewish home in the old country.'

Well, I would have felt more at home in the French Hospital in Jaffa, but they had not responded to my calls. Perhaps they had closed up for good. With a sense of foreboding, I felt uneasy about staying at the Savoy. Nothing happened though, and I continued to contact influential people in agricultural research and development in Tel Aviv.

Four years later, the Savoy Hotel hit front page headlines in South Australia's daily newspaper, *The Advertiser*, on 7 March 1975:

> At least twenty hostages were killed or wounded as well as the Arab guerrilla captors when Israeli commandos stormed a waterfront hotel in Tel Aviv today ... the guerrillas took Israeli defences by surprise when they landed in two rubber boats on the beach in the centre of Tel Aviv just before midnight and started shooting wildly along the waterfront, sending people running for cover. The Palestinians then seized the cheap hotel close to the beach and grabbed the hostages. Fierce fighting erupted as the guerrillas fired sub-machine guns, automatic rifles and bazookas in all directions.

The six Palestinians had demanded the release of ten imprisoned Arabs, but the Israelis rejected their demands. Instead, 40 commandos burst into the hotel at dawn and killed the terrorists. Unfortunately, the hostages — mostly the United States, British and German tourists — were also killed. I shuddered to think of having to go through that experience if it had happened while I was there.

Before leaving Israel I met up with a South African, Paul, who was keen to walk around the Sea of Galilee and focus on Jesus' time with the disciples and the multitudes. He invited me to go with him.

We set off with rucksacks from Tabgha, a village on the north-western shore of the Sea of Galilee, and the traditional site of Jesus' miracle of the multiplication of the loaves and fishes. The pale, blue millpond-sea beckoned us to swim across, but we left that for the swimmers in their annual tradition.

From Tabgha we hiked south to Bet Degania, the second kibbutz established in Israel. Paul and I stayed the night there before trekking northwards on the eastern shore, hugging the water's edge. The Golan Heights, captured by Israel from Syria in the Six-Day War of 1967, towered above us.

We reached a branch of the Jordan River which was too deep to wade through. So, while we tried to work out how best to move our rucksacks across without getting them wet, a fisherman came to our rescue and offered to take us to the other side. We thanked him and set off again only to come across another branch of the river. We faced the same problem, but another fisherman came to our rescue. I thought of the song, 'One more river to cross,' but this time we had no more rivers or branches and we continued to follow the northern shoreline of the Sea of Galilee until we passed close to the site of the ancient city of Bethsaida where Jesus fed the multitudes and healed the blind man. Further on, we stopped at the ruins of Capernaum, an ancient fishing village, where Jesus taught and healed a possessed man. After hiking for more than 50 kilometres, we arrived back at Tabgha.

Paul and I went our separate ways. I tried to correspond with him later from Australia, but, perhaps because of the turbulence in South Africa, he didn't reply. The Sea of Galilee walk, though, with its spiritual significance, will always be a memorable one.

Soon after the hike I flew back to Australia, feeling disappointed that nothing certain had opened up. But this was just as well for Liz as she was expecting Linda — well, we had not named her yet.

Liz had stayed with Max and Marjorie Hart who had opened their home to Liz in her late teens. Max had been the principal of the Teachers Training College in Butare, Uganda. Unfortunately, Marjorie contracted polio before giving birth to her two sons, David and Peter. On their return to Adelaide, Max questioned the prevailing policies for Aboriginal education for his masters of education. From his findings he advocated new initiatives for Aboriginal people to be taught in their own cultural context and in their own language.

Max made regular trips to Aboriginal communities and recorded the vitality of the Church among Aboriginal people by allowing their leaders to tell their own stories. The stories, published in *A story of fire: Aboriginal Christianity* and *A story of fire continued*, expressed a more positive side to their lives than the ones often associated with Aboriginals.

On one of Max's trips to Ernabella, a remote Aboriginal community south-west of Alice Springs, he suggested I drive a Mini Moke to hand over to the Aboriginals living there. Max would follow in his Ford station wagon. I accepted and drove up the Stuart Highway, and, before coming to the border with Northern Territory, followed a reddish dirt road westwards over washouts, creeks and corrugations, to arrive coated with red dust and looking more like one of the Aboriginals at the centre.

Max introduced me to Aboriginal people living at Ernabella, now called Pukatja, and their traditional ways. What impressed me was their art of listening, expressed in the Pitjantjatjara language as *Kulila* which was most important in Aboriginal life. The whole experience was an eyeopener with an insight into their culture and values. Many of Aboriginal blood had been caught in a trap between two worlds with loss of connection and identity. Max went out of his way to communicate and relate with Aboriginals in a quiet and unassuming way, but it seemed there were too few like him.

On returning to Adelaide, a friend of Liz's said that her father, a dairy farmer, desperately needed a holiday. Would I take over the milking of 100 Friesian cows for three weeks? After a wild goose chase overseas we were desperate for money, so I accepted the challenge. The dairy farm was located not far from Victor Harbor and in a high rainfall area of the south coast region. The milking went smoothly and we all loved the fresh feel of farmland.

On the day of handing over to the dairy farmer, Liz's brother, John, parked his car close to the farmer's car which I had been driving. I took care in avoiding his car on reversing out of a parked area but had not noticed a tree stump on the other side. I crashed into it and sustained a $100 damage to the rear boot and bumper. The farmer had not insured his car, so we agreed to share the cost, but that meant parting with my last week's salary of $80. We were poor again.

Looking on the positive side, another dairy farmer, Max Gale, in a neighbouring valley had heard about my dairy relief efforts. Max, too, wanted a three-week holiday. All three of us shifted to our new farm with 80 milking Jerseys. The Jerseys were more temperamental than the Friesians. In between milking the cows were strip-grazed on tall-growing Sudan grass. I shifted the electric fence wire every few days, but, to my horror on one day, the cows had broken through the fence line and disappeared into the two-metre tall grass adjacent to the strip-grazed area. I eventually rounded them up after following the flattened trails of grass. On looking back it could have been a world first for the *Guinness book of records* — losing a herd of dairy cows in a paddock.

Rachel, our two-year-old daughter, loved the cows and often joined me, but on one occasion I spotted her patting the head of a Jersey bull that was lying down in a small enclosure, and, fortunately, showing no signs of aggression.

The milking ran out, and I turned to taxi driving in Adelaide. I worked for St James taxi service and took home 40 per cent of my earnings, at times little more than the dole. They divided us into 'Gays' and 'Foxes' — that was before 'gay' took on another meaning. I was Gay 68, although I should have been a 'Fox' with my past experience. When I made a serious error in taking a passenger to the wrong destination, the other taxi drivers knew about it. At the home base where I was about to stop for refreshment, a taxi driver came out and said, 'Have you heard about what happened with Gay 68?'

'Yes, I know. Crazy driver,' I said. I hopped back into my taxi and left the base.

Taxi driving was not my line and so I changed tack, this time as a builder's labourer. It went well at first with a plastering job at the Tivoli Hotel. I worked with someone who knew all about plastering, so there was not much that could go wrong if I followed his instructions. My next job was digging a trench and some carpentry work at a building site. The builder inspected what I had done and did not approve of my efforts. He expected me to have had building experience. I told him that he had not asked about my experience at the interview. I fired myself. The builder was happy and paid me out.

Nothing substantial showed up, so I tried my hand at pruning vines for Penfolds Magill Estate, the original home of Penfolds Wines and Australia's most prized wine, the Grange. Under Gino, an Italian who worked like a Trojan when he wanted to, I learnt how to prune each vine with its tangled mass of canes in a few minutes. Gino's boss, Don Wilson, often worked with us, and so Gino set a fast pace. When Don was not there, Gino relaxed and we did, too. At the end of three months I was one of two temporary recruits who had survived the intensive pruning, wintry weather and calluses. In the night my hand went into spasms but somehow I had kept going. Don offered me a permanent position as a vineyard worker, which could lead to being a manager of a vineyard. I nearly took him up on his generous offer, but felt that there was something in the pipeline that would be more in tune with my leanings towards agriculture and teaching.

After my pruning experience, I taught science, biology and mathematics for a term at Marden High School, where a large number of the students were of Italian or Greek origin. Discipline was a problem and trying to encourage students who lacked interest in these subjects proved another hurdle.

Linda arrived on 15 September 1972. I attended the birth again, and Liz had an easier delivery compared with Rachel's.

With a fresh start to teaching, I taught agricultural studies, science and biology for the next term at Immanuel College, a Lutheran school. I studied for a diploma of education at Adelaide University and felt I gained ground as a teacher but still had a long way to go before mastering the art. In the meantime I applied for a position at Roseworthy Agricultural College as a livestock research officer.

Chapter 9

Roseworthy Agricultural College

I FORGOT ABOUT MY APPLICATION for the position at Roseworthy Agricultural College. Six months after I had applied, however, I received a call from the college for an interview if I were still interested. Dr David Taplin, the head of animal science and production, and Milton Spurling, the deputy director of Roseworthy College, interviewed me. The interview passed off well, and a short time later, they offered me a position as a livestock research officer. I would lecture and carry out sheep breeding research to improve wool production and fertility in a closed flock of South Australian Merinos.

I accepted and began in January 1974, on the same day as the new principal, Don Williams. We shook hands and wished each other well.

Roseworthy Agriculture College was established in 1883 as Australia's first agricultural college; it was situated about 50 kilometres north of Adelaide and about 10 kilometres to the north-west of the town of Gawler. The college had struggled to find a foothold in the farming community, but persevered to succeed in meeting their aspirations through its training programs, research and extension.

One of the college's eleven principals was William Lowrie — a Scotsman no less — who arrived at Roseworthy College in 1888. He advocated the use of superphosphate and advised on crop rotations to increase yields. He won respect from the rural community with his research experiments on farms.

We rented a timber-framed house next to the winery on the college farm. The farm itself covered over 1,000 hectares of mostly cropped land for wheat, barley, oats, peas and beans, and grazing land for sheep, goats, dairy and beef cattle. Closer to the residential area were the intensive sections for poultry and pigs. Experimental grapevines grew close to the winery.

Most of us lived on the college — about 30 academic staff, 40 ancillary and administrative staff, and over 200 students studying for diplomas in agriculture or oenology.

We soon felt part of the community with afternoon tea get-togethers in the main building, weekend social barbecues, and a host of other events for staff and students. Rachel started off her primary school at Roseworthy, a small town, about 3 kilometres from Roseworthy College. Through the school and going to the Baptist Church in Gawler, we expanded our friendships with people outside the college.

Don Williams' vision and innovation led to new courses in natural resources and the environment, business management, agricultural production, horse husbandry, wine marketing and an international diploma in dryland farming. As well as opening its doors to international students, the college welcomed female students for the first time. Except for wine marketing I became involved in all of these courses.

At the start of my 20-year stay at Roseworthy College I supervised the running of the experimental Merino sheep flock involving the selection for increased clean fleece weight and fecundity in South Australian Merinos. A large bank of data of wool and body traits had accumulated and needed to be analysed. I enrolled for a master's degree at Adelaide University with Dr Oliver Mayo, my supervisor at the Waite Research Institute.

Along with looking after 600 Merinos and a Poll Dorset flock I took up lecturing in sheep husbandry and sheep breeding. Ian

Gregory, with a doctorate from the University of New South Wales, joined the research team and he wrote programs in Fortran to analyse the wool and body traits. I found Ian hard to understand at first as he mumbled away through his beard. He looked more like a bushranger than a research scientist. We became good friends as we teamed up. On one occasion I took potluck and threw a gumboot over the top of partition dividing us. It landed on Ian's desk and not on him. Ian never forgot that.

When money from the State eventually ran out for research, I had to become a full-time lecturer. That meant, as well as lectures in sheep husbandry and breeding, I lectured in soil science and assisted in courses in climatology, anatomy, chemistry, plant science, biometry, pastures and dryland farming systems. With so many unexpected subjects thrown at me, the staff often asked when I was going to take over their area. 'Soon,' I would say. 'You'd better watch out.' But I would have drawn the line at wine science, marketing, business management and agricultural engineering. I filled in once for a lecturer in courses on land use and land rehabilitation for the natural resource students, but felt that I had sold them short.

At times I felt overwhelmed with a high contact load for lectures, tutorials and practicals, creeping up towards 30 hours a week. A one-hour lecture often took three hours to prepare, even if I had given it before. I always searched for new material and tried to put a new angle on it, along with a challenge to the students. I varied the delivery to keep the students motivated and interested. But they were swamped, too, and often responded like robots. The contact time for students was over 30 hours a week, and, with the rising number of complaints from both staff and students, we had to reduce the loads. Practical work suffered the most while computer time increased.

In my spare time, I continued with my master's degree, and after four years I presented my thesis 'Selection studies in South Australian Merinos' to Adelaide Universty. It was accepted and I graduated at a ceremony held in Bonython Hall of the North Terrace Campus in 1978.

In our welcome holiday breaks we jumped into our Galant station wagon and headed east to Sydney, the New South Wales Central coast, Canberra, or to the Victorian Alps. We also went locally to Victor Harbor on the south coast, explored the wildlife sanctuaries of Kangaroo Island, hiked in the Flinders Ranges, and visited Liz's sister, Meg, and her husband, Malcolm, on their vineyard property at Renmark in the Riverland. Malcolm always went out of his way to show me around his vineyard and explain the finer points of growing vines. He was always thinking up new ways to reduce costs and save on labour.

Rachel and Linda never allowed me to forget one of our holiday breaks at Ulladulla, on the coast south of Sydney, where we landed one evening at a caravan park. It was getting dark and we took a chance in booking a caravan for one night without seeing it first. That was the worst thing I could have done as it was the most rundown, unclean, spidery caravan you could imagine. After seeing their first spider, the girls panicked and decided to sleep on campbeds outside. I walked back to the office to see if we could get a clean caravan, but the owners had left for the night. Instead, ferocious-looking dogs, in charge of warding off unwelcome intruders, growled at us.

On another occasion near Lake Jindabyne I tried to put up our newly bought tent in bucketing rain while the girls looked on from inside the car. No help, of course. The plastic T-piece on one of the two supporting outside poles broke. The tent collapsed on top of me, and the girls, including Liz, just laughed. Drenched, I bundled up the tent and we headed for a night's stay in a caravan park in Canberra. The next day I found someone to weld on two metal T-pieces so we could continue on our camping holiday.

Most of us, as young families, lived on the college so we thrived as a community. The farm environment was ideal for bringing up children.

One of the lecturers was happy to get rid of a French Pleyel piano. After a professional tuner had worked on it, Rachel and Linda competed with each other for playing time. We booked them in to a piano teacher who lived in a small cottage not far away. Tina Dimmick was a professional singer and pianist and had already established a reputation for teaching young children. Linda's career in music had begun.

We offered our home to students for their Christian fellowship meeting in which 20 or more students would come and often hear a guest speaker. A friendly atmosphere seemed to allow the students to open up and speak about their faith in a non-threatening way. Grant Thorpe, a frequent speaker, reminded me of Dr John Hercus' approach in challenging students.

During the summer break, students only stayed on the college if they were involved in farm work. That meant they were often short of cricketers for local matches. Having found out I had played cricket in Scotland they invited me to play in most of their summer matches. I loved being out on the field once again, but the heat was trying if there was no shade on a 40-degree Celsius day.

Enough money was found to build a 25-metre swimming pool, but they drew the line on squash courts that I had planned and promoted.

Squash for me was a quick way to de-stress; I enjoyed the game immensely and always looked forward to squash matches and competitions. I started off in Grade D and then moved to Grades C, B and finally A Grade. During the week I would rush down to Elizabeth for a regular game with Peter Keane — a punter and florist, a strange combination. Peter was just as keen a player and showed irrepressible optimism in anything he did. Punting for him was his hobby, as well as an occupation for a number of years, before he became a florist. Angus, his offsider, had developed a computer program that brought in thousands of dollars. Why work if all is going well was Peter's philosophy. As the second highest punter in South Australia there seemed no barriers for Peter. Several times, Peter and his wife Effie invited us out for the evening.

In one of my squash matches I played Jim Strachan, who had migrated at a young age with his family from Elgin in Scotland.

With our common ties we continued to meet on the squash court and with his family.

I continued with cross-country running, often after work around part of the farm. Since high school days, a six to 10-kilometre run a week had become a feature and fabric of my lifestyle. Then the first Festival City Marathon event for Adelaide appeared on the horizon in November 1979; it would run from Gawler to Adelaide. In preparation, I stretched my distances to 15 and 20 kilometres. After enduring several 20-kilometre runs I decided I was ready for 42 kilometres, come what may. On the day of the marathon, I ran slowly and hit the wall, as they say, at about 30 kilometres. After that, if I had stopped, I would never have started again. I survived with a time of just under four hours, much slower that Grenville Wood, who came in first at two and a half hours and the premier of South Australia, John Bannon, at three hours. After that one-off effort I went back to my usual run.

In 1976, Don Williams had successfully negotiated with the Food and Agriculture Organisation (FAO) and other world organisations to fund an international one-year course in dryland farming. The courses would run for five years and, if successful, could continue for another five years. Students arrived from Middle East countries, North Africa, Cyprus, India, Pakistan and Afghanistan; they added a new cultural dimension to the college. Liz and I welcomed them and often had one or two around for a meal. We tried to make them feel at home and offered them any assistance they needed. Quite a number were Muslims, but often they relaxed their practices for occasions like Ramadan.

Naidu, from Madras, and Dhoulay, a Pakistani, complained to me about the lack of noise on the campus. It was so quiet to them. I had not heard of that complaint before, but realised that they had been so used to all kinds of city noise that the quiet had unsettled them; not only the quiet but a lack of people. So I took them to a Barossa Festival where hundreds had gathered to taste gourmet food and wine. They felt right at home again.

Part of the program for the international students included tours to the other states in Australia. As one of their lecturers I went with a group of 20 to visit farmers and places of interest in Western Australia. The mini-bus towed a trailer with lots of camping equipment and supplies for the trip across the Nullabor Plain to Esperance and on to the south-west of Western Australia, visiting farms, research centres, parkland areas, and Muresk Agricultural College. The students protested at our attempts to enthuse them with camping. Putting up tents, camp barbecues and roughing it was not their style, especially as we had been paid heaps of money, so they said, for much better facilities and services. After a few days of poor sleep and continued grumbling we yielded — not that I minded — to stay in hotels or caravan parks. We decided to return by train after all that running around.

On the way back we stopped at Kalgoorlie to view the gold mining and swim in the public swimming pool. There were plenty of Aboriginals swimming and some gazed in wonder at the darker Africans of our group. I tried to keep them out of the red light district but a couple of Africans found their way there after the evening meal. Perth was also a hot spot for some of them. When three hadn't turned up for breakfast I found they were still sleeping with their newly acquired girl friends.

The following year I took another group of students to New South Wales and into south-east Queensland. On the way we stopped at the Hay RSL (Returned & Services League) for dinner. One of the students from Jordan asked how to bet on the one-armed bandits so I demonstrated how to play the pokies, just for fun. 'You try,' I suggested. He did, and to everyone's amazement coins tumbled out — $50 worth. That was the end of my hope for a relaxing RSL-style dinner. They all tried and kept on trying until they had exhausted their money supply. Only the Jordanian came out on top. I had warned them.

We got to know other overseas students who appeared on the college to pursue either an undergraduate course or a post-graduate diploma or master's degree. One of the students, Mariano Deng Ngor, had fled Southern Sudan as a refugee. He became an active campaigner for the rights of Sudanese facing oppression from the Muslim military regime in the north. We often talked about the conflict in which millions of South Sudanese had been displaced and left without access to food and livelihoods.

On another student tour, I took the third year agricultural students (aggies) to New South Wales the day after the ploughman's ball. Not recommended. Some were still in evening attire as they rocked onto the bus. Others looked as if they had been washed up on a beach with that droopy-eyed, hangover-glazed look. One student even climbed up onto the luggage rack and fell asleep.

We toured the Riverine Plain of New South Wales to learn about the extensive range of farming practices — extensive sheep and cattle grazing, dryland farming and irrigation of pastures, maize and rice growing. The Riverine Plain was traversed by a number of rivers including the Murray, Murrumbidgee and Lachlan Rivers. After stopping at a number of properties we stayed the night at Yanco Agricultural Institute, located 2 kilometres south of Yanco, between Leeton and Narrandera in the Murrumbidgee area. Like Roseworthy College, the Yanco Institute offered agricultural courses to students.

Terry Davis, a lecturer in agronomy, spoke to the students about irrigation practices, such as water requirements of rice, timing of water application, and the problems of salinity and water logging. At the end of the day, Terry and his wife Chris invited me over for dinner. I left my lieutenants, Rod, Les and Alan, in charge of the students. No blame on them, but who would have expected anything untoward after midnight.

The aggies, bar two sensible ones, left the Yanco pub to walk back to their sleeping quarters at the Yanco Institute. Unfortunately, they let loose on the way, forming themselves into two battle lines in an orange grove. The missiles were research oranges which they tore off the trees and flung at each other. One orange broke a skylight.

The next day the students assembled in a lecture hall for another talk by Terry. None of us in charge knew of what had happened the previous night. And none of us suspected anything since the students were quiet and lamb-like as Terry addressed them. The principal, accompanied by a local policeman, walked into the lecture room. My heart sank. What didn't I know? The principal drew me aside and explained what had happened. The worst part was the ruination of a research program to compare different varieties of oranges. The principal would inform our principal what our students had done, and he would expect compensation. I felt like crawling into a dark burrow. Although I had been out to dinner that evening I had to bear the brunt of their foolhardy actions and had to explain what had happened to our director when I arrived back at Roseworthy College.

Jim Watkinson, our unofficial college poet, wrote about the 'Yanco trip … or whom the bell tolls' for the college newsletter. An abridged version:

> There's a sleepy little hamlet
> Yanco is its name.
> 'Twas there in 1986
> Our Aggies made their name.
>
> It was a trip for learning
> Well led by Thomas Mann
> Happy Les and Rocket Rod
> Were his right and left hand man.
>
> At various stops along the way
> Our students soaked in skills
> But all the time as students do
> Were seeking extra thrills.
>
> On a Tuesday night quite pleasant
> They hit the Yanco pub

And very soon had settled in
Just like the Community Club!

The Landlord he was very pleased
He was raking in the cash
But what would happen when they left?
What would they flamin' smash?

They all trooped out at closing time
Into the cool clear air
What could they do to stir things up?
They really didn't care

On and on the rabble sped
They didn't have a bus
They came upon an orchard green
The fruit of which were lush

Through the night air like coloured bats
The Citrus Aurantium flew
They didn't know it was a trial plot
O what a flamin' blue!

I've heard of Cylcone Tracy
And the wind they call Maria
But for this silly band of Aggies
The consequences might be dire!

One last thing before you ask
For whom the bell does bong
It tolls for all you Aggies
Who don't know right from wrong!

Chapter 10

Algeria, Scotland and West Berlin

ROSEWORTHY COLLEGE WON A CONTRACT for a three-month course in sheep husbandry for 20 agricultural officers from the Middle East, so that earned me another trip to the eastern states as well as organising lectures, practicals and visits to local farms and research centres. All spoke reasonable English except for a polite and smiling Syrian who had bribed an official to pass him on his English test in Syria. We all got on well, including the Syrian who didn't appreciate the finer points of my sense of humour but laughed anyway.

Our lecturer in soil science, Iain Grierson, signed up for a three-year consultancy in Algeria, on a World Bank funded project. Knowing that I had studied soil science at Aberdeen University, our head of agronomy, Hugh Reimers, asked if I could run the course for the natural resource students (nat rats), wine students (plonkies) and agricultural students (aggies). I took up the challenge, and Iain said he would leave all his lecture notes to help me get started. But he had locked his filing cabinet, so I started from scratch to prepare the courses. Word got around the college that a sheep husbandry lecturer, of all people, was about to lecture on soil science. What could he know?

The head of oenology, Bryce Rankine, an internationally acclaimed researcher on soils influencing the performance of vines, appeared at my first lecture to his wine students. My heart sank — he had come to test out my credibility. Anyway, I had a comprehensive set of slides for the introductory lecture and tried to ignore him as I flashed up different soil types and highlighted poorer and better soils, taking into account texture, structure, organic matter and fertility. I would sink or swim. Towards the end of the lecture Bryce left and that was it. No comment from him, and the course went well, according to the students at the end of the semester.

The extra course loads meant I had to work harder and longer hours in the evening and at weekends. Liz felt she was battling on her own to bring up Rachel and Linda. Sometimes, when I arrived back in the evening, Liz seemed at the end of her tether, and I didn't help with sharp words to the girls. We needed a break from the college. It came unexpectedly; most things did as I discovered later.

SAGRIC International, a consultant firm linked to the South Australian Department of Agriculture, was looking for a replacement for a livestock consultant who had participated in a World Bank funded project in Algeria — the same one that had engaged Iain Grierson. The consultant had decided to come home before his three-year contract had expired. Would I be interested in replacing him for the final eight months of the project?

I had thought of taking study leave, but this sounded more of a challenge. Bob Hogarth, the manager of the South Australian side, and Harry Nash, a livestock officer with the Department of Agriculture, interviewed me.

'We are involved in a rehabilitation program for 850,000 hectares of the steppe region,' Bob said, 'an area sandwiched between the Sahara desert and the Atlas Mountains. The lack of grazing and water in summer for the Saharan area south of the steppe involves movement northwards of livestock to the cereal areas where they can graze on straw, stubble and unharvested grain. With increasing population, though, this type of movement, known as transhumance, along with nomadic movement, has put more pressure on the steppe, and increases settlement of the nomads and cropping in marginal areas, all leading to land degradation. Our task is to come up with plans to rehabilitate the land and encourage vegetation to grow, and to start implementation of those plans.'

'Are our South Australian dryland farming practices applicable?' I asked.

'That's what we are trying to find out. We believe they are to some extent. If so, how can we best implement them, taking into account the social and cultural changes which have occurred under French occupation?' Bob replied.

'A huge project,' I remarked.

'Yes, the Algerian steppe stretches about 150 kilometres southwards from the Atlas Mountains in the north, covering more than 15 million hectares. The region supports 2 million people, 600,000 of whom are nomads living in tents. The whole area has become very run-down with overgrazing from sheep and goats.'

'How is the project going?'

'We have had severe setbacks with getting the project underway, in working with our Algerian counterparts, and with carrying out the survey work.'

I thought about these points for a moment before Bob said, 'If you were offered the position, you would help complete the livestock survey of the area and take part in the resource survey which is running behind time.'

After a few more verbal exchanges Bob offered me the position, and I accepted.

I took leave from the college and also asked for study leave of six months following the Algerian stint, at the Animal Breeding Research Organisation, located at Edinburgh University in Scotland. Fortune favours the bold, I thought. The college approved the study leave as well.

Rachel had just started high school at Gawler, and we felt it best if she settled in for a few months. First, I would go to Algeria, and

Liz and the girls would follow after Rachel had completed a term at high school, and arrangements made for correspondence courses while overseas.

From what I read, after eight years of savage fighting with the French from 1954 to 1962, the Algerians had finally won their independence. The French president at the time, De Gaulle, had had enough and bowed to the inevitable demise of colonial rule, which lasted for more than 130 years; not without a huge number of casualties on both sides. Ten percent of the Algerian population had died as a result of the war. Houari Boumediene, president of Algeria from 1965 to 1978, knew he had to promote reforms in agriculture.

The Ksar Chellala project was signed in January 1979 in Adelaide by the deputy minister Des Corcoran and the minister of agriculture Brian Chatterton. A 21-gun salute, heralding an anniversary of the Algerian Republic, ensured that the project went off with a bang. Australian specialists were appointed to work with a team of Algerian counterparts over a three-year period (1979–1982).

The Algerian Ministry of Agriculture and Agrarian Reform had never undertaken such a huge project. They were in the dark, and we were, too, as I found out. The enormity of the project, involving 850,000 hectares of mostly degraded steppe rangeland, would overwhelm us.

The Algerian Government wanted permanent settlement around new centres and to discourage the south to north migration. Sheep farming would be carried out in designated pastoral cooperatives.

With a stopover in Rome to pick up my visa, I flew off to Algiers on 15 January 1982. From the plane, the Atlas Mountains came into view, followed by tall apartment blocks and red-roofed houses of Algiers, the capital and seaport.

Christine who was employed as the project administrator met me at the airport. 'Welcome to Algeria. It's different,' she said, enigmatically.

Our Algerian driver Ahmed drove through the bustling traffic of Algiers and sped like a man possessed over the Atlas Mountains.

It grew dark and the road twisted its way down onto the lower lying cereal and vine regions.

Five hours later and 300 kilometres south of Algiers, we arrived at the Ksar Chellala project base. I gathered my nerves to meet the leader, Wal Buddee, at the project site, which housed both the Australian and counterpart Algerian contingents. 'Welcome to Ksar Chellala. We are going to be busy,' he said.

Wal had been appointed as the third leader in July 1980. The previous two leaders had resigned — an inauspicious start to the project. He introduced the Australian crew: Wal Buddee's wife Leila, Chris, who was in charge of the resources survey, and his wife Carol, and Terry an agronomist from New South Wales with his wife Christine who had accompanied me from Algiers, Colin, the irrigation engineer, his wife Consuelo from Colombia, Maurie, the admin officer, and David, the cartographer, with whom I would be staying.

Later, I met the Algerian counterparts when we had a four-hour meeting in French to discuss the lack of progress for the project. My French was sorely tested — I wished I had done more.

David, a single easy-going guy in his mid-twenties, seemed to see the lighter side of things no matter how serious they were. He had worked on the project site for three months and knew his way around.

He brought out an Algerian red wine for our first dinner. 'Welcome to Ksar Chellala,' he said. 'Quite a change from our Australian lifestyle, but you'll get used to it. We'll take it in turns to cook the evening meal.'

'Thanks, David,' I said. 'How come our Algerian counterparts live in stone houses and we live in Australian-style homes?'

'Well, that was the first mistake: the Australian managers had insisted on Western-style prefabricated homes, provided by Italian contractors. The Italian company went insolvent and the Algerians improvised, but the completed homes give little protection from the cold and the hot desert winds. The more sensible stone-built homes for the Algerian counterpart staff and families are ideal.'

'I see. Any other problems facing us with only eight months left to complete the project?' I asked.

'We are well behind with the resource survey, and the land mapping should have been completed. They had delays in building our houses, and in acquiring equipment, staff and vehicles, and wasted time learning French in a resort in the south of France.'

'Learning French in France! How long did that take?'

'Three months, all expenses paid.'

'Wow! How do you get on with the Algerian counterparts?' I asked.

'Ah, we don't get on too well. Everyone pushes their own ideas.'

Later, I gathered, too, that no attempt had been made to involve the major stakeholders — the nomads and settled farmers. Their knowledge, understanding of the issues and what needed to be carried out were not taken into account. With little communication at all levels, we blundered on.

The next day, I viewed a desolate scene — hardly a blade of grass. The flocks of sheep and goats were handfed. Tents dotted the landscape, and Ksar Chellala, a village of 25,000 people, stood close to the project base with a jumbled assortment of stone-built houses and open-fronted stalls.

I joined my small Algerian team of four. Mohammed and Nourredine had already begun the livestock survey of the steppe area. We also had a driver and another interpreter. Mohammed, a Berber, spoke reasonable English. The Berbers, he told me, were an indigenous ethnic group, living mostly as settled farmers in the Atlas Mountains of North Africa. I found Mohammed a pleasant and engaging person to work with. We corresponded for many years after completion of the project.

For my first venture, we followed some pistes or bush tracks through denuded areas and into valleys or oueds with signs of cultivation and well-eaten sage bush, and then on to Stipa country similar to our pastoral areas. Flocks of sheep, numbering between 200 and 300, grazed on stunted bushes. To supplement the diet for survival the owners handfed with barley grain.

The livestock owners seemed to live in mostly isolated areas in simple stone buildings, the roofs weighed down with heavy stones or straw and compacted earth. Others lived in goatskin tents. It was hard to imagine what their life was like.

The shepherds easily managed their flocks of sheep and goats. Donkeys or horses pulled two-wheeled carts loaded up with supplies from neighbouring villages. Unkempt and tousled-hair young children looked on — very few of them went to school, I gathered, as it was too far.

As part of the survey, Mohammed and Nourredine thrashed out one question. What type of movement did the owner carry out with his sheep and goats? Had he settled down with limited movement of his flock? If he was a tent dwelling nomad where did he move to and how often?

On arriving back at Ksar Chellala, the streets were crowded with mostly men who wore a brown, long overcoat — a *djellaba*; the men purchased items from open-fronted shops. Occasionally, I spotted a woman completely covered except for one eye.

In the evening we played volleyball, our Australian side up against our counterpart Algerian side.

In the days that followed we continued with the livestock survey. Livestock owners always welcomed us with coffee — strong and flavoured with white sage. In the course of the day we had ten or more cups of coffee. Not recommended. If we arrived near lunchtime our host provided us with a meaty pea soup, couscous and battered pancakes, or something similar, but always with couscous. We asked all the questions in Arabic as few spoke French in the steppe areas.

On one occasion our Land Rover crossed a small oued after a rainstorm and we sank deep into the mud. We tried for three hours to free the vehicle. A farmer nearby revived us with a filling couscous meal. A rescue group arrived from the base, and, after being hauled out, we called on some people who had already promised us a meal. We could not refuse our second couscous meal! Our team for once did not wolf it down. We all felt bloated, and I had to cancel my evening meal that David had prepared.

One weekend, I accompanied Mohammed, Ahmed our driver, and an accountant, to Tipasa, on the coast. In the evening we went to a disco in the evening where young men packed the dance floor. We drank passable red Algerian wine. A male dancer pulled me onto the floor so I had to perform.

The next morning, bleary-eyed, we wandered through the Roman ruins of an amphitheatre, temples, forum and Christian burial tombs. I found an inscription from Albert Camus's writing on a stele: '*Je comprends ici ce qu'on appelle gloire: le droit d'aimer sans mesure.*' Translated it read: 'I understand here what one calls glory is to love without ceasing.' I pondered on it for some time, trying to comprehend the suffering experienced on both sides during the war for independence. Could the loss of so many lives have been averted if they had taken more heed of words by Albert Camus, the French Nobel Prize-winning philosopher and novelist? And yet, Camus sided with the *Pieds-Noirs*, people of French and other European ancestry, who supported colonial French rule in Algeria and were opposed to Algerian nationalist groups such as the Front de Liberation Nationale (FLN). Did he not see the writing on the wall for Algerians seeking independence?

By the middle of March a few tinges of green dotted the steppe as we journeyed into our 21st zone. The dry state had weakened the sheep with limited grazing on sparse patches of Artemesia and Noea shrubs.

On one of our visits, we called on a well-to-do steppe dweller with five sons and 25 grand children. Enclosed feeding areas were used for growing out lambs. Inside his home, we sat down cross-legged on luxurious carpets to coffee flavoured with white sage. Shoorba followed — an oily soup with noodles and spices, and then a meat dish with potatoes and sauce, and finally a sweet flavoured tea. Curious children kept in the background and eyed me. Our host didn't speak French so I trotted out a few Arabic phrases.

On another occasion, a man on a donkey arrived like Lawrence of Arabia, I thought, to help us carry out a vegetation survey. He hugged me like a long lost relative with a heart-warming embrace. We visited his stone dwelling for lunch — couscous and chicken.

In our tent-dwelling visits, women made clothing, carpets and wall hangings, from wool, goat and camel hair, using simple looms and sewing materials. Older women only left their homes bare-faced with their husband's permission. Tent-dwelling women wore no veil or mask. If a stranger approached they hid in the tent and the man served a meal outside. Women married young in arranged marriages and had many children.

About the middle of March I switched to surveying the land and vegetation in a resource survey. Dhaleb, our driver, assisted us in a wheel point survey of vegetation and in quadrat sampling. Nourredine protested that the land class capability mapping wasn't detailed enough.

Bob Hogarth, our general manager from Adelaide, flew in from Morocco on 1 April. I put him up in my house, which had been allocated in readiness to receive Liz and the girls.

We spent a sleepless night in one of the worst storms we could imagine. In the afternoon the day turned to night with powerful winds swirling masses of degraded topsoil into the air. And then the rain! I'd set a mouse trap, and Bob watched it sail past his eyes from the kitchen to the living room with water everywhere. I thought the roof was going to go, but it held. Bob and I bailed out water for two hours.

Ted Chapman and his assistant director arrived for two weeks. The only worthwhile thing the minister performed was a party trick; then he played cards into the small hours of the morning. The trade commissioner, Hugh McLelland, got drunk and behaved completely out of tune to the code and conduct of a diplomat.

We held a number of meetings with the Algerians in Algiers to set priorities on the work to do. While there, I had my first opportunity to visit the Casbah — a walk through narrow lanes separating houses built several centuries ago in the Ottoman Empire. We drove slowly through the streets to avoid boys playing soccer. A ball whistled over my head, and I realised that the soccer craze had gripped a nation with Algeria qualifying for the World Cup.

At one of the get-togethers at Ksar Chellala, I put forward a livestock program for the planned steppe experimental station, and it seemed to be acceptable to the Algerians. As a treat I cooked stuffed zucchinis for everyone. The whole concoction looked awful, so I loaded the zucchinis with condiments. The chef de mission surprised me by coming back for seconds. On a similar occasion, in a competition to promote good will between the Algerians and Australians, my curried garbanzos took second prize while the dish prepared by the chef de mission was judged the best — a diplomatic outcome.

Slimane, one of the international students who had studied at Roseworthy College, invited David and me to go to Constantine. We stayed on the research station, El Kroub, in a two-storey house. People lived on top of each other in high-rise apartment blocks. I felt sorry for the children with no parks — they played on the streets, footpaths and vacant lots. The next day we wandered through the Roman ruins at Timgad and visited Djamila, not far from Constantine — regarded as one of the finest Roman cities in North Africa. The baths and toilets seemed to be in good shape with a well-designed underground drainage system.

While at Constantine, we attended a village fair to watch a spectacle of decorated horsemen charge into an open arena, encircled by a huge number of people. The horsemen, dressed in various costumes, lined up with raised guns, awaiting a signal to gallop, and then fired their guns in unison.

In the second week of June I travelled to London to meet up with Liz and the children. After spending a few days in London we flew with British Airways to Algiers. Our driver sped once again through the Atlas Mountains — no concession for a family — and we arrived at dusk when the scorpions had come out of their daytime hiding places. Liz gasped at our flimsy-built quarters with little protection from the elements, and with no power or water on tap.

Liz sighed for home comforts but adjusted somehow to the lack of mod cons, and Rachel and Linda did their home schooling exercises after some persuasion. Lentils provided our chief source of protein, but we had to screen them because of similar-sized stones mixed in with them. Where would we find a dentist anyway?

Water, our big problem, came from nearby wells. Young boys on donkeys carried the water in large tractor-size tubes. For us water arrived by tank and was pumped into the house or into our bath if there was nothing coming through the shower.

At nighttime, the girls did not mind the scorpions, but they would have shrieked at spiders back in Australia. That kind of logic defied me. The black scorpions were more deadly than the yellow ones; you had to be treated within three hours. A young woman in the town was stung and died with the delay in going to hospital. With a sting from the yellow scorpions you had a chance of survival, allowing you a little longer in time to reach a hospital for the anti-venene. Most times yellow scorpions entered our prefabricated home so we had to shake our clothes and shoes. I would flick them into a jar half-filled with alcohol and later set them in a clear plastic mould for taking back to Australia as paper weights.

One of the project drivers took Liz and others into Ksar Chellala to buy essentials. The driver threw everything, including the French-style baguettes, into a boot caked with dirt and grease. No matter, the baguettes were crisp and crunchy for a morning breakfast or snack, but by lunchtime were rock hard and could be used as weapons. There was little chance of buying fresh vegetables and fruit or cheese and eggs. Chickens were scrawny and the meat questionable with the number of flies hanging around.

Market days were held on a discarded rubbish site. Clothing, pots and pans, and you name it, were for sale. Carcasses of sheep, goats and cattle were hung up; everything, including heads, innards and testicles, were for sale.

Home schooling, volleyball, and a number of daytime get-togethers or dinner evenings kept us all occupied. I continued with the resource survey during the day, often getting baked in the summer sun of over 40 degrees Celsius. Once I nearly collapsed with sunstroke while out assessing the type and degree of plant cover with David. I had to recover in a stone shelter provided by a small flock owner.

In the evening, I struggled with a livestock report, knowing that we had not got to grips with the real issues to bring about change, and with little attempt to utilise the knowledge and capabilities of the local people. Perhaps we would all learn how not to run a project of this kind and magnitude.

By August the dust storms were frequent with hot, dry winds — the Sirocco — from the Sahara. The dust found a way through our shutters and coated everything inside. We endured constant water and power shortages. Liz developed a nasty ear infection which caused a lot of pain. Slowly with antibiotics the pain subsided and the infection died down. She was surprised when she went to the local doctor to learn that painkillers and antibiotics were given as a suppository. That knowledge hurried up the healing process.

We visited Tipasa and the girls enjoyed jumping around the Roman ruins. They bargained with local girls selling trinkets and amazed us by coming back with nothing. On the way back we sighted camel trains and nomads on the stubble fields with all their flocks.

Rachel was so taken with the camel train that she wrote a poem:

THE NOMAD
Moving slowly yet consistently they reach nowhere and
   stay.
Up goes the tribal canvas for a night or a season?
Their pitiful home with goatskins long since lost their
   satin-like sheen
From moody, restless sands which call frequently when
   stirred by wind.
Gaudy-coloured woven rugs and trinkets made of silver

Pots and pans and firewood are their only needs for
   possessions.
The camels lurch and off they're hauled along with the
   pregnant daughter
Darkness is near, tea won't be long for a lamb's last bleat
   is its slaughter.
A fire sparkles and crackles and sways like a tree seen
   long ago in the
chilly, starry night. Sheep are sleeping, nevertheless used
   to the day long hike.
Rough, throaty, gibbering language overtakes the
   infinite-like silence.
Silver earrings clinkle, sending delicate sound waves
   through the sand when they swing,
Whilst she is serving the sweetest Turkish tea to her
   contented, handsome Saharan.
Leather-skinned, squinty-eyed boys grow weary and
   uncertain
For a scorpion's bite does not guarantee life by the
   morning.
Daybreak and the camels are taller once more.
What unknown destination is there for today?
The heat of the morning penetrates its scorching rays
   on the place
Where the Nomad has been and may pass again one day.
The Sahara, the home of the Nomad
Where they wander, careless and free.
The life, the land, a place I'd long to be.

Rachel was 13 at the time and, according to Arabic custom, of a
marriageable age. Well, it should not have affected us, but I became
aware of an 18-year-old, Tayeb, coming to our house in the evening
to check up on data for a report. When he knocked on our door his
eyes scanned inside for any sign of Rachel. When I realised his true
intention, I became more circumspect; otherwise, we might have
lost Rachel prematurely.

The girls, though, did learn how to dress up as covered Algerian women, bake bread and make couscous. Well, maybe they could have made good Algerian wives after all. We would never know.

On another weekend we visited Bousada, a town at the northern edge of the Sahara. We stayed at a tourist hotel with a swimming pool fringed by palm trees, a taste of the sublime compared to Ksar Chellala. Rachel and Linda even discovered they sold coke.

With about two weeks left of my contract, a letter arrived from one of our squash players to say that my weekly squash partner Peter Keane had taken his life and the lives of his wife Effie, and their two children. I was shocked. I just could not believe it. Peter had everything to live for with a thriving florist business. No one seemed to know why he had done this. I wandered around in a daze for about a week, trying to come to terms with this tragedy.

My eight-month contract ended towards the end of August, and we planned to fly to London on 31 August.

We headed north to Algiers, over the Atlas Mountains for the last time. We were on our way to Edinburgh for my study leave at the Animal Breeding Research Organisation (ABRO), attached to Edinburgh University.

Algiers airport was packed, and at the check-in-counter the airline staff tried to cope with the volume of passengers. It seemed a shambles, and the girl was flustered as she handed back our passports. But only one boarding pass, as I discovered half an hour later. I rushed back, but the girl had been replaced by another official. Fortunately, after a lot of explanation from our interpreter, the official handed over three more passes. We could all officially leave Algeria.

Later, when I thought about our Algerian experience I realised we were fortunate to have been there at a relatively peaceful time in its violent history from the 1950s to the turn of the century. An Algerian civil war raged between the Algerian government and an Islamist rebel group, which began in 1991 following a coup which denied an Islamist electoral victory. Like so many other countries taken over by colonial powers, not only did independence come at a cost in human life, but also post-independence with political parties vying for dominance, which often resulted in bitter conflict.

On the home front, the Algerian project came under severe criticism, especially by Labor member Brian Chatterton who claimed we had ignored important socio-economic factors. As far as I know, the recommendations for the development of the Ksar Chellala agro-pastoral zone were never implemented. A sad outcome for the people of the steppe.

Large-scale funded projects, I discovered, were fraught with potential problems like the ones we experienced. The biggest problem, I felt, was a top-down approach that ignored input from local stakeholders.

From a personal point of view, I valued learning about Algeria and its steppe-dwellers, who received us with friendliness and simplicity of lifestyle. But I wished we could have done more for those struggling in their livelihood.

Scotland

At London airport Rachel and Linda made a beeline for chocolate — three months deprivation proved too much. On arriving at Edinburgh the Edinburgh Tattoo was in full swing and so was the rain. It drenched us as we sought accommodation in vain. Eventually, we found an old farm house by the sea at North Berwick. It was comfortable enough and, with beach walks nearby, we soon felt at home, with the harshness of the steppe fading into the distance.

At the Animal Breeding Research Organisation (ABRO), Dr Charles Smith introduced me to his colleagues and provided me with an office for my research task: to analyse a large bank of data to compare crossbred ewes from five sire breeds, from 1976 to 1981. The breeds involved the traditional Border Leicester, three imported breeds — the East Friesian, the Oldenburg and the Texel — and a new prolific breed, the Cambridge. Rams from these breeds were joined to Scottish Blackface ewes on an upland farm in Scotland. Crossbred ewes derived from the sheep were compared over three lamb drops on a lowland farm in England. I set up the data for analysis on a Prime computer with the help of a statistician.

After three weeks at North Berwick we moved to Lasswade, a satellite town of Edinburgh. We rented the lower floor of a two-storey home. Rachel and Linda attended a local school. No one understood them, and it took them a while to pick up the 'ayes', 'dinna kens' and other strange words. Linda always joined her words like a true 'emmachisit' (how much is it) Aussie. But by the end of her school term she had acquired a Scottish accent which no one understood when we returned to Adelaide.

In between my wrestling with data we explored Edinburgh's past and ventured into the countryside. Our intended weekend trip to the Isle of Mull was postponed several times with the chilly onset of winter. Liz went along to a university welcome wives evening and heard about the history of Edinburgh University dating back 400 years. That spurred her on to explore the many places of historical interest in the city.

We ventured into the Scottish Highlands on a few calmer days. Waterfalls trickled down mountain sides, and, on a walk through the Hermitage in the Tay Valley, trees stood on the brink of the falls, surrounded by ferns and autumnal leaves showing tinges of golden-yellow and red in a dappled canopy of light and shade. The scene took our breath away.

Later, we stopped at Soldier's Leap at Killiecrankie, where a government soldier had leapt to his escape at the Battle of Killiecrankie in which 3,000 government troops were defeated by a highland army led by Viscount 'Bonnie' Dundee.

We stopped at Aviemore Centre for the night. Rachel and Linda went swimming, played space invaders, go-karted on a track, and dry-skied on a slope of fine plastic brushes instead of snow.

The next morning we hiked for four hours through the forests in the Cairngorms near Loch Morlich. We rested at a bothy, a simple stone hut set aside for those caught in a snowstorm or wild weather. Two reindeers came right up and nosed their way into my rucksack as I photographed them.

After lapping up the highland ruggedness of the Cairngorms, we motored on to the Kyle of Lochalsh, a village on the north-west coast of Scotland, where we boarded the ferry for the Isle of Skye. On landing we headed for Talisker House, a Georgian mansion built in the 17th century and home to the Clan Mcleod for most of the time. Friends of my mother, Mark and Rosemary Wathen, had rented the house and invited us to stay.

'Johnson and Boswell, well-known authors of their day, visited Talisker House in 1773,' Mark said. 'Johnson was so impressed that he wrote in his diary that Talisker was the place beyond all that he had seen, where the hermit might expect to grow old in meditation, without possibility of disturbance or interruption.'

We climbed Preshal More, a hill that overlooked Talisker, and after taking in the hill and coastline scenery, Rachel and Linda made a fast descent, sliding down on the seat of their pants. They shrieked and whooped as they went down on the wet heather and mud, while Liz bewailed the state of their clothes when they reached the bottom.

After a privileged stay with our hosts at Talisker we made our way back to Edinburgh. The weather turned colder with the threat of snow so we decided to leave the Isle of Mull for another day.

For Christmas we loaded our luggage into a Rover which I had bought cheaply from an ABRO scientist. The girls set off by train to Norwich while I planned to drive all the way down in snowy weather — not such a good idea, as the snow kept falling and blinding the windscreen with my imperfect windscreen wipers. I nearly made it — only six miles to my place of birth, Woodgate House, in Aylsham, Norfolk. Then, as I concentrated hard in the fading light of the evening, a car careened in from a side road on my right at high speed. I swung away from the vehicle to avoid a crash and ended up against the embankment of a churchyard — how convenient! The car's front end crumpled, the radiator hissed steam and the impact threw me forward, with luggage that was stacked on the back seats landing on top of me. The offending car did not stop, but a nearby house light came on. The occupants of the house had already donned their safety clothes and helmet to extricate me from the car. They had done it all before — many times, they said. I was shaken but not hurt, and I thanked them for their trouble.

I phoned Peter Purdy, my cousin at Woodgate Farm, and he arrived about half an hour later to tow the Rover for the last six miles. I let Peter have the car — I was glad to get rid of it.

We stayed at Woodgate, joining in with all the Christmas activities with cousins, aunts and uncles on Mum's side. The girls loved playing charades.

After Christmas we visited another two aunts and uncles at Winchester and celebrated the New Year with Scottish dancing.

We headed back to Edinburgh to complete my writing up of the research. The Cambridge crosses were the most prolific but had high lamb mortality and lower litter weights at weaning than the traditional Border Leicester crosses. The East Friesian crosses were appreciably superior in several production traits.

West Berlin

Liz and the girls flew home in time for the first term of 1983, while I stayed on for two weeks to finish up the research study. I then flew to Berlin to stay a few days with Heiko, my canoeing partner in France, and his family. It seemed like winter wonderland with their snow-roofed and two-storey house overlooking an iced lake, Krumme Lanke, on the edge of Grunewald Forest.

I enquired about a tall flag-pole positioned in the front of their garden. Heiko said, 'Oh, the chief SS officer had commandeered the house during the Second World War, and that pole marked his place. In this street, detached and terraced houses were allocated to SS officers according to rank. You are probably sleeping in his room.'

Feeling uneasy about that thought, we discussed the Russian attack on Berlin. 'Would you like to visit East Berlin?' Heiko asked.

'Is it possible to arrange?' I said.

'No problem. In two days time you can go on a tour of East Berlin. The bus will pass through Checkpoint Charlie.'

Heiko fulfilled his promise but declined to accompany me. I boarded the bus and we waited at the border crossing point for about an hour before we were cleared to go through. We drove close to Alexander Platz, through drab-looking streets and uninspiring apartment blocks. We stopped at a lakeside tearoom, but even the dishwater-coloured brew seemed to match the environment. We climbed aboard the bus for another well-rehearsed spiel of the sights by our guide. All in all, it was quite depressing in contrast to the vitality and brightness of West Berlin. I felt sad for the East Berliners, who, because of an end-of-war agreement between the major powers, had lost their right to be part of a prosperous growing nation. The Berlin Wall symbolised the divide between Russia and the West. A comfortless reflection on our humanity, I thought.

After more sightseeing in West Berlin, I left to fly back to Norwich and to prepare for a two-week stopover in India.

Chapter 11

India

RICK SHIPWAY, A FORMER STUDENT at Roseworthy Agricultural College, encouraged me to visit the Good Shepherd Agricultural Mission (GSAM) orphanage farm situated on the outskirts of Tanakpur, in the province of Uttar Pradesh and close to the border with Nepal. Rick had grown up on a dairy farm in the southeast of South Australia and had taken up the challenge by Len Reid, president of the society For Those Who Have Less, to deliver Australian dairy cows to the farm and carry out a breeding program to improve the milk yielding ability of local cows. He stayed on the farm and fell in love with Maxine, the daughter of the founders of the orphanage farm, Max and Shirley Strong.

The opportunity for me to visit the farm was too good to miss, and I had three weeks before the teaching term began.

After arriving in New Delhi, I met up with Rick, Max Strong and Len Reid. A haze hung over Delhi as we drove through a network of streets, jostling with rickshaws and taxis for premier space. I braced myself for the constant lurching of the Land Rover as all kinds of traffic hogged and honked the road, from fast moving buses and gaily ornamented trucks to carts, cyclists, foot walkers and wandering cows. Road gangs pounded rocks and heavy stones into lighter weight material for road making. In fields bordering the roads, Indians irrigated, weeded and fertilised plots of vegetables.

Our first roadside stop was a welcome relief. While the others checked out the café for breakfast I stretched my legs and straightaway a group of four Indians — my first encounter — approached with open arms. I drew back, startled by their wizened noses and curled-up fingers. At that moment Max came out of the café and, noticing my predicament, handed them a small amount of money. 'They have leprosy,' he said. 'We have some of them staying on the farm. No one will accept them.' After cups of sweetened tea and battered patties of potatoes, peas and onions, we journeyed on to Bareilly.

At Bareilly we picked up Peggy, from the GSAM farm with her eight-day-old Robert. We squeezed up for the last two hours. As the shadows lengthened we arrived at Tanakpur, a town 10 kilometres from the orphanage farm and lying at the foot of the snow-crowned Himalayas on Nepal's western border.

'Centuries ago,' Max said, 'Tanakpur probably was a small village; however, with the coming of the railway it had become a trading centre for Nepalese, Tibetans, hill dwellers, farmers and indigenous groups. Fortunes were made through smuggling. The town had become famous for fine seed potatoes brought down from the mountains to market. Sal and shisham from the surrounding jungle made a booming timber business. Nomads walked out of the Tibetan mountains driving sheep flocks loaded with borax; the sheep were shorn and the wool shipped by rail to distant textile mills. The nomads then drove the sheep back loaded with salt and cloth.'

At the farm, children came out to greet us and help unload. A cup of tea revived us while we met Mrs Strong, Maxine their daughter, and Malcolm and Florence, who had grown up on the farm. We talked for a while, and then two of the older boys took us to the guest-house.

I arose early the next day to catch the dawn. A slight mist hovered over the Himalayan Ranges and the wheat glistened with the early morning dew. The howling of jackals had stopped, and the farm was quiet except for a flurry of activity in the mango trees as parrots chirped and darted to and fro. Two boys carried pots of tea across the central compound. Tall eucalypts towered above them like kings protecting their minions. A chill was in the air, but they had told me that the wintry day promised to be a little warmer than usual.

I wandered to the farm gate, and the main road was already full of life — Indian life — bullock carts, cyclists, rickshaws, and, occasionally, a fast-moving, gaily-coloured truck. But the farm itself seemed like a world within a world. Once through the guarded entrance everything changed. A calmness which stirred the senses prevailed.

Then music filled the air: Christian hymns echoed loud and clear, filtering through to all parts of the farm, and even beyond. After several minutes a voice came over the loudspeakers — 'Good morning, boys and girls. How are you this fine day? It's a very special day for Matthew today. Happy birthday, Matthew. The Lord be with you.' The music continued and after the hymn a gong sounded. It was seven o'clock — time for breakfast. Max was there greeting everyone by name, all 115 of his family. The smaller family units of about six to eight children sat at their respective dining tables. A hush prevailed as Max gave a word from the Bible and explained the day's portion of scripture, making it relevant for the day's times. In prayer Max gave thanks to God for his great love and goodness towards them, for his provision of all their needs, for his protection against the enemy and for his strength to persevere. Grace was said and the serving girls from the kitchen swung into full operation. With an animated buzz children quickly tidied up their portions of porridge, dhal and chapatti.

After breakfast the children slipped away — morning duties and the first session of school. Rick went as well, to help look after the maintenance in the farm workshop and to supervise the trainees. Max introduced me to the farm work supervisors, Malcolm, Chester and Anil. I met also Maxine, Florence, Valerie, Eunice, Violet, Patricia, Josie, Maureen and Grace, all of whom had responsibilities — the schooling program, the trainee girls, the nursery, the pig, dairy and poultry sections, the kitchen, washing and mending departments, and, of course, raising an adopted family.

The children affectionately called me 'Uncle'; each of them had a story to tell of how they had been abandoned, some even dumped at the farm's gate, and some on death's door with starvation. Some of the carers were Anglo–Indian, who, after India had gained its independence in 1947, were not accepted by either the British or Indians. They had grown up with the farm and continued to care and support new ones arriving.

Later in the day, I played cricket with the boys on an uneven pitch in the central compound. After the game the boys and I set off to the jungle which bordered the farm to bring home firewood — we forded a river, jumped over a stream and passed through a small village. A green carpet of growing crops on the farm and the jungle beyond seemed to symbolise two different ways of life, rubbing shoulders, and in tension.

'When did you come here?' I asked Max at the evening meal.

'Well, we established the Good Shepherd Agricultural Mission farm in 1948 as a home for homeless young people after pitching our tent on a plot of land, which was covered with scrub, forest and elephant grass. All we had was a vision and a firm trust in God. We had no money or support from an organisation, but young people joined us, sent by those in India who had heard of our adventure in faith. You know, we drove all the way up here from Bombay in 1948 by tractor with a four-wheeled trailer.'

Max then continued to captivate me with his account of how they had to struggle against wild animals, diseases, jungle grasses and scrub forest yielding meagre harvests of grain. The 120-acre farm was formerly part of a Terai jungle estate which bordered West Nepal and India.

Amidst all the hardship, Max and Shirley lost their two sons, one to cerebral malaria, and the other as a result of a tractor accident. Of their three daughters who grew up on the farm, Maxine remained and married Rick.

'Despite our personal adversities,' said Max, 'we are still convinced that God is good and has called us to this work. We have extended our services to the villagers who came and settled on the land around the farm. The farm benefits almost every home in some way or other. Some spend months in hospital at the farm's expense. Others have come for free medical aid, schooling or advice and assistance in farming.'

The farm story grew on me — a story that seemed to belong more to the David Livingstone era with intrepid adventures into the unknown. Max and Shirley Strong had come to India soon after the partition of the British Indian Empire into India and Pakistan, which at that time included Bangladesh. Up to 14 million Hindus, Sikhs and Muslims were displaced during partition. In a retributive genocide which followed, involving mostly people of the Punjab province, atrocities left up to half a million people dead. Into this precarious aftermath of violence and uncertainty, Max and Shirley settled in an inhospitable area of northern India to make a home for Anglo–Indian children, left in the wake of the collapsing British Empire. Later, Max and Shirley could not ignore the plight of any abandoned child. What a story to be told!

Near the time to leave, I asked Max whether he would mind me coming again to write up his account of the orphanage farm. 'Yes,' he said, 'that would be just fine.' Could I do it, though? With never having written a book, but, with an interest in writing, a challenge awaited me.

Nothing in India goes to plan as I found out in trying to leave. First, the Indian Airlines flight to Mumbai was overbooked, and, only at the last moment, they found a spare seat. Then, as the British Airways plane from Mumbai gathered speed for take-off something fell off the wing. The pilot made a split-second decision to bring the plane to a shuddering stop before running out of runway. More than 200 of us sweltered in the heat with no air conditioning for four hours until a decision was made to disembark and stay at the airport hotel until another plane arrived from London. We went through all the formalities again and ended up in a brightly-lit hotel — far too bright until we realised we were part of an Indian movie set. Cameras rolled, the stars performed, and we were the extras.

After starring in an Indian movie I arrived safely back in Gawler.

* * *

With the next summer break for students I flew Air India in January for a three-week stay at the GSAM farm. Rick warmly greeted me at the airport, and, after a rest overnight at one of Rick's friends, we journeyed by Land Rover through the province of Uttar Pradesh to the farm.

I met up with Max and the other carers to hear their stories of how the farm first started and attracted helpers to care for the children.

'We faced many pioneering hazards,' Max said. 'In the early days of settlement, one of the boys pulled straw from the thatch wall of the dining hut, set it alight from the stove and then lit a kerosene lantern. The lighted straw burnt his finger tips; it dropped onto the dry grass and within seconds flames leapt up the side of the hut and onto the roof. A bucket brigade did their best, but there was no chance of saving the structure. With burning bits of thatch falling about us, we managed to save some meagre furnishings, a trunkful of books and the heavy wood-burning cook stove. For some time after, we cooked on that stove sitting out in the open.

'During the dry season, the 30-metre wide river, descending from the Nepali Himalayas, passed only 200 yards away from our campsite at the edge of the jungle. Shirley and the children made daily trips for laundry and bathing. They soon became accustomed to pythons hanging in trees at the river's edge.'

'What about the wet season?' I queried.

'In the wet season the Himalayan mountains unleash floods of rainwater onto the plains of the Terai. The river that borders the farm becomes a swollen torrent with its momentum from the hills almost the same by the time it reaches the farm; it triples in width and often floods its banks.'

'Did the floods affect your homes?'

'A number of times water came up around us and even into the houses. It was not unusual to rise in the morning during the monsoon and find the legs of the beds sunk into the earth floor so that the occupants were lying at the level of the mud floor itself. Other pieces of furniture adopted lopsided positions at various angles, which had a disorientating effect on whoever entered the house.

'A newly-formed road added run-off to the farm, increasing the flood potential. Since the land was flat there was little prospect of an efficient drainage system. Once we had to rescue Tharu villagers perched on roof-tops. We rafted them down on tractor tubes and provided a home for them on the farm until the waters receded.

'During the wet season we had another threat — the rising water forced snakes to seek higher ground. Once, Shirley eyed a large cobra hanging down from the wooden beam of our thatched roof. On another occasion, at nighttime, Shirley flashed her torch back at a slight rustle she had heard at her feet and was horrified to see a large, coiled banded-krait. There were many close encounters with snakes in those early days, though no one was bitten. As well as snakes we faced danger from tigers, leopards, wild pigs and elephants.'

'Did the animals damage the crops?'

'Yes, especially the elephants. They flattened and devoured our crops.'

'What kind of crops did you grow?'

'We planted rice at the beginning of the monsoon; it was cut and threshed in October and November. The grain was spread on the ground and run over with the tractor, the rice being quite easy to thresh in this manner. The wheat was planted in December and harvested in April. We also grew lentils, called *masoor* — a low growing bush with a small pod; the grain was cracked and the outer husk taken off by running it through a small hand mill which consisted of two flat, circular stones with the top one having a hole in it. With our wheat we made chapattis and yeast bread, and cracked wheat was made into porridge for breakfast.'

'Any meat or vegetables?'

'Game from the jungle provided meat, but this was not a regular item on the menu since work on the farm took priority over hunting. The vegetable garden, though, gave a ready supply of vegetables in season — peas, carrots, beans, cabbages, cauliflower, potatoes and onions. Cooking oil came from *lai*, a mustard-like plant, also grown on the farm.'

Max recounted more about the farm, and I felt that I had enough for the time being to go on with. Perhaps, I would have to come again to complete the story.

Back in Gawler I began writing up the story in my spare moments.

By 1993, I had written the first draft of the Good Shepherd Agricultural Mission (GSAM) farm story — a slow process with home life, teaching, and other projects. I needed to go again, not only to check what I had written but to update the story. Max had corresponded regularly with me over the years and invited me back. His wife, Shirley, sadly had passed away in America only two weeks prior to my intended departure, but Max urged me to come anyway.

A postal strike had delayed my letter informing Max Strong of my arrival time so there was no one to meet me when I arrived in New Delhi. I took a deep breath and stepped outside the airport to face India. It was surprisingly chilly.

As a country of the unexpected, with many facets of life not seen or experienced by Western style of living, India assaults the senses, some of which leave indelible memories. Visit me if you dare, it says.

After haggling with the driver, I hired a taxi for 350 rupees to the Nirula Hotel in the city centre. The hotel was booked out so an auto rickshaw driver, a Sikh, whose name was Mr Singh, of course, took me to the Sheesh Mahal hotel. The vulnerability of being in an auto rickshaw seemed to increase tenfold with the dense peak hour Delhi traffic and darkness falling prematurely with a thick pall of smoke hanging over the city. There were no rules that I could fathom. The near collisions must have been commonplace, but Mr Singh didn't twinge a muscle as he deftly wove a way through all the offending vehicles. The hotel room was quite comfortable — anything was reasonable after surviving Delhi traffic. Next day, I would sort out the bus trip to Tanakpur.

Through a tour operator I booked on an evening bus to Nainital. He assured me that another bus from Nainital would only take an hour to reach Tanakpur. The only other foreigners on the bus were from England — Tim, Fiona and Kerry. They planned to explore some of the lower Himalayan Ranges near Nanital. The bus started off with only a few passengers, but Indian buses don't stay like that for long and soon we were full to overflowing. Hindi music deafened us — maybe the taped music helped to keep the driver awake. A constant stream of heavy transport vehicles passed us — thank goodness. We stopped a couple of times for *goram chai* (hot tea). At about 8 am the next morning we had breakfast at a roadside café; nearby, a group of monkeys scrounged for scraps.

The bus then climbed steadily while negotiating numerous hairpin bends. The mountain sides were at first richly adorned with fir, spruce and pine trees, but these became sparse as we reached Nanital. I wished the English tourists happy travelling. A young lad offered to carry my suitcase to the bus station. Another bus left immediately for Auldwani, and, fortunately, I had the last seat. The passengers appeared to be more like Nepalis or Tibetans.

On the next bus from Auldwani to Tanakpur the last seat was mine again. I clambered over luggage in the aisle and fitted awkwardly into a cramped-size space with no chance of leaning back or feeling comfortable. Despite the seat growing harder and more uncomfortable, I became absorbed with the rural setting of fresh green wheat fields, fallowed rice paddies and sugar cane which set an attractive outlook amidst farm homes and scattered trees. As the bus neared Tanakpur the Nepali hills came into view.

I was stiff and sore and very thankful to leave the bus at the farm. Max Strong was in his office and greeted me warmly, just prior to the evening meal. We caught up briefly with past events before I slept on a hard bed in the boys' quarter — after 15 hours on Indian buses, it didn't matter how hard it was.

The next day it was 'Hello, Uncle' as I met up with some of the 130 boys and girls living on the farm. Some of the older ones remembered me from the last time, and some of the younger ones, even nursery children, made sure they didn't miss out on their new visitor. I toured the grounds and buildings — the workshop, fish ponds, hostel, school, piggery, dairy, wheat, rice and lentil fields, the vegetable gardens and guava orchard. The boys' hostel had been built with financial support from Holland in 1987. Three schools were supported by the farm — their own built a few years ago, a Hindi school over the road, and an English medium school in Tanakpur for 200 children.

On Sunday, Max led the service and talked about patience as an enduring quality of Christian life. The girls sang without music, and then there was a prayer for the sick. After lunch I played cricket and visited the boys' home for a smoky get-together by a smouldering fire. Joseph, I learned, came from a Mukti home, and Tim from Bombay was abandoned as a child. On the girls' side, Cherry and Angela were left in a bundle on a railway line.

The following day I met Anil who looked after the dairy cows. He explained some of the problems of the progeny from the Australian Friesian and Jersey cows sent to the farm over ten years ago. 'They suffer from parasites and foot rot, and don't do so well in the summer heat,' he said.

I met with carpenters making a bed, a woodchopper, womenfolk cutting berseem clover for the dairy cows, and women winnowing the mustard seed used for cooking. I also met leprous people who lived on the farm. A number of the children were from leprous parents; they had been dumped on the farm. I met a couple of girls, Cindy and Dixie, who would have died if they had not been rescued.

In the evening I walked down to the river bordering the jungle. Vultures, perched on the tops of trees, were settling down for the night, and myriads of tiny fish were jumping in the river. Indian workers were crossing the river to return to their homes in the jungle. The Indians on the farm side of the river lived in thatch-roofed, mud-built homes; their cows and goats were housed in open stalls.

For the next ten days I had numerous talks with Max, the farm manager, the teachers, the pastor, the accountant, maintenance people, farm workers and, of course, the boys and girls. I had free rein to move around. The boys and girls, even the youngsters in the nursery, collared me wherever I went. When I started showing my family photos, one girl asked, 'Which is your favourite daughter?'

'I don't have a favourite one,' I said.

She asked again, 'But you really must like one a little more?'

'No.'

'Well, which is the naughtier one?'

'Aha, I can tell you that.'

The young boys kept showing me around, and one took me for a walk through the jungle — no pythons, tigers, leopards or elephants, though. Another lad, Bunty, often came to my room to scout around, and on one occasion made cold coffee with powdered milk. Yuk! After that experience, the lads nicknamed him 'Cold Coffee'.

I taught Australian and Scottish geography in the farm school — four lessons altogether, and one session with 200 kids at the Tanakpur School where I spoke on Australia, and faced tricky questions on politics and religion. I sang a verse of 'Waltzing Matilda' and tried to dance a highland fling.

The ongoing problems for the farm concerned tribal disputes over land, persecution by Hindi extremists, educational needs for the children so that they could find their way in the outside world, and sponsorship of children — 30 children required sponsorship. Liz and I were able to sponsor Elena Rai, a Nepali child, who went on to be educated at Dr Graham's Homes in Kalimpong.

One of the main concerns for the farm folk was what would happen when Max died. Malcolm, the farm manager, should be able to cope, but Max was the main contact for the sponsors and was heavily involved in administration.

The goodbyes went on forever, it seemed, before I caught a bus back to New Delhi, where I hired a Nepali chap for two days as my auto rickshaw driver. We toured all around New Delhi, visiting a 13ᵗʰ century Mughal fort, temples, art emporiums, monuments, bazaars, and the awe-inspiring Bahai Temple. Gladys McLean, an American, officiated at the door of the Bahai Temple and talked at length about the Bahais and their spiritual beliefs.

Later, I met Zeena who had grown up on the GSAM farm and had left to work as a domestic helper with a doctor's family. She cooked a terrific chicken curry, the best I had had while in India. Although tied to her new home, her life was reasonable, and she travelled on occasion to Calcutta, Kashmir, Bombay and the farm. She praised Max Strong but wouldn't go back there to stay. She feared the outside world, but felt safe in a well-protected home even though she couldn't go to church on Sunday.

Back in Gawler, I realised that the story of Max Strong and his family had been an adventure in faith. Having no organisation to support them, Max and Shirley put their faith into action, taking on, most of us would consider, impossible odds in an inhospitable region of northern India to make a home for the young homeless, to raise and educate them, and to nurture them in the Christian faith so that one day they would be equipped to rejoin Indian society. I had to admire the Strongs' tenacity, perseverance and trust in God.

With this in mind, I titled the book *Launching out in faith: a farm home for children in India*. I published the book with Seaview Press and ran off 100 copies for passing on to the Good Shepherd Agricultural Farm in India and for some of Max Strong's supporters in America. I passed on the remaining copies to people in South Australia. One of Rick's relatives read the book and sent $5,000 to the mission farm. So I felt that the book did have value in promoting and supporting the farm.

The title seemed to confirm to me what we all should be doing in some measure — a key to life itself, perhaps — to recreate ourself in harmony with God's purpose. Being open to challenges, and a readiness to search out and discover, were all part of that process to fulfil our destiny.

Chapter 12

Bangladesh

WITH THE FINANCIAL BACKING OF Lions Australia, Len Reid, who had accompanied me on my first trip to the farm in India, had arranged for ten Suffolk rams and a number of ewes to be sent over to a Bangladesh government livestock centre for the improvement of the local breed. In early 1985, he suggested I go to Bangladesh to check on how the rams were settling into their new environment and to make sure they were properly cared for.

'You can travel with Badal,' Len said. 'He has recently graduated with a Bachelor of Social Science from Melbourne University. Sponsored by our organisation, Badal will set up a sub-branch to help run social welfare projects that offer hope and a livelihood to Bangladeshis.'

Badal and I arrived at Dhaka airport on 10 March 1985; we lugged our bulging suitcases towards the customs barrier. He passed a suitcase onto me. 'Now we are more evenly balanced and less likely to cause an upset to the customs official,' he said. 'You can never predict what games they play at Dhaka airport. It's a golden opportunity for them to make some money on the side.'

'All right,' I replied. 'Hope there is nothing dangerous in the suitcase.'

'No problems at all. If I didn't come home with gifts for all my relatives I would be regarded as tight-fisted.'

Badal, a youthful-looking Bangladeshi with bushy eyebrows and jet black hair, handed me an electronic typewriter and said, 'Here, this is better with you, too.'

I shuffled towards the customs barrier with two heavy suitcases and an electronic typewriter. The customs official showed scant interest in Badal's personal effects and accepted his descriptions of the gift-wrapped presents after unwrapping two of them. The official then examined the typewriter and asked for my passport. I handed it over, and he wrote a couple of words on the page opposite my passport details before turning to the last page and adding a few more words of Bengali script.

'It's nothing, really,' Badal assured me. 'It means you have brought this typewriter into Bangladesh for personal use. If I had brought it back home they might have detained me unnecessarily.' I accepted Badal's comment and dismissed the intrusion from my mind. That is, until one month later, when I tried to fly out of the country.

Bangladesh had gained its independence from Pakistan in 1971, but not without a huge loss in life from Pakistan's extensive military operations and air strikes. The country had endured a famine in 1974 that affected millions of people.

From what I had gathered about Bangladesh, it was mostly a fertile alluvial plain on the delta of three main rivers, the Ganges, the Brahmaputra and the Meghna, and subject to frequent floods and cyclones, causing significant damage to crops and property.

Sandwiched between India and Burma, Bangladesh was one of the poorest countries in the world with a population of about 94 million in 1985, which was concern enough for a country only two-thirds the size of the state of Victoria in Australia. That meant the density of people was one of the highest in the world at 640 persons per square kilometre. It put tremendous pressure on rural resources, forcing people to migrate to the cities or seek work overseas. Over 30 per cent of people were likely to remain below the poverty line in years to come, with a projected population of 160 million by the end of 2015 — a 70 per cent increase in just 30 years.

I met up with Latif Siddiqui, the assistant director of Livestock Services for Bangladesh. Latif had studied for his master's degree in agricultural science at Edinburgh University. With our links to Scotland we soon developed a firm friendship.

The next day Latif and I set off for the government-run Savar dairy farm, about an hour's run from Dhaka. We threaded our way through heavy village-life traffic — crowded buses, trucks, carts, and people walking along the highway.

At Savar, we met Dr Ziauddin, who guided us around the farm. We visited the artificial insemination centre, and director Dr Chowdury joined us for a discussion on the future needs of Savar and outlying centres. 'We urgently need doses of Friesian and Sahiwal semen,' he said. 'Without these the breeding program for improving our local breeds will grind to a halt.'

I examined two of the Suffolk rams and a number of ewes that had been sent to Savar; they seemed to be in a forward store condition. With the six-month dry spell limiting grazing on pasture, they had been fed a concentrate ration of wheat bran, rice polish, a pulse variety and oil cake. Despite the lack of medicines, vaccines and proper equipment, the sheep had been managed well, in large measure due to the services of a retired farm hand who had taken a special interest in them. The sheep pen was cleaned daily and a large fan applied when the sheep showed signs of discomfiture due to humidity and heat. In the hot season during their non-grazing time they rested in the pen close to the fan.

I tagged the sheep and foot-trimmed them. Two Suffolk rams were lame and three ewes were pregnant. One ewe had a lamb at foot but showed signs of mastitis in one half of the udder.

From talking to one of the veterinarians, the two original rams had suffered footrot. The rams had been foot-bathed and given antibiotics, but, although outward signs of footrot had diminished, the hooves of the rams were misshapen and appeared tender in the pastern area.

Later, I examined the local sheep from different flocks. The poddy-shaped sheep were much smaller in size, about 50 centimetres in height and weighing 15 to 20 kilograms. The white or brown coloured hair — not wool — was about 5 to 8 centimetres long. The black-coloured face and legs were bare apart from short pigmented hair fibres.

Most families owned two or three sheep and a few goats, which were looked after by a woman. A man often shepherded the larger sized flocks of 20 to 25 for roadside grazing. Occasionally, a concentrate of polished rice bran, groundnuts and mustard oil cake was given. The sheep were not shorn; they shed their hair naturally. They were dipped once a year. A small number of rams were left entire for mating and the rest castrated for lamb or mutton, but goat meat was preferred to mutton. The ewes lambed down twice a year giving birth yearly to a total of three or four lambs. The skins went to the tannery and the hair was not valued.

Despite their short-comings in size and quality of fibre the sheep appeared well-adapted to their environment and highly fertile.

The veterinary surgeon pointed out the difficulties of communication for treatment of sheep in the *upazilas*, the administrative regions in Bangladesh. Treatment and preventative care were further hampered by a lack of facilities and medicines at the veterinary clinics.

I met up with Badal who was working hard to establish a sub-branch for Len Reid's new organisation, Human Rights — First the Child. He hoped to help finance microprojects for women living in poverty at the village level. Mohammed Yunus had already piloted this approach with the launch of the Grameen Bank in 1983 to offer loans without any collateral.

With about one month remaining of my stay, a national election threatened to interrupt his efforts. 'Everything will come to a standstill,' explained Badal. 'People will return home and the government offices will close. The military and police will be on standby everywhere. A referendum on military rule will confirm the rule of Hussain Mohmmad Ershad, the Army Chief of Staff who seized power in 1982. Being an unpredictable time with so many radical elements at our universities it would be better for you to leave the country.'

'I could lie low,' I said, 'but I'll accept your advice and go to Nepal. I have always wanted to visit that country.'

I flew from Dhaka airport, and, as the Biman Fokker soared upwards, lightning arced across the sky and black thunderous clouds enveloped the plane. The rainy season of the summer monsoon had begun.

I thought about the millions of impoverished Bangladeshis who would never fly on their own airlines. Then, from my aisle seat, I looked around and most of the passengers on board were Nepalese with their almond-shaped eyes and high-set cheekbones. Instead of an air of expectancy and joy in returning home, I sensed a mood of dread and foreboding. Even the stewards were subdued, I thought, in attending to the needs of their passengers. I closed my eyes to dispel the negative vibes.

Two hours later, having circled twice through thick blankets of cloud and driving rain, the plane began its final approach. The Nepalese froze and gripped their seats as though they were about to meet their maker.

The pilot eased the plane onto the runway and when it finally stopped the Nepalese burst into a spontaneous round of applause. Broad smiles replaced taut lines of fear.

As the passengers rose to retrieve their luggage and prepare for disembarking, I caught sight of the flashing lights of ambulances and fire engines.

'We were expected to crash?' I asked the flight attendant.

'I'm sorry, sir,' she replied. 'Not us, but the previous flight from Dhaka. We tried to play it down — no sense in alarming the passengers. Unfortunately, news leaked out and everyone feared the worst. That plane crashed when it overshot the runway. The airport authorities thought it wise to have the ambulance and fire brigades on standby for this flight as well. You were lucky not to have been on that flight.'

After recovering from that thought, I stayed two days in Katmandu viewing temples, shrines and holy men. Then I took a bus to Pokhara, about 200 kilometres west of Katmandu. The city provided a base for trekkers into the Annapurna ranges of the Himalayas. I enquired about day hikes and set off early in the morning to tackle the foothills of Annapurna close to Pokhara. I met up with walking groups from Japan and other countries, and a group of school kids joined me for a while as I wandered through hill settlements, a forested area, and terraced rice fields.

On the return flight to Dhaka the plane — Bangladesh Airlines — had a faulty reactor and we sat on the tarmac for three hours. When it did take off there was a resounding round of applause, which I was getting used to. On nearing Dhaka storm clouds bumped us considerably, but we landed without incident. No applause though. Once outside, I faced the usual beggars and peddlers.

For my next trip, Dr Siddiqui accompanied me to Noakhali by train. We arrived at the station at 1.30 pm and actually departed at 9.30 pm — the longest time I had waited for a train at a station. The previous train had collided with a goods train and several people had died. We passed by the crash site with the mangled pieces of carriages strewn everywhere. At numerous stops Bangladeshis crowded onto the platform to sell their wares.

I examined two local flocks in the Noakhali District; no special care was provided for the flocks, and lambs born in the monsoon season often died. The sheep grazed mainly on couch grass and were shifted towards the coast when cultivation was in progress, grazing in forested and saline areas. Liver fluke seemed to be the biggest problem and then roundworms. Natural selection again favoured a small-sized, hardy animal that was highly fertile.

On visiting a nearby Danish project, I spoke to researchers who were keen to establish legumes and promote a wool-bearing sheep rather than one with hair. Their overall project extended over three districts with 5 million people and it involved building construction, womens cooperatives and livestock improvement. I partied with the Danes before I left, drinking Swan beer and munching on Bengali cookies.

The following day we visited the government-run Sonagazi sheep development farm, where eight of the Suffolk rams had been taken. Dr Arun Kumar Das welcomed us and said, 'Once the rams had settled down they were joined with local Bangladeshi ewes to improve meat production in the progeny. Of the eight rams that were sent to Sonogazi two years ago, only three rams have survived and these have to be given a supplement because of overgrazing and a dry season.'

I examined the rams and two were in fair condition, while the third was in poor condition and lame in the hind leg. 'What happened to the other rams?' I asked.

'We attribute their deaths to pneumonia or bloat,' Dr Das said. 'Footrot was also a major problem. Vaccines are mostly not available. Medicines are in short supply. There is no refrigerator and no running water. The sheep shed in which they were housed overnight doesn't provide adequate ventilation and the flushing out of the shed could have aggravated the footrot condition.'

The rams, I noticed, had flabby testicles and that wasn't a good sign for breeding; they took little interest in the local ewes — confirming my misgivings that the large-framed Suffolk rams had difficulty in acclimatising to the hot, humid environment of Bangladesh. I suspected that the crossbred progeny would not fare well either under Bangladeshi growing conditions.

Next, Latif and I flew to Rajshahi to examine the local sheep at a proposed site for a new sheep and goat development centre. On arrival a crowd of onlookers quickly gathered. In this poorer area of Bangladesh, no one owned a tractor and the harvesting was carried out by sickle. Bullocks worked the rice paddies.

Mutton and lamb were popular in the district and the hair was given to some local blanket makers for spinning and weaving. The hair was washed prior to being teased apart and spun by a simple-designed spinning machine. A ball of coarse material was then wound onto a shuttle for weaving, and with different coloured fibres a patterned blanket was made. Chalky white hairy fibres stood out in the finished product.

After another memorable week in Bangladesh, I arrived at Dhaka airport with my travelling bag and proceeded to the check-in counter via a baggage clearing station. The official scanned my opened bag for illegal items and noted the front scribble on my passport. He fingered each page in turn until his eyes fastened on the one-liner on the final page. 'Where is your typewriter?' he asked.

'My typewriter? I don't have one!' I replied.

'When you arrived at Dhaka airport you had a typewriter and it was for personal use.'

'Oh, that one! I left it for my friend. He'll take care of it until I return.'

'We have no information about that. Here it says the typewriter is for personal use and not for anyone else. It's a crime to take this item into the country and leave it here. You have to take it with you. Please wait here.'

After waiting 20 minutes, my frustration turned to desperation with the last boarding call. I appealed to a crew member of Thai Airlines who was about to board the plane, 'Can you help me?' I asked. 'They won't allow me on the plane because I don't carry a typewriter that I had brought into the country. It wasn't mine. I had carried it for a fellow passenger to help carry his luggage load.'

The crew member accepted my story and pleaded with the customs official to let me pass. The official raised his voice in protest but finally shrugged his shoulders. The crew member signalled thumbs up as the official talked to his superior on the phone.

'You are free to go,' he said after the phone conversation.

On the return to Adelaide I stopped over at Singapore and stayed with Mr and Mrs Jean de Jong, a Dutch couple who worked for Nestles and who were the parents of Mike who had come to Roseworthy College to study farm management.

I visited Changi prison, one of the notorious Japanese war camps. Most of the Australians captured in Singapore during the Second World War were interned in Changi in 1942. A large number were sent to work on projects, such as the Burma–Thailand railway. The prisoners on those projects had much less chance of survival.

On arrival at Sydney, an airport official examined my passport and said, 'You haven't been to Bangladesh, have you?'

'Why not?' I replied.

A month later, in May 1985, a cyclone from the Bay of Bengal struck the coastal islands of Bangladesh. In spite of early detection of atmospheric turbulence and the history of severe cyclones in the area, an estimated 11,000 people lost their lives.

* * *

Towards the end of 1985, Dr Siddiqui invited me to return to Bangladesh to accompany him on field trips to check on the livestock programs.

So, on 15 January 1986, I first spent a couple of days with Joan and Len Reid at their Melbourne home. We had long discussions on current progress with peace walks, livestock projects and a number of the society's activities. 'We don't have enough support,' complained Joan. She was quite concerned for Len who had taken on too much. 'It's almost a one-man show,' she said. Len asked if I could travel on to India after Bangladesh to check up on a consignment of Poll Dorset sheep.

We also talked about the development of an improved Taurindicus breed of cattle for India. While the benefits of crossbreeding were acknowledged, there still needed to be a research effort for ongoing improvement of breed type to ensure its adaptability and performance for smallholders at the Indian village level.

I first flew to Bangkok for an overnight break at the Airport Hotel. At breakfast I met Barbara Brooks from Tasmania; she was on her way to Dhaka to arrange adoption procedures for a young girl,

Rosie. She hoped to take her back to Australia. Barbara had a lot of red tape to cut through, and I admired her determination.

On a previous trip to Bangladesh, Barbara and her husband, with son Luke, aged four, and Joseph, aged twelve, were travelling in a first-class compartment on a train when a girl, no bigger than Luke, had boarded the train after the ticket inspector had passed through. Rosie, named by Barbara, played with the balloons that Barbara had given her children for the six-hour trip. When they alighted from the train, Rosie held Barbara's hands with a pleading look on her face. Barbara understood that her father had died and that she had been abandoned; she let Rosie accompany the family for the rest of the trip and then managed to place her in Mother Teresa's home for children in Dhaka. They were returning to Bangladesh to see how Rosie was faring and to continue with efforts to adopt her — a frustrating process.

We talked non-stop until landing at Zia International Airport. The Bangladeshis hauled piles of luggage, and all came under close scrutiny by the customs officers. Badal was there to meet me, his head popping up over the heads of everyone. Barbara was surprisingly calm amidst the confusion. 'Bangladesh is my second favourite country,' she said. I tried to hold on to my baggage but the insistence of a baggage porter won. We parted, wishing each other the best.

Badal and I hopped into a baby taxi which putt-putted to his place. The buses still had the usual hangers-on. There were plenty of mosquitoes, but I had a net this time. For our lunch the chillies in the salad proved too hot, but the rice meal prepared by their cook, Kalam, cooled them down.

The next day I would arrange my itinerary with Dr Siddiqui. Later on, I would fly to India to sort out a consignment of Poll Dorsets.

I awoke at 5.30 am with the muezzin calling loudly for prayer: 'Allah, hu akbar.' Dr Siddiqui and Dr Ali, a veterinarian and close associate of Len, arrived. We met the director, Dr Nazi Ahmad, who gave me my brief — to explore the potential for local breeds;

to examine the sheep and goats at Sonagazi. Could the Sonagazi centre be used for growing Napier grass, and could this be fed to the sheep in sheds? What about the direction of the whole sheep breeding program for Bangladesh? How much importance should be attached to selection in various strains of local breeds? Where did Suffolks fit in? Could I obtain information on the Droughtmaster? And what equipment did we need? Well, nothing like a tall order for a short trip.

Dr Siddiqui outlined a suitable itinerary — Savar, Mymensingh, Noakhali and Chittagong.

In the evening I had a surprise visit from Barbara and Rosie. Barbara had made some headway with procedures for adoption. With her defiant street attitude, Rosie's education caused concern at Mother Teresa's home.

The following day, for my education in the potential of small-scale farming, Latif and I visited an American Baptist farm where Rick Farley, the American in charge, welcomed us. Rick's determination and enthusiasm shone out as he showed me his goat crossbreeding program, duck and sheep projects and the fish farming venture. His aim was to move towards integrated systems and part of his plans was to build duck housing — a simple bamboo and thatched house raised off the ground — over the fish ponds.

As we stood admiring his meaty crossbred bucks, a villager arrived with a half-sized black Bengal doe. The Barbary cross buck was taken out of a pen and straightaway mated the doe, size difference being no problem. He served her again and the villager slapped the doe on the rump.

Napier grass stood out. This was sold to the villagers or used as fodder for the goats. About 300 small-framed sheep kept in sheds were fed rice straw and supplements. We talked about the prospect of using Suffolk rams. Two large pens enclosed several thousand Khaki Campbell ducks, their manure washed into the fish ponds. A worker demonstrated how he caught the fish with a net flung over the pond surface; on one haul he caught ten carp.

After the farm visit I returned to Savar dairy farm, where I stayed a few days in my old guest-house — my friend the rat was still there. The cook and his wife looked after the meals, and the farm staff received me like a long lost friend.

The director and his officers all wanted more dairy cattle. I would pass on the request to Len Reid.

In the meantime, I accompanied the artificial insemination team. A dairy microbiologist spoke in rapid fire English as the van hurtled along, stopping at several places to offload the vials of semen.

Back in Dhaka, Barbara and Rosie joined me for a Chinese meal. Rosie took everyone by surprise with her high-spirited romps. Barbara had everything in hand for the adoption with support from her solicitor and World Vision.

The next day Latif and I caught the train to Mymensingh. Squashed in like sardines, we had no view at all of the countryside flashing by. Most travellers had not even paid for a ticket. When the inspector arrived, the students and others were let off.

Our guesthouse at Mymensingh overlooked the mighty Jamuna River. Early in the morning, shrouded mist on the river slowly lifted to reveal placid waters and boats laden with goods making their way downstream.

We met Dr Hadar Ali who gave us a run-down of the district's problems concerning the dairy cross breeding program: not enough selection on local breeds; emphasis needed to be on Sahiwal — the Frieisan crosses needing more care and extra food for calves; lack of transport to outlying areas; no educational program; no vet surgeon to identify reproductive diseases; lack of facilities; needing deep frozen semen, that was mobile; lack of medicines. 'And we need a family planning program,' Dr Ali said.

'I'll discuss all these matters with Len Reid when I return to Australia,' I replied, offering some hope, but realising that funding would be limited.

Latif then invited me to accompany him into a remote area of Bangladesh bordering Burma. We first journeyed to Chittagong, a city of 3 million people and Bangladesh's main seaport, handling a large volume of the country's imports and exports. Situated near the Chittagong Hill Tracts and to the south-east of the country, the city was built on the banks of the Karnaphuli River which flows into the Bay of Bengal.

After experiencing the openness and trundling pace of rickshaws, the belching fumes of three-wheeled auto-rickshaws and the close packing of Bangladeshi travellers on buses and trains, I welcomed the Chittagong express which was in a class of its own, an incongruous touch of progress. As the train swept by innumerable paddy plots and clusters of thatched-roof dwellings, my thoughts drifted back to my last encounter with an Australian. An airport official had cast a quizzical eye over my departure card. 'You're not going to Bangladesh, are you?' he asked.

Latif, who had invited me to come and see some of the wonders of the Chittagong Hill Tracts, sensed my thoughts. 'To know the true Bangladesh you must have some good experiences as well as some that are not so good,' he remarked.

After arriving at Chittagong, Latif haggled with several drivers at a bevy of gaily-coloured rickshaws parked outside the station. A shake of the head, though, indicated nothing doing. One driver muttered, '*Ji*', after ten *taka* was offered. The wiry lad, dressed in soiled shirt and traditional skirt-like *lungi*, pedalled into the heavy traffic — a life-shortening experience, as every type of vehicle bore down on us with blaring horn.

Later, from my hotel window I marvelled at the kaleidoscope of Bangladeshi street life amid a sunset that cast a marigold draping over the Bay of Bengal.

The next morning our jeep driver carefully skirted several hundred demonstrating students before setting off into the Hill Tracts. The plains with their patchwork of bare cloddy plots and rice plantings gave way to lush green foliage. The road traffic thinned to a trickle of bullock-drawn carts, rickshaws and foot travellers.

Was this still part of the Bangladesh I had come to know with its teeming millions?

A new kind of face emerged along the highway — a subtle blend of Burmese, Arakanese and Bengali. Youngsters appeared almost doll-like in expression; attractive women wore colourful sarongs. About 20 kilometres from Rangamati, Latif guided the driver onto a dirt track which climbed towards a knoll that overlooked an expansive valley, richly endowed with tropical plants and carpeted in the lower reaches with rice.

One of the nearby villagers came out to greet us, his face beaming as he approached Latif, a long-time friend. He ushered us to a table outside his bamboo dwelling and brought out a bottle of clear, home-brewed spirit distilled from fermented rice. Latif, being a strict Muslim, declined, but our driver, of Burmese descent, had no qualms. Our host topped up our glasses, with virtually no acknowledgement to my half-hearted refusal of the fourth pouring. The conversation, clearly polite at the outset, became quite animated and even heated as the brew began to take effect. Latif explained to me the delicate situation with the Hill Tracts people, mostly Buddhists, facing an influx of ethnic minorities, under a government resettlement plan.

After much discussion, our host brought out some hard-boiled eggs — presumably to dilute the effect of the liquor. After our visit, we walked down a precarious, narrow-winding hill track back to our jeep.

We journeyed on to Bandarban, gateway to the interior where primitive tribes lived. The attractive green foliage of the rain forest seemed even more impenetrable. I imagined the Bengali tiger in this deeply rutted land with steep-sided valleys. Thankfully, Latif's friends welcomed us with cups of tea. We admired the locally produced bamboo work and cotton-woven material with tribal patterns.

Towards sunset we decided to stay the night at Cox's Bazaar, a premier tourist spot. Here, they said, was the longest stretch of golden beach in the world — 120 kilometres — and safe for swimming and surfing. The following day we visited a bazaar where Burmese vendors displayed an array of shells, jewellery, handbags and woven material — ideal for souvenir hunters.

Then we set off into the Hill Tracts to Naikongchari, further south and close to the Burmese border. On arriving at a large village settlement, a young man in his late twenties, who was the chairman of the *upazila*, welcomed us like royalty. A crowd of villagers assembled while soldiers stood in the background. Because of recent skirmishes between the local tribes and the authorities, an armed escort accompanied us to a nearby tract of land, newly-acquired by the government for a crop and livestock improvement project. The chairman was clearly very pleased that his *upazila* had been chosen. We feasted on curried rice, beef and chicken pieces, fried mixed vegetables, all heavily spiced and eaten Bengali style — with one's fingers.

After speeches and farewells we journeyed back to Chittagong. On the way our driver became suicidal, passing everything with the aid of two blasts of the horn. He clipped a rickshaw and dragged it over — fortunately with no harm to the driver. We left the driver to deal with the police and caught a bus back to Dhaka. Bangladeshi farmers dotted the countryside guiding their bullock-drawn ploughs or attending to irrigated plots. They were a people on the move and desperate to survive. The land pulsed with life.

On another trip we took a jeep through some of the most ravaged cyclone areas right to the seashore where thousands of people and animals lost their lives. We visited the seashore after a very bumpy ride. On the way we saw some of the destruction of the cyclone — uprooted trees, and smashed homes and shelters. I examined the local sheep, a flock of 200 with two rams and some lambs. Many of the lambs were born in the monsoon and many died. The sheep fed on the fallows before returning to the coastal areas for grazing. A crowd was waiting for a ferry to a neighbouring island which was also devastated by the cyclone.

I then flew to New Delhi to meet with Dr Basutha, Commissioner of Sheep, and we talked about the prospects of Dorsets and Suffolks for India. He was convinced that the Poll Dorset would suit best for prime lamb production. We discussed the best ways to acclimatise the sheep. After that, I travelled with a livestock officer to Rajasthan to meet with livestock officers to discuss the export of mutton breeds to India.

I returned to Dhaka for a few final meetings with Dr Siddiqui and Dr Ziauddin to discuss the urgency of sending cattle to Bangladesh, before flying back to Australia.

Later, I was happy to learn that Rosie had been accepted as a migrant to Australia.

I continued to correspond with Latif over the years. We were both concerned about the growing incapacity of Bangladesh, a predominantly agricultural country, to feed its rapidly rising population, which was projected to reach 230 million by 2050 and 250 million before the population stabilised. Added to this was the continued rural to urban migration causing problems, such as the increase of urban slums, rising disease, sewage disposal, and the drawdown of the water table. Arsenic contamination was still a problem with shallow water tables. And climate change could cause flooding, drought, and rising sea levels with salinity affecting crops. Irrigation networks were insufficient for the dry season. Overall, a lot to tackle in the years ahead.

Chapter 13

Pakistan

In April 1987, when Rod Reeves from SAGRIC International, a company based in Adelaide, acting as consultants and international project managers, rang up from his office to ask if I was interested in going to Pakistan for a year as a livestock advisor, I jumped at the opportunity — crazy me. I found it very difficult to refuse a challenge of that order. Life at Roseworthy Agricultural College, while interesting and varied, was demanding and time-consuming with extra workloads in a number of different courses. I needed time out. The college granted me leave for a year without pay. I would go to Pakistan as part of a three-man team from Australia.

In hindsight, you never think of all the consequences — some good, and some you could definitely do without. You plunge in where you ignore reason and sensibility, and I certainly did that. SAGRIC advised against the family going — it was not a suitable place for women and children.

Liz agreed that she could cope with the children and everything else, and the extra money coming in would go on a deposit for a house in Gawler. She had noticed that I had become stressed and a time away might revitalise my energies. Actually, I came back stressed out, but in a different way.

I had worked with Rod at Roseworthy College in the agronomy department. We had got on well together and often combined our efforts in student courses. As an organiser Rod was ideal as a project manager for SAGRIC International which tendered for overseas projects with an emphasis on agricultural development in poorer countries. SAGRIC linked in with the South Australian Department of Agriculture as an international consulting firm.

Rod had successfully bid for a multi-million dollar project funded by the United Nations Fund for Drug Abuse Control (UNFDAC) in Dir District of the North West Frontier Province of Pakistan. The objective of the project was to help establish an economic environment which would provide people with opportunities to achieve an acceptable income and standard of living without recourse to the production of opium poppies. Numerous sub-projects concerned agriculture, forestry, road improvement, drinking water supply, irrigation channels, horticulture, health and education. And livestock improvement was where I came in. Overall, it was a huge project. As a veteran of large-scale projects — well, one in Algeria — I was doubtful of their capacity to improve local lives and their livelihood. Perhaps this time it would be different, so I pitched in.

As part of the contractual agreement I could return to Australia every three months for three weeks.

I am always amazed how the groundwork moves in a confirming way once the door opens. For Pakistan, Liz's sister-in-law, Sandra, knew of a Pakistani woman, Shaheena, in Adelaide, whose family lived in Islamabad. Her father was the brother of the nawab of Dir District in the North West Frontier Province. The nawab was apparently the most powerful ruler of the princely state of Dir District before it became part of Pakistan. While the nawab's rule had largely been taken over by the district officer, he was still the most important figurehead in the district, commanding the highest respect. A good person to know if I ran into trouble! Shaheena was a well-educated young woman engaged to an Australian doctor who had converted to Islam. We met a number of times, and I attended her wedding about a year later in Adelaide. She had let her father and the nawab know that I was on my way.

I flew to Islamabd on 19 August 1987 and met up with Amir, a nephew of the nawab of Dir District — another fortunate coincidence — who had been assigned to me as my driver for the duration of the project. We first visited Shaheena's parents in Islamabad; they welcomed me into their home, and I met Shaheena's brother and sister. Her father, who ran an automobile repair workshop, said, 'The Pashtuns are a proud race. Here is a letter of introduction to my brother, the nawab, who lives in Temergara, Dir District. Come and see us next time you come to Islamabad.'

After thanking him for his kindness, we drove to Temergara, the capital of Dir District, where I met Tony, an agronomist from Queensland, one of my two Australian colleagues. He had worked on a number of overseas development projects and seemed like a 'techno-whiz' with solutions for every problem he encountered. Alby, the project advisor, would arrive in mid-October.

We settled into a purpose-built accommodation for foreigners with three single rooms, a dining room and a kitchen for the Pakistani cook — Bill, we named him — who would prepare all our meals. Our 'home' on a hillside overlooked the township of Temergara and the Panjkora River. Muddied with the soil swept down from deforested hills of the alpine regions to the north, the river flowed on its way to join the Indus River. The mountains to the north stood like monuments to the Hindu Kush.

Tony gave me a rundown of my role and said, 'The assistant director of the livestock department is so far uncooperative. Your job, I understand, is to work with the assistant director, four vets, 39 stock assistants, and the newly appointed animal husbandry officer under project funding, Rahimullah Farooqi, to build up the animal husbandry side.'

'Any guidelines on how to do that?' I asked.

'Up to you how you go about it. Most of the work in the district has been of a veterinarian nature. The villagers often come to the centre or a livestock outpost with or without a sick animal and request medicines. Artificial insemination has just started at three sites.'

'Anything I should know about the poppy growers?' I asked.

'Most people in the numerous valleys of the district have agreed to stop poppy growing in exchange for agricultural, infrastructural, and other inputs. However, poppy growers in three valleys have refused to have anything to do with the project. We have to avoid them; if we dare enter the valleys they might shoot first and ask questions later.'

'Well, I hope my driver knows which valleys those are?'

'He will,' Tony said in a less than comforting tone.

The Dir District Development Project was only one element of a wider program to eradicate poppy production for opium in the North West Frontier Province of Pakistan. Poppy had been grown in the area before the turn of the century, but production had become more widespread since the Second World War. The government of Pakistan had taken a number of steps to stop poppy production since 1973 but efforts were focused on the North West Frontier Province with the aim of wiping out poppy production.

Tony next introduced me to the project staff, the counterparts, drivers, peons and the Pakistani project director, Saiful Maluk. I met my counterpart, Rahimullah Farooqi, a slim bearded man in his mid-twenties, appointed as the first animal husbandry officer with the local livestock department. Together, we would come up with plans to improve livestock production in the district.

The following day, Tony and I travelled to Dir, the main town, although not the capital, and an hour's journey to the north of Temergara. We passed through Temergara with its open-fronted shops lining narrow streets, and with hundreds of men out shopping or just strolling. On the way, men squatted on roadsides and huddled together in small groups; young men often walked with linked arms or hands. All men wore the *shalwar khameez* — a long shirt and a baggy, pyjama-like trousers. 'Better for us to wear western clothes so we can't be mistaken for Pashtuns,' Tony advised.

'Why?' I asked.

'Well, we don't want to be caught in the crossfire,' he said. 'Many Pashtuns have scores to settle.'

What have I come to? I thought.

Where were the womenfolk in this drab and unnatural setting? Then I spotted a woman, fully covered in a burqa. A veil covered the woman's face with a small slit-like opening for her eyes. She accompanied her husband but kept several paces behind him, as a mark of respect, Tony said.

The winding road followed the Panjkora River with the view constantly changing — sometimes cut off by steep-sided slopes which had been cleared of timber. Along the roadside, tents housed Afghan refugees who had fled the war in Afghanistan. The Afghans were up against the might of the Russian Army which had invaded their country in December 1979. 'The mujhadeen from Afghanistan come and go as they please,' said Tony. 'Many have AK 47s. The locals also covet Russian-made Kalashnikovs for protection.'

'For protection?' I asked, wondering who exactly they needed protecting from inside Pakistan.

'For protection from their own people,' Tony said. 'You will find out.'

We arrived at Dir, which lay at the foot of the Lowarai Pass that led to Chitral District. Men — not women — crowded the shops in the bazaar; many were armed with knives, Kalashnikovs or other weapons. 'You wouldn't want to be on the wrong side of someone here,' Tony said.

'I am not sure if I am going to get used to these armed characters,' I replied.

'You will.'

After returning to Temergara, Rahimullah and I worked out a program to meet with the veterinary officers and stock assistants in the outlying parts of Dir District. It would give me an opportunity to become familiar with the varying livestock production scenarios in each area.

First we met with the assistant director of the livestock department at his office in Temergara. A grey-bearded man in his fifties, he outlined the main problems limiting livestock production

— the lack of veterinary facilities, the need for improved animal breeding and feeding regimes, the difficulties of the stock assistants living in isolated areas and the lack of medicines … the list went on.

As part of my brief, we had to design and establish a poultry breeding unit for at least 1,000 birds — egg and meat-laying birds — raising them from fertile eggs. We would keep the birds for six to twelve weeks and then farm them out to the villagers. We would also organise an extension program for the migratory people who moved from the hills in the north to the south during winter, taking with them flocks of sheep, goats and cattle.

For the next few weeks I toured the district as much as possible. Slowly I built up a picture of the Pashtuns, their land, livelihood and culture.

Dir District was still firmly entrenched in tribal traditions but had come under government control in the 1960s. The whole district was mountainous with a rugged terrain ranging from 600 to 5,700 metres in height above sea level. The major part of the area comprised a series of mountain ridges and intervening valleys. With the opening up of the district, deforestation by logging companies had led to severe water erosion of soil into the Panjkora River.

The average annual rainfall varied from 500 to 1,000 millimetres, coming mostly in the monsoon season (June to September) and the winter season (December to March).

The main crops were wheat and maize in the rain fed areas; in the irrigated areas, wheat, maize, sugar-cane, rice and fruit were grown. And, of course, poppies. On the lower slopes, below 1,200 metres, most trees had been removed for firewood. Higher up were a pine zone (1,000 to 2,000 metres), a fir zone (2,000 to 3,000 metres), and, above the fir zone, alpine pasture. There seemed plenty of scope for reforestation and encouragement of rangeland species for grazing.

I learned that the poppy situation was serious with heroin addiction in Pakistan increasing from near zero in 1980 to over a million persons in 1987. Part of the opium supply went over the border to Iran or Afghanistan, and probably to Russia. The Mafia had established well-organised trade outlets. The farmers who grew the poppies received up to twelve times the return of the next best crop.

Not only did the government have to deal with the poppy crisis, but also attend to the thousands of tent-dwelling Afghani refugees who had taken up residence on the banks of the Panjkora River and lived on handouts from the government. The local Pashtuns regarded them as brothers and helped them out as much as possible. Also coming over the border from Afghanistan were Russian refrigerators, televisions and Kalashnikovs — prized possessions for the villagers. Men carried Kalashnikovs or some kind of weapon for protection or to settle an old score as part of their revenge code. During the day gun-shots could be heard — mostly testing or for wedding celebrations, they said. But you never knew for sure.

The Pashtuns appeared to accept strange people like me openly. It was a man's world, though, with women confined to houses as much as possible. The women who did venture outside were carefully covered, some completely veiled so that no part of their face was recognisable. What a challenge for liberationists!

As a Muslim, the Pashtun was entitled to four wives. To have a son was the best possible news. A wealthy man in the district, I learned, had four wives and 24 daughters. He had desperately wanted a son and he would not be defeated. Having six to ten children was quite common in Pashtun families, but most had only one wife.

Friendship, I noticed, was rekindled each day with an effusive ritual of salaams, handshaking and bear hugs. Hospitality, also, was part and parcel of the Pashtun way of life; sometimes it was overwhelming. For the stranger, it usually started off with a *chai whisky*. Nothing to do with Johnnie Walker or any other brand. It was an invitation to take tea. If you accepted, there was a further choice: *shin chai* (green tea) or *tor chai* (black tea). Black tea was usually boiled with buffalo milk with heaps of sugar added — a sickly sweet brew. Green tea, on the other hand, came from China and was flavoured with the addition of black or green cardamom seeds — rather like a jasmine tea, with a calming effect on the digestive system if taken after a spicy meal. I opted for green tea if given a choice.

My hosts always took Rahimullah and me to a guest room which was part of the *hujra* or men's houses. In wealthier families the *hujra* consisted of a line of rooms, each with a separate entrance, and fronted by a verandah. As an important meeting place for guests, it adjoined the rest of the house which was out of bounds to a visitor. They often seated me on the most comfortable *charpoy* with a cushion as backrest. After tea, an invitation to have *roti* (a meal) followed. If you accepted, it was the best the family could afford. Nothing was spared — spiced chicken, rice, clarified butter, curd and vegetables — all eaten with fingers and with the help of *naan* — a flat type of bread. The youngest man usually served you and piled your plate as high as possible, dousing everything with ghee. Fortunately, *bas* (enough) shouted loud enough stopped your host from going to absurd lengths. Afterwards, more green tea. And then an invitation to stay the night.

Hospitality was offered in a formal way, but the feeling was sincere and friendly. The household owner's wife also felt that her honour and respect were at stake. I was invited to many homes but never once did I see the wife of the host.

If you remarked on an attractive object or painting in the guest room, you were more than likely going to take it home with you. With Pashtun hospitality, once you became their guest, you were at their mercy — all right sometimes, but too much on other occasions.

Hospitality and violence, I found, were strange bedfellows, but they existed in Pashtun society. For a newcomer like me it was hard to reconcile the Pashtuns' generosity with their deep-seated jealous and warlike disposition. Everywhere family seemed to be arrayed against family, and tribe against tribe. According to a proverb 'the Pashtun is never at peace except when he is at war.' Feuding amongst themselves was ongoing. In one valley in Dir District, over 60 people had been killed in feuds in a 6-year period. The police did not interfere; it was too dangerous. The disputes were mainly over land and power. If a man's cousin had become wealthy and powerful then there was pressure on him to display his own strength. The *jirga*, or village council, could intervene to protect families but violence still erupted. Fighting for honour was the main theme.

Revenge could be a long time in coming. One man, I discovered, was killed in the early 1950s. His killer offered the victim's family blood money, which was accepted. But that was not enough compensation, and after 30 years the son of the murdered man killed his father's killer while he lay on a hospital bed. This action was praised. Even minor incidents could end disastrously, as when a child once refused to join in a game with a cousin; this led to whole families being locked in mortal combat.

Only with a common outside enemy do the Pashtuns join together as one. Regarded as some of the fiercest of fighters, no outside force had subdued them. The British could not control them. To the south of Dir District, Winston Churchill recorded the Pashtun uprising in 1897 at Chakdara. On one occasion, when faced with several tribesmen brandishing swords, Churchill ran for his life and hid behind a knoll. About 3,000 Pashtuns had gathered in a wide and spreading half-moon around the flanks of the British soldiers. Fortunately, reinforcements arrived in time to keep them at bay.

Would the Pashtuns become more peaceful in today's world with progressive education, development and more contact with the outside world? I doubted it since inter-tribal conflict had existed for hundreds of years and would most likely escalate as a result of Russian and United States interference in Afghanistan upsetting the balance of power.

The government had not long taken over Dir district, but, in reality, tribal law still prevailed. The North West Frontier Province chief minister was committed to the enforcement plan in the poppy growing areas. Eradication would go ahead whether by manual labour or aerial spraying of the poppies, all in conjunction with development programs aimed at the rehabilitation of poppy growers.

Of the million people or so in the district we were the only resident foreigners. Most tourists visited neighbouring Swat Valley rather than Dir District. We were an oddity, and I am sure that for many children in the valleys we were the first Westerners they had seen. We could have bypassed a lot of that attention if we had dressed in the *shalwar khameez*, as a lighter skin-coloured Pashtun was quite common.

Rahimullah and I came up with plans to improve livestock production in the district. Unfortunately, United Nations for Drug Abuse Control (UNFDAC) made a huge mistake in giving the money to the Pakistan Government, and it took ages for the money to be released. The Pakistani manager of the district project also had other ideas on how to spend the money. Livestock improvement was a low priority. A new road or a newly-built irrigation channel were the showpieces.

Rahimullah and I visited Rabat and Ouch in the lower part of the district and met stock assistants who decried their isolation, the difficulty in moving around without transport, and the lack of medicines for livestock — all problems which would come up again and again as we continued to visit other areas in Dir District. The low priority given to animal husbandry was evident. At Ouch we met with Dr Manzoor Hussain at the veterinarian hospital and discussed the potential of improving facilities and the outreach program.

As we headed north to Petrach in Kohistan, the lushness of tree-clad hillsides, the winding Panjkora River and attractive valleys surprised me after the barrenness further south. The roads, however, were jarring; several times my head hit the roof of our Land Cruiser. Amir over-honked the horn and slammed on the brakes at the slightest hint of an approaching vehicle on the wrong side of the road or too close to us.

At Petrach the farmers admitted to growing poppies, but, with good will, treated us to a rice meal served in a cool, darkened room. After the meal they stood stiffly to attention for photos, and the village elder invited me to stay the night. I thanked him and declined.

At the weekend I joined in the practice sessions of a local team playing cricket. With raw talent evident, you didn't know how many Imran Khans or Javed Miandads would turn up with coaching. Cricket had taken over as the number one sport in Dir District. Level wasteland had been cleared and given a boundary of sorts. A pock-marked pitch guaranteed an unexpected bounce of the ball which added a new dimension to the game. One local team had marked out a pitch on the Panjkora river flats because the fine grey silt and clay had compacted well.

Teams appeared late in the afternoon and played until the fading light caused them to disperse. Tournaments were the rage; one had 27 teams competing over a 50-day period. I participated in one tournament and a knock of 25 helped to preserve Australia's image.

Australian cricketers were always held in high regard. I made sure everyone knew I was an Australian ex-cricketer and in one celebrated game I had bowled the best batsman in the world out — test cricketer Rohan Kanhai. Word soon got around the district and my status rose to that of an honoured guest. I gave speeches, opened tournaments, awarded trophies and even commentated on the game as it progressed. Everyone treated me like royalty. No harm in that, I thought. I would come down to earth on my return to Australia.

On one occasion, while I was commentating on the game, a group of spectators leapt to their feet — a snake had wriggled in amongst them. Even the bowler stopped in his stride to let the commotion subside. On another occasion, the traditional *shalwar chameez* which most cricketers wore was used to advantage. A fielder at silly mid-off was struck in the mid-ribs and doubled up in pain causing the loose folds of his shirt to enfold the ball. The fielder recovered quickly to appeal and the batsman was given out.

Entertaining Botham-style play provided lots of fours and sixes. Cricket should go a long way here. I wondered, though, why Afghanis were not represented in world cricket matches. After all, the Pashtuns lived on either side of the border and you would think that the game would have attracted the same degree of enthusiasm in Afghanistan.

Cricket in the North West Frontier Province received a real boost following the playing of the World Cup matches in Pakistan. No matter that Pakistan lost to Australia in the semi-final; cricket still remained high in everyone's eyes. Pakistanis were delighted when India, their traditional foes, also failed to reach the final of the World Cup.

In the last week in September I received the sad news from home that Liz's brother-in-law, Malcolm, had committed suicide. I had always enjoyed Malcolm's company with his readiness to show me the latest developments in his vineyard at Renmark. He was an innovator; he quickly adapted to new varieties with top grafting. One of his inventions was an automatic snipper operated by compressed air to make it easier for hand-pruning of vines. He was also a prominent member of Renmark's ambulance service. I had lost a friend; it was a sad loss for his family and for everyone who knew him.

At the beginning of October, Tony upset his counterparts in agronomy and was asked to leave. The Pakistani director of the project, Saiful Maluk, didn't like Tony; he didn't like our assistant livestock director for that matter, so no money was released at first for livestock programs. To further complicate matters, Helmut Sell, our UNFDAC advisor in Islamabad on the opium crisis in Pakistan, was under pressure by the Pakistan government to quit his post.

Fortunately, our counterpart to Saiful Maluk, Alby, arrived on 19 October with fishing gear, golf clubs and a plentiful supply of whisky. He had come on a holiday jaunt, I thought. After settling in he met with the district officer of Dir District and Saiful — who had become 'Sinful' in Tony's way of speaking — and pacified him enough to have Tony stay on. Tony would apologise for his outlandish behaviour and not throw his weight around in working with his counterparts.

The three of us conversed on a wide range of topics at the evening meal table with Bill cooking us Western type food —Tony had primed him. We differed a lot in our attitude and approach to the project. Tony had worked on a number of overseas projects and emphasised a technical solution for every problem he encountered. I favoured a participatory approach with building up the capacity of the livestock officers so that they could work with farmers more effectively. Alby was sceptical of any progress being made and often downed a half bottle of whisky at a time. Where he got his supply from was a mystery — Pakistan was officially a 'dry' country. Alby and I did not get on that well, but we coexisted.

We rarely watched the Pakistan news on TV, partly because it was in Urdu and partly because it showed a monotonous account of President General Zia-ul-Haq's daily engagements.

I twice visited the nawab with Amir and an interpreter. Although 80-years-old the nawab seemed to have his finger on the pulse of what was going on in Dir District. I also took time out to visit Shaheena's family in Islamabad and stayed with them overnight. This gave me an opportunity to get to know Shaheena's father, and brother, Javed, who talked at length about the changing political fortunes of Pakistan.

From Islamabad, Rahimullah and I journeyed north-west to Jaba sheep farm in the hills, where we met the director for discussions of the potential of the Merino sheep in Dir District.

We also travelled to Murree which was alive with tourists and locals wandering through the bazaars. Everywhere, Kashmiri carpets were on sale.

I dined with Helmut Sell and his wife Susi at Abbottabad, a city located about 110 kilometres north of the capital, Islamabad. Helmut had full oversight of all the activities in Pakistan with programs designed to stop the growing of poppies. He had inside knowledge of those in government and Inter-Services Intelligence who benefited from the status quo. The quandary was: How best to use this knowledge? Would he expose those responsible?

Not much later, a bomb went off at their residence, but caused no personal injury. The Pakistan government again requested Helmut to leave, and this time for safety's sake, he and his wife left Pakistan. I valued their friendship and was sad to see them go.

On our return to Temergara from Abbottabad, we drove up the winding path of the Malakand Pass where Mohammed Mullah fought the British. I discovered that Winston Churchill was a war correspondent covering the battle, and my great-uncle from Banff, Scotland, had died fighting the Pashtuns at the pass.

Back in Temergara, snow appeared on the distant mountain peaks to the north. Unfortunately, the rains had failed to come during the summer and the rice and maize plants had suffered. With floods and a hail storm the crops were further damaged.

With the cooler weather, the Kohistanis, who lived in the northern part of the district, started their slow march southwards towards the plains, moving with them sheep, cattle and goats. The women covered their faces when a man approached; they played a major part in the movement. The men often went ahead by car.

I spent a day at Mingora in Swat district where a livestock training session was held. On the way we passed the burnt out shell of a bus. A terrorist had placed a bomb under one of the seats and it had gone off killing nine and seriously injuring twenty-seven.

I tried to put the bombing acts out of my mind and, at the weekend, I officiated at a cricket tournament in Ouch. I opened the game after shaking hands with all 22 players and umpires — rather like the Duke of Edinburgh at Wembley Stadium. Lots of young boys sat cross-legged near my seat and looked up from time to time to see if I was enjoying the match, or maybe to see if I was for real.

The poppies were on the move by the third week in January. I toured around the north and observed women weeding the plots.

In a persuasive manner the district commissioner talked to many groups of villagers; some had heeded his advice and some hadn't. More in a gesture of defiance, the commisioner and volunteers pulled out poppy plants from individual plots by hand. Armed soldiers went along, too, ready for any action.

A few weeks before, helicopter pilots were supposed to have flown over the poppy fields and sprayed them with 2,4-D, but perhaps the pilots had not been paid enough. The local growers had armed themselves to the hilt with Kalashnikovs, rocket launchers and missiles.

In a ground clash between the poppy growers and the Dir scouts, hundreds of rounds were fired in a typical wild Western shoot out. The government had promised law enforcement action in certain designated poppy areas for this year.

Soon after, we had our first fall of snow and the hills looked majestic in their new white coats.

We drove up to Wari, a town about an hour's drive north of Temergara, and the poppies were about 15 centimetres in height. The people seemed touchy as we checked a few fields.

Then, out of the blue, like fleas to a fresh dung pat, officials swept in to organise activities for the British Secretary of the Commonwealth sent by Mrs Thatcher. With charts, seating arrangements and security set up, the district commissioner and deputy director focused on the events and all the trimmings. It started at the helipad with Neil Hughes, an UNFDAC advisor, and high ranking officials arriving from Peshawar. We joined them for a Pakistani spread, with poppies as the main topic of conversation.

The following day, 7 February 1988, a helicopter touched down at 10 am and the British ambassador and a customs officer stepped out. The briefing lasted for an hour, then a cavalcade of 20 vehicles with double police escort took off for Wari. Driving rain kept most in their cars.

We stopped at a refugee settlement and the best part of the day from my point of view was a speech by a refugee advocate appealing for more United States assistance to oust the Russians from Afghanistan. 'The Afghans have suffered enough,' the speaker said. 'The last Russian must be kicked out.' The storm then unleashed lightning and thunder as if to confirm what the speaker had vented.

The heavies departed, none the wiser, I suspected. Following their departure, the poppies shot up to nearly a metre in height and began to flower. Parts of Dir District looked ominously attractive with red, pink, purple and white flowers providing a colourful contrast to the golden yellow of ripening wheat.

A few days later, I had a cup of tea with a very courageous Punjabi army officer. One of the servants to the deputy commissioner and our project director had discovered a brief case containing 30 kilograms of high intensive explosive, close to the district commisioner's office and other office buildings. The Punjabi officer managed to clear over 200 people away from the buildings before cutting through the case and severing the wires leading to a battery; it was a remote-controlled device and could have gone off at any time. 'Over 100 would have been killed,' he said. He proudly showed a certificate for his bravery. The district commissioner's office was just down the road from us, so we all felt vulnerable.

Amidst all the furore and attacks, I tried to concentrate on plans for livestock development and to establish a livestock centre at Wari to cater for the northern part of the district. I managed to get the scheme on the agenda for the next project review board meeting at Peshawar. Wari was in the heart of the poppy growing area so every move called for Solomon's wisdom.

I visited the veterinary research institute in Peshawar to organise training for our chief veterinary officer and to help set up our own diagnostic laboratory.

While in Peshawar, I also met with the director of animal husbandry for NWFP, and he was keen to assist us in the supply of improved chickens for the villages. He encouraged us to carry out nutrition trials for sheep and cattle using urea, molasses and oilseed cake.

Peshawar, the capital of the North West Frontier Province, appeared like a frontier town and was full of surprises for the visitor. Wandering through the bazaars gave me a colourful insight into the Pashtun way of life. Shady dealings abounded.

The Pearl Hotel in Peshawar where we stayed was heavily guarded; a soldier on the third floor with a rifle made us feel uneasy. We had arrived at a difficult time in the Afghan–Russian conflict; we heard the crackle of gunfire on the streets. Armed Afghani communists crossed the border to terrorise Pakistanis because of the American support given to the Afghani mujahideen — the guerrilla-type military units fighting the Russians.

In the early days Peshawar had become an important centre for Buddhist pilgrims. Then the Moghuls arrived in the 16th century. One of the Moghul emperors, Akbar, had a trunk road constructed from Delhi to Kabul via Peshawar and the Khyber Pass. The Sikhs and British followed, and it was regarded as one of the most fanatical cities in India (before Pakistan came into existence). The tribespeople of the area at that time had a fearless passion for freedom and were excellent fighters. The British had a hard time containing them. The Khyber Pass, only 60 kilometres away from Peshawar, was the scene of several battles between the British and Pashtuns. In 1893 the Durand line was drawn cutting the Pashtun country in two — India on one side and Afghanistan on the other. After 1947, Peshawar and the North West Frontier Province became part of Pakistan.

Peshawar in 1987 was still the main link between Pakistan and Afghanistan. Scores of heavy-laden trucks crossed into Pakistan via the Khyber Pass. Without too much checking, Pakistani soldiers allowed them through with their cargoes — Soviet refrigerators and air conditioners, TV and hi-fi sets and a variety of alcoholic beverages — off-loaded into warehouses dotting the road to Peshawar. A bottle of vodka sold for $12 Australian; officially, Pakistan didn't allow consumption of alcohol by Muslims.

The Khyber Pass was not the only route for these goods. Donkeys and mules used some of the hundreds of mountain tracks along the 2,000 kilometres border with Afghanistan. One mule could carry up to four refrigerators or ten TV sets, I was told. Once over the border, pick-ups transported these goods to Peshawar.

Half a million refugees had taken up almost permanent residence in Peshawar, and on the fringes of the city I saw their mud and stone dwellings — an arresting feature of the Peshawar plains. The refugees were free to move about. A number of foreign refugee agencies in Peshawar assisted with the provision of food, social and medical services, and encouraged local handicraft skills. There were even veterinary services for those who owned livestock. The impact on the environment, though, had been devastating with overgrazing and the stripping of shrubs and trees for firewood.

Rahimullah and I visited the poultry breeding centre at Seluza to confirm their interest in our project and then on to Harichand dairy farm to see the popular Friesians; however, Jerseys were preferred for the cooler areas.

On the way back to Temergara we passed by a funeral service for a highly respected Pashtun leader, but we learned from a bystander that a bomb had gone off and killed some of the 40,000 mourners.

Back at Temergara I tried to focus on livestock improvement programs and called together the local vets and stock officers. Rahimullah put forward our plans for discussion — establish a poultry breeding unit, improve milk production in dairy cows and buffaloes, egg production for village households, improve livestock services, carry out nutrition and rangeland trials, and explore marketing options.

As a start, we designed the poultry breeding unit, and the Pakistani project manager approved the program for its establishment at Wari. Rahimullah supervised implementation of the nutrition trials.

For relaxation one weekend, I climbed up into the hills north of Temergara. Near the top I became exhausted with the thinner air or was it just the lack of exercise? A couple of lads appeared, unnerving me with their Kalashnikovs and a double barrelled shot gun. Fortunately, they were not Afghani communists and they guided me down to safer regions and advised not to go up again, especially on my own. Quite wise of them and unwise of me! I ended up having *chai* and an egg dish with them. They asked in their broken English how many children I had — a constant question at guesthouses — and they couldn't believe I had only two, in contrast to their five or more. Was I sad with no sons? 'The daughters make up for my loss,' I replied. They looked at me with disbelieving eyes.

The snow was fast disappearing from the hilltops. The Panjkora River had swollen up with the recent rains and the wheat was heading up and the poppies were flowering — almost like white and red tulips. Anti-feeling toward the Pakistan government was building up with the slow release of funds for the line agencies. Only a small amount of money had been released for the livestock programs.

Rahimullah and I visited the Punjab, which was altogether different from the North West Frontier Province. A quirk of history had brought them together under the Pakistani flag, but the Punjabis and Pashtuns were diverse in language, culture and physique.

Fortunately, our driver Amir spoke Punjabi so there were no problems in finding our way around. We travelled to Punjab via the Malakhand pass, where from the top of the pass there was a magnificent view of the fertile plains below, irrigated by a British-built canal. We journeyed south after reaching Islamabad and passed through the heavily scarred landscape before meeting the lush green plains of the Punjab with its extensive network of canals for irrigation.

Five major rivers flowed south to join the Indus. Along the banks of the Jhelum River, Alexander the Great fought and won his last battle, but his faithful charger, Bucephalus, died.

The Punjab was rich agriculturally with a population approaching 50 million. It was the most go-ahead province and attracted Pakistanis from all over. But there were problems: the continual supply of water to the wheat, rice, maize, cotton and sugar cane fields had raised the water table to within two metres of the surface. In many places surface salts shimmered under the blazing sun with a snow-like elegance. On the industrial scene, in some of the larger cities, such as Faisalabad, the textile, chemical and engineering plants gave rise to a smoky haze which diffused everywhere. No pollution laws.

On the road, a profuse variety of vehicles jostled with each other — motorised rickshaws, donkey carts, bullock carts and even camel carts, tongas — horse-drawn carriages — cyclists, motor cyclists, flying coaches and gaily-coloured trucks. We passed trucks and carts loaded high and wide with sugar canes. On a couple of occasions the top-heavy load had caused them to overturn, throwing canes everywhere. The flying coaches spared no mercy to anyone. They blasted you out of the way with screeching horns if they came up behind you, and they flashed lights, which meant 'get out of the way, I'm coming through'. So you were obliged to move off the road. *Inshallah*, or 'if God wills', we arrived.

On the way to Lahore, the capital city of Punjab province, we encountered several buffalo dairy farms. The Nili-Ravi breed was favoured over the famous Sahiwal cows because of the richer milk (6.5 per cent fat). The buffaloes were stall-fed and hand-milked. Berseem clover was a popular green feed and transported by donkey or bullock cart. The buffaloes also had free access to a rice straw stack. During a 300-day lactation period they produced about 2,000 litres of milk. The buffalo bull was not as harmless as it looked — at one of the farms one chased us. Although bulky, heavy-boned animals, they could run like tigers for short distances.

With a population about the size of Sydney, Lahore attracted many tourists to view the magnificent Moghul and British buildings, mostly constructed from a deep red brick, which took on a fiery nature with the setting sun.

We visited the Fortress Stadium for the horse and cattle show — a Pakistani equivalent to the Adelaide Show. One thousand pipers played a stirring medley of Scots and Pakistani tunes. Horse and camel dancing followed with the animals prancing to music on their hind legs. Nochi goats performed a quick step quite naturally, because of a peculiar anomaly in their front leg tendons. Tent pegging proved a popular event, where teams of four riders urged their horses to gallop as fast as possible towards partially buried stakes and attempt to strike them with lances. Resounding applause followed if all four lances and stakes were presented to the audience.

We returned to Temergara to learn that the district commissioner, Alby, and others had gathered up enough courage to pull out poppies as a show of strength. The police, chief officials, and any notable, took part. Not for me, though.

Time seemed to slip slowly by — I was not happy with the progress but persevered nevertheless. It rained for three days non-stop. The chocolate-brown, turbulent Panjkora River doubled in width.

Rahimullah and I ran a training program for the stock assistants — an eight-day course which included a visit to Peshawar and Jaba sheep farm, near Mansehra.

A shoot out occurred in a nearby village when a policeman tried to stop a vehicle. Seven were killed and a number injured.

Then on 10 April 1988, an ammunition depot in Rawalpindi, that supplied the Afghani mujahideen fighting the Soviet forces, exploded killing more than 1,300 people. The United States were involved in a covert operation to supply arms to the mujahideen in Afghanistan from bases in Pakistan. The attack, as a reprisal, could have been carried out by Afghani or Pakistani agents or the Soviet KGB; no one knew for sure. One of the rockets landed close to the Australian Embassy in Islamabad, fourteen kilometres from the explosion site. A man climbed a tree for safety but a shell decapitated him.

I flew home at the end of May for three weeks rest and to recover from poppy syndrome.

We bought our first home in Gawler with the deposit we had saved. Liz and I managed to squeeze in a few days holiday on Kangaroo Island. It took most of the three weeks for my mind to change gear from living on the edge with poppies and Kalashnikovs. The next and last three-month stint would prove the toughest healthwise.

Arriving back in Islamabad from Karachi, the 41 degree heat hit me like a shock wave at 10 am. Amir Nawab and one of Sher Ali Khan's sons, Javed Iqbal, greeted me at the airport.

Javed wanted to talk about a serious family matter.

'Good to see you,' I greeted him.

'And you too,' Javad replied. 'I am glad you liked the chappal shoes. It is only a small token of what is in my heart. Also, I am happy you have come to no harm with your driver. Thank God. You know, I didn't have much confidence in him.'

'Have you news of Shaheena?' I asked.

'Yes, and that is what I want to talk to you about. Shaheena has informed us of her intentions to marry an Australian — an orthopaedic surgeon. She claims that he has become a Muslim.'

I sensed an ominous tone but said nothing.

'You have been in Pakistan for a year now — a short time. But you can tell me: How can we allow this? You know fairly well the social values prevalent here and with what fanaticism they are grounded. For a man to do so is somewhat acceptable. But for a girl to do so is unheard of and no less than a taboo.'

'But if they choose to live in Australia, I am not sure what you can do.'

'Well, I would like to ask you a favour. That is, if you would be kind enough to appreciate our dilemma and also provided you can find time. I would be most obliged if you could have a word with her and remind her of us and her roots. It is not that we don't want to see her happy, in her own house, with her own family. But the shame her actions will bring upon this house are unbearable, awesome. I can't even bring myself to think how we could ever cope with the situation.'

'I am sorry to hear that you feel this way. I am not sure how I can help, especially if they choose to live in Australia; they are free to marry.'

'I know I am asking far too much. But we have no one there to remind her of us and the social and cultural values that we here have to abide by and live with. She is an anthropologist and should know better that anybody else. She is also a Pashtun and comes from a most conservative background. Her family indeed has made the grave mistake of reposing such trust in her and burdened her with such responsibilities that she could not and did not shoulder. There is nothing anyone can do. But it would have us forever indebted if you could talk to her of this most urgent matter. Who knows, maybe your impassionate reasoning makes her see the light of day.'

Perhaps I should have said 'it is not my place to interfere — they are both adults and are free to make their own decision.' Instead, I said, 'I'll see what I can do but I don't hold out much hope.'

The words of one of my bosses of the Department of Agriculture, Harold Chamberlain, came back to me: 'Remember that different cultures have different ways of thinking, each in its own way quite logical so that perhaps often it is better to listen, think hard, ask an occasional question and let them do most of the talking.'

When I returned to Adelaide I said nothing about Javed's concerns. I felt it wasn't my place to interfere as an outsider. Liz and I attended Shaheena and John's wedding and reception.

Back in Temergara the mangoes in the market tasted delicious. The melting of the snow had caused the river to turn a milky chocolate colour.

On one weekend we journeyed north over the Lowari pass. We followed a swift flowing river into one of the valleys and wound up at a border town, famous for its hot springs. The whole place was alive with the wildest, bearded characters you could imagine, mostly Afghanis who had come over the border for replenishments. Many openly displayed Russian Kalashniknov guns, rifles and shotguns, and even young lads brandished rifles. Hundreds of horses and donkeys crowded into a large compound. The mujahideen eyed us suspiciously as we negotiated our way through the narrow lanes of the bazaar.

Further north, on the way to Chitral, we stopped in one of the Kalash valleys to meet with one of the tribes known as Kafir

Kalash — the wearers of black robes. The legend was that they were descendants of soldiers from the legions of Alexander the Great and settled there. The Kalash lived a simple life and loved music. The women wore colourful clothes and did all the work. They lived in windowless, mudstone huts and had no need for money. And they didn't bury their dead — enough said. We sat down on a log while one woman played the flute and another danced, imparting a sense of peace and joy.

In Chitral we stopped to watch a polo tournament, another pastime inherited from the British. The snow-capped peak of Trich Mir towered behind us at 7,700 metres.

Another weekend trip took us to the Kaghan valley in Mansehra District, the jewel of beautiful valleys. The long winding hill roads were quite tiring. A number of shepherds gently moved their flocks of sheep and goats up the mountain trail towards the alpine pastures. Amir lost his cool when the goats refused to budge. From Mansehra we passed through Basham to the Swat Valley and then back via Mingora to Dir District — about ten hours of driving.

By the middle of June it was unbearably hot but there was some relief at night. I usually woke up bathed in perspiration. At night I walked along the river bank and imagined cooling off in the snowy, milky-green waters of the Panjkora River.

I started to get dizzy, with weakness spells, and felt that I was losing my sense of balance. I became anxious and fearful, and afraid of losing my sanity. What was wrong with me? Could I survive to mid-August to fulfil my contract? I wasn't sure and phoned Rod Reeves in Australia to advise him of my predicament. He encouraged me to see a doctor and continue if I could.

Perhaps my fear and anxiety had come about from the war-like nature of my working environment. I did not know for sure. Although I was aware of potential danger and violent events that had occurred, I had not confronted danger head-on. The tension perhaps had built up gradually without my realising it. Then I wondered if the malarial tablets — Lariam (mefloquine) — I had been taking had affected my mental state. I had been on Lariam since the start of the project. I stopped taking the tablets just in case.

Then my duties changed with Saiful Maluk requesting that I spend time travelling around the district with a movie camera, recording details of the various sub-projects — all to show the executive director of UNFDAC on his arrival from Vienna.

I set off the next day to a local village about 30 kilometres away — one-and-a-half hours drive over bumpy roads. We filmed a suspension bridge being constructed, although, the first time we started to film, the labourers stopped working, so we had to do a retake, this time with all shovels and picks in action. The foreman ordered tea and chicken pieces, all at 7.30 am. Children rafting down the Panjkora River in rubber tubes were keen to have their pictures taken, too, so we obliged.

We climbed up a rough mountain track with the Afghanistan border on one side, and the tribal territory of Bajaur on the other. Down below in the lower reaches of the valley, irrigation channels brought water to flood the rice paddies. The channels had been constructed with concrete sides since the earthen works built by the villagers were continually rupturing with the force of the water. I walked to the intake head and filmed the irrigation officer describing the construction which had been financed by the project. Monsoonal rains soaked us as we wended our way back across the edges of rice fields to the Land Cruiser. One of the locals said that a labourer had been murdered at a point where I stood. The irrigation officer commented that the people here were very religious. Was that the reason for the man's demise?

We passed a number of refugee settlements that had existed for many years with the more permanent type home of stone and mud. Guns were on display as usual but not pointed towards us. Our driver bogged the Land Cruiser in one of the muddy river crossings and a tractor eventually pulled us out. Every part of my body was bathed in sweat or rain as we journeyed back to Temergara.

For another week I travelled extensively, taking film of the different sub-projects — mainly for the director of UNFDAC, who was to have stayed with us for one night, but he left after lunch to meet President Zia-ul-Haq without seeing the film.

Two days later I set off for Peshawar for a bridge on my teeth — 3,000 rupees ($250). The traffic in Peshawar came to a halt frequently, and I just sweltered as they tried to work it out. The fumes from exhaust were dense and bazaar life carried on at a subdued rate with shades and fans appearing to offer some relief from the intense heat.

Then on 3 July 1988 a civilian passenger flight from Tehran to Dubai was shot down by a guided missile from a United States naval cruiser. The plane came down in the Persian Gulf with the loss of all 290 on board. The attack, understandably, generated a great deal of animosity towards the United States and that meant potentially us since we could easily be labelled as 'American' in Pakistan. We were told to take extra care. For the remaining time in Pakistan, Amir examined our Land Cruiser for anything suspicious. We added 'revenge killers' to the existing threat of belligerent poppy growers and Afghani communists.

In the last two weeks I wrote up a livestock report for the project and spent time with Rahimullah to ensure ongoing progress and to discuss Rahimullah's desire to pursue a master's course in Australia. And then there were goodbyes to everyone.

On my last day in Dir District, 18 August 1988, in I was ready for Amir to take me to Islamabad on my first leg back to Australia. Alby knocked on my door at about 6 am and said, 'You should think twice about going to Islamabad. General Zia-ul-Haq, the president of Pakistan, has just been assassinated.'

I gasped and tried to take stock of what that would mean and the possible repercussions for foreigners like me trying to leave the country. 'I will take my chances,' I said.

I could see the headlines: 'Australian tries to leave Pakistan following assassination of president.' Despite increased surveillance and military presence, the trip to Islamabad and flights from Islamabad to Karachi and onwards to Australia went without a hitch. Perhaps I was meant to return home. In any case, I was eager to see Liz and the girls and leave the fighting behind.

Adjusting back into Australian society was much harder than I had imagined. The mental unbalance I had experienced in the previous two months continued and there was no way I could take up lecturing duties again. I requested study leave until the end of the year. In one sense I had become accustomed to tribal life in Dir District with the gradual immersion into a Pashtun way of life that had brought me into contact with so many different kinds of people. True, it was not pleasant at times, but it was meaningful and satisfying, beyond expectations of my role as livestock advisor. Life in Australia had lost its simplicity, its earthiness, its slower pace and engaging nature. Life had become unreal — perhaps, this was all part of my stressed-out paranoia.

Roseworthy College granted compassionate study leave at a government research farm close by at Turretfield. I would look into various aspects of South Australian dryland farming systems and write up a chapter for a book on dryland farming.

A new threat emerged in 2007 with the planned takeover of lower Dir district by the Taliban, an Islamist fundamental organisation. The Pakistan Army launched an offensive operation to retake both Dir and Swat districts.

Later, I learned that poppy growing in Dir District had declined substantially, but neighbouring Afghanistan still put Pakistan under threat from drug abuse and trafficking, using Pakistan and Iran as a supply route to Turkey and Europe.

Whereas Pakistan had reduced production of poppy, Afghanistan and Myanmar had steadily increased its supply. By 2013, 200,000 hectares of Afghan fields were growing poppies, according to the UN's Afghanistan opium survey. Because of violence and instability, both Afghanistan and Myanmar had become major opium producers.

Two large-scale projects — in Algeria and Pakistan — were enough. On my return to Gawler I was happy to rejoin our Community Aid Abroad organisation and raise money for small-scale projects.

Mohammed and I visit the Roman ruins at
Tipaza on the coast of Algeria

Encounter with an Algerian steppe dweller on a donkey

Young boys growing up on the Indian orphanage farm
of the Good Shepherd Agricultural Mission

Dr Latif Siddiqui and I examine the local sheep in Bangladesh

Accompanied by Barbara from Bangladesh,
Rosie starts a new life in Australia

A group of students from the Middle East, Africa and
the Indian sub-continent undertake a 1-year course in
dryland farming at Roseworthy Agricultural College

Rahimullah and the poppy fields in Dir District of
North West Frontier Province, Pakistan

My driver, Amir, introducing his family members

Awe-inspiring Victoria Falls on the Zambezi River,
at the border of Zimbabwe and Zambia

My West Timor team, Martin, Erna, Ning
and Samson, for the village study

Joyful Sabian Mandeans on their release
from Woomera detention centre

With the Harbin teachers of English from north-east China

Chapter 14

South Africa, United Kingdom and Sri Lanka

WITH ROSEWORTHY COLLEAGUES ASKING, 'WHERE to next?' and not 'Where have you been?' I tried to live down a growing reputation as a wanderer.

But it's strange sometimes how things work out and you never plan anything. That's how it was with a visit to South Africa and onward to meet Liz in London. It all fell into place, as though someone else had planned it.

I had contributed to a paper on rangeland management, along with two Roseworthy Campus colleagues, Vic Squires, a principal lecturer, and Martin Andrew, deputy director. Following the Algerian and other African experiences, the paper described the problems in implementing improved range management on common lands in Africa: an Australian perspective. The South African Journal of Grassland Society accepted the paper and invited us to present our findings at a rangeland conference in Pretoria. Only one of us could go. Vic could not go because of a clash in his schedule and Martin was too busy. Could I go? Well, no need to think about that. With leave accruing, I could also visit for the first time two elderly aunts in Johannesburg and Durban, and fly on to England and Scotland before returning home. Liz was happy for me to go to South Africa but would have loved to join me in England. 'It might work out somehow,' I said lamely.

I flew to Perth on 28 April 1991 and met up with Pim and Graham Reid who had lived on a farm near Elgin in Scotland and had also migrated to Australia at the same time as my parents. We ambled through Kings Park native bushland and along the banks of the Swan River, taking in its wide, meandering course through the suburbs.

Then on my fiftieth birthday I flew to Harare. With no wild birthday celebration there I flew on to Livingston.

As the plane approached Livingston I caught glimpses of misty plumes of spray jetting skywards. Not long after landing I walked to the River Zambezi on a relatively isolated road — perhaps a little foolhardy. A track led off to give spectacular views of the Victoria Falls.

Having walked into a sea of spray from the main falls, I turned back through the rainforest, flush with grasses, palms and bushes. A bushbuck grazed peacefully by the track. I arrived at a village where I became entranced with dancers and musical performers playing drums and marimbas.

I then flew back to Harare and on to Johannesburg, or Joburg, as they say. I met my aunt Ella for the first time and chatted away in her flat about our common relatives on Mum's side.

'Your great-great-grandmother died in the Indian mutiny in 1857; her husband, James, was an engineer building railways in India,' Ella said. 'And Alice Hunt, my grandmother, and your great-grandmother, was an active photographer from the 1880s until the early twentieth century. Her photos have formed a valuable collection of life in north-west Norfolk. It was so unusual for a woman to take such an interest in photography at that time. And she had eleven children to raise.' (www. selwyn-family.mc.uk/AliceHuntCollection)

'And one of those was your father, Donald Hunt,' I remarked.

'Yes, at Haileybury my father was a keen sportsman and a long-distance runner. He joined the Cape Mounted Rifles in 1896 and served in the Boer War, where he was mentioned in Kitchener's despatches. Later, he married Grizel Scott and they set up home in Petermaritzburg, where they brought us up.'

'How did he fare in the Boer War?' I asked.

'Well, Donald and his younger brother Reggie were fighting the Boers and holding off an attack at one stage in a town. During one night, a corner of the town was being shelled, so Donald got up out of bed and went to get his men under cover. On returning, he found a shell had gone through his room, hit the bed, and gone through the blankets. That was a close call for my father. Reggie said that it was 'virtue rewarded'.

'In charge of a unit, Reggie also talked of the sickening smells, the crawling mass of lice in his clothes with no chance of a bath for a month, the terrible wounds of his men and, of course, the dead men and horses. He worshipped his men but had no idea how men could stand what eight days of holding a line meant with such a barrage of shells. Three of his men did go insane, but others smiled when he met them, and one said that they would do it all again for him. Reggie was severely wounded later and laid out for dead but was saved by wagging his finger. He recovered and later served in the Great War, after which he was in Iraq helping to raise and train a new Iraqi army.'

'Someone must have been watching over Reggie,' I said.

'I am certain. On another occasion in May 1902, Donald took a small scouting party to locate a militant group of Boers east of Edenburg. Just on dawn they saw smoke from the chimney of a farm house supposedly cleared of inhabitants. Donald demanded admittance but got no answer, so he kicked in the door, bending his spur as he did so. It was then that they found themselves in the midst of an assembly of Boers who greatly outnumbered them. They rode away in a hail of bullets, untouched. Later when it became light they could see the Boers riding parallel to them on the right and left. Perhaps the Boers had feared a trap and had not closed in on them. Donald had accomplished his mission in locating the enemy.

'His good fortune continued when he served with the South African Scottish regiment during the Great War. He fought and survived the Battle of Delville Wood, one of the fiercest battles in France as part of the Battle of the Somme. He was one of the few South African survivors. After the war he went to the Caucasus to assist White Russians in fighting the Bolshevik communist forces in the Russian civil war.'

What possessed him, I thought, to go on fighting? 'What did he do when he returned to South Africa?' I asked.

'After a charmed life with no injury, he came home and joined the administration department of Sekukuniland as an inspector of mines, until he retired in 1931.'

Ella then let me know in regard to the apartheid policy that the laws governing geographical and racial segregation would soon be repealed, and a national conference of the African National Congress would take place in Durban, the first to be held since 1959. She foresaw a new post-apartheid era, in which Nelson Mandela would play a leading role, and the restrictive policies for black and coloured people under apartheid would be replaced by ones giving equal rights and opportunities to everyone. It all happened three years later in 1994 when the African National Congress party won the election and Nelson Mandela became the president of South Africa.

Ella's simple and austere flat was one of many in a multi-storey apartment block, in which mainly coloured families lived. She had no qualms about her environment but she had been mugged in the street and her handbag stolen.

Ella introduced me to a panoramic view of Joburg from the top of the 46-storey Carlton Tower. Mining dumps encircled the town and the black townships beyond were just visible.

We walked for several blocks to reach the library museum to learn about the gold miner days, Boer War I and II, miner's strikes and notables, like Paul Kruger. The streets were chock-a-block with traffic and pedestrians — mostly black and coloured people, well-dressed, and well-fed. At least I didn't see any poorly nourished people.

On Sunday we attended a cathedral service with several hundred others, mostly Blacks. With christenings galore it seemed we were in factory-line mode. I shared a prayer book with a coloured girl, Shehad, who had come from Cape Town to be a midwifery nurse.

Aunt Ella then drove me to Pretoria, and I booked in at the Manhattan Hotel.

The conference opened on 6 May 1991 with a prayer and address to encourage us. I met delegates from Swaziland, North Transvaal and from Zimbabwe, and talked to Mike, a tobacco grower from Zambia, and a Pakistani from Peshawar.

Most of the talks, I found, were long-winded and dry. I drifted at times as the trite expressions rolled off with too many facts to digest.

When my turn came, I began to sweat under a barrage of bright lights. With difficulty I marshalled my thoughts and launched into our rangeland experience in the Algerian steppe. I pointed out the barriers in making progress: a lack of involvement of the nomads and settled farmers in determining their own destiny; little attempt to use local knowledge and capabilities of stakeholders; and our failure to establish a working relationship with our counterparts. As a result we pushed our own ideas and technology without taking into account what impact they would have on the way of life of steppe dwellers and their livelihood.

The extra bright lights taxed my eyes as I tried to focus on the first question: 'How can you ensure the improvement of future rangeland projects?' someone piped up.

'We would have to give much more emphasis on communication, local knowledge and participation in decision-making by all interested parties,' I replied.

A few more questions and on to the next speaker, Brian Roberts, also from Australia, who entertained: 'The South African accent has caused a stir with households becoming "arseholes", he said. 'So we have had endless arsehole computer outputs in the system.' Talks followed on land tenure and communal grazing problems. The game management talks commanded a great deal of interest.

Ella rang later to find out how it went.

The next day we visited a beef and mutton Merino farm. A consultant discussed grass varieties, irrigation of ryegrass and fescue, growing sorghum, making silage, and the importance of the veld — an open grassland with scattered shrubs and trees in southern Africa — which we saw just before sunset.

I rang Anne, Ella's sister, to let her know I was on my way to Durban.

The journey by bus through the Orange Free State passed through flat country grazed largely by beef cattle. Small African settlements dotted the landscape with maize as the main crop. The Drakensburg range of mountains provided a strong, picturesque contrast with rolling hills, table top buttresses and greener pastures.

Anne greeted me like a long lost relative, and I stayed in a cottage next to her place. At an evening meal, I let Anne know that Ella had passed on information about her father Donald and his exploits during the Boer War.

'Did she tell you about the concentration camps?' Anne asked.

'Concentration camps? Ella had not mentioned these,' I replied.

'Yes, well, it is not a proud part of our history,' she replied. 'The fighting around Edenburg had intensified, and, in response, the British columns chased Boers throughout the southern Free State. They also cleared farms and brought in Dutch inhabitants — men, women and children — to pack off by train to the concentration camps at Bloemfontein, Springfontein and Norvals. My father was in charge of packing them off. He probably sent more people to concentration camps than anyone else in South Africa.'

I tried to take in the enormity of what that meant. I could only think along the lines of Nazi concentration camps, but surely they could not have been so severe.

'What was the purpose of these camps,' I asked.

'Well, Lord Kitchener's idea was to intern all women, children and men unfit for military services, as well as the Blacks living on Boer farms; it would be the most effective way of limiting the fighting capacity of the Boer guerillas. The camps were first classed as refugee camps but then became known as concentration camps. From what we know now, the camps caused the deaths of more than 4,000 women and over 20,000 children. An English lady, Emily Hobhouse, found out about them and tried her best to make the British authorities and people know of their plight.'

'Was there any response from the British parliament?'

'I understand it was finally discussed in the House of Commons in 1902. The opposition party at the time deplored the mortality and living conditions in the camps, but their motion was defeated. Joseph Chamberlain, who had responsibility for directing the Boer War, said that it was the Boers who had forced the policy of establishing the concentration camps. But public voices grew in protest, and soon after, the Treaty of Vereeniging was signed; those still surviving in the camps were gradually released.'

'How did it affect your father?'

'He was devastated when he realised the true extent of what had happened in the camps. And he blamed himself for the part he played.'

'He was under orders,' I suggested, as a consolation.

'Yes, but it didn't help much.'

'I am sure it has affected you and Ella, too.'

'Yes, it has.'

We let the subject go and talked about Anne's growing-up days and her time as a nursing sister. After two days in Durban and meeting Anne's friends, I hired a car to visit Umfolozi, a game reserve.

I drove northwards through bushland, cane fields and forests, and, finally, small village settlements as I neared Umfolozi. After booking in for an overnight stay, I drove slowly through the game reserve and spotted impala, nyala, wildebeest — ugly looking beasts — zebras and two rhinos. The rhinos were massive and solid, not stirring a muscle as I drove slowly by, which was just as well.

The next day I had excellent close-ups of giraffes, impala, nyala, waterbuck, hyena, warthog and zebra. The giraffe towered over the acacias, picking at the fresh, thorny foliage.

I returned by Richard's Bay, a town in KwaZulu-Natal having one of the country's largest harbours. I also stopped at Shaka's Rock, a village on the coast where the Zulu chief Shaka was said to have thrown his enemies to their death from a promontory.

Several Africans wanted lifts, but I thought it unwise with a hired car.

I drove up to Cathedral Peak Hotel and on to the Drakensberg mountain ranges which were covered in haze because of a recent fire. Gradually the haze lifted, and a two-and-a-half hour walk to Umbrella Rock and Doreen Falls allowed me to take in sweeping views of the peaks and hillsides.

Back in Durban, Anne and I celebrated our last night at a pub with Anne's friends — Reg, Joan, Moly, Anton and Joy.

I travelled back to Johannesburg by bus and joined Ella for a cathedral service, which was deafening with the brass timpani, but I suppose impressive to some. Ella read out the passage on 'those dry bones'. Later, I wished Ella well with her intended settlement into a retirement home in Pietermaritzburg.

Although distant relatives, we were all interconnected in an enriching way through our family tree, and I felt privileged to have spent time with Ella and Anne. Just one opportunity to meet with them as they passed away a few years later.

United Kingdom

On my flight from Johannesburg to London with British Airways I was sandwiched between Corinne, a psychologist from Sweden, and a grandmother who had visited her sister in Port Elizabeth. The films went all through the night, all five of them. There was not much sleep, so after arriving in London I booked in at the Eagle Hotel for a two-hour kip.

I then took an underground train to Westminster to enjoy a warm spring day browsing around the Abbey, Lambeth Bridge, Buckingham Palace, No. 10 Downing Street, Regent's Park, the War Cabinet, and Trafalgar Square with still the same number of pigeons.

I hired a car from Kenning's and motored on the M 25 to Tunbridge Wells to stay with my cousin, Margaret Jackson, and her husband, Tony, a retired bank manager.

We walked through a local wood with a host of bluebells, and then through Sheffield Gardens, among rhododendrons, azaleas and all kinds of conifers and cedars.

I continued on my way to my birthplace, Aylsham, in Norfolk and stayed two days with Uncle Tom and Aunt Peggy and once again met all my cousins. We watched a home movie of sailing on the Broads.

I then drove up to one of my favourite hiking grounds — the Cairngorms and Glenmore Forest Park — and trekked for three hours through blooming heather and the soft green foliage of spruce and birch.

I journeyed onwards through picturesque lochs and mountains, going by Inverness, Dingwall and Ullapool to Elgin in Morayshire. In Elgin I caught up with school friends: Alaistair Bissett, editor of the Press and Journal, Alaistair Russell, a solicitor, and Duncan Davidson, a clerk and receptionist at Moray police station.

The following day I visited Garmouth by the River Spey and viewed our house, Woodview, where we had stayed for a number of years — it brought back sad and joyful memories. The Garmouth day drizzled in the morning so I called in to see Davy MacPherson with whom I had worked on a farm. He poured a dram for the chill. And he hadn't changed in his slow-moving gait and soft humour.

After dropping in to see others in the village I called by the Garmouth pub for a beer and met up with Sampi Fraser who had drunk too much. 'Is that you, really you, Tommy?' he said.

'Aye, it is, a' the way from Australia,' I replied. Others joined in, and it seemed as though I had never left Garmouth.

I offered Sampi a lift back home in his tipsy state. 'Na, na, Tommy. I'll be just fine.'

But as he ventured outside, he overbalanced and fell over a large pot plant. He landed awkwardly, cutting his face on the sharp-edged gravel of the road. I coaxed him into the car and took him back to his place. I rang the bell and Mrs Fraser appeared, took one look and threw her arms around me. 'Come inside, Tommy, come inside. There's a cup of tea brewing.'

'Thanks, Mrs Fraser, but Sampi needs some attention first. Look, he's cut himself badly.'

'Och, dinna worry about him. He'll tak' care o' himself. Come on in.' So I did and caught up with the village news.

On the road to Aberdeen I stopped at Meiklefolla where some of my forebears lived, including my great-grandfather who moved to Banff. Others worked on farms or went to fight with the British Army overseas. At the cemetery where a number of Manns were buried, I came across the gravestones of John, my great-great-grandfather; his son William, who was killed at the Malakand Pass fighting the Pashtuns; and another son Alexander, who was killed in China at the time of the Boxer Rebellion.

I searched for Meiklefolla farm, where another son worked, and while stopping in front of a letterbox, I realised I was staring at the engraved name of Meiklefolla on the letterbox itself. The farm owner happily showed me around, and he directed me to two other farms, Backhill and Mill of Burns, where other Manns worked. The ancestry effort was very worthwhile and fulfilling.

At Aberdeen I stayed with school friend, Allan Carmichael, who worked as an accountant for an Aberdeen firm. His son, John, joined us for dinner at the Gordon Arms.

Then I motored south to meet up with Stewart Binnie, another close school friend from Elgin days, and his wife Florence. Their home at Freuchie was large enough for several families, but with three daughters maybe they needed all that spare room.

At Auchtermuchty, I joined Colin and Ruth O'Riordan, friends of the family, for a shivering walk up West Lomond, but with a magnificent view of Fife stretching before us. I sampled Colin's homemade beer before a dinner of roast beef and vegetables, accompanied by red wine.

I drove back to Aylsham and phoned Liz from Woodgate House. She had some great news. In about ten days' time she would accompany one of her patients from the nursing home who wanted to spend his last days with relatives in England. All expenses would be paid. I could hardly believe our good fortune.

With a few days to spare I flew to Amsterdam to meet up with a former Roseworthy College student, Mike de Jong. We toured the polder region nearby and called into a modern dairy where our host explained all the mod cons of dairying, including computerised feeding. Then we savoured Dutch conviviality at a local pub which hosted a full mix of people.

After farewelling Mike and wishing him the best in job searching, I delighted in a canal trip in which the guide explained the historical worth and design of the buildings we passed by. Later, a city tour provided an insight into the founders of Amsterdam, the Diamond Museum, and Rijksmuseum where I lost myself in admiring the landscape scenes and portraits.

I decided to take the plunge and travel to Berlin to meet once again with Heiko and his family. The East German countryside appeared more rundown than the West side, showing a lack of lustre in factories and houses, and less productive farms.

With Heiko as tourist guide we first visited the Reichstag, which, following German reunification in 1990, was made the seat of parliament in Berlin. Next, we visited a memorial to the Russians in the Second World War, and then the remnants of the Berlin Wall. There was no checkpoint Charlie this time as we crossed into what was the East German side. The bus took us to Alexander Square and we visited St Mary's Church.

The next day we toured Wannsee Lake where churches and castles seemed to sprout amidst trees bordering the lake. Later, exhausted from all our sightseeing, we relaxed over fine dining with Heiko's mother, her granddaughter and husband who joined us for lively conversation, helped on by a generous flow of German wine. We parted in the best of spirits.

Back in London I had time before meeting up with Liz to visit the Imperial War Museum. Displays of VC holders, gassed soldiers, Belsen, trench warfare were well laid out and absorbing, though a sad reflection on our humanity.

It was great to see Liz appearing at the airport. Her patient, an elderly chap in a wheelchair, was whisked off by his daughter.

We decided to revisit Tony and Margaret at Tunbridge Wells; they had offered their holiday home in Wales for a week. Wales beckoned for the first time for both of us and we took full advantage of a quiet cottage retreat set in undulating hilly country, populated only by sheep, near Llanwrthwl by the River Wye. We explored the Welsh Highlands later on and soaked in the idyllic setting of Betws-y-Coed in Snowdonia National Park.

All too soon we flew back to Australia with a stopover in Hong Kong for a week on Lantau Island. Another former student of Roseworthy College, Jan Viruly, from Holland, had offered his flat for a week. While he could not be there his Filipina servant looked after us. Jan, who had become a high profile salesman for a fertilizer company, travelled all over Asia to promote his product. Amazing what some Roseworthy students end up doing!

Later, Jan travelled around Australia with Sir William Gunn, past president of the Wool Board — an unlikely alliance. They visited us at Roseworthy College. A big and impressive man, William spoke over lunch with passion about his life and the wool industry. I let him know we might be related way back with Mann being a sept of the clan Gunn. The Vikings from Norway had settled in the top of Scotland and had gradually worked their way down into the heart of the Scottish Highlands. 'Either peace or war,' I said. He smiled in acknowledgement of the clan motto.

Sri Lanka

Back in Gawler and towards the end of 1991, Len Reid suggested I join him in his efforts to foster livestock development for dairy cows and sheep in Sri Lanka.

Len Reid, a fighter pilot during the Second World War and a politician, worked tirelessly for the poor in India and Bangladesh. He organised a number of walks throughout Australia and overseas to highlight the plight of the underprivileged and to raise awareness of what people could do. Mahatma Gandhi had started the idea of a journey on foot, or *padayatra*, with his famous salt march in 1930. Prominent citizens or politicians used the *padayatra* to inform and educate people on issues facing their livelihood and well-being, and to galvanise people into action.

I hadn't realised the full intent of Len's plans when he rang me. He had just completed a successful walk from Coimbatore to Madras, and, full of optimism, wanted to carry out a similar walk from Colombo, the capital of Sri Lanka, to the Jaffna Peninsula to 'create peace and goodwill'. This was at the height of the conflict between the Tamils and government forces in Sri Lanka in which the Tamil Tigers, a militant separist group, sought an independent state in Sri Lanka.

Our bus from the airport to Colombo YMCA was stopped seven times for security checks. One of Len's contacts had arranged for us to meet the prime minister, Mr Wijetunga, to advise him of our intended walk to the Jaffna Peninsula. Before doing so, we had discussions with International Red Cross who informed us of arrangements that could be made for our visit. I felt my knees weaken at the prospect of walking into Tamil Tiger held country. A walk anywhere else in Sri Lanka would have been acceptable.

We met the prime minister and other ministers, along with army generals, in a small conference room. After introductions Len informed the prime minister that his organisation had sent hundreds of gift cows and sheep to Sri Lanka in the early 1970s, and these had performed well. Also, with farmer tours from Australia, a close association with farmer organisations in both countries had developed. Len had tried to send 200 dairy heifers to the Jaffna Peninsula, but could not send them while ethnic violence persisted. 'Can we go to the Jaffna Peninsula to assess the situation?' Len asked.

The prime minister raised his eyebrows. 'It would be better to send your cows and sheep to government farms in other parts of Sri Lanka,' he said. The ministers and army generals nodded in agreement.

Len considered that for a moment. 'We could do that as you request, Prime Minister, provided freight costs and health tests were met by the Sri Lankan government.'

And then to my amazement, Len said, 'We propose a crusade from Colombo to Mallakam on the Jaffna Peninsula, as a continuation of our long South Indian Crusade from Hyderabad via Guntur, Madras, Coimbatore in which thousands of students have participated.'

'Who do you plan to see at Mallakam?' the prime minister asked.

'We wish to see the vice chancellor of the university and professor Srihaskaran.'

'We will bring them to Colombo, but we cannot grant you permission to visit the Jaffna Peninsula.'

I heaved a sigh of relief. But Len was not satisfied and persisted with his request. He said, 'Our organisation has been working in India, Pakistan, Nepal and Sri Lanka for 30 years, and we have introduced livestock breeding programs which have been highly successful. We are still involved in India and Bangladesh with their continuous requests for livestock. The decision not to allow our organisation to visit Jaffna concerns me greatly as our intentions are genuine in wishing to help the local people.'

Frowns appeared on the faces of the ministers and army generals. The prime minister continued to hear Len out.

As Len continued I realised another problem. He tried, unnecessarily, to repeat what he had said but misquoted previous facts and had difficulty in remembering dates and places. He stumbled and paused as though his mind had slipped out of gear. I felt embarrassed for him and entered the conversation for the first time to correct what he had said and to confirm our interest and participation in the livestock breeding program for Sri Lanka. For the prime minister it was enough. He thanked us for our concern and cooperation and wished us well.

After the meeting, Len felt let down and said, 'It was obvious that the prime minister had grievous doubts as to my credibility and was not prepared to allow our small group to go there to assess the situation for ourselves. Atrocities had obviously taken place in the Jaffna Peninsula and the government was determined to prevent us from visiting the area.'

I sympathised with him, but secretly was glad of the prime minister's response as I had no wish to walk into conflict areas involving the Tamil Tigers.

Back in Australia I learned from Len's wife, Joan, that Len had developed early signs of Alzheimer's disease and that he would be winding down his organisation. Len had brought attention to the plight of the poor and undernourished in the Indian subcontinent through his peace walks and livestock improvement programs. I admired Len for his zeal and capacity to bring about change for the underprivileged and marginalised.

Chapter 15

Danger in the driveway,
forging links, and cAmerica

ALTHOUGH ROSTERED TO FINISH DUTY at 11 pm, Liz continued until near midnight with the updating of case notes and completing of quality assessment forms. She was always glad that I had insisted on driving her home after tiring nursing shifts. On an August night in 1992, though, Liz's life changed forever. After I had picked up Liz we detoured by the railway station to pick up Linda's car. Linda had rung earlier to say that she had forgotten about her Subaru being left at the station and could we drive it back as she was about to go to sleep.

I followed Liz home and saw her drive the Subaru up the driveway into the carport on one side of the house while I drove the Toyota into the garage on the other side. It was pitch dark save for a glimmer of light from a nearby street lamp.

Liz, standing just inside the carport and behind the boot, reached up to pull down the roll-a-door when the Subaru bumper bar nudged her calves. Liz tensed her body to hold the Subaru in place so she could bring the door down. The nudge became an overwhelming push as the car started to roll down the drive. The awful truth dawned on Liz that she must have left the car in neutral and with the handbrake off. She had no strength to escape the path of the car that was now starting to reverse down the driveway. Liz felt her feet give way as she fell forwards and under the chassis of the car. Then a terrific whack on the back of the head and Liz passed out.

I heard a piercing scream and hurried to the carport fearing that someone had attacked Liz. To my horror there was no sign of Liz or the Subaru. I looked back along the steep, 17-metre driveway. Nothing! And then I saw the shadowy form of the bonnet of the Subaru facing me from the opposite side of the 10-metre wide street. The car had come to rest with its rear wheels against the pavement's kerbing. The boot of the car had broken through the paling of a pine wooden fence that, together with the kerb, had prevented the car from plunging down a steep-sided valley of a conservation park. Liz's legs were barely visible underneath the bonnet while her body lay face down under the chassis and with her face pushed hard and upwards against the kerb.

I realised the immediate need to lift the car. Fortunately, next-door neighbours, Allan and Don, rushed out after hearing the cry. Don shouted to Allan, 'I'll phone the emergency services.'

Allan quickly appraised the situation and responded, 'Hang on. I'll go and get a jack.'

Within seconds Allan had a powerful hydraulic jack lifting the back of the Subaru clear of Liz's legs and lower body. Liz was free from one of the wheels that had caught the fleshy part of her thigh and from the muffler that had burned and pressed hard against her shoulder. By this time, Liz had regained consciousness and showed remarkable calm as she struggled to say that she could still move her legs and arms, despite searing pain in her shoulder, her legs, and from a whack on her head. I didn't know the extent of Liz's facial injuries and reached under the raised car to support her neck and head before easing her away from the body of the car, all the time keeping her body flat against the road.

'There's gravel in my mouth,' whispered Liz. I examined her mouth and what had passed as gravel were pieces of broken teeth. Apart from lost and broken teeth and some lacerations, Liz's facial features seemed to have survived intact.

The ambulance crew arrived after a long 20 minutes; they immobilised her before taking her to the local hospital in Gawler where Liz's doctor attended to her immediate medical needs before sending her on to the hospital in Elizabeth. As there were no spare hospital beds, she lay on a barouche for six hours while X-rays were taken and her wounds dressed. The X-ray showed a crushed thoracic vertebra, so the doctor arranged for Liz's transfer to the spinal injuries ward of the Royal Adelaide Hospital.

Fitted with a brace that immobilised her body from under the armpits to the thighs, Liz endured an uncomfortable two-week stay in the ward. The egg-sized haematoma from the thump on the back of her head started to shrink and the flayed skin from her legs and shoulder showed signs of healing with the numerous dressings. There was good news: the fractured thoracic vertebrae had not damaged the spinal cord.

Liz felt lucky to walk out of the ward unlike most of the other patients, including an Aboriginal who had becomd a quadriplegic as a result of diving into a shallow river from a fishing boat. Six months later, Liz continued her nursing at the aged care home.

I found out later that, after swimming pools, driveways to Australian homes are the most dangerous places. Driveways with slopes sometimes as steep as 1:5 are common with homes built on undulating or hilly terrain, a common feature of capital cities and country towns in Australia. Reversing vehicles on steep driveways often have restricted vision. Every week a child is run over in the driveway of a family home.

Forging links with Chinese researchers and an Indonesian study

While Liz was recovering from her driveway injuries, I turned my attention to looking after a delegation of three Chinese from

Xingjiang Agricultural University, Urumqi. We organised a three-week stay at Roseworthy College for the president of the University, Yin Jin-Zhang, and two research scientists in plant protection and plant breeding.

They arrived in September 1992, and, fortunately, the two younger research scientists spoke English to keep the president informed since his English was poor. They met counterpart researchers at Roseworthy College, Department of Agriculture, CSIRO, as well as innovative farmers. The door had opened for collaborative research, and the Chinese president extended an invitation for us to visit Urumqi.

Bob Barrett, a Roseworthy colleague, had suggested a few months prior to their visit that we should both go to China to explore avenues of cooperative research in our respective fields, poultry and sheep.

I had not taken Bob's suggestion seriously, but not long after, a Chinese student, Tim Sun, arrived at Roseworthy College from Urumqi in Xinjiang, a province in the far west of China, to undertake a master's study in rangeland management. We welcomed Tim and his wife Melinda and five-year-old daughter Rachel into our home.

I introduced Tim to the pastor of the Gawler Baptist Church who invited Tim to talk about the Underground Christian Church in China, of which he was a discreet member of a group of believers in Urumqi. His home, like all students and staff, was on the university campus grounds.

Tim suggested we pursue a cooperative research program involving plant and livestock production. I approached Professor Woolhouse, the director, about the idea. At first he put up a number of objections including the outlay of cost. Then, unexpectedly, he gave the green light, and it was up to me to organise an itinerary and meetings for the Chinese delegation.

My Chinese odyssey had begun. After the stay of the president and the research scientists, the president invited me to visit their university for a month. I thanked him but didn't know if that were possible given the likelihood of changes affecting the College.

Ironically, it was a former student of Roseworthy College, John Dawkins, who, having become minister for employment, education and training in the Keating Labor government, brought about the forced changes of mergers of universities and advanced colleges of education in Australia.

Professor Woolhouse piloted the changeover of Roseworthy College to become a campus of the University of Adelaide. If we were to stay on in the new merger we should have more opportunity to do research. Up to that time most of us had been constrained by full teaching loads, whereas staff at the University of Adelaide had much less contact time with students and more for research. We had to fall into line, so I decided to enrol for a PhD. I still had 15 years of working life.

I contacted Professor Graeme Hugo of the Geography Department of Adelaide University. I had read about his research on Java studying rural to urban movements on the island of Java. The Indonesian government had also sponsored movement of people from the densely populated Java to less populated islands to the east of Java. The resulting mix of ethnic people affected the livelihoods of rural and urban communities.

I thought about carrying out a similar study of movement of people on West Timor, one of the poorest islands of Eastern Indonesia with scant rainfall in drought years and reliant on one-season crops. Over time, spontaneous migration, rather than government-sponsored migration, had occurred with Indonesians from neighbouring islands settling in Kupang, the capital of East Nusa Tenggara province, or in villages.

I expressed my interest to Graeme in studying the impact of rural-to-rural movement on villagers and their livelihoods. How, for example, did the mix of rural movement and ethnicity influence resource management? Graeme advised me to contact the University of Nusa Cendana in Kupang to establish a base for my research.

I flew to Kupang on 4 November 1992, and Tomi, a tourist guide, greeted me on landing at the airport. He seemed genuine and suggested I book in at the Flobamor Hotel.

The following day I met the rector, Professor Mozes Toelehire, of the University of Nusa Cendana and the head of the centre for population studies, Cornelius Serangmo, who offered an office from which I could carry out my field study. Cornelius seemed an easygoing, likeable chap who had come from Yogyakarta to take up his position.

Later I met up with Don and Di van Cooten — keen missionaries with Don exploring ways for farmers to adopt sustainable practices and technology appropriate for small-scale cropping and livestock-raising. They offered me a place to stay on their missionary complex if I were to stay in Kupang.

I then flew to Jakarta for talks with officials of the Indonesian Institute of Sciences (LIPI), to assess whether I could undertake a village survey in West Timor.

I also travelled to Bogor by train to meet with the dean and staff of Bogor Agricultural University to discuss rural development in villages and the need to carry out further research in remote parts of Eastern Indonesia.

Finally, I attended the 2nd International five-day seminar, from 15 November 1992, on livestock services for smallholders at Hotel Santika in Yogyakarta. The seminar addressed the importance of the delivery of animal health and production services. About 300 delegates representing 38 countries participated. It was the first time for many years that South Africa had been allowed to attend a conference in Indonesia. The barrier had come down with the moves to abolish apartheid.

Robert Chambers challenged the delegates in his keynote address to acknowledge the professionalism of farmers in his farmer-first approach. 'The farmer must participate fully in decision-making affecting his livelihood,' he said. The grassroots concept appealed to me as the best way forward at the village level.

I presented a paper that Rahimullah and I had written on livestock improvement to smallholders in Dir District of the North West Frontier Province of Pakistan. I tried to convey what the Dir

District Development Project was doing to encourage farmers to move away from poppy growing.

Not long after returning home, another trip opened up.

America

Based on our combined experiences, Vic Squires and I wrote up a paper for a five-day conference on sustainable village-based development, to be held at the Colorado State University in Fort Collins from 28 September 1993. Vic could not go to the conference, so I decided to go on my own.

To attend the conference I first flew to Los Angeles (LA) with North-West Airlines from Sydney. We had one sandwich for dinner and later a chocolate ice cream which had already melted in the wrapper. No one could say we had been overfed on the flight. Occasional drinks though. Breakfast was French toast — soggy and tasteless. At least the senior stewardess was a bright soul and called us to exercise with the help of a video program on seat aerobics. Given our empty stomachs most on the plane opted out.

At Los Angeles I joined a tour which visited Marina Bay, where we strolled alongside luxury yachts on the quayside. The tour included Century City, Movie Studios, Sunset Strip, Beverley Hills, Bel Air, Rhoda Street, Sunset Boulevard, Down Town and the Chinese Theater. Hand cut footprints of famous actors and actresses went back about 50 years with the most recent being Mel Gibson. At a Chinese café nearby, a down-and-out collared me with all his personal problems and was in full flight with some of the world's problems, including the Vietnam War, when it was time to board the bus. Whew!

As we passed the mansion of a movie star, our guide said, 'One home and 127 rooms and the family are still trying to find each other.' The troubled area of LA was conveniently left out of the trip

— better for us to see mansions belonging to Tom Jones, Humphrey Bogart, Alfred Hitchcock, Marilyn Monroe than to see the poorer side of LA. Some shops were only by appointment. I would ring up later.

The next day I caught a bus to Fort Collins and stopped off at Las Vegas and Denver on the way. After leaving the hotel to book my ticket at a travel agency, a black man pounced on me. I'm up for a mugging, I thought, so I stepped back.

'Hey man, are you scared of me?' he said.

Then for non-stop palaver there was no equal; rather like Eddie Murphy in full flight. I stopped him by asking, 'How much do you want?'

'Twenty-five dollars will cover a day's expenses,' he said.

'I can manage two dollars,' I replied. Then he agreed to lower his demand to $14, then $12, by which time we had reached the travel agency. I went in and left him standing outside and by the time I came out he had disappeared without his two dollars.

I travelled by bus to Las Vegas, the first stop on my way to Denver. The glittering lights of the gambling city came into view, making the evening sky like a fairy wonderland — a heavenly site, or maybe not in reality. I stopped at the Nevada Hotel after a heart-stopping moment of losing my luggage — temporarily. It had been put on the express bus and dumped off. I walked down the boulevard while thousands of people gambled on one-armed bandits. The tax on each machine, I learned, was $500 dollars, and the money went to schools, parks and sport facilities. There were plenty of shows to choose from — sleazy, gaudy, and all eye-catching. Pick-pockets were a big problem, I was told, so I returned to the hotel without trying my luck — my Scot's heritage winning out.

The next day, on a bus tour to the Grand Canyon, Jerome, our Indian guide, kept up a humorous patter. The opulence of the stars' homes boggled the mind, and the new Hotel Luxor, costing $500 million, had been paid for by MGM before construction had started.

At the Grand Canyon, Jerome took us to within a metre of a 2,000-metre drop. 'I will whoop with you as you go down,' he said. There were no guard rails — Australians would have had a fit — so we had to be extra careful, lie down on our stomachs, and crawl to the rim and peer over. I tried not to imagine the rock edge crumbling away as I viewed a majestic, natural wonderland of coloured rock strata, with the brown Colorado River just visible at the bottom of the canyon, snaking its way into the distance.

After, the bus didn't start but one of the passengers was a mechanic and there were cheers as it chugged into life again. The local Indians provided a savoury meat dish — 'coyote and rattlesnake,' joked Jerome.

The trip to Denver took 18 hours, but having a front seat gave a panoramic view of rugged mountain country of Arizona, Nevada, Utah and then Colorado. From the desert shrubs of Las Vegas we passed into dry range country — mostly sage bush and other small shrub species. The mountain landscape in Utah showed up in multi-coloured formations — grey, yellow, brown and red. The countryside was sparsely populated with a succession of irrigated farms on valley floors.

On the bus was a mixed bag of people — Black, Mexican, southerners, and odd ones like me. The Mexicans were friendly; they were illegal immigrants, I gathered, seeking their fortune in cities like Denver. An old lady beside me had a booming voice and was emphatic about her views on her little ol' country town of Harrington. Her own home was best. She wasn't flying there. And she didn't go out in the snow.

Whenever the bus driver stopped he repeated his mantra: 'I'm stopping here for ten minutes, and if you are ain't on this bus in ten minutes you'll be left high and dry.'

As we neared Denver we passed into rich, green farmland with forests on mountainous slopes. Then there was a succession of wealthy holiday towns — Swiss type chalets, mansions, and ski lifts everywhere. A paradise if you had the means. The bus descended into Denver City with a 2 million population. We arrived at about 8 pm with the lights of the baseball stadium shining out more than anything else.

At the city centre next day, a guide in a museum described Colorado from early settler days. A tapestry depicted some of the influential figures in Denver's history that included a silver pearls lady and a pretty dancer who helped children during a smallpox plague.

I moved on to Fort Collins which nestled below the Rocky Mountains — snow-capped with a recent snowfall. I checked into Holiday Inn, the venue of the conference. A day before the conference, I rented a car, a super deluxe Dodge Intrepid, and drove to the Rocky Mountain National Park. Surprisingly, I soon adapted to the other side of the road, after first driving on the left out of the rental yard. I drove up to Ester Park, a tourist town, through gorge country. At a magnificent viewpoint of about 14,000 feet — half Mount Everest's height — my head throbbed with altitude discomfort.

The five-day conference went off well with talks, discussions and workshops. My working group elected me as their leader in our discussion group to discuss ways in which villagers at the local level could be empowered to make important decisions concerning their livelihood. The delegates were mostly from developing countries, a number of them inviting me to Argentina, Hawaii, India, Bangladesh and Pakistan.

I flew back to LA and met up with my penfriend Judy from New Zealand and her husband Howard. We breakfasted downtown overlooking Laguna Beach and then watched beach volleyball. In the evening we enjoyed a lively performance of Mexican Mariachi music.

Chapter 16

West Timor, Cambodia, and home scenes

On returning to Roseworthy Campus, the merger with Adelaide University had affected all staff. Some preferred to call it a takeover with courses like winemaking going to the Waite Campus in Adelaide; other courses were axed or radically changed. University staff started to appear on campus; some didn't know where Roseworthy was and rang up for directions. To make it worse, we were 'in the red' and the university offered us staff packages. Many felt like me, at the crossroads of their career. Which direction should we take? I had applied to become a senior lecturer but was turned down with Professor Woolhouse advising that the university had too many chiefs. That clinched it. I would resign and take the package offered. Liz, Rachel and Linda all agreed, saying 20 years was long enough at Roseworthy, and I looked stressed out from workloads.

About 20 of us were farewelled at a low-fanfare, no-frills luncheon in April 1994. The mood, unlike the usual pomp and speeches celebrating a staff member leaving, was sombre, with little acknowledgement of our contribution. Anyway, in a few words, a senior lecturer did wish us well in our new lives outside the campus.

To give focus to this new beginning and not to lose contact with my agricultural life, I decided to continue with my PhD. It was now more a research interest than a means to enhance career prospects. Fortunately, I was still enthusiastic about finding out what went on at the village level in terms of resource management as a result of movement of people. What part did the government and non-government organisations play in determining village outcomes for livelihood practices? How sustainable were the village systems? How did people of different ethnic backgrounds work together?

At 53, I still had twelve years of working life in me at least before I could officially retire. I had taken a two-month course in teaching English as a second language. Perhaps I could gain work in this area later on. Odd jobs here and there might come up, I thought wistfully. And I could always try becoming a freelance writer having completed a course in freelance journalism. Both teaching English and writing would lead me into areas I could never have dreamt of.

Roseworthy College, though, had been great as a workplace and was ideal as a measure of permanence for Rachel and Linda in their schooling and growing up. Linda had commenced studies in music at Adelaide University, while Rachel had undertaken a course in social work at the University of South Australia.

Life in the agricultural teaching and research realm had been varied, absorbing and challenging. I never wanted to fall into a humdrum routine which could have happened if I had stayed on to retirement age. Leaving in the early fifties at least gave me scope to start afresh and find new avenues.

After confirming my research study at the geography department of Adelaide University with my supervisors, Professor Graeme Hugo and Associate Professor Lesley Potter, I planned first to fly to Jakarta to begin the ground work.

I stopped over in Darwin and joined a tour to Litchfield National Park, about 100 kilometres south-west of Darwin. The park, attracting many tourists every day, featured a rich community of natural forest species and waterfalls. We swam at one of the falls, but I lost my bathing trunks while in the water. I waited until all the tourists had started walking back to the bus before retrieving my towel and shorts — no sense in scaring the tourists.

I flew to Jakarta, the capital of Indonesia, and reported to the police and Sosspol, which was Indonesia's counterpart to the Australian Intelligence Security Organisation (ASIO). I also contacted the Indonesian research organisation, LIPI.

On the flight to Kupang, I espied Java's volcanoes, terraced rice fields, forests and coastal plains. On approaching West Timor, a drier and more barren-looking landscape came into view.

A mild panic with my *bagasi*; at first, it didn't appear, but a youngster located my luggage, and I was soon on my way to Don and Di's place by taxi.

Don welcomed and introduced me to Ori, a young Indonesian lad, employed to help with household and agricultural chores. I had to complete all the formalities within a week of arriving, but I was one day overdue. Ori offered to take me to the immigration office.

An immigration official asked, 'Why are you late? How come you do research here if you don't speak Indonesian?' I explained that I could not complete the formalities sooner and I would hire an interpreter. Form followed form and most had to be photocopied across the road where others waited in line. Finally, with a letter of recommendation from the University of Nusa Cendana, Kupang, I had to notify the local police and Sosspol of my activities.

I took a *bemo* — a type of minibus — up to the university, which revealed stark, concrete buildings perched on a rocky landscape with hardly any shrubbery. The front steps of the university overlooked Kupang Bay and mountains to the east, the views softening the impact of the university's harsh surroundings.

Cornelius Serangmo introduced me to his staff, who had assembled in a sparse office setting where the sun beat through the unshaded windows. 'With no gas, power shortages and infrequent water on tap, it is difficult to run our basic sciences course,' Cornelius said.

Cornelius suggested I could examine villages along the coast from Kupang and highland villages inland from the coast. Rotinese from the nearby island of Roti, and other islanders of the province of East Nusa Tenggara, mostly from Alor, Savu and Flores, had settled in villages along the coast, mixing in with the local Timorese. The highland villages, on the other hand, were mostly inhabited by Timorese.

At the university I met Graham Eagleton, an Australian agronomist with an Australian aid agency. He talked about the value of the lontar palm in which the male trees were tapped for their prized juice. The juice could be fermented into a strong alcoholic beverage. 'The palms originate from the nearby island of Roti,' Graham said. 'The juice provides a valuable nutritional supplement in times of hardship, especially when crops have failed to grow because of the lack of rain.'

'Do the villagers carry out slash-and-burn farming?' I asked.

'Yes, they do, but we are trying to discourage it as more and more land becomes denuded of natural vegetation and infertile after years of cropping.'

After an introduction to farming practices, Graham said, 'How about joining us on our regular Saturday hash day? You'll meet up with the locals and about 40 expats.'

'Great, I look forward to it,' I said, always relishing a cross-country run.

The hash event featured a 15-kilometre run towards the hills; we set off through the scrub along a rocky, single-file path. Then we walked, as running on the coral outcrops was hazardous. We climbed to the top of a ridge to view Kupang Bay, mountain ranges and flooded rice paddies.

On the way back I fell heavily onto a sharp piece of coral which sliced into my leg. Graham's wife, Fah, patched me up with betadine and a bandage she had for just such an occasion. 'One of the hazards of running on a coral island,' Fah said.

The thorny bushes, sticking seeds and trailing undergrowth all provided minor obstacles to the 'Down Down' site with the traditional hash song: 'Here's to the gang. They are true blue, They are hashers through and through. They are hashers so they say, but they'll never get to heaven in a long, long way. Drink it down, down, down ... .'

Derek, in charge of the hash day, asked, 'Any new runners?'

And it was 'down, down, down' for us new ones.

Back in the office, Cornelius managed to obtain statistics data on several *kecamatan* (districts) close to Kupang. We selected six *desas* (villages) for the field study. Two villages, Nunsaen and Oelbiteno, would be in the highlands, and the four coastal villages would be Pariti, Oeteta, Nuataus and Poto. I would have to get letters of introduction from the *bupati* (head of the regency or *kabupaten*).

Cornelius and I then headed to Teddy's Bar to relax with an Indonesian beer in a tranquil setting overlooking Kupang Bay. He talked about his lucrative hobby of diving for lobsters and selling them for 6,000 rupees each to Teddy who then served them to his customers at 27,000 rupees.

I met up with Justin Lee, also from Adelaide University, who was doing his PhD on non-government organisations (NGOs) in Eastern Indonesia. He had contracted malaria and was staying with his father-in-law, Abia.

Justin and I went to the regional planning and development office (*bappeda*) office to examine maps of the project area, but surprisingly the maps were very poor on detail. The older Dutch maps were detailed but difficult to read and out of date. I returned to the university to discuss the project with Cornelius and requested curtains to shield my desk from the burning sun.

I hired a vehicle for a trip to Sulamu on the coast. Abia joined us and we picked up a number of villagers on the way. Sulamu looked more like a holiday beach resort; the locals followed us with interest. We met Abia's relatives who offered me my first unfermented drink from the lontar palm, which tasted like a banana milkshake. I declined the betel nut, the seed of the areca palm, valued as a mild stimulant.

Back in Kupang, Justin volunteered to act as interpreter for a visit to Camplong in the hills. A clerk provided information on the highland villages of Nunsaen and Oelbiteno, where I hoped to carry out a household questionnaire before the wet season arrived.

I needed a local interpreter, and it wasn't long after I had spread the word that I met Samson Fangidae, who had graduated from a private Catholic-run university in Kupang. Samson lived with his family in Kupang and was of Rotinese background. I hired him, and we came to an amicable agreement on his wage.

Samson smiled a lot — a bright side to many of the islanders, as I would find out. With an air of authority he engaged people with ease. We bargained for the hire of a Toyota Land Cruiser — the biggest cost item, which would turn me into an impoverished researcher. A friend of Samson's, Martin, was hired as our driver for visits to the villages.

My new office curtains arrived, and we held an official opening ceremony with Cornelius giving a short speech to his staff before drawing them across to block out the sun's rays.

During a walk to the shops or a ride in a *bemo*, the 'Hey mister' was sprinkled with 'Hello', 'How are you?', some unintelligible sounds, giggles, furtive looks, and lovely smiles from Timorese girls. The *bemos* 'bomp bomped' a mesmerising beat as they hurtled along, playing American rap songs that were vulgar, but no one seemed to mind.

The next day I ran into a *demonstrasi* with students blocking all *bemos* going to the campus. Instead of trying to run the gauntlet I caught up with Justin Lee who had just returned from Sumba. His findings about corrupt practices involving NGOs on the island had sparked fireworks, but he survived. We adjourned to Teddy's Bar where we met a world cyclist travelling around Timor.

Samson and I officially started the field work for the research study on 21 October 1994. Our vehicle survived a rough road trip to Nunsaen and Oelbiteno, the villages in the mountains. We passed by Fatulehu, a sacred mountain that stood out from the surrounding countryside. Banana trees, palms, mangos and cassava grew in the home gardens.

The *kepala desas* (village heads) seemed to welcome the survey. Samson kept up a running commentary to convince them of the value of the research.

Next we visited the coastal *desas* of Poto and Nuataus. Seven Australians fleeing from the Japanese were rescued by a submarine near this part of the coast in 1943. The *kepala desa* of Poto offered us a rice and spinach dish. Then at Nuatuas we had another rice dish, accompanied by dry fish and fatty slices of pork — no meat. The fish was off and I had difficulty in swallowing the fat. Fortunately, scrawny dogs appeared for scraps.

Later, back in Kupang, Pak Abia taught me how to say *selamat tingal* and *selemat jalan* (goodbye wishes) and other common words in *Bahasa Indonesia*. He accompanied us to Pariti and Oeteta, the two remaining coastal villages for the survey. The *kepala desas* also welcomed our study.

We returned to Oelbiteno and the village folk met us at the church. The traditional chief wore colourful garb befitting a monarch, which included a hat more appropriate for John Martin's Christmas pageant. We discussed the survey, and I spoke for a while explaining its purpose with Samson translating. We then retired to the *kepala desa's* home where his wife presented me with a handwoven scarf. I reciprocated with an Australian-designed tea towel of a koala bear, suggesting she hang it up rather than use it.

We left with a throng of villagers waving goodbye. Young ones cheered and chased our vehicle while grown-ups looked on from the entrances of dimly-lit homes.

The road had become slippery after a shower of rain, and the Toyota failed to climb a steep incline. After two hours of trying, Samson and I left Martin, our driver, and set out for the main road, 20 kilometres away. It was dusk when we reached Nunsaen so we picked up a torch and carried on for another three hours in the dark until we reached the main road, where we hitched a ride back to Kupang. I thought, surely, there must be an easier way to carry out a PhD study. Martin eventually returned with the vehicle.

The trip to the villages of Pariti and Oeteta on the coast, however, went off smoothly with the *kepala desas* receiving us warmly. At Pariti, three hundred hectares of common land had been taken over by forestry officials; it extended all the way up into the hills. A forestry nursery raised teak, mahogany and other species. The government had forced the householders on this land to relocate their homes in the mid-1970s to nearer the coast. What were the impacts? I would have to factor this unexpected movement into the study.

At Oeteta, a front yard was converted into a wedding reception area for Saturday, and we were invited for the first of two receptions. The Timorese bride and Rotinese groom shook hands with everyone. Music played, and there were speeches, formal and informal, with lots of laughter. Later after the meal, the bridegroom asked if I would like to dance with the bride. I realised that Pak Abia had been up to his tricks and had arranged it. Fortunately, we danced a western waltz without mishap, courtesy of my dance teacher when I was in Leeds.

Then, because it was a mixed ethnic marriage, we sped through the night to the second half of the reception at Camplong. Everyone again was in a festive mood and danced. Samson plucked up courage to ask a woman in red and I was given a partner.

From what Samson said, mixed marriages were becoming more common with the different ethnic groups in West Timor.

We launched the pilot questionnaire at Oelbiteno, and the *kepala desa* organised five household heads to meet with us. We ploughed through the questions in a painstaking manner. The farmers waited with patience for their turn.

A funeral intervened, and the *kepala desa* insisted that we, with about 50 others, pay tribute to the dead man. We filed past his bed; the villager looked old and at peace. Then the questionnaire restarted with Samson developing some rhythm after a while.

The *kepala desa* said that no Australian had visited Oelbiteno since the Second World War. Even the Japanese, I learned, didn't stop there — they passed through, probably chasing Australians.

Samson and I visited the traditional chief and enjoyed his banter about characters in the Bible. His memorabilia included a dagger from early Dutch times. The *kepala desa* joined us and practised his English: 'I am drinkinck tea,' he said, which had everyone laughing.

The secretary of the village handed over a list of all the names — all Dutch ones, incredibly. I chose at random 12 per cent of the village householders to interview — for Oelbiteno it was thirty-one. We completed the questionnaires just in time.

The rain descended in torrents — the rainy season had arrived, and it was time to go back to Australia. Street boys kicked and splashed a football to each other. Everyone's face lit up, as though they had never seen rain before. Along the roadside, gardens became swamped with water, which lapped against doorways and the sides of homes.

Cambodia

Before I returned to Australia, I spent a few days in Cambodia with Gordon Paterson, a former Roseworthy College student who had visited our home on a number of occasions. Gordon worked with the Mennonite Central Committee (MCC), a non-government organisation, to encourage community-based management of forests. I visited one of the integrated community development projects in Takeo Province and met with local villagers who were actively participating in the planning of agroforestry systems.

The bombing of Cambodia, a neutral country, in the 1970s, was authorised by Richard Nixon, the president of the United States, and Henry Kissinger, the national security adviser; it gave rise to Pol Pot and the genocidal Khmer Rouge.

The Pol Pot regime of the 1970s led to wholesale forest destruction. After 1979, local villagers returned from forced displacement and continued to exploit the forest resources to survive. 'Slowly,' said Gordon, 'we are trying to encourage sustainable forms of management so that the villagers will benefit from the forest products and maintain the forest in good condition for the future.'

On returning to the capital, Phnom Penh, Gordon said, 'For your education you should visit Tuol Sleng Genocide Museum. They estimate that 25 per cent of the population was murdered by Pol Pot and his Khmer Rouge regime. The prison housed thousands of Cambodians who were tortured and killed.'

'Okay,' I said with some apprehension.

We walked slowly through the prison, a former school. Only a few were there besides us, so the quietness added to a growing sense of unease as you confronted the nature and evidence of man's brutality — in one room, a rusted bed frame and the tools of torture. On a wall in another room were photos of those who had been tortured and executed. Every person who entered the prison was photographed and documented. Those who were educated or intellectuals were especially targeted. When the Vietnamese army liberated Phnom Penh in early 1979, they found only seven prisoners alive.

'The legacy of that terrible war continues today,' said Gordon, 'with so many suffering. A high percentage of the population are amputees because of landmines, and this affects entire families.'

Gordon introduced me to one of his field assistants, a landmine victim who hobbled on one leg. The MCC non-government organisation had given him a sense of purpose and dignity after what he had been through.

I left Cambodia with a heavy heart for the people who had endured such horrific times under the Khmer Rouge reign of terror.

Linda

About a month prior to Christmas 1994, Liz and I had invited a Japanese couple, Tomoya and his wife Jumko, to dinner. Tomoya, an agriculturalist in Japan, had come to Roseworthy College on study leave for a year. Linda joined us for dinner and, during a rather innocuous conversation about life in Australia, Linda piped up, 'Mum, Dad, I am going to marry Andrew.' Life in Australia went by the board as we gasped, more at Linda's timing than anything else.

Linda and Andrew had known each other for about six years from schooling days. Linda had just graduated from Adelaide University with a degree in music and had her sights on teaching music in a school. Andrew, who looked the image of Tom Cruise, even with his sheepish smile, had qualified as an electrician and had secured his first job. Although we hadn't seen a great deal of Andrew we were happy for them. Probably primed by Linda, Andrew let us know of his desire to marry her. Times had changed; gone were the days of asking permission. We bowed to modernity. Linda asked if I would be master of ceremonies for their wedding reception at a golf club venue in the city. I felt that was an honour so I accepted.

What could I say about Linda? Then I realised — Linda had not been one to say outright how she felt on some disagreeable occasions. But she did write down her feelings on scraps of paper which were pushed under a door for us to read when we stumbled upon them. I had collected all these jottings over the years, not knowing exactly what to do with them until this moment.

At the reception I read them out in my speech. Linda's jaw dropped with the words, 'Mum, Dad and Rachel is a pig.' But, she joined in with the laughter as I read out the other notes. Some were sweet and innocent, like her note to the tooth fairy requesting a special gift of money beyond what she should have expected for a tooth coming out. Over the years Linda's tastes were expensive so I turned to Andrew and asked, 'Can you afford to keep Linda?' With a bemused look on his face Andrew must have wondered what was in store.

Vintage

After Christmas I felt I must try to find my first job post-Roseworthy Campus so we could continue to survive. I applied for a job as a weighbridge operator at Orlando, Australia's largest winery in the Barossa Valley and home to the best known wine in the world, Jacob's Creek.

After two interviews, a maths test, a problem solving test, a medical examination, a physiotherapist assessment, a two-hour written test on health, safety, welfare and proper behaviour, and a one-day training course — the mind boggled — the new recruits were ready for action. 'Learn to expect the unexpected and don't panic,' our trainer said.

As well as weighing and checking the grapes for quality, a Baumé value measured the sugar and gave an indication of potential alcohol. We liaised with the crusher guys, winemakers, grower liaison officers, growers, our wine bosses and viticulturists.

Mistakes, mishaps and misadventures happened every day. And like a prime minister we patched them up as best we could. Cartnotes were checked and reprinted if necessary. The phantom load arrived on one shift. The crusher broke down and the computer system failed. And on one occasion, while using the Maselli sampler, I managed to augur the probe into a U-shape.

In the wee small hours of the morning shift, plunger coffee, pancakes and the occasional pizza kept us going. The semis rolled in throughout the day and night while the local Barossa growers came with tractors and trailers in the late afternoon. At times drivers piled up on each other, but their patience and good humour usually carried them through.

Once, in the evening shift, I worked over at Orlando's Richmond Grove Winery with Phil. He filled me in with the routine. 'Our work is stress-free here,' he said. Well, that night, the computer system broke down, the printer refused to print, hydraulic oil appeared in a load of grapes, grapes from different blocks were inadvertently mixed, the crusher packed up, and the crusher staff came to Phil for advice on all their problems. Phil's normal stress-free composure showed signs of wear.

And the finale at the end of April featured the vintage weighbridge breakup lunch on the lawns at Richmond Grove Winery, accompanied by a selection of some of Orlando's finest wines. The way everyone worked together, despite a few mishaps, impressed me.

Chapter 17

Return to West Timor

IN MAY 1995, AND AFTER another vintage as a weighbridge operator for Orlando, Liz and Rachel accompanied me back to Kupang. We spent a few days on the island of Semau where we snorkelled amongst a dazzling array of coral life.

We visited the coastal villages of Pariti and Oeteta, and the scenic spots at Soe in the highlands. Staying too long at Kupang did not appeal to Liz, however, and Rachel insisted Liz have a *real* holiday with her friend Joan in New Zealand.

We recommended the survey questionnaire at Pariti. Liz and I sat outside the *kepala desa's* house while Samson interviewed the farmers as they rolled in. We interviewed a number of women because they were widowed or because of their husband's fishing activities. Fishing featured strongly as part of their livelihood. I drank away the taste of a salty flavoured rice and fish meal. 'You like *daging ular* (snake meat)?' the *kepala desa* asked.

'No, never tried it,' I replied, fearing he might produce a live python which was known to be in the area.

Liz and Rachel returned to Adelaide while I set out for Poto and Nuataus with Samson. Everything had turned a lush green after the recent rains. I renewed acquaintance with the *kepala desas* and officials. John, a farmer in Nuataus, was keen to help with providing a list of villagers. He spoke out against the Industrial

Tree Plantation Estates, known as *Hutan Tanaman Industri* (HTI), which had taken up land once used for grazing and cropping. He requested a copy of the New Testament while the *kepala desa* wished for a camera.

Two women, Erna and Ning, from Kupang and chosen by Samson, joined us to interview the womenfolk, an essential part of the survey.

Most of the villages in the Kupang district, I found out, had land taken from them by the Industrial Tree Estates, which allowed private or government-owned enterprises to replant with teak, mahogany and other species, to feed the pulp and non-pulp industries. The loss of farming land had dealt a severe blow to the villagers. Some of them had been arrested and even tortured after demonstrating against the takeover of land that was owned by the village communities under customary law.

In the villages of Poto and Nuataus there was fear of losing land to the government forestry program if they did not use it. At one *dusun* (sub-division of a village), the HTI had taken over 75 per cent of land seven years before, and this still annoyed the villagers a lot. Each villager had been given a small block of land, but it was not enough for a livelihood. Everyone in the *dusun* had been forced to move closer to the coast.

At another *dusun*, with no skills training, Timorese had learnt how to fish and tap the lontar palm from Rotinese. Dried fish was a staple part of their diet; fish and prawns were sold to eke out their existence.

There had been no benefits from the government forestry program. Only a few had found work in Kupang. After more visits to the six villages, I returned to Adelaide and tried to make sense of the responses to the questionnaires.

Two years later, in June 1997, I revisited the six villages in West Timor to obtain more data.

I first travelled south to Katherine from Darwin by bus to spend a few days with Linda and Andrew. I felt I was back in the fast lane — they barely had time to say hello before shooting off to Mataranka to take part in a band competition. Meanwhile, I relaxed and took their dog Charlie for a walk to the hot springs on the outskirts of town. Charlie let me down. He jumped into the hot springs pool with all the bathers. The bathers came out annoyed, and Charlie stayed in. I couldn't cajole him to come out so I walked away. Charlie realised the game was over and came bounding out. Then I saw the sign saying 'No dogs allowed'. No wonder they were upset. Linda and Andrew didn't come back till Sunday morning having come second in the competition.

After lunch Andrew showed me around the RAAF base, Tindal, where he worked as an electronics engineer. Everything was turned on for the airforce personnel, no expense spared — Olympic-size swimming pool, gymnasium, irrigated playing fields, lush garden surroundings, tennis and basketball courts, restaurants and whatever you could imagine for airforce personnel. And we wonder where our taxes go.

Later, at Katherine High School, Linda showed me her music room where students practised on a wide range of musical instruments. I met the principal of the school, John, who told me that the music department had been at a low ebb but had picked up a lot with Linda's efforts. He invited us all to a travelling army band concert that evening. The army band put on a variety performance which included an impersonation of Elvis Presley.

Linda accompanied her all-girl choir the following evening in the Darwin Entertainment Centre for the Northern Territory Eistedfodd. A polished performance, I thought, and highly praised by the adjudicator.

I flew with Indonesian Merpati to Kupang and bumped into Tomi, my faithful guide, when I first came to Kupang. Once Tomi was in charge all the others took a back seat. He organised the taxi and driver to Hotel Ina Boi, situated in a peaceful location overlooking Kupang Bay — great for sunsets and for viewing the mountainous ranges to the east. Although the rainy season had just finished, it still looked like picture postcard with lush green growth and frangipanis and bougainvilleas in full bloom.

Samson was still his happy self and keen to come to Australia — probably to find a wife, if the truth be known. He had shown a lot of interest in Rachel on her visit to Kupang, but she had had other ideas.

The roads to Oelbiteno and Nunsaen were still *jalan stengah mati*; that is, you were half-dead by the time you had travelled on them. The villagers welcomed us again, and I assured them that I would complete the study soon and forward the report to them and to the Indonesian research institute, LIPI.

I collected more data on the forestry activities to include with other data on movements of people in the villages, ethnic background and agricultural practices. More people had moved to Kupang from outlying villages hoping to find employment. Many were disappointed, even after obtaining a secondary or tertiary education, because the few manufacturing industries and poor incentives for business investment did not offer sufficient opportunities.

Overall, we had interviewed 265 village household heads and most had been affected by the takeover of land for industrial forest plantations. The coastal villages of Pariti and Oeteta were more dependent on irrigated rice farming and were in a better position to cope with the loss of land. On the other hand, the coastal villages of Poto and Nuataus and the highland villages of Oelbiteno and Nunsaen were more disadvantaged, due to their greater loss of dryland farming resources on which their livelihood depended.

In all villages, I found, the takeover further exposed the vulnerability of villagers because of their isolation, the centralised approach of government, the insecurity of land tenure and the lack of political and economic empowerment.

On the positive side, the close association of ethnic groups, along with their social and cultural aspects, contributed to the relative harmony under which the Rotinese, Timorese and other ethnic groups lived in the same community. This contrasted with the ethnic tension arising with the government-sponsored programs of resettlement in which there were greater differences between ethnic groups.

In my final week, I went snorkelling with Cornelius Serangmo over the coral reef at Tenau, about 10 kilometres from Kupang. We waded out over the jagged coral, minding the starfish, sea urchins, sea cucumbers, sea worms and deadly stonefish. Fortunately, I'd taken a good look at the stonefish in the Darwin coral aquarium and reckoned I could spot them. Once out into the deeper parts I relaxed and swam above the many kinds of coral, becoming lost in another world with many colourful species of fish.

I completed the survey and spent the next year writing up the thesis — a time-consuming and daunting process. I tried to keep focused on the thesis in between weighbridge operating and other part-time jobs, including teaching English to migrants.

Towards the end of 1998, my supervisors gave me the green light for the thesis, 'Population movements, ethnicity and resource management', to go to two external examiners. And on 15 April 1999, I was admitted to the degree of Doctor of Philosophy in the Bonython Hall of the University of Adelaide by Bruce Webb, the Chancellor. It was a great moment for me to think that all the efforts had been worthwhile. I had found deep satisfaction in the nature of the study and of meeting with so many people in West Timor to appreciate their way of life and culture, and how the villagers pursued a livelihood in the face of difficult circumstances.

I decided that I should visit West Timor one more time as soon as possible to thank those involved in the research study and to hand over a copy of the thesis to the University of Nusa Cendana.

With a United Nations sponsored referendum on independence for East Timor planned at the end of August, it was a troubling time for both West and East Timorese. If independence were granted to East Timor, then violence could easily spill over into West Timor.

On 15 July 1999 I flew to Darwin, and Linda welcomed me with a tour of Darwin city, Cullen Bay, and a bite of tortillas with sour cream, avocado and chilled tomato. Charlie greeted me like a long lost friend and whimpered for a walk. Later we feasted on an Indian meal at Nirvana.

I walked along Casuarina Beach in the early hours before Linda dropped me off at the airport for the flight to Kupang. What happened to Merpati airlines? Leg space adequate, no dripping water from a supercooled ceiling, food quite tasty and service above average. And the seat was springy and supportive.

Jimmy from Flobamor Hotel greeted me at Kupang airport; Tomi was on tour.

I caught up with Don and Di and thanked them for provision of a home on the ex-missionary air base. Don had suggested I work as an agriculturalist in East Timor, but I chose not to join the missionary outreach. As events turned out I would have had to flee for safety, as Don and Di did, when foreigners, especially Australians, were targeted following independence of East Timor from Indonesia.

Don described how he was coming up with low input machines for harvesting rice — pedal power rather than petrol power. The duck farm with India Runners and Muscovies seemed a good idea with the eggs ideal for cooking and with the ducks having less disease problems than chickens.

Samson was into all sorts of new business ventures — investment in cashews, buying and selling cars and import/export. We dined at Timor Pantai on prawns, rice and vegies.

I met Cornelius, his wife and daughter, and we discussed the policies of the government, the East Timor crisis, and the wealth of fishermen from Alor who could sell shark fins at $150/kilogram.

Cornelius and I watched the 17th of the month flag hoisting ceremony to commemorate independence and to remind us of goals and ideals of *pancasila*, the five principles for Indonesia's peaceful co-existence. Speeches, prayers and various salutes all gave the ceremony a touch of dignity.

We met with the rector of the university and I thanked him for my sponsorship and facilities, and for working with Cornelius and his department. I handed over a copy of my thesis.

Then, Samson and I set out to the coastal villages for the last time to say farewell and thank all those who helped in the survey. The rice harvest was complete and the grasses were drying up, signalling the long dry season ahead.

I met John, a devout Christian, at Poto. The New Testament I had given him four years before lay on his desk, weather-beaten and dog-eared. A mango and cashew project, supported by World Bank, had commenced in my absence.

We stopped at Pariti for dinner, and Samson's uncle, Pak Fungidae, talked about study in Australia for his daughter. On the way back Samson sang at a a karaoke club.

Tomi Toh arrived at the hotel and we chatted over a beer about his latest fortunes — a slack time for tourists, though. He had become a senior guide with his English improving. He was still single and struggling to survive. I treated him to lunch at the popular Palembang restaurant.

I went up to the university with Pak Cornelius and his wife to discuss all kinds of topics with his staff including studying abroad, Rotinese and Timorese differences, and English requirements for Adelaide University. The head of agronomy, Pak San, invited me to come again next year for a lecturing spell.

On my final day, Cornelius Serangmo invited me to a lunch party for a reunion of his colleagues from Jogyakarta. Singers entertained the guests while a pianist accompanied Cornelius, the life and soul of the party, and others in singing Indonesian songs.

Before flying back to Darwin I planned a short trip to Flores. From the 20-minute plane ride, coconut palms came into view as we passed over the coast. Being a volcanic island, Flores showed an abundance of natural and planted vegetation, in contrast to the coral and less fertile island of Timor.

After landing at Maumere, I hired a taxi to Larantaka on the coast. At a holiday resort, I chatted to a Catholic priest, Heinrich Bola, who had been there for 40 years. Over dinner we talked about the government and NGOs, leprosy control, training courses for Flores people in Austria, and herbal remedies for snake bites.

I visited Ipir on the south coast where fisher folk worked from simple bamboo huts close to the sea. The fish were dried and sent to market.

I then took a bus to Moni and talked to Franco, an Italian from Turin, who appeared like an inveterate traveller with a white goatee beard and slouched hat. He and his Indonesian wife from Denpasar were quite content to rough it. The bus zigzagged through thick groves of coconut palms, bananas, bamboo and vines and shrubs.

We settled into a wayside hostel and awoke at 3 am for a trip to the Kelimutu Lakes. With 25 foreigners I travelled by truck to the summit. It was a clear moonlight night and perfect viewing for the turquoise, brown and black lakes, one of which belched forth sulphurous fumes. Sunrise revealed a surreal scene of mist-shrouded slopes.

I then caught a bus back to Maumere for the flight to Kupang and on to Darwin.

Soon after July 1999, violence erupted in East Timor with the granting of independence. Some of those, who thought of themselves as Indonesian, carried out vicious attacks on innocent villagers, aid workers and nuns. They left a trail of devastation.

I had reservations about East Timor's strive for independence. On the one hand it seemed right that people should have their independence after more that 400 years of Portuguese occupation. But the cost of more than 200,000 lives, when the Indonesian Army invaded East Timor in 1975 to claim it, was too great a sacrifice. Australia had deserted its former wartime ally; the government knew about the impending invasion but did nothing, and it knew of the senseless killing that followed with little protest to the Indonesian government.

The whole island of Timor was about a third the size of Tasmania with the country roughly split into two parts — West and East. If sense had prevailed, Timor could have remained as one country, even with the less desirable outcome of being part of Indonesia. West Timorese had adjusted to Indonesian rule with the Indonesian takeover from the Dutch after the Second World War. East Timor could have done the same.

East Timor was fortunate, I thought, to secure its independence under incoming president Habibie who yielded to a referendum offering East Timorese a choice between special autonomy and independence; they chose independence. The previous president, Suharto, resigned in 1998; if he had remained president he would have maintained his ruthless stance on East Timor to remain part of Indonesia.

Chapter 18

Family

WHILE SETTLING IN ADELAIDE FOR a period of 25 years Mum developed a wide circle of friends. She valued everyone as a person, and found great interest, in being with people. As testimony to her interest she kept notebooks containing all the bits of information collected from friends, such as birthdays, anniversaries, dates of birth of the sons and daughters, along with anything else of significance. She was a constant letter writer and kept in contact with many people in Australia and overseas.

Mum's interests were wide-ranging, including her love of bushwalking, flowers, trees and the natural beauty of Australia. She was keenly interested in the history of Australia and the Australian environment. Life for her was a learning experience. Well on her agenda was finding out about the behaviour of animals and birds.

She loved English literature, poetry and classical music. At age 61, she joined a literature class in which her teacher, Liza Morriss, was ten years older. The 'poetry circle', as Liza often called her group of girls, ran for 19 years. Mum attended the class for 16 years and then, with my father, moved to Urunga on the mid-north coast of New South Wales in 1990.

Towards the end of 1996, Mum's health started to fail with swelling in her legs and having to endure seeing out of one eye following a burst blood vessel. She rarely complained and felt helpless in looking after Dad who still suffered from severe depression. Mandy had taken time out from her nursing job to spend time with them but needed a break so I went up for about three weeks. Mum was just holding up, but her legs had swollen to twice their normal size indicating circulatory problems; and sure enough, the specialist discovered she had a faulty valve in the left ventricle. At age 83 he advised against an operation and Mum would not have one anyway.

Mum had all the grace and charm to face the unknown, never fretting, just accepting her fate with a serene faith. Mum was the spiritual soul of the family, always exuding a selfless love and concern for others. Every night in the eventide she replenished her soul with meditation, prayer and reading of uplifting books. No one who met Mum was not touched by her friendly openness. She was a treasure, a rare gem.

Mandy returned to look after Mum for the Christmas and January period, and then I relieved her at the end of January. She was moved to palliative care in Bellingen Hospital. I spent her last day on the lawn of the hospital garden. A lawn mower clattered away so that we could not hear each other — how absurd if this were Mum's last day, I thought at the time.

The following morning, 5 February 1997, I walked along the riverbank just prior to going to the hospital again. Suddenly, I became aware of a release or lightness — I knew at once Mum had gone. I looked at my watch; it was 8.10 am.

A nurse from the hospital rang and let me know that Mum had passed away before breakfast at 8.10 am. I went over to the hospital to see her for the last time and she looked at peace.

Robert Draffan, a pastor originally from Elgin, took the funeral service and later we compiled all the words most meaningful to her into a book which Rachel and Linda referred to as *Grandmother's little book*. We printed about 50 copies for her friends here in Australia and her relatives and friends in England and Scotland. But Mum's brother Tom wanted more to hand out to all the Norfolk folk. In the end we printed over 500 copies.

Her quotes included one by Cardinal John Henry Newman which meant a lot to me as I searched for meaning in life. He wrote: 'God has created me to do Him some definite service, He has committed some work to me which He has not committed to another ... he knows what he is about.'

Mum was a blessing to everyone who knew her. She always remained open to thought and ideas, never succumbing to the blind acceptance of conventional understanding or literal interpretation. She wrote:

'One just has to keep a very balanced view of everything,' she said, 'and absorb and digest all the current views. The truth lies somewhere in your understanding and your own interpretation of all that is.'

Dad found a place in a retirement home and stayed there for a few years before he needed extra care. Mandy and I visited him and walked with him along the shorefront at Redland Bay in Brisbane.

Liza Morriss, Mum's English teacher, moved into a full-time residential care facility in 1993, where Mum requested I visit her.

On visiting her for the first time I soon realised that her legs had almost given up on her and she could barely walk. But she had an indomitable spirit and lived each moment to the full. While her physical body declined even further over the next few years, her mind remained as active as ever. Never did I see her asleep like the others in the ward. Her writing and love of reading kept her alert and in tune with current events and people. On one occasion I watched Liza write the finishing touches to a poem, with ease and words flowing from her pen. Like Anne she saw the best in people, and her writing reflected this.

Liza Morriss died three days short of her 99th birthday. Mandy passed on to me more than 60 letters that Liza had written to Mum. I had kept the letters for a several years before reading them and realising they were a treasure trove. With her way of tapping into the English word, no wonder Liza had inspired students with her English teaching at Adelaide Girls High School for 27 years. She was awarded an MBE for her services to education in South Australia.

For *Two fine ladies*, I selected a number of Liza's letters, along with words of inspiration chosen by Mum. An Iranian refugee, Hani Ashtari, designed the cover and we printed off copies of the book for friends and relatives. Liza's well-written letters gave glimpses of her life as a student and lecturer at the University of Adelaide, memories of Adelaide in her youth, and as a traveller in Australia and overseas. Her letters covered the growing friendship of Liza and Anne, bonded by a passion for literature, art and the beauty of nature. They were expressive of thought, feeling and experience, and touched on notes of intimacy, discovery, reflection and inspiration, values so readily glossed over in modern forms of communication. In essence they captured the elegance of what sadly might be a dying art.

At the same residential care home we visited Liz's mum and a Scottish lady, Madge Anderson, from Elgin, my home town in Scotland. Liz's mum remained in reasonable health until she suffered a fractured hip from a fall in the middle of the night. A surgeon operated on her at the Royal Adelaide Hospital, but she fell again and undid all the operative work. Infection set in and she passed away shortly after at a nursing home in Tanunda. Her life seemed a sad one with having to part from her four children when her husband drank excessively and had become violent — attributed, Liz and I believe, to post-war trauma. She never expressed any bitterness and tried to adopt a cheerful spirit to all the changing fortunes in life. About two years prior, Liz's dad died at 79, not long after being run over by a car in Melbourne. We visited him in the intensive ward in hospital, but there was little hope. He seemed resigned to the inevitable, and we comforted him as best as we could. With all his drinking and smoking, his liver and lungs had stood up remarkably well.

Madge Anderson surprised us with her tenacity to hold on to life. She recalled intimate details of her early life and had always topped her class in Elgin Academy. Then at 97, she appeared to lose her memory and hallucinated. Nothing made sense when she talked to us. The nursing staff withdrew all medication on expert advice, and she recovered her sanity to live until one hundred and one.

Chapter 19

Tassie bound

LIZ AND I NEEDED A break and flew by Qantas to Melbourne in November 1997 to revisit our favourite honeymoon spots after 30 years together. We had a blueberry muffin for breakfast — Qantas was economising. Once on board our flight to Hobart we had another blueberry muffin for lunch. In less than an hour we flew over parched rural areas of Tasmania's midlands and central highlands.

A cool, breezy atmosphere and former Roseworthy College colleague Ian Gregory welcomed us to Tasmania at Hobart airport. Ian, a keen yachtsman, drove us across the Tasman Bridge to Constitution Dock for a meal of fish and chips. If we could have returned there in about another month's time we would have seen the yachts coming in on the final leg of the Sydney to Hobart race.

We walked along the esplanade, passing Parliament House, to Salamanca Place which boasted a terrace of Georgian warehouses dating back to the whaling days of the 1830s. They were occupied by restaurants, taverns, galleries, craft shops and offices. Nearby was Battery Point, the original seamen's quarter of the city. Wrest Point Casino stood out prominently, further around on Sandy Bay.

The rolling countryside around Ian's place at Collinsvale looked inviting with green pastures in the vales and lower foothills and with the forested slopes of nearby mountain ranges.

Sam, their 14-year old son, showed off his driving expertise with tight manoeuvres of his Holden in the backyard. We held our breath at his reckless showmanship, but Ian and his wife Sue seemed unperturbed. Later we reminisced over a warm log fire. They had adapted well to their new life in Tasmania. Ian worked as a computer programmer while Sue painted in her spare time.

The following day Ian took us to Mt Field National Park, where the first of many rainforest walks entranced us. The lower parts of the park featured forest stands, while the highlands showed off their peaks, lakes and alpine vegetation. The rainforest with its closed canopy left us awed in a tangle of mosses, ferns, vines and trees. Russell Falls appeared as a series of cascading curtains of white spray.

Our next stop was further inland at Strathgordon, an almost deserted town straddling Lake Pedder and Lake Gordon in the Southwest National Park. Strathgordon was the construction township for the development of the huge hydro-electric scheme in the Gordon/Pedder region. The two lakes together comprised the largest inland freshwater storage in Australia, about 27 times the volume of water in Sydney Harbour. On the way to the lakes we stopped for another rainforest walk, known as the Creepy Crawly Walk. It was a photographer's paradise with every step a magical scene, and a little spooky, too, with forest eyes watching from the dark recesses of dense foliage and limbs — well, it was easy to imagine that.

We tried our hand at fishing on a fast flowing river. But no luck after an hour — several nibbles though. On the way back Ian felt something cold and clammy on his neck. I looked and discovered a black leech, bloated with Ian's blood and the size of a slug. Ian preferred to wait until we arrived back at his home before removing it. By that time it had already dropped off, but Ian's neck was coated with blood; he recovered after a couple of beers.

The next day we visited Richmond, half an hour's drive from Hobart. Here was Australia's oldest freestone road bridge built in 1823 by convicts. We also called into nearby St Lukes Church, the oldest Catholic Church, built in 1836. After lunching on a local pastie we drove back to Hobart to visit ex-Gawlerites, Ruth and Brian Harrison, at Rokeby. They had recently joined their son Mike and daughter-in-law Joni, and all seemed happy with Tassie life, but needed plenty of firewood in the shed to ward off the wintry days.

We braved the windswept and stinging blasts of sleet on Mt Wellington's summit. From an enclosed viewing area we absorbed a panoramic view of Hobart and the numerous bays bordering the River Derwent.

Liz and I motored down to Huonville — famous for its apples, and we bought some from a road side stall to munch on. At Hartz Mountains National Park we braved a chilly alpine walk before retreating to a secluded picnic area bordering the Huon River.

We motored up the Tasman Highway through hilly countryside toward Bicheno on the eastern coast, and picnicked with another couple at the Three Thumbs Lookout in the Wielangata State Forest. The couple praised the cuisine and views of a Japanese restaurant 'Kabuki by the Sea' near Swansea. So we stopped there for Devonshire tea, seated by a large plate glass window that overlooked the surf pounding onto rocks below us. In the distance we sighted Oyster Bay, Maria Island, Schouten Island and Freycinet Peninsula. Maria Island had served as a former penal settlement for convicts, established in the 1820s.

We booked in at a cabin overlooking the bay at Bicheno. A stretch of silver white sands lay beyond the immediate rocky foreshore. Fishing boats nestled in a calm bay behind our cabin. A one-legged seagull wasted no time in adopting us.

The next day we explored Freycinet National Park, one of Tasmania's best known attractions on the east coast. The terrain included islands, wetlands, precipitous mountains, lagoons, beaches and rocky shores. This great diversity resulted in a wide range of habitats for flora and fauna.

We tackled a steep climb to a crest overlooking Wineglass Bay with its white sandy beach and crystal clear turquoise-coloured water. South of the bay lay lagoons and open forest, dominated by rugged granite peaks. We could have descended to the bay, but then we would have had to climb up again, and Liz's legs had started to wobble. On the way back to Bicheno we stopped at the pristine and white coastal sands of Friendly Beaches. In the shrubby area behind the sands we stumbled across an echidna. Liz saw it first and shouted, 'hedgehog'.

Liz recovered the next day from her climb while I ventured forth on a six-hour bush and beach walk in the Freycinet Park. I followed the Peninsula Track to Hazards Beach. The walk along the firm golden-yellow sand was a welcome relief after scrambling up and down rocky tracks. After another two hours of walking on the beach and through open forest I reached the white sands and tranquil waters of Cooks Beach. At this point I could return by Mt Graham and Wineglass Bay, but this would have taken at least six hours and my energy reserves had only a three-hour supply left. I returned by the same route.

From Bicheno, the following day, we drove up the coastal road to St Helens, with a stopover at Beaumaris for another beach walk — golden sandy stretches as far as the eye could see and deserted. Moving inland from St Helens we visited a cheese factory at Pyengana on the way to St Columba Falls and went on another rainforest walk.

The steep ascending Tasman Highway provided us with sweeping views of sparsely populated mountainous areas, thickly forested for the most part and with patches of green pasture on the lower slopes and valleys. We turned into the forest at one stage for a picnic lunch at an attractive grassy glade. A variety of birds serenaded us. We continued on to Launceston via Scottsdale, stopping to take in the view of the rich agricultural and forest countryside at Sidling look-out.

Just as we checked into the guesthouse, a huge pall of smoke filled the sky. A furniture store down the road had caught fire. Later we learned it had been gutted with an estimated damage bill of over one million dollars.

The following day, we set off to explore Cataract Gorge Reserve, formed by an earthquake. The Esk River followed the depression, widening and deepening the gorge over time. When William Collins first observed the area in 1804, he wrote that 'the beauty of the scene is probably not surpassed in the world'. The slow speed of the chairlift allowed us to appreciate this ancient rock gorge before sailing over the top of rhododendrons to the gorge restaurant, where five peacocks put on a showy performance to impress one uninterested and unavailable peahen.

We headed west towards Mole Creek, stopping for a picnic lunch on the tranquil, tree-lined Meander River at Deloraine. The colonial buildings reflected the area's early history, the town itself set in a gentle pastoral landscape against the more awe-inspiring range of the Western Tiers. The Mole Creek Guest House, in the foothills of the Western Bluff, placed us back in the nineteenth century with its quaint Victorian style furnishings.

From Mole Creek we explored Sheffield, known to some as the Town of Murals, nestling under an impressive Mt Roland. We wandered up and down the main street, fascinated by the murals which had been painted by professional artists to feature the district's pioneer history. Later we discovered more murals in places outside Sheffield.

Not far away lived Tina Dimmick, Linda's first piano teacher, who had inspired her in those early days. So we caught up with Tina and her husband, Terry, over lunch in their country cottage. After, we visited a honey and lavender farm where Liz went to town on her Christmas shopping list while I sampled some of the many varieties of honey — Swiss Brandy Honey a favourite.

After visiting Lake Barrington, the site for the International Rowing Course, we followed the Mersey River down to Lake Rowallan and to the start of the Walls of Jerusalem walk. We settled instead for an alpine walk to the Devil's Gullet which had been formed by glacial action accompanied by the deposition of thousands of boulders. The Devil's Gullet look-out, well-fenced in from a precipitous fall of 1,000 metres to the valley floor, provided a breathtaking view of the main peaks of the nearby national parks. These included Cradle Mountain, Mt Ossa, Mt Rufus, and, in the distance, Frenchman's Cap in the Franklin-Gordon Wild Rivers National Park.

Cradle Country Chalet offered a secluded cabin on the edge of a forest. Our hosts, David and Sue, welcomed us to Cradle Mountain country. They were newcomers, too, from Adelaide — arriving only a week before to take over the chalet business.

A visit to Lake Dove and Cradle Mountain had been the highlight of our trip to Tassie 30 years ago on our honeymoon. On the drive to the lakeside carpark we stopped by a river for refreshments. A wallaby and a cheeky currawong joined us. The currawong hovered over our sandwiches and took a swipe at one of mine. The wallaby, more polite, waited patiently for a nibble.

The first view of Lake Dove, basking under the clear blue sky, with Cradle Mountain as a backdrop, was stunning. When we walked around the lake on our honeymoon it took about six hours, following a path that almost led up to the snow-capped peak. I was lucky to get home alive with an intact marriage. This time the walk around kept pretty well to the edge of the lake and was well-boarded. On the far side of the lake we walked through the tranquil Ballroom Forest, under the shadow of Cradle Mountain. A far better proposition!

We found that the vegetation of the park varied from mixed forests with stringybark eucalypts and rainforest species of myrtle, native laurel, sassafras, pandani — a giant heath plant — and celery-top pine to open buttongrass moorlands and alpine vegetation with snow gum and yellow gum. The flowers around Lake Dove included the red Tasmanian waratah, Christmas bells, lemon-scented boronia and yellow mountain rocket.

The following day I set out on my own to follow part of the Overland Track. Liz rested at the chalet, catching up with Christmas cards. A steep climb to Marions Lookout was rewarded with spectacular views of Cradle Mountain and Lake Dove at its foot. Then I followed an easy walk across the open, exposed Central Plateau to Kitchen Hut, an emergency shelter. The final ascent of Cradle Mountain could have been tackled from there, but I chose to circle around the back of the craggy peak and return via Rodney Lake. I passed by rocky outcrops and small glacial lakes. The track then descended with some difficulty to Lake Rodney, passing Artists Pool and Flynns Tarn. Nearby was Scott Hut, a memorial to Ewan Scott who died of exposure in this region. Then one more climb to Hansons Peak before descending to Lake Dove and the carpark. After six hours of hiking my legs ached, but I felt rewarded.

We visited Wilmot, where the general store had a link with the start of the Coles family empire. We also stopped at a local winery before driving to Zeehan near the west coast. Our luck with the weather ran out. Heavy showers were broken by brief periods of sunshine as we drove through mountains and forests. We lunched at Rosebery which owed its early existence to the discovery of gold, and was named after Lord Rosebery, the prime minister of England at the time.

The history of Zeehan dated back to 1642 when Abel Tasman, from his brig, Zeehan, sighted the mountain peak which was later named Mount Zeehan. Silver and lead were discovered in the 1880s and the population rose to over 10,000 with 26 hotels, but only two remained. Tin mining also allowed the area to thrive. We visited the Pioneers Memorial Museum which held one of the finest collections of minerals in the world; in addition, the museum included a native animal display, a photographic display of town life at the turn of the century, and a display of steam locomotives and rail carriages.

From Zeehan we travelled on to Strahan with a stop at the Henty Dunes — our first taste of the west coast. Situated on Macquarie Harbour, Strahan catered to tourism, fishing, aquaculture and forestry. At one end of the wharf stood one of the few remaining Huon pine sawmills which still cut logs felled in the rainforests of western Tasmania.

We walked along the 40-kilometre long Ocean Beach to a protected mutton bird colony. We learned that all the birds were out at sea and would later return to their individual dune holes. At some stage in the year they would fly off thousands of kilometres towards the Arctic Ocean north of Japan and return several months later to the same holes.

How could any visit to Tasmania be complete without a cruise on the world-famous Gordon River? Well, not to miss out, we joined about 60 other passengers for a six-hour cruise, taking in MacQuarie Harbour, the penal settlement of Sarah Island and turbulent Hell's Gates. As we glided down the tranquil Gordon River, endless tracts of untouched rainforest, with their crystal clear reflections in the still, tea-coloured waters, opened up before us.

At Heritage Landing we disembarked to stroll on the elevated walkway, to take in the rainforest wonders, especially the 2,000 year-old Huon pine tree — possibly the oldest living tree on earth. Part of the tree had weakened and had to be brought down for safety reasons, its glorious column with moss-covered bark now resting besides its twin — dare I say, pining away.

On the return journey we passed Sarah Island where the convicts received brutal treatment. The worst ones were sent there; it acted as a base from which working parties were sent ashore to harvest the tall timbers for shipbuilding. The penal settlement existed from 1822 to 1833, and the escape route was either through Hell's Gates or through impenetrable forests and over the snowy mountains of the south-west wilderness. Most who tried to escape were either caught, drowned, or died of starvation or exposure. One who did escape was Matthew Brady who later formed the Brady gang of bushrangers.

After leaving Strahan we soon arrived at Queenstown, an anomaly of the Tasmanian landscape. Its bare hills, looking more like the lunar surface, provided a bizarre testimony to the sulphurous smelting processes of years gone by. For more than 100 years mining had been based on the huge Mt Lyell copper deposits.

We moved on to Derwent Bridge where we stopped the night in a spacious chalet overlooking a scrub belt. Not far away was Lake St Clair situated at the southern end of the Overland Track.

On the final leg to Hobart we stopped at Hamilton which had retained many of its colonial buildings. We picnicked by the River Clyde hoping to catch sight of a platypus. No luck. After, we spent an hour in a craft gallery featuring the timbered products of Huon pine, blackwood and sassafras. Some of the burls from the Huon pine trees had been hollowed out and lacquered. It was very tempting to buy one but the price put us off — most were over two hundred dollars. A small cross-section of Huon pine cost ten dollars so we settled for that.

Arriving back in Hobart at the Sandy Bay Motor Inn we had easy access to the casino and to the restaurants for our last evening meal. We settled on a smorgasbord of hot and cold salads and meat and seafood dishes. Well, the holiday was not quite over. We had been given a free casino fun-pack. But there was one problem — we didn't know how to play Tas Keno or play the pokies. No one had enlightened us. We watched for a while, and then read all the information on the front of the machine, but we were still little the wiser. Finally, we followed a couple of schoolgirls who seemed to be novices as well. And after winning some money, so we thought, we decided to press the collect button but nothing came out. Eighty-five cents did show up on the screen so we reasoned that a further 15 cents would bring the total up to one dollar. The machine crashed and one of the attendants came over and said, 'You know, we'll have to spend over $1,000 to fix this machine up.'

'You have to be joking,' I said. Tas Keno brought us $7, and a game on a machine playing poker another $3, and then we retired, still not really understanding the complexities of modern gambling.

Would you believe it, on the return Qantas flights to Melbourne and on to Adelaide we expected blueberry muffins but had a proper breakfast and lunch.

And for Liz on the occasion of our thirtieth anniversary:

Rose of Delight

A rose of delight, glistening in dew
With sails unfurled – rapturously new
A rose of passion, expansively bloomed
Textured in velvet and fully perfumed

Petals lapped over, a burgundy red
And light purple veins with dewdrops to shed
Margins rolled under with soft mitred tip
And cupped out centre like a sailing ship

A rose of my heart and softly woven
Like the love of my life, love she has given
The rose of my heart with beauty so deep
Blooms ever and ever, such treasure to keep

Chapter 20

China — Xinjiang and Gansu

China's West

As I HAD LEFT ROSEWORTHY, I didn't really expect the president of the agricultural university in Urumqi to honour his invitation. But he did with several letters to indicate his readiness to finance my trip and stay at the university.

The transfer of sovereignty of Hong Kong from the United Kingdom to the People's Republic of China was due to take place on 1 July 1997; this significant event officially marked the end of Hong Kong's 156-year colonial governance under Britain. The British Empire ceased to exist with its last crown colony.

Hong Kong people appeared happy with the conditions set out under the terms that applied to the Special Administrative Region of China. This would allow Hong Kong to go ahead much as it had done in the past. I would have to be content in seeing the celebrations on Chinese TV.

Two weeks before the takeover of Hong Kong by China I took the half-hour flight from Hong Kong to Guangzhou (former Canton) with Chinese Southern Airlines. I tried not to think about the conversation I'd had with a British businessman on Lantau Island describing some of the Chinese air crashes, especially the one where a young lad took over the controls of the plane with the same airline.

At Guangzhou I made my way to the domestic airport lugging my baggage for half a kilometre. I managed to find a seat close to the check-in counter and patiently waited for two hours amidst the scurrying of countless passengers. Finally, after checking in and saying goodbye to my luggage, I was told the plane was late — a day late!

An official collected all the would-be passengers and said we'd go to a nearby four-star hotel for the night. I couldn't even fax the people in Urumqi who would meet me at the airport — the fax number was in my checked-in luggage. Anyway, the hotel was comfortable and I tried to watch Chinese TV. Hardly anyone spoke English, even the hotel staff.

For our evening meal, the dishes kept coming and piling high. At our round table for twelve, I was the only foreigner, it seemed. I waited for a cue. A Chinese man helped himself to chopstick portions of all the dishes. Everyone else waited in silence. This man was taking the lead but no one followed him. Why? A small mound of food appeared on his plate. He must have an enormous appetite, I thought. Then he handed the plate to me. Well, his politeness overwhelmed me and I muttered thanks for his efforts.

I was a bit rusty with chopsticks but soon got into the swing again. The battered finger-like pieces turned out to be chicken feet — very crunchy.

Next day the plane to Urumqi took off on time. Every seat was taken, the rows of seats so close together that I couldn't budge once I'd settled in. Hardly any padding on the seats made things worse. Five hours later and I thought I would need a small crane to lift me out.

On the way, spectacular snow-capped peaks of the Tianshan mountains — a vast mountain range bisecting Xinjiang Province — came into view. At Urumqi airport, English lettering stood out on a building amidst all the Chinese characters: 'Grasp the opportunity, consolidate the enterprise, strive for the take off of Xinjiang Civil Aviation.' Chinglish, I thought. Quite a number of the planes were branded 'Air Volga' in large letters and with 'Xinjiang airlines rented' in smaller letters underneath. Renting planes from Russia! What next? And how safe were they?

Tim Sun, the ex-Roseworthy student, met me with a broad smile on his face. And two ladies welcomed me from Foreign Affairs — the director, Madam Zhang Feng Lan, and an interpreter, Madam Ma Yong Mei.

We drove through Urumqi along tree-lined streets bordering numerous apartment blocks, wayside shops and street markets. It was about eight o'clock in the evening and the shopping centres in the centre of town were still open and crowded. Most of the traffic consisted of buses, taxis, 4WD-vehicles, blue-coloured trucks, bicycles and a few sedan cars.

The university complex seemed like a compact jungle of 6-storey apartment blocks and various departmental buildings — home to some 6,000 students of varying ethnic backgrounds and about 500 staff. My room was dimly lit with a small bathroom, lounge and bedroom. There was hot water for about an hour a day, but I never knew which hour — they kept changing the time. Fortunately, two large thermos flasks provided hot water — enough to have a shower and a cup of Chinese tea. Tim's wife, Melinda, and their daughter, Rachel, came over, and we caught up with past events.

The president of the university, Yin Jin-Zhang, welcomed me. He had invited me to participate in a program of lectures, seminars and discussions for the animal science department. We finalised details for the next three weeks. Refreshments included slices of watermelon and honey melon along with glacial water and green tea. In the evening the president formally welcomed me at a banquet — the first of many — on the 24th floor of the Palace Hotel.

The lectures went well for the next two weeks with about 20 to 25 staff and students coming to each lecture. My interpreter, Professor Yao, translated as best as he could. Several times he found himself in a pickle and had to be helped out by staff members in the room. Once there was a long argument as to what I had said, so I waited patiently on the sidelines as time drifted by. Eventually I asked if there was a problem. 'No problems,' Professor Yao replied, and I continued. It made lecturing much easier — you had time to think what you might say next. The students and staff appeared interested in hearing about livestock production in Australia.

In the afternoons I had discussions with staff members of each department. Facilities and equipment in the laboratories were fairly basic. Occasionally, I'd see a modern piece of equipment donated by the World Bank or some other organisation. All the buildings could do with renovation and definitely a coat of paint to make them more attractive. But no money, they complained.

Everyone was attentive, especially Mei from Foreign Affairs who checked up about my meals and room. Well, I did complain about the toilet being blocked. She eventually found someone to fix the problem. In the meantime I used a communal toilet on the second floor of the guesthouse. It was vacant the first two times. Then, on the third day, a woman was cleaning it. She screamed something in Mandarin, probably saying that I'd walked into a ladies toilet and had no business being there. After that incident, I was more careful in deciphering the Chinese characters for gents and ladies.

The meals in the dining room tended to be rather oily. The pickled vegetables for breakfast swam in sunflower oil. As they always served too many dishes I didn't have any qualms about leaving the less enticing ones.

One afternoon, Tim escorted me into town for my first taste of city life — visiting a Uighur market place, small Chinese stalls, a traditional medicine shop, a modern department store and a friendship store. We also visited the geological museum displaying an overall impression of Xinjiang province with its vast reserves of natural wealth of minerals, coal and oil. Xinjiang was about the size of Queensland with the Tianshan Mountains dividing the province and forming the Tarim and Junggar basins. The water supply depended largely on mountain precipitation and the melting snow, the average annual rainfall being only 150 millimetres.

The main crops, irrigated with the melted snow, were winter and spring wheat, highland barley, rice, maize, oilseeds such as sunflowers and canola, and sorghum. There were also cash crops such as cotton, sugar beet, hemp, mulberry for silkworms, tobacco and vegetables. Fruits included apricots, pears, walnuts, figs, apples, pomegranates and melons. Xinjiang's industries were prolific with petroleum and chemicals, textile factories, coal, cement, cars, electronics and sugar refining.

The most fascinating part of the natural history museum we visited was the display of about 50 mummified bodies — all over 2,000 years old and collected from tombs in the desert regions. The dry heat had preserved them from decay. Their features had remained intact, as well as most of their woven garments that were worn at the time of burial. In another hall were artefacts and costumes of the ethnic groups living in Xinjiang.

The 20 million people in Xinjiang, with 1.6 million living in Urumqi, comprised 45 percent Uighur, 45 percent Han Chinese and 10 percent of different minority ethnic groups, including Kazak, Hui, Kirgiz, Mongol, Tajik, Tatar and Sibo. Most of the minority ethnic groups and the Uighurs were Muslims. A fundamental Uighur Moslem faction wanted independence from China. The majority of Han Chinese had migrated into the province in the previous 40 years and, according to the Uighurs, had taken over land and resources. Just before I arrived Uighur rebels had planted bombs in buses, killing nine people and injuring a large number. The alleged ringleaders were rounded up and executed.

On the first weekend the president invited me, along with the ladies from foreign affairs, to visit Heaven Lake. We passed fields of wheat, barley and yellow-flowering sunflower crops. Then we climbed into mountainous terrain for about an hour. Heaven Lake, bordered by pine trees and green pasture, lay at the foot of Mt

Bogda, with its 5,000 metre high snow-capped peak barely visible through the clouds. The crystal clear water looked inviting but was icy cold. Mei said, 'You are seeing the lake at the best time — in summer.'

Back in Urumqi, with Tim, Melinda and Rachel, at about 10 pm, we climbed a nearby hill to the university. It was still light as we watched the flickering lights appear all over the city. Then at precisely midnight the sky lit up with bursting shells of flames, stars and bright-coloured lights. The light show entranced us for more than an hour, coming from six separate firework displays in different parts of the city. Hong Kong was now part of China.

On another occasion we travelled along the ancient silk route to Turpan, one of the lowest places on earth, situated in the Gobi desert. Near Turpan we visited the valley of the grapes — 8 kilometres long and half a kilometre wide, and home to some 5,000 Uighur, Hui and Han people. The seedless, white grapes were just ripening and welcome thirst quenchers in the 40 degree heat. A complex irrigation system, known as *karez*, channelled the water from melted snow into a vast network of underground canals — I could almost stand up in them. Wells, conveniently located, allowed access to the water by pump or donkey.

A little further on, we visited the ancient city of Jiaohe, built during the 2nd century BC. Here stood Buddhist monasteries, clay-brick houses, an underground temple, stupas and ancient tombs.

For our banquet-type spread, fish appeared on a platter with the head pointed towards the distinguished guest. So the person at the head and the person facing the tail charged their glasses with a strong whisky-like drink made from sorghum, to down in 'bottoms up' or *ganbei*. A heady experience! With many dishes you could avoid the more questionable ones like sheep and chicken stomach, and chicken feet — not going to get caught again — and anything which resembled intestines.

We visited a number of small farmers who had been given loans by the state to help establish their private enterprises — chicken farms for meat production and eggs, lot-feeding farms for fattening sheep and cattle, and small dairy farms.

At Shihezi we visited an exhibition centre dedicated to Chou en Lai, the first premier of the People's Republic of China. Photos and stories depicted his life. He served under Mao Zedong to orchestrate the Communist Party's rise to power and China's foreign policy.

We also visited Kazak flock-owners in the mountain grasslands. The nomadic pastoralists took their flocks of sheep, herds of cattle and goats, and horses into the higher mountain pastures during summer time.They returned in the autumn to the lower regions where the flocks grazed and were shedded in the winter. A Kazak family invited us into their yurt for a cup of green tea boiled with sheep's milk.

The last week involved a trip every day to the rural areas. I would start the day with a walk or jog round the campus at six in the morning. Older Chinese performed Tai-Chi or just walked, and students studied in the open for exams. We returned after our visiting at about 10 pm, having had a Chinese banquet on the way. On the final night, staff of the college of animal science farewelled me with gifts and, of course, another Chinese banquet.

Well, if I thought that my Chinese adventure was at an end, that thought was soon dispelled with another door opening, when Peng Wukui, a senior agronomist with a department of agriculture in Gansu province, and a former postgraduate student at Roseworthy, invited me to go to Baiyin city, on a one-month non-paying consultancy to explore the potential for improved lamb and pasture production.

While staying at Roseworthy College, Peng had often visited us at home. His English was passable, but we found him difficult to understand because of his peculiar way of speaking with an almost closed mouth. I tried my best to cajole him into changing his ways, but he made little progress. However, we became good friends and we kept in touch

China's Northwest

At the Ansett check-in at Adelaide airport, on 20 October 1999, the surname on the ticket was 'Thomas' — the Chinese system, I explained. 'Have a good trip, Mr Thomas,' said the attendant, as she handed me the boarding pass.

At Sydney airport I bought Australian gifts, but I skipped on the small kangaroos with 'made in China' on the back. On board the Eastern China plane, service was excellent with ample cups of water and orange juice. On the 10-hour trip to Shanghai I chatted to a couple of friendly Chinese men — one returning home to Shanghai to sort out problems in his furniture business and the other visiting relations in Beijing.

On the two-hour leg to Beijing I chatted to a Canadian lawyer about world politics. He had been in China for the last 14 years assisting Chinese to migrate to Canada. At Beijing airport, a Chinese man greeted me with a large sign showing 'Mr Thomas'. I was getting used to my new name. He drove me to the Airport Garden Hotel and handed over a ticket for my onward flight to Lanzhou the next day.

The plane to Lanzhou, capital of Gansu province, was packed with most seats taken up by well-dressed businessmen. At Lanzhou, Peng Wukui, my host, welcomed me, along with his wife, Zhang Yongning and 6-year old daughter, Peng Cheng. Peng Wukui looked the same as he had six years before when he had been a student at Roseworthy Agricultural College.

We journeyed for two hours by minibus to Baiyin, catching glimpses of the barren hilly landscape in the fading light. Arriving at my hotel in Baiyin, a foreign affairs official, Mr Lu Xinglai, welcomed me. Mr Lu would have oversight of my stay in Baiyin, arrange official engagements and sightseeing, and generally keep tabs on me. He spoke English well, and, although appearing formal, had a keen sense of humour. The diphthong in his name made it difficult to pronounce but calling him Louis did the trick.

The first of many Chinese banquets followed — a lavish affair with a variety of vegetable and meat dishes followed by grilled fish and soup, all interspersed with green tea and goodwill toasts of beer or spirit — 60 per cent proof made from sorghum or barley. How was I going to survive a month of Chinese hospitality?

The following day there was a formal introductory meeting with Mrs Dai Hai Yan, the director of the Foreign Affairs Office of Baiyin municipality, Louis, Peng, and Mr Wu, the divisional chief of livestock production of the Agricultural Bureau. Mr Wu outlined details of my daily program for the next month while Mrs Dai introduced me to Baiyin municipality as part of Gansu Province.

Mrs Dai explained that Gansu province was located in the northwestern part of China in the upper reaches of the Yellow River. The province, mainly made up of mountains and plateaus, was about twice the size of Victoria. It had a continental climate with an annual rainfall of about 300 millimetres falling mostly in the warm summer months. Thanks to the Yellow River irrigation schemes, much needed additional water was available for growing crops like maize and wheat. Living in Gansu were a number of ethnic groups including the Han, Tibetan, Dongxiang, Mongol, Kazak and Manchu.

More than 3,000 years ago Gansu was the cradle of the Yellow River Valley civilisation in which the earliest forms of agriculture in China began to appear. The Silk Road made it possible for an active outlet for Chinese technology and silk to the West while bringing in gems, spices and cotton.

Baiyin, renowned as the copper city in China, was also involved in the mining of gold, lead, zinc, coal, gypsum and limestone. Overall, Baiyin municipality had become the largest nonferrous base in China, as well as an important energy base in Gansu. With so many mining plants on the outskirts of Baiyin city one wondered about the environmental and health impacts.

The area had become the key development zone for high-lift irrigation agriculture along the Yellow River; it also had several hydro-electric power stations. As well as small farm plots of mainly maize and wheat, there were larger commercial enterprises producing melons, rice, vegetables, fruits, hops, fish, lamb and poultry.

Following our first discussions on the prospects for the lamb industry and pasture improvement, we strolled through the main shopping area. On crossing the street I coped with vehicles driving on the right and numerous bicycles threading their way through the mainstream traffic of buses, trucks, vans, minibuses, taxis and the popular three-wheeler taxicabs. It was a nerve-racking experience to have a number of cyclists bearing down on you as you attempted to cross the street, but the trick was to stay calm and still, and they pedalled by on either side. Sometimes they looked back at the strange foreigner, and one cyclist nearly had an accident doing this. With only a few private vehicles there were few traffic jams.

We also sauntered through one of the main open-air markets. Several thousand shoppers milled in two laneways that stretched for about 200 metres, separating three rows of adjacent stalls. The variety of food items on display, especially the colourful array of spices and internal organs of animals, took your breath away. An animated buzz of buyers and sellers permeated the whole marketplace and this, combined with a kaleidoscope of scent and colour, conjured up an atmosphere that would rival the best of our Western supermarkets.

Peng and I visited a large department store and compared prices of TVs, washing machines, refrigerators, lounge and bedroom suites, with Australian ones — not a great deal of difference. Most were out of people's reach, according to Peng, with earnings of less than $10 a day. Still, there were some rich people in China, a lot different from the days of the Cultural Revolution. Baiyin was one of the new rising cities in the north of China with row upon row of multistorey residential buildings, department stores, high-rise commercial centres and many modern textile and industrial plants. I was surprised to see the Chinese abacus being used alongside a computerised calculator in a department store.

For the next four weeks I stayed at the Baiyin Hotel — probably one to two-star rating by Australian standards. With few other residents it promised to be a peaceful stay. Well, not quite. At nighttime the local disco, just outside the hotel, swung into action with sounds filling the cold night air. But, fortunately, they stopped at about midnight. The bed mattress was as hard as a board and kept me tossing from side to side, and after two nights I was hip-sore. But with an ensuite, and even a hand-held shower, I was over the moon. Coal-fired burners provided central heating and most times the water was warm. A TV covered about 40 channels and on occasion there was an English news, and even an odd English-speaking movie, like 'Gone With the Wind'.

I awoke to the sounds of Chinese band music coming from the loudspeakers placed strategically throughout the city. I guess if I were a Chinese patriot the music would have stirred me into action for the day ahead. Occasionally, a Western piece of music was played — notably 'Auld Lang Syne' and the love theme from the film, 'Titanic'.

On the first Saturday, Peng and I enjoyed a relaxing stroll through the Baiyin city garden area. With winter fast approaching, trees lining the footpaths were losing their golden-yellow leaves. We hired a paddleboat to go on Goldfish Lake to take in views of gardens interspersed with bends and bridges, and 10-storey apartment blocks in the background.

Later we celebrated the birthday of Peng's son, Peng Cheng, an adorable 6-year-old boy one moment and a brash tearaway the next. Another couple, Xie Junrong and his wife, Wang Shuanghai, joined us with their 7-year-old son. The tea party was more like a Chinese banquet, prepared by Peng's wife, with donkey meat, peas, lamb, noodles, almonds, cabbage, spinach, mushroom and prawns — all downed with Chinese beer, Sprite and green tea.

For the next few days we discussed the potential for lamb and pasture improvement with Mr Wu, Peng's boss, and a number of Peng's associates. I was slowly building up a picture of what was happening in the countryside, but I needed to get out into the rural areas to see for myself. That didn't happen for a week because of arrangements that had to be made and Peng's own work in the agricultural bureau.

Finally, we made our first visit to Lanzhou, the capital of Gansu province, to visit an agricultural and industrial exhibition. As we left the industrial mining works on the outskirts of Baiyin, we passed through brown loess hills with patchy, parched-looking grassy clumps and sparse perennial shrubs. The hills overlooked low-lying cultivated plots of land bordering the road. This land was mostly irrigated with water piped from the Yellow River for summer crops of maize, vegetables and rice. As we crossed over the Yellow River at Lanzhou, the industrial centre for the North-West lay before us. A haze of smog hung over the city which Peng said was quite common.

The exhibition displayed advances made in areas of mining, petrochemicals, irrigation agriculture, horticulture, aquaculture, animal and plant production. There were lots of joint projects with Holland, Germany, France, Israel, Japan, America and New Zealand, but only a small contribution from Australia. After, we visited the central square with its attractive fountains and green surrounds. We also toured one of Lanzhou's garden parks that included a zoo — but no pandas. I had to settle for the Black Siberian bear that put on a dancing performance.

In the days following, we visited the counties of Ruining, Jingyuan and Jingtai and crossed the mighty Yellow River several times by road bridge and by ferry. Flocks of sheep grazed on shrubs on rather barren hill slopes and on crop stubbles in the lower lying areas. Most of the land had been tilled but here and there donkeys pulled single ploughs, and on one occasion a camel was used.

Wood was scarce so the farmers stored the maize stover in preparation for the coming winter. Roofs of homes were covered with corncobs — maize being the main irrigated crop. Everything in the rural areas suggested a hard and simple life style — quite a contrast to the development in Baiyin. Older farmers often wore a bluish uniform with a peaked cap reminiscent of the days of Mao

Zedong, who, surprisingly, was still much revered despite those hard times.

We met Peng's father, a farmer who had survived the Mao era, whereas many thousands of peasants had died of starvation because of the poor production from rainfed crops. Now, thanks to the extensive Yellow River irrigation schemes, farmers could eke out a living on small plots of land.

The officers of the agricultural bureau looked after us well, taking us to different farming areas to meet with farmers. We climbed high up into the vast stretches of bare rugged hills to view the terraced plots for maize production — brown tilled land with a few patches of snow. I would have to come again in the summer season to see a complete transformation. Here and there, plots of dryland or irrigated lucerne offered the potential for improved lamb production. We discussed ways in which it could be used, along with the production of other legumes and feed materials such as maize silage.

We passed by an open-air sheep slaughtering place by the side of a main road. The sheep were taken out of small trailers, killed by having their throats cut on the ground, and then hung up on a horizontal bar for dressing. The carcasses were then transported to their various destinations by motorbike. Our local meat inspectors would have a fit, or, should I say, a field day.

Apart from all the agricultural expeditions, I spent three days with the Foreign Affairs Office translating a Chinese-style English or 'Chinglish' document entitled, 'Guidelines for investors in Baiyin' into proper English. Long-winded and flowery expressions would have put any investor off, but I think I managed to reduce it to essentials. Louis was more than grateful and we celebrated at one of Baiyin's most popular restaurants for lamb. All the previous formality disappeared as Louis, Peng and I partied over a sumptuous banquet.

Through another request, I took part in an English-speaking program to schools in Jinguan, organised by Mr Ma Jun, a friendly host and entertainer. I spoke to about 50 English teachers and tried to give them clues for their English teaching to students. All students had to learn English as a second language, and I could see there was a vast potential for English teachers in China. The teachers rarely had any contact with foreigners so they were rapt in anything I had to say. After three hours of talking and answering many questions, they arranged that I meet some of the students.

Well I did, but, to my amazement, with more than 500 students packed into a hall more suited to half that number. After Ma Jung introduced me, I spoke slowly in simple English about Australia and they listened intently. About 40 minutes later, they forwarded their questions on paper. What do you think of China? What do you like about China? How old are your daughters? How many wives do you have? I'm sure that was a mistake. They laughed as I replied, 'Only one.' Then, could I sing an Australian song? I knew I should I have practised one beforehand for such an occasion. Anyway, two verses of Waltzing Matilda went down well with everyone clapping.

After many more questions Ma Jun suggested it was time to visit a few classrooms. But getting away was easier said than done with about 60 students milling round afterwards asking questions and seeking autographs. In the classrooms the teachers invited me to speak to the students on Australia again, as well as answer questions. Some students showed a lot of promise in the way they spoke. Altogether, I found the experience illuminating.

A highlight of the visit was a meeting with the mayor of Baiyin City to discuss the potential for a joint Chinese-Australian project to improve lamb production. I said I would see what I could do when I returned home. A first-class banquet followed with well-prepared dishes of meat, fish and vegetables, accompanied by almond milk, green tea, spirit and wine.

One last farewell banquet was put on by Ma Jun, and then Peng and I took the train to Beijing — a 27-hour journey through Inner Mongolia. Travelling first class in a clean and comfortable room with bunks we passed by extensive plains of irrigated and dryland crop areas. Many flocks of sheep and herds of cattle and goats grazed the stubble left over from the harvest. In the drier areas of Inner Mongolia, grasslands and mountain ranges in the background stood out. The pace of development in the larger cities with multistorey apartment blocks and industrial plants was in sharp contrast to the mud-built dwellings and simple lifestyle seen in the rural areas.

The train arrived right on time in Beijing. We clambered out weary and headed for a central hotel where Peng left me. The next day we visited Tiananmen Square, Mao's Mausoleum, the Forbidden City and a Buddhist temple. I viewed Mao's embalmed body for about ten seconds; it was hard to believe he had changed the course of history for China.

The Forbidden City (Imperial Palace) kept us occupied for hours with so much of China's history on display. The entire city, covering 74 hectares, was the home of emperors from the fifteenth century until Puyi, who reigned briefly as the last Qing emperor, left it in 1924. Thousands of Chinese people and tourists visited the Palace that day; millions must go there every year.

What was it about the Forbidden City that attracted so many tourists? Conveniently located in the heart of China's capital city, Beijing, an aura of intrigue and mystery enshrouded the Forbidden City as it had done for over five centuries.

In imperial times the Forbidden City was a world within a world — a pass into another world, it seemed, with names like the Hall of Supreme Harmony, the Palace of Earthly Tranquillity, the Palace of Longevity and Peace, and the Hall of Mental Cultivation.

The Forbidden City was completed in 1420 under the orders of Emperor Yongle and was the imperial palace for emperors of the Ming (1368-1644) and Qing (1644-1911) dynasties. At each of the four corners of a 10-metre high wall enclosing the Forbidden City was a watchtower and outside the wall a moat. The buildings faced south to benefit from the principles of *yang* and to protect against the harmful *yin* effects from the north — cold winds, evil spirits and invaders.

Nearly every house in the Forbidden City was roofed with yellow glazed tiles while red, the symbolic colour of imperial power, showed up elsewhere.

From the central pavilion overlooking the entrance to the Meridian Gate the emperors presided over the departure and return of military expeditions. Also, on the 15th day of the first lunar month, the Ming emperors received high-ranking officials there for a great banquet that also provided an occasion for composing poems.

After passing through the Meridian Gate we arrived in a courtyard with five bridges stretching over an inner moat, named Golden Water River. The five bridges represented the five Confucian virtues of humanity, sense of duty, wisdom, reliability and ceremonial purity. At the end of the courtyard was the main entrance to the Outer Court, the Gate of Supreme Harmony, which led into the largest courtyard of the whole palace. Here the Hall of Supreme Harmony and two other main halls of the Outer Court stood on a three-tiered marble terrace with finely carved balustrades.

Decorated in red and gold, the Hall of Supreme Harmony was regarded as the most magnificent of all the palace buildings. In this hall the main events of the Chinese empire were celebrated, such as the enthronement of the new emperor, the emperor's marriage, and results of the imperial examinations — often accompanied to the rhythmic chimes of golden bells.

Pu Yi, the last emperor of the Qing dynasty, was enthroned in the Hall of Supreme Harmony. He was only three years old and cried out, 'I don't like it here. I want to go home.'

His father tried to comfort him by saying: 'Don't cry. It'll soon be over.' Officials took this as an omen and within three years the young emperor was overthrown. Pu Yi's life and the grandeur of the Forbidden City were portrayed in the film 'The Last Emperor'.

In more fortunate times, one of the earlier emperors of the Qing dynasty, Qianlong, ruled for almost 60 years. He presided over a military expansion of the Chinese empire that took over Mongolia and new territories in the west and parts of Russia. He commissioned a collection of all Chinese writings, was a patron of the arts, and devoted himself to painting and calligraphy.

Carvings of dragons, symbolising imperial power, featured everywhere and a special point of interest was a marble carving of dragons playing with pearls behind the Hall of Preserved Harmony. Anyone who was caught touching this holy stone would be executed. According to historical records, thousands of peasants had moved these immense stones over iced paths made by pouring water on the road in winter.

Behind the Outer Court was the Inner Court with a number of palaces and the Imperial Garden — impressive with its natural beauty and harmony. Following the principles of Taoism, the Chinese had always tried to express their appreciation of nature through landscaping art, painting and poetry.

Hugging a box full of cans of almond milk — a gift from the mayor of Baiyin — I said goodbye to Peng at Beijing's newly opened and modernised airport, rivalling any in the world. The plane was packed with Chinese again with most of the passengers stopping off at Shanghai. From there I had a relatively quiet and smooth trip to Sydney and finally home to Adelaide.

Chapter 21

Teaching English

On my return to Gawler, work became a priority. I applied for a number of jobs and found part-time work with Modbury TAFE as a mathematics support teacher to help mature students reach a level of ability that for one reason or another they had not achieved at school. Improved maths skills would improve their opportunities in the workplace.

After fulfilling one contract I took up another, but this time teaching English at an advanced level to migrants who had come to Australia to settle as permanent residents. In the first group I had 22 students from Asian, European and Middle Eastern countries. We pitched in with all kinds of activities to mimic scenarios in everyday life with plenty of conversational practice, which often ended up in laughter at a faux pas or misunderstanding. I tried to steer them through the course so that they would acquire skills in reading, writing, listening and speaking. At the end of the course we celebrated with an international flavoured lunch in which everyone brought their own creation.

I was ready to apply for another contract at TAFE, but my eye caught an article in *The Advertiser* which appealed to me. A teacher in English was needed for asylum seekers at the Woomera detention centre. I applied for the position of an education officer with Australasian Correctional Management (ACM). After an interview and police clearance, ACM gave the green light to start on 30 September 2000 for a six-week contract. I knew little about what was going on with asylum seekers at the detention centre.

On the phone the interviewer had said the salary for a six-week appointment was at the rate of $87,000 a year. I had never come close to earning that kind of money. I had misheard, but I was happy to be earning anything to recoup some of the expenses for carrying out the research in West Timor. The interviewer asked, 'Have you had any experience in dealing with people from Middle Eastern countries?'

'Yes,' I replied and described the contacts with students at Roseworthy College and with those in Algeria and Pakistan.

The purpose of mandatory detention, I gathered, was to ensure that unauthorised arrivals were confined while their identity was established, and to facilitate health, character and security assessments. It enabled the processing of their claims for refugee status and their availability for removal if they had no lawful basis for remaining in Australia.

Underpinning the policy of mandatory detention was Australia's *Migration Act 1958* that required all non-Australians who were unlawfully in mainland Australia to be detained and that, unless they were granted permission to remain in Australia, they must be removed as soon as possible.

Successive governments of Australia had maintained a mandatory detention policy with bipartisan support since its introduction in 1992.

The overall responsibility for the care of detainees at the detention centres belonged to the Department of Immigration, Multicultural and Indigenous Affairs (DIMIA). DIMIA staff decided whether or not the detainees were to receive a three-year temporary visa.

Most detainees were from Afghanistan, Iraq and Iran, with smaller numbers from Morocco, Algeria, Palestine and elsewhere. Some detainees had arrived with their families, others were single adults or unaccompanied minors. After a sea voyage from Indonesia the asylum seekers usually landed at Ashmore Reef or Christmas Island, having undertaken a journey from their homeland with the help of people smugglers. DIMIA officials then organised their ongoing flight to one of the detention centres — usually Woomera, Curtin or Port Hedland.

My flight from Adelaide to the modern township of Roxby Downs took about an hour — time enough to wonder what I would be doing for the next six weeks, away from Liz and grown-up daughters Rachel and Linda. With images of August riots at Woomera still fresh in my memory I wondered, too, what I had let myself in for.

The preceding events might have deterred me if I had thought about it rationally. I doubt it, though, as the pull of finding work and being a teacher once again would have drawn me across the threshold.

I flew to Roxby Downs which seemed like an attractive oasis set in a reddish-brown landscape of scattered shrubs and small trees. Nearby, Olympic Dam prospered with its mining of high quality copper, uranium, gold and silver.

The security officer from the Woomera detention centre, who had been assigned to pick me up, had fallen asleep. He appeared after 20 minutes and apologised for his catnap.

We travelled for nearly an hour along a sealed road to Woomera, passing sand dunes covered with mulga, native pines and hopbush, and intervening tracts of mostly saltbush, bluebush and western myall. As we neared Woomera, the water tanks, a prominent feature of Woomera, came into view, as well as the fenced perimeter of the Woomera Immigration, Reception and Processing Centre — just 3 kilometres outside the town.

An apt name for the town, 'woomera' was used by the Australian Aborigines as a throwing stick for propelling a spear. From spears to rockets, Woomera in the South Australian outback was established in 1947 as a joint project with the United Kingdom for testing experimental rockets and missiles. Later the European Launcher

Development Organisation (ELDO) designed and built the Europa series of rockets.

Len Beadell, who has been called the last of the true Australian explorers, carried out the initial surveys needed to establish the Woomera Rocket Range.

In its heyday Woomera boasted a population of more than 6,000. But in 2000, with some 350 residents, basking in its once secret past, the town provided services for the detention centre as well as passing travellers, and looked forward to a new phase of aerospace development.

When I first arrived at the Woomera detention centre on 1 October 2000 the perimeter fencing topped by razor wire unnerved me with its prison-like appearance. What had I come to? I thought.

Internal fencing separated the administration and services area from the compounds in which the detainees were housed. I observed detainees walking slowly across the dusty, gravelly area while others swept the concrete surrounds of the administrative area. A few isolated trees and a row of shrubs nearby offered little consolation to the stark layout.

Trish, the programs manager, introduced me to all her staff — Mary, Frossine, Jamal and Mehrdad, the interpreters; Christine and Margota, the education officers; Harold, the psychologist; Alley and Kylie, the welfare officers; John and Jennifer, the recreation officers; and Rosetta and Janine, the counsellors.

Christine and Margota showed me the educational facilities in the main compound — all fairly new as everything had been burnt down in the recent riot. Christine had done a mammoth job in starting all over again. With three classrooms and a library we were in business. Each classroom was twelve metres long by three-and-a-half metres wide — totally unsuitable for teaching, as we would find out later. After the tour the three of us discussed how we might run the classes. Teaching would start the next day.

After one day at the Woomera detention centre I realised I had crossed the divide to a different world, a world that was about to unfold, more than I would realise, to expose the character and plights of people fleeing from their home countries. The world inside the centre would also expose us as Australians — our weaknesses and strengths, our compassion and contempt, our attitudes, beliefs and fears.

The young children were rowdy but keen on colouring and drawing. Then I had a session with the intermediates, followed by an older group for mathematics. I tried to stay afloat and soon realised that teaching children with little understanding of the English language was going to be a challenge. In the afternoon I taught about kangaroos and wombats and read an illustrated children's storybook.

Everyday I passed through a gate into the main compound. A security officer unlocked the gate; another sitting at a desk would then record our call number — education three in my case — and the time we entered. If we were carrying our radios and not bringing in contraband we would be allowed through. Often detainees would mill around the gate waiting to pass through to the administrative and services complex for medical treatment, work duties, phoning or making contact with the interpreters and DIMIA.

I started to get into the swing of teaching mathematics and English to the young children, aged from five to seven. They were rather restless, but when they settled down to their exercises they seemed happy. Any colouring combined with the elementary mathematics was always a plus. One who appeared a little more restless than most was a bright young lad, Shayan. His parents said they had fled political persecution in Iran. With a bit of coaxing and extra attention Shayan responded and joined in with the activities. I had no idea at the time of the trauma and suffering that would befall him.

The older children were lively and needed to be challenged as well as entertained. The art and craft activities absorbed their interest. Our assistant detainee teachers explained in Farsi and Arabic what we would do and this helped a great deal; otherwise, if we had a class on our own most of the exercises had to be almost self-explanatory.

We walked through the compounds to see for ourselves the evidence of the recent riots in August: scorched earth and stones, the removal of concrete facing from the barrack-type buildings, which had been used as missiles and where the fencing had been broken through using iron bars. According to reports, there had been a peaceful protest the previous day but, during the night, security officers had gone into the dongas to round up ringleaders to take them to a compound named Sierra. One of the women must have thought she was back in her home country and had begun screaming and tearing her clothes. The whole compound had erupted and gone on a rampage. The school had been among the six buildings destroyed.

DIMIA had arranged three interviews for an applicant claiming refugee status. Where an application was refused, a person could seek a merits review of that decision from an independent tribunal — either the Refugee Review Tribunal (RRT) or the Administrative Appeals Tribunal (AAT), depending on the basis for refusal.

We decided to test the waters for adult teaching of English and life skills. After spreading the word, about 30 people crowded into one of the small teaching rooms. I spoke about the importance of learning English for living in Australia before answering questions on employment prospects, finding jobs and buying a car.

English teaching to the adult men in the main compound started in earnest the following week, with about 20 turning up after the last children's class in the afternoon. They responded well and seemed keen to learn. I could see that we should really split the class into two: one for beginners and one for the more advanced. We were limited, though, because of the priority given to children's classes.

The days started to fill up with teaching children from 9 am to 3 pm, followed by adult English classes for men. Margota and Christine taught the women. Initially the response in India compound was good with about twelve Afghani men turning up. It was very informal. They found out I had been in the North West Frontier Province of Pakistan for a year and that I knew some Pashto. When I asked for *tor chai* (black tea) they were very happy to oblige. I brought in some newspapers and we looked at the employment advertisements and talked about how we might find a job. After a week I could sense that they were becoming more depressed with the apparent hopelessness of their cases. Some of them preferred to withdraw into themselves and even sleep the day away.

As the Afghanis had been separated from the others, the English teaching was mostly to the Iraqis and Iranians in the main compound. It was more organised and we settled into a routine of conversational practice sessions interspersed with information on Australia and life skills. The lessons seemed to go well with lots of participation.

Generally speaking, about 85 per cent of detainees had experienced the devastating effects of war and were traumatised because of losing close friends or family members. As well, there were many who had experienced fear, persecution, hunger and the loss of homes and livelihood, and some had suffered imprisonment and torture. I started to discuss these tragedies and sad stories with Father Tom Atherton, a Uniting Church minister at Woomera, in the hope that he might influence DIMIA and the ACM officers to show more compassion and respect for people who had suffered so much.

Two of the most reliable detainees, who helped us with our teaching classes, were Wahib and Morteza. We needed them because of our limited ability to communicate with the children and because they represented a cultural link. They were always punctual and capable of looking after the children if required. Morteza, a 15-year-old, spoke Farsi and had come with his family from Iran, while Wahib, a 30-year-old, and a veterinarian from Iraq, spoke Arabic and had come on his own. Their cases looked bleak as the months rolled by but it did not deter them from helping. On any spare occasion I would take Morteza for English instruction and reading.

Wahib was always asking questions about Australia and eager to make a new life when the time came. It looked more like 'if' for both of them as most of their fellow passengers were succeeding in their visa applications. Just after my six-week contract, Margota let me know that Wahib had gained his temporary protection visa, while Morteza, the most deserving person I had met, if that could be taken into consideration, had failed to have his case accepted by the Refugee Review Tribunal. We both felt very sad for him and his family.

On Thursday, 19 October 2000, 40 detainees were released and the general mood lifted. But it was only temporary. In the next three weeks only small numbers were released and those left behind began to become even more despondent. Intelligence suggested there could be the makings of another riot.

The last two weeks of my six-week contract passed without a serious incident, and I left to gather my senses. Trish hoped I would be reappointed at some stage. I did not know, though, whether I would take up another contract if offered. Doing a job was one thing but becoming embroiled in a bigger scenario was something else.

One of the things I had realised, even after a short spell at Woomera, was that you see the asylum seekers from a different perspective. They were people desperate for a new start in life, for whatever reason. They were full of hope at the outset, but gradually that hope whittled away if their case officer, and later the Refugee Review Tribunal, rejected their cases. And their cases could still go to the Federal Court and the High Court. Finally, once all avenues had been exhausted, there were two options: they could obtain a passport and return home (of course, at any time a detainee could opt to do this) or, if a passport were not forthcoming, try to seek asylum in another country and meanwhile stay in the detention centre. The interpreters, welfare officers, medical staff and security officers had to cope with a whole range of problems as the detainees became more and more dysfunctional. It was little wonder that some of the staff had to be counselled as well.

I had some time out and, after a hot summer, I applied again.

'We're moving away from the six-week contracts,' said Vic, the human resources manager. 'We'd prefer the one-year contract so as to give opportunities for families to come. The longer contracts would be better for everyone.'

I thought I wouldn't survive a one-year spell at Woomera so I replied, 'How about six months?'

'Yes, we can do that. When would you like to start?'

So, with that brief phone conversation I started on 5 March 2001. It was still hot, athough I had missed the very hot summer for which I was thankful. Liz would join me in three weeks' time. She had resigned from her position as a registered nurse and was looking forward to a well-earned rest.

If I had any illusion that the next six months were going to be like the previous six-week spell it soon disappeared. In November 2000, there had been about 250 detainees with only a handful of children — making life relatively easy in terms of teaching. Intelligence reports were now indicating that this could blow out to 2,000 with the expected arrival of further boatloads.

As we approached the detention centre the four-metre high palisade fence topped by razor wire was pervasive. The razor wire had been installed after about 500 detainees had broken out of the previous fence in June 2000. The galvanised all-steel product of the palisade fence resisted cutting and ramming, I was told. And the helical coil of razor wire with needle sharp barbs at ten-centimetre intervals was superior to flat tape or barbed-wire products; heavy bolt cutters were needed to cut it.

The double-sided five-metre high palisade gate dwarfed us as we entered the Woomera detention centre. In the administrative block we met Trish, the programs leader, Sharon, a recreational officer, and Margota and Liz, the two teachers who had stayed over summer. A few people wandered around the compounds, though the board in the operations room showed the numbers of different nationalities — 45 Iraqis, 100 Iranians and 225 Afghanis.

I was eager to find out more about what was going on this time and resolved to have more contact with the detainees and staff. Everyone seemed to have their own perspective on the asylum seekers — DIMIA, the various ACM staff, the Government in Canberra, the refugee action groups, and, of course, the public. Did anyone have a full picture of what was going on? I doubted if anyone or any organisation could or would know the full story. Being at the grassroots level, though, the programs staff were in an ideal place to gain some detailed knowledge.

On Friday, Peter, our newly appointed teacher from Brisbane, and I held a teachers' meeting. We met our assistant detainee teachers, Ali, Yusef, Musa, Tawakoli, Hussain, Maher, Mehdi and Salem. All were keen to have English teaching themselves and practical aids for their classes, such as conversational exercises and tapes. They were reasonably fluent in English as well as speaking Arabic or Farsi. We agreed to have a meeting every Friday morning so as to empower the teachers, as Peter put it.

The 13 to 17-year-old girls were a lively bunch — Bunin, Shaima, Gulshan, Betul, Sarah, Sahar, Nazeerah, Maryam and Tayyaba. Shaima from Afghanistan was the most outspoken and had a good command of English. She belonged to the Hazaras, an ethnic minority who had suffered brutally at the hands of the Taliban — a fundamentalist political movement. The Taliban demanded that her father hand over their land. He refused, and so the Taliban came one night and took him away. Her mother, fearful for the fate of her five daughters and two sons, fled to her cousin's home. That family was also in fear and had decided to escape with the aid of a smuggler. Shaima's mother had urged her daughter to go with the family. They had fled Afghanistan in late 2000 and eventually boarded a fishing boat in Indonesia. After a six-day voyage, in which there had been no food and precious little water, an Australian naval vessel had intercepted them.

In the afternoon about twenty 13 to 17-year-old boys, many of them unaccompanied minors, came for social studies. They settled down well as we talked about Australia. I spoke as slowly as possible and used the more proficient English speakers to translate when necessary.

The next day I took the girls on an imaginary shopping expedition to the supermarket. We had a lot of fun as we discussed some of the items and how much we would have to pay. Then Javed, a new assistant, and I took on more than 20 exuberant youngsters, aged eight to 12, for mathematics and then the 13 to 17-year-old boys for a lesson on travelling in Australia. We covered distances and how long it would take to go by car from one place to the other, as well as fuel costs.

In the compound I met two fellows who had fled from Ghazni, Afghanistan. Their relatives had had to sell land to pay the smugglers. From Quetta in Pakistan they had flown to Singapore and on to Jakarta, where they were bundled into a van and hidden in the jungle for two weeks before being taken to the coast. There they boarded a small Indonesian vessel that took them to Ashmore Reef. This was typical of many stories that I would hear over the next few months.

We organised computer classes for the adult men and women in the afternoon, trying our best to share the computer time between Iraqis, Iranians and Afghanis. Amir, from Iran, volunteered his help organising the classes in the computer donga. With only six computers, Amir rostered everyone as fairly as possible without causing upsets among the nations.

About 25 men, mostly Iraqis, came to the advanced English class. I made the class as practical as possible by setting up a range of conversational scenarios, such as making an appointment with the doctor, booking a room for the night and answering the phone. After a practice session with the whole class they practised among themselves. We then talked about Australia and introduced various life skills, such as driving a car, shopping at the supermarket, using credit cards, paying bills, buying a mobile phone, looking for a place to rent and rental agreements, and taking care of our health.

They enjoyed themselves and for a brief moment forgot about their Woomera woes.

One of the detainees, a 27-year-old from Iran, Bijan, usually came in late and sat at the back of the classroom. His shoulder-length hair made him stand out from the rest. He listened intently without saying much, his dark eyes friendly but sorrowful. He reminded me of a drawing of Jesus I had once seen. After one of the classes he said he would like to help in our teaching program.

'What would you like to teach?' I asked.

'I would like to take classes in meditation and hypnotism,' Bijan responded.

Surprised by his response, I thought for a moment and said that would be good, but we had better call the classes 'meditation and relaxation'. I was happy to give him a go and I would arrange a classroom. I was sure Bijan was no Svengali, and it certainly could do no harm in this type of environment. I talked it over with Pam, a newly appointed recreational officer, and she agreed to keep an eye on the classes.

Two others who were keen to assist in teaching English were Shahin, and his expectant wife, Samira. Shahin was like a breath of fresh air with his slim boyish appearance belying his mature approach to life. As a 25-year-old graduate from an Iranian university he spoke fluent English; he longed for a new life in Australia. As a compassionate man who quickly appreciated the complexity of the legal situation for Iranians held in detention, he would do much for them in the future. He had held an important office before his escape from Iran. Samira's father had been involved in some anti-government political activities which caused serious problems for Shahin in his workplace. There had been no other option but to sell their house to provide money for passports, travel to Malaysia, and for the smugglers.

Accounts of the voyages from Indonesian coastal ports to Ashmore Reef in over-crowded, unseaworthy boats would make anyone think twice about putting their life in peril. Some of the teenage girls told how they had been packed like sardines on a 15-metre boat. The waves had lashed at them all night, with everyone screaming. They all thought they would be swept overboard. With no food except biscuits and a glass of oily water, and with no toilets, their arrival at Ashmore Reef seemed like entering paradise.

The sea voyage was the last leg of a harrowing sequence of events for children. Knowing their personal backgrounds and especially their traumatic experiences it would not be surprising for them to have behavioural problems. A small number of children — usually about 10 per cent — aged five to twelve, did not come to classes. Some had withdrawn from contact with other children. Some had come initially and not again. We referred those who persistently refused to come to the psychologist.

The children all worked away with an animated buzz enjoying a whole host of simple language-learning activities and basic mathematics. While the parents anguished over their future, the children seemed more resilient. They were a lively lot, participating in classroom activities as well as those arranged for them by the recreational officer. In the longer term, however, even the children would suffer because of their parents' distress.

Ali Reza, an aspiring teacher, had hopes of continuing his chosen profession in Australia. He said the government of Iran had targeted him because of his involvement in student demonstrations at Tehran University. He had fled to Australia to escape imprisonment and torture. He provided excellent assistance in November compound with the teaching, and we were able to make progress in the children's ability to speak, write and read English. Fortunately, we did this without the usual shifting and disruption of classes by DIMIA's policy of movement of detainees to other compounds with the stages of processing. Ali Reza would often look after the children until I arrived a few minutes late from the main compound. When I entered the mess the children would burst into a deafening cheer. Then we settled down and started our English hour followed by mathematics.

Two Iranians, Mosen and Mouiad, also came in to help us. They could not speak much English but were keen to teach.

Although there was an educational centre comprising a classroom for 30 adults and a computer centre allocated to both Mike and November compounds, there were no chairs, tables or whiteboards. Despite this, we decided to launch out and either use the mess or have the detainees take chairs from the mess to the classrooms. With the recent arrival of detainees there was a spurt of initial enthusiasm for learning English. The Arabic and Farsi interpreters joined in, and we coped with large classes of more than 50 at a time. As we co-opted more detainees to assist and run some of the classes, we reduced the class number of each to a more manageable group of twenty-five. On our roll book we had over 30 assistants and we were running about 25 one-hour classes a day.

One of the problems that the detainees faced was boredom. English classes for adults were provided for only one or two hours at most. Even for children it was difficult to slot in more than two hours of contact time. So the recreational and social welfare officers devised a whole range of activities, such as women's meetings, children's club after school, art and craft, board and card games, sewing, special sports events, mural painting and Aussie dingo. Aussie dingo was a huge success and run like Aussie bingo which was a gambling game — we could not have that without raising questions.

Most days after arriving home I would be emotionally drained, not from the teaching but from everything else. The clamouring of voices and disquiet of the centre were in complete contrast to the quiet, ghost-like town of Woomera. Liz, in contrast to myself, was completely relaxed and relished the change of pace in her life, not minding at all the almost surreal peacefulness of the town. At the end of the day I would force myself to jog a little into the bush surrounding the town. Often I would spot kangaroos or emus or even a few sheep grazing on the saltbush. After, I would relax a little, but the voices of unrest were still there and I would wake up in the early hours of the morning and hear them again.

Winter began with a warm sunny day and two emergencies. Shahin in November compound asked me to help write a letter to the Department of Immigration, Multicultural and Indigenous Affairs (DIMIA) requesting that they answer questions about the delays in processing. We discussed the situation and wrote a letter to the DIMIA head at Woomera, coming from Shahin as the representative of November compound:

> We have been here for two to three months and would like to ask some questions concerning the delay in our processing. We would appreciate meeting with you or your representative to discuss the situation.

There had been talk about a demonstration, but I suggested that a letter would be a better way. 'If there is no progress you could think about a peaceful demonstration,' I advised.

After two days, they gathered near the front of the compound to protest more vigorously. The chanting of about 100 detainees outside the fence went on for over two hours: 'DIMIA, DIMIA, DIMIA'. Some raised their banners with messages: 'SOS', 'Freedom' and 'Visa'. The water cannon moved closer, and the intelligence officer recorded everything on video. It was peaceful, however. Shahin had said so. Finally, the DIMIA manager appeared, accompanied by the psychologist, medical officer, interpreters and security officers. The manager agreed to restart their claims if everyone said that they were seeking protection under the refugee convention. He sent application forms for the detainees to fill in.

The intelligence officer was pessimistic about any chances for them. He confided to me: 'Why do you think DIMIA have kept quiet? They've been screened out. If they tell them this there would be a riot, just like at Curtin. There's nowhere to go. They'll have to stay here until they decide to go back.'

Jeremy Moore, a lawyer from Adelaide, had given Shahin the phrase, 'I am looking for protection and refugee status under the

Refugee Convention'. This would permit the processing of applicants to continue. About a month later, those who had filled in the forms had their second interview.

The Sabian Mandeans, followers of John the Baptist, believed there was no need to align themselves with the protesters. When they realised there was no progress with their applications, they, too, asked for help and filled in the appropriate forms. They had felt justified in their cases, because of fears of being persecuted for their religious beliefs. That was no guarantee for automatic acceptance, as many would realise later, when their case officers and the Refugee Review Tribunal would reject them.

One of the Sabian Mandean families was more fortunate. I met Masoud and his wife, Hamidh, and their 13-year-old son, Youhana, and 12-year-old daughter, Seemen. They were a delightful and charming family. Masoud explained how many of the Sabian Mandeans had been denied the usual occupations in Iran and had become goldsmiths, as Masoud had, or silversmiths. Masoud's faith was very real. He believed God had led them to Australia. On one occasion, after seeing a video on the Great Barrier Reef, he went into raptures about God's creative handiwork. His son, Youhana, volunteered to help in the classroom and lapped up the English lessons. I feared for them, like the other Sabian Mandeans, but, after a little more than two months, the good news came through about their protection visas. Masoud was overjoyed and with a broad smile on his face went around hugging everyone.

Fearing no progress, my compter organiser, Amir, and meditation teacher, Bijan, and four others ran off into the bush behind Woomera. They were free and 'felt like birds', Amir told me later. They had walked close to the road, making their way to a small town, Pimba, to the south. When a car passed they had retreated back into the bush. At Pimba, from their hiding place near a train, they had seen two police cars going back and forth through the town and, at one stage, could hear police voices. The police had set up roadblocks on the Stuart Highway and on the road to Roxby

Downs. Eventually, the police caught all of them and sent them back to Woomera.

As the months rolled by at Woomera detention centre, children would usually stop coming to classes or, if they did come, they were more withdrawn and listless and not so willing to join in classroom activities. Two sisters, Nola, 11 years and Sandra, nine, came to the class initially and then withdrew. I tried to encourage them to come but they preferred to play in the dirt surrounding the classrooms. I informed the psychologist who tried to convince them that activities in the school were a better option. They came to classes for a short time and then sadly withdrew again. Their brothers, Alan and Matthew, showed a similar response to long-term detention. They showed great potential in the classroom at first and then 'switched off'. Alan's drawings were displayed at a number of venues outside the detention centre.

Michael, an 11-year-old Iranian boy, arrived at Woomera detention centre at the end of April 2001. He was the best gift any teacher could have — bright, keen and tackling assignments with studious care. He seemed a thoughtful lad and full of promise in our November compound classroom. Later, he became stressed and dropped out altogether.

Sarah, an Afghan girl, also showed signs of detention stress. No one was really sure of her age, including Sarah herself, who thought she might be 12-years-old. At the beginning of her detention she was enthusiastic about her lessons and always turned up to class with a smile and headscarf faithfully in place. As the months passed, though, she became listless and withdrawn. There were occasions when she returned to her former bright self and came to class. Again the detention syndrome prevailed. About a year later, in the 2002 Easter protest, the outside world caught a snapshot of her emotional distress as one of the Australian protesters hugged her outside the razor wire. The Refugee Review Tribunal rejected their application for refugee status and, from then on, the whole family showed signs of depression. The children withdrew from school or only turned up sporadically. From animated and expectant faces they became lifeless in a sea of despair. Sarah's mother suffered from arthritis and couldn't function properly as a parent. Sarah herself became a parent by default. It was not uncommon, we found later, for a child to assume that role. Sarah was angry and would often say, 'Why are they doing this to my family?'

I began to realise that the danger zone for children in a detention centre environment from my observations was definitely six months. We actually witnessed their demise over time, and it was reinforced by an environment essentially devoid of compassion and counselling with a culture of despair that repeated itself across the detention centres of Australia. This emotional abuse was not picked up straight away, it was an insidious affliction, like a benign tumour, burning inside but not devouring. Children became more listless, often angry and more aggressive, sometimes assuming a parental role and responsibility for their family members. They turned to self-harming and absorbed negative elements of the detention system culture.

On 6 June I turned up to work at 6.30 am. A storm had raged all night. I arrived in a surreal setting of camp lights cascading their beams on pools of muddy water. A virtual quagmire greeted us everywhere; it was easy to spot the low-lying areas — one in front of a classroom. The boys had no qualms about wading through it and dragging red clay mud on their shoes into the classroom.

Then all the new arrivals from Mike compound overwhelmed us. Packed bodies filled each room. There were more than 50 unaccompanied minors in one room.

For the advanced classes in English I talked in simple terms about Australia and each State separately. With the help of maps of the States showing the capitals, towns, geographical features, resources and industries, they conversed in pairs, one asking questions about each State and the other replying. I would spend a little time in each lesson on new vocabulary before devoting the rest to Australian life skills. The kind of scenarios I set up included opening a bank account, making an appointment with the doctor, paying bills at the post office, buying a mobile phone, taking driving lessons, buying a second-hand car, using credit cards, travelling around on buses and trains, looking at maps and job hunting. And someone even asked to speak 'Strine', so they learned how to say the more common expressions such as 'g'day' and 'fair dinkum'. One of the idioms they learned was 'Buckley's chance'. Hamkar, one of our teachers, was always using it, especially in relation to the visa, so I cooled his ardour a bit by saying we did not use the phrase that often.

During the lunch hour I stayed back to run a computer class with some keen Afghanis in the main compound. At about midday a lot of banging and shouting came from Oscar compound. Shortly after, the noise seemed closer. I looked out of the computer room and, about 25 metres away, about 70 detainees were pushing on the five-metre gate separating the compound from the administrative area. The gate swayed back and forth, moving five to ten degrees off the vertical. It was going to go, I was sure. Then the water cannon moved in and the detainees retreated. Meanwhile, an emergency alert came over the radio and all staff beat a hasty retreat out of the compound — even the security officers had sought refuge behind the protective fences. I closed up the two computer rooms, and about ten detainees escorted me about 120 metres to another gate. I was moved by their compassion to protect me from possible harm. As we strode across the compound the security officers, interpreters and other officers looked on from outside. I thanked the detainees for their concern and unofficial escort.

As a result of the prolonged waiting, the detainees, I observed, in Oscar compound reacted adversely with cases of dysfunctional behaviour, self-mutilation and attempted suicide. Surprisingly, through all the difficulties they faced, there was a bonding and a camaraderie that were not so obvious in the other compounds.

By 24 July there were two more attempted hangings in Oscar, more slashings and one detainee attempted suicide by burning a mattress while he lay beneath it. Someone noticed the fire and raised the alarm. The detainee pulled through after treatment for his burns. His room was gutted and blackened so much on the outside that it provided a chilling reminder of what could have happened if he had not been discovered.

In my last two weeks a new lot of arrivals, mostly Iraqis had come. There were altogether about 1400 detainees; 331 were children, with 58 of them unaccompanied.

I started off new classes in India compound — normally only a temporary holding area for the newly arrived. We met in a recreational room, and Hayat, a 33-year-old Iraqi doctor, spoke English well enough to act as an interpreter.

Hayat's story was that he had begun work as an orthopaedist in a hospital when members of the Baath party approached him and said that he must give up his chosen profession and become a soldier in Saddam Hussein's forces. He had tried to protest but to no avail. The response was unequivocal: 'We don't need any more doctors. We need soldiers.' There had been no alternative for Hayat — he had to leave his six-month-old bride and flee Iraq.

About 60 men, women and children came along for an introductory session and with Hayat's help we divided the group into beginners and advanced. With great enthusiasm everyone joined in the alphabet and simple conversational exercises. Then, after one week of enjoying their company, I had to explain to them that my contract was coming to an end.

Leaving the detainees behind was hard, knowing that some had little chance of being released under the current hardline policies. It was heart-rending to say goodbye to the children. Little Azita and Sapedeh, from the eight to twelves class in November compound, clung to the fence and pleaded with me not to go. I said I had to — my time was up. I wished them the best and hoped they would be out soon. I dragged myself away from the November fence and stopped at nearby Oscar compound. Thamer, Adnan and Amir from Iraq were there. We talked for a few minutes, and I wished them the best with their cases. Both Thamer and Adnan looked skywards as they raised their arms to Allah.

Chapter 22

Post Woomera

OUTSIDE THE RAZOR WIRE PASSIONS ran high on both sides: the ardent supporters of prime minister Howard's 'We will decide who comes to this country' policy and of those who recognised the inhumane treatment given to boat arrivals, especially compared to those who arrived by air. Australia's 'unfair go' aggravated the despair and distress that many asylum seekers had faced in their countries as a result of persecution.

Many with whom I spoke asked what was going on at Woomera. Howard and immigration minister Ruddock had spoken, and the media presented what they knew, but the true picture remained a mystery because officials and those employed by Australasian Correctional Management were sworn to secrecy.

I decided to put pen to paper to unravel some of the mysteries surrounding the plight of asylum seekers and what really went on in the Woomera detention centre. In the meantime, I continued teaching English to migrants, first with a private company, and then with Modbury TAFE.

In August 2001, I watched an ABC *Four Corners* program on the case of six-year-old Shayan, who by then had been in detention for 17 months, first at Woomera, and subsequently at Villawood detention centre where he had completely withdrawn from life. I barely recognised him as the lad I had known in the classroom. At

Woomera, Shayan had seen guards beating refugees with batons during riots. And at Villawood, Shayan had not spoken since he had seen blood pouring from the wrists of a refugee who had tried to commit suicide. He refused to eat or drink and had to be taken to hospital every few days for rehydration. Aamer Sultan, a medical practitioner and a refugee from Iraq, had identified Shayan's condition as immigration-detention stress syndrome.

At about this time, the Woomera detention centre became a 'hot' topic in leading international newspapers. Journalists flew into Adelaide, eager to pick up first-hand accounts of refugee stories. One of them, Southeast Asia Bureau Chief, Richard Paddock, of the *Los Angeles Times*, rang me at work. He wanted to speak to one of the unaccompanied minors who had been released. I said that might be difficult, but we might be able to speak to someone who had just turned eighteen. Essa, a former Afghani unaccompanied minor, was happy to tell his story so we met on a balmy, late summer's evening at the Hyatt Regency Adelaide. Essa explained that he had lost family members and that he had no knowledge about whether any of his family were still alive or how to go about finding out about them. After Essa's account of his life in Afghanistan, his journey to Australia and what it had been like at the Woomera detention centre, Richard interviewed me and was keen to know anything about the Bakhtiaris — another story, he explained, for the *Los Angeles Times*.

I met with the Immigration Detention Advisory Group on 17 May 2002 to discuss ways on how to improve facilities for the new Baxter detention centre near Port Augusta. I talked about the pervasion of a culture of despair across all detention centres. Later, I wrote to Ray Funnell, chair of the Immigration Detention Advisory Group, and said:

> I believe the overriding concern is still the processing of applicants' claims in a reasonable time. In conjunction with this is the need for applicants not to be held in limbo without communication on the progress of their

cases; the need for independent legal representation; and the need to provide a category of visa, such as a humanitarian visa, that allows the asylum seeker into the community pending the outcome of their cases if not resolved within a specified time period, say three months. The special visa would also take into account those people who wish to return to their country of origin or go to a third country but cannot because of political or other reasons.

If the processing aspects can be addressed then I believe we can offer valuable services in education, counselling and other activities, especially if we allow ready access of concerned people from outside organisations such as STTARS. If we are just improving the environment for asylum seekers in Baxter then I think we will ultimately face the same problems as we have had up to now.

Ray Funnell replied on June 4, 2002:

Thank you for your letter of 20 May 2002 and for the information and the impressions passed on to the IDAG during our recent meeting in Adelaide. I hope you and the other people with whom we met that day are aware of the importance that we as a group place on such meetings.

We continue to work at improving the lot of those being held in detention and we remain hopeful and, we trust, realistically hopeful of being able to bring about some changes in policy that will result in a much better system of processing asylum seekers.

After nearly two years in the Baxter detention centre, nothing had changed for the better. The culture of despair remained. And the condition of the children had grown steadily worse. Many reports from psychiatrists, other health and social workers, and from the Human Rights and Equal Opportunity Commission confirmed this.

Michael, who showed so much potential when I first met him in the November compound of Woomera, had joined his father and mother in various dysfunctional and self-harming behaviours. 'They are like caged animals, with the father going crazy and the mother going under. They are so far gone as a family,' a social welfare worker at Baxter said.

Anita, 13-years-old, and her brother, Samuel, 16, had come from Iran at the same time as Michael. Anita and Samuel were a cheery and chirpy duo in the classroom at Woomera, always happily engaged in school activities. Anita became angry and despondent with their case being rejected at each stage of the tortuous processing system. Anita wrote to me:

> Mr Tom hello,
> Excuse me that I have nothing that I send you. I don't think I can come to see you again very soon because we have [been] rejected. I miss you and I still remember your face. Never forget you. I would like that I had something to send you good teacher but if God we can get visa and we will see [you] very soon. Thank you for your picture. Anita

Could anything be salvaged from the wreckage of families like Michael's and Anita's? The Howard government refused to intervene. I spoke to Neil Andrew, federal member for Wakefield and Speaker of the House of Representatives, and he said 'The government is stuck between a rock and a hard place. We're damned if we do and we're damned if we don't.' At least he conceded that families were suffering in detention.

The symptoms of the failure of the detention system were obvious. I knew from my experience at Woomera that, if we were going to have a system of mandatory detention, three months was the limit; otherwise, we would irreparably damage the lives of children. Mandatory detention as a system didn't work unless we were interested in making people suffer and behave abnormally. To justify using it as a method of prevention of mass boat people coming to Australia would set us up as torturers.

The new morality under John Howard as prime minister could accommodate this, as seen with the Tampa and Siev X affairs, the Pacific Solution and the war in Iraq. After espousing the evils of Saddam Hussein's regime and Robert Mugabe's Zimbabwe, and if hypocrisy were a virtue under the new morality, then the Australian government had nothing to fear. But I wondered about the Australian people. We were responsible for the people in detention. Where were we heading if we engaged in this kind of human rights abuse? Would we be so complacent if our own children were in detention?

I wrote about what had happened at the Woomera detention centre and recounted a number of refugee stories so that the reader could appreciate the reasons for seeking asylum. In July 2003, author Eva Sallis launched my book *Desert sorrow: asylum seekers at Woomera* at the South Australian Writers Centre. The atrium filled to capacity with more than 200 people attending the launch. Eva spoke passionately about the government's inhumane treatment of the refugee boatpeople.

Following the publication, and for the next two years, I had invitations to speak to organisations such as Rotary, Lions, Probus, church groups, high schools and Circle of Friends.

I spoke to the first Circle of Friends — the Belair Circle — in 2002 which had formed to discuss how to help those in detention. The concept, sparked by a councillor, was to befriend refugees, especially families in detention, who had a good chance of getting out on a bridging visa. This group had to guarantee total support for housing, food, health care, education and social activities, as the government would not grant any income or settlement entitlements.

I was amazed at this growing grassroots support in the community. People did care about the inhumane treatment stemming from the government's mandatory detention policy.

Following the birth of the Belair Circle of Friends, new Circles involving more than 30 in each group began to form throughout the metropolitan area of Adelaide. The support extended from those on bridging visas to families and single people living in detention in Adelaide without a visa, to those on temporary protection visas and to long-term detainees in the Baxter detention centre. By the beginning of 2006 the grassrooots movement had mushroomed to over 70 Circle of Friends groups throughout Australia.

Overall, there was a deep resentment from the Circles of the government's intransigent policy to lock up asylum seekers indefinitely and to treat them inhumanely. Not being able to trust the government to give the boatpeople a 'fair go' was a shocking revelation. Manipulating the truth and destroying people for political gain broke the innocence of belief in a just and compassionate leadership. Part of being involved in the Circle of Friends was personalising all of that.

I juggled the teaching of English with speaking engagements in Adelaide and country towns. Most people I met were supportive of a friendlier approach towards asylum seekers, but there were a number, too, who supported the hard line policies of the government and they made their views felt in question time.

One of the Iranian asylum seekers, Shirin, approached me through the Semaphore Circle of Friends, for help in writing her story. She had read my book *Desert sorrow* describing personal stories of detainees.

As a teacher at the Woomera detention centre, I first met Shirin's sons, Shadmehr, aged 11, and Shahrooz, aged one, in early May 2001. The family had fled Iran and was seeking protection in Australia under the United Nations Convention for Refugees.

Shirin recounted her story, through a series of interviews, of her upbringing and marriage in Iran, the voyage to Australia, her long-term stay in detention, and of her settlement into the Adelaide community. At times we had to cut short or postpone the interview as the emotional upsurge proved too much.

Shirin's anguish and torment, I found, mirrored that of others who had experienced long-term detention for more than two years. The damaging effects were ongoing. All were caught up in an unforgiving and soul-destroying system.

Boatpeople like Shirin coming to Australia without a visa could be kept in detention indefinitely. As a prisoner, convicted of a crime committed in Australia, you knew your charge and you knew your sentence. As a boat detainee you knew neither and you were unable to challenge your detention in a court. Shirin's case was difficult to resolve by the courts, but she could have remained in a community-friendly environment while the case was being processed.

In Gawler I met the president of the Gawler Refugee Association, Pat Sheahan, to talk about the possibility of sponsoring Sarwar from Afghanistan. I had first met Sarwar in early 1980; he had come to Roseworthy Agricultural College from Afghanistan to undertake a one-year's course in dryland farming.

Sarwar was a likeable character with a quiet, easy-going manner and a heart-warming smile. Behind his modest manner he was a proud Afghani believing that whatever he did in his education or profession would be for his country's benefit. He had been working at a government agricultural research station when the Russian army had invaded Afghanistan to prop up the new communist regime.

On returning to Afghanistan, Sarwar was arrested in 1981 because he had an affiliation with the West. He was tortured while in jail for a year. He then fled to Pakistan and became the provincial manager of Afghan Aid, a British non-government organisation.

Sarwar had tried to come to Australia through the appropriate channels but had been rejected as an applicant for refugee status. I made a fresh application under the special humanitarian program for Sarwar and his family to migrate to Australia. Backed by the Gawler branch of the Australian Refugee Association the application was approved. Sarwar, Soraya and their three sons arrived in Australia in mid-October 2003. The family stayed in temporary quarters on the Roseworthy Campus of the University of Adelaide. The two older sons, Seleman and Ghufran, were outgoing and engaging, while Numan appeared to have a quiet, more withdrawn nature.

Near Christmas time, the Gawler Refugee Association held its annual refugee social for which I was the master of ceremonies. As the 25th social rolled underway I welcomed the mayor of Gawler, Tony Piccolo, and Hieu van Le, the deputy chairman of the Multicultural Ethnic Affairs Commission. We recalled the time when seven families from Vietnam spent their first days in Gawler. Hieu van Le spoke passionately about those early days in the 1970s. On landing in a flimsy boat in Darwin Harbour he first heard the expression, 'G'day mate'. In 2014, he became the Governor of South Australia.

I then introduced Sarwar who danced to Afghan music while his son, Seleman, played the piano. We all sang 'Advance Australia fair' and, after tucking into ethnic dishes, we finished with a bracket of Irish and Scots songs.

We helped Sarwar and his family find a house to rent in the Para Vista suburb of Adelaide. Sarwar tried to find work in the agricultural field but was unsuccessful; instead, he became a taxi driver. After staying in Adelaide for just over two years, Sarwar and his family moved to Frankston, Victoria, where they had friends and Sarwar had employment prospects. Sarwar found work as a driving instructor.

Later, the family moved to Endeavour Hills, a suburb of Melbourne, and bought a home. All three boys studied well at school and the two eldest sons pursued university courses.

I thought the family was well on the way to settling in Australian when I heard in September 2014 of the terrible news on national radio and TV that Numan, the youngest boy, aged 18, had been fatally shot in the head after stabbing two policemen. At first I could not believe it. Another person with the same name, perhaps, but with the photo of Numan I knew it was true. The news shocked me, and I felt deeply for Sarwar and his family.

Liz and I had visited the family a few months before, and we gained the impression that they had settled in well with the local community. Sarwar proudly showed off his prolific supply of home-grown vegetables.

Following the tragic loss of Numan, I talked with Sarwar and his eldest son Seleman, and with Sarwar's close friend, Akber, to try and understand Numan's change in behaviour. He had apparently lost interest in his studies and had become more distant from his family. He appeared to be more religious, and had had contact with hardline Muslims at the Al-Furqan Centre in Melbourne.

I realised how easy it was for disaffected young Muslims like Numan to be influenced by those who held extremist views. Later, Hamkar, who had assisted me in the teaching program at Woomera, outlined how important the Afghan culture was in holding the family together. 'I believe a clash of cultures has led to a loss of identity and bonding of Numan with his family,' he said. If this were the case, Sarwar had been powerless to prevent the breakaway, and would not have forseen the terrible consequences as a result of extremist elements filling the void.

Hamkar rang Sarwar with concern for his family; they had known each other from their studies together in agriculture at Kabul University. Later, Sarwar, his wife Soraya, and their eldest son Seleman, drove over to Adelaide from Melbourne. We all met at Hamkar's home, and Sarwar shared more of the story that perplexed them. For Soraya, it was too much, and she left the room sobbing; she was convinced that Numan had not become radicalised. Hamkar's wife, Hafizah, comforted Soraya as best she could. I felt very sad for what they all must be going through.

Hamkar had been in charge of a government experimental farm in Afghanistan. During the Russian occupation, he had driven his vehicle over a land mine causing permanent damage to his right foot which forced him to walk with a pronounced limp. On his release from Woomera, Hamkar had found a place to rent in Collingwood, a suburb in Adelaide. When I visited him he was lying on the floor with the Adelaide telephone directory as a pillow. Liz and I supplied him with pillows, towels and other basic necessities for his new life in Adelaide. Hamkar hoped that his wife and six children from Peshawar in Pakistan could join him.

Yousef, another of my assistant teachers at Woomera, and from Iran, had settled into his accounting course. I reminded him that I didn't give his case much hope. It seemed to hinge on defamatory statements he had made about the government of Iran. 'You never thought I had a chance,' he laughed.

'You're right, after reading about your case details,' I said.

After refusal by his case officer in Woomera he had tried to commit suicide. His review officer granted him a three-year temporary visa, and, in September 2005, he proudly showed me his permanent visa which had been granted without a hitch. Most of the Iranians I knew at Woomera were now part-time or full-time taxi drivers.

Tricia of the Belair Circle of Friends rang to ask if I would visit a 57-year-old Iranian man who had been in detention for six years. I had never come across anyone who had spent that amount of time in detention. No wonder he was in Glenside Psychiatric Hospital. One year in detention was enough to destabilise you mentally.

At the Baxter mental quarters of Glenside, a grey-haired man with a blank, forlorn expression walked out of the small unit. I went over to him and introduced myself. Zombie-like, he moved towards a car that had just pulled up, and a nurse directed him to the front seat. That was our brief encounter. I would try again.

After he had departed, Shafiq, an intelligent and well-educated man from Bangladesh, who had been in detention for five years, appeared. After a warm welcome, his mind seemed to switch off, despite Yousef, a Palestinian, joining us and talking about their cases. We chatted for about an hour and Shafiq emerged from his cloud of melancholy to join in the conversation. Kamrun Ali, an Afghani, also joined us; he had been in detention for four-and a half years and was eager to contribute to society, but he had been one of the unfortunate Hazaras who had been refused a visa at every step of his legal avenue saga. He had just been told he had a temporary protection visa. Accompanied by Jill, a Circle of Friends person, he tried to cope with his mentally rundown state and start life again.

The day after the visit to Glenside, Khaldoon, an Iraqi I had known in Woomera, called in on a taxi trip to Gawler. We talked about the deteriorating situation in Iraq where he saw the outcome as a no-win situation, with 60,000 Iraqis being killed a year, and no sign of the Americans leaving or the insurgent attacks abating. The Sunnis, who were backed up by Saddam supporters from Syria and Saudi Arabia, were building up a bank of hatred against the Shias.

Khaldoon's Iraqi friends, Uday, Thamer and Amin, all had their permanent visas, and he would get his in three months. He would fly to the Iranian border with Iraq to meet his relatives and bride-to-be.

Hundreds of asylum seekers were on bridging visas. They had no financial support, were not allowed to work and had no access to financial benefits. The government threw them on the mercy of Australians. It was no wonder the charities were in full demand, and the Circle of Friends in Adelaide filled a vital role to support refugee families in the community.

Jean Oates, who lived in Whyalla and had regularly visited the detainees in Baxter, rang to say that Said had just been released after three years in detention and wished to speak to me. Jean passed the phone, and Said said, 'I've been released at last. I have read *Desert sorrow* and I was the one in the photo on page 163.' The photo showed a bare-chested detainee escaping through the palisade fence after it had been prised apart by an iron bar.

By October 2005, after six years of activists fighting for the rights of asylum seekers detained on the mainland of Australia and offshore centres, most had been released. Three Afghanis were left in Baxter and two on Nauru. What a legacy for future generations! Australia had fallen victim to a dehumanising culture which ignored human values and rights. We retreated into an island, fortress-like mentality rather than actively engaging the world — a world of conflict, desperate plight of homeless refugees, and of extreme poverty for 1.2

billion people. On the home front an incredible silence, interspersed with belligerent tones and denigration, dominated the political arena.

But I had to admire the Australians who did go into bat for those in detention or who were out in the community on temporary protection or bridging visas — lawyers, artists, dentists, playwrights, musicians, actors, social workers, educators, psychologists, psychiatrists, retirees and even an odd Green and Democrat politician. And not forgetting farmers, fruit growers, business people, TAFE and university people, and no doubt many others. All protested in their own way about the inhumanity of mandatory detention and its aftermath. The coming of the boatpeople was a boon for Australia — it revived compassion. A fair go surfaced for concern of the underdog, pulling our weight when needed, and riding roughshod over the paranoia of a brainwashed and misinformed community. Fear was still alive and well, though.

What would be the next battleground? Pulling out of Iraq? Poverty in the Third World? United States domination? The Palestinian question? Global Peace? Uranium mining in Australia? Our poor and homeless? Our mental health system?

Amir rang me on 1 November 2005 to say that his family had fled Iraq to Jordan and they were awaiting their visas for Australia. His sister-in-law and brother-in-law had disappeared and perhaps caught in the crossfire with the insurgents and the United States Army as they travelled from Jordan back to Iraq. Amir had found a house in Adelaide to rent and hoped his wife, son and daughter would soon join him, after six years of him not seeing them and waiting for a permanent visa. As a microbiologist, Amir seemed to have settled down and was not as anxious as when his family was in Baghdad. 'The United States are desperately trying to find a way out of Iraq but can't,' he said. 'One way to resolve the crisis would be to carve Iraq up into three separate parts for Shias, Sunnis and Kurds. This would provide a window of opportunity for the United States to withdraw, if they're sensible enough. Really, I don't see any hope for a very long time.'

I had to agree. Bush sense was non-existent. The United States and its allies had fuelled the fire for years to come. In Iraq, Muslim brotherhood ceased to exist with Shias fighting Sunnis, and other factions in the conflict. With hate rampant, Muslims lived by the sword.

I could see that one of the difficulties with Islam, in contrast to Christianity, was legalism under sharia law with rules for everything — private, family, business and government. The close binding of a Muslim to a faith which allowed little leeway for dissent or discussion led to an intractable no-win situation. Law-abiding obedience constrained rather than liberated. True freedom ignored spurious tenets of faith.

Imposing sharia law in Iran by the ruthless dictatorship of Khomeini from 1979 not only stamped out hopes of democratic reform but also led to thousands being killed or imprisoned, many in the infamous Evin prison in Tehran.

In the extreme, and in contradiction to texts from the Qu'ran advocating peace, an unthinking and literal adherence to other texts advocating violence and retribution meant justifying terrorist activities.

In October 2005, the beheadings of three innocent Christian girls by Muslim extremists in Sulawesi, Indonesia, showed the extent of misplaced zeal and the aberrant nature of fundamentalism.

On 6 December 2005 the media had a field day with the coverage of Saddam Hussein's trial and his berating of a witness for the prosecution, and of the judge. Then, as an adjunct to Saddam was Uday, a past member of Saddam's bodyguard, and roaming the streets of Adelaide. According to the premier of South Australia, Mike Rann, Uday was up to all kinds of mischief and should be locked up. Better still, sent back to Iraq. The media hounded Uday and lay in wait at his home. Shahin drove his van to Uday's place and picked up his belongings and then tore off through the streets of Adelaide bursting through red lights to escape from Adelaide's paparazzi.

In the evening, Uday's subdued voice on the phone let me know he had taken a hammering. It was a setback in a long series of obstacles since coming to Australia six years before. He had already been through the mill with DIMIA and ASIO, but had at last gained a TPV, no doubt helped by Bernice, the doctor at Woomera, who married him.

Uday had lost his father to poisoning and his life was in danger, too, from Saddam. His job had been as an administrative officer and he had nothing to do with the terror regime. His freedom on a TPV was a welcome relief from being in detention and then on a bridging visa. The three years in the community had been harrowing enough with his continual battle for refugee status. With no adverse press until this time, the media had made up for lost time by trying to associate the terror regime of Saddam to one of Saddam's relatives. Uday had to lie low and hope it would all blow over and his permanent visa would not be compromised by scaremongering tactics.

The government leaders, Bush, Howard and Blair, and others, were united against a common foe — Al Qaeida. But what if the real foe was the United States — the neocons who represented the modern crusaders? Their crusades had taken them into Iraq and Afghanistan to bulldoze people into submission and put down the 'forces of evil'. The American goal of liberalisation and, perhaps Americanisation, justified the violent invasion and the loss of hundreds of thousands of innocents.

I called in to see Audrey who was a member of the Circle of Friends that looked after Shirin. I wanted to hear more about Shirin's story, but Audrey found it too hard to contain her emotions. She choked back tears as she recounted how she first met Shirin at Baxter detention centre. It was a shocking realisation of how Shirin and her two sons had been trapped with her role as sole parent squashed with the severity of her confinement. Shirin's mental torture had prevented her from being a parent for Shadmehr and Shahrooz. It was too much for Audrey to reconnect with this outrage. She wiped the tears from her eyes as she bravely continued with the story of Shirin's eventual release after nearly three years and of the ongoing trauma of the effect of the detention experience as she tried to cope in an Australian community.

I realised that the story repeated itself with other unfortunates. Parents with children who stayed in detention for more than three months went downhill in coping and mental stability. For single men, six months was the limit, but for parents with children the time was much shorter.

Through the Australian Refugee Association (ARA) I assisted those refugees seeking employment and checked up on people who had been in detention, especially long-term stayers.

I met up with an Iranian man who had been in detention for six years. He was leaning over the front wall of his rental place when I went along to see him. His face spelled gloom and his movements were slow and awkward; he was in no condition mentally or physically to work. I could not believe that he had spent nearly six years in detention. Hafez, the employment officer at ARA, had assigned him to Pinnaroo for a packing job. The country town was far too isolated, the lifting work too much, and his pay would barely cover his rental expenses. But, most importantly, he needed to receive proper care and treatment for his traumatised state. I let Hafez know that his chances of holding down a job were slim, but he was still keen to give him a go.

Yousef, the Iranian who had helped in teaching at Woomera detention centre, joined me in visiting Mashallah. What a story! Mashallah had gone through hell and would have a long way to go to recover his former self. On his last visit to hospital from detention he had been without food for 72 days. On an intravenous drip he was close to death, the closest of all detainees.

Allan, a friend, introduced me to Corneliau Rau, an Australian resident, who had spent four months in the management unit of Baxter — locked away for 18 hours a day without any proper treatment. According to other detainees, she screamed, often removed her clothes, and showed signs of being mentally disturbed, extremely anxious and tearful. The fact that no one had alerted the authorities to the severity of Cornelia Rau's state indicated that this type of treatment and behavioural response was in the realms of possibility for boatpeople at Baxter and a sad reflection on DIMIA's responsibility for proper treatment of detainees. Fortunately, Cornelia's parents identified her after they had read a newspaper article referring to a sick German in detention.

'They liked the power thing,' Corneliau said. 'I didn't do anything in Baxter, yet they locked me up in those cells most of the time. No one questioned my background, my health status or even treated me properly if I did have serious health problems. But I didn't. I feel really bad about the detainees having to go through what I went through.'

Shirin, like Cornelia Rau, had spent time in the 'management unit' — an isolated cell; in fact, the most of any woman who had come by boat. Coming by boat without a visa was Shirin's liability — unfair treatment was justifiable. Being an Australian citizen was Cornelia's asset — it shouldn't have happened to her. The treatment of Cornelia by DIMIA galvanised politicians into action for the first time in five years. Corneliau Rau ultimately received $2.6 million compensation for her wrongful detention. Shirin was unlikely to receive any compensation.

While visiting a number of people on temporary protection and bridging visas I continued to work part-time with Hafez at the Australian Refugee Association. Many who came to us at that time were refugees from Sudan who had spent a number of years in refugee camps in Kenya, Ethiopia or other nearby countries. Most were keen for temporary work so they could earn enough money to bring their relatives out to Australia. I tried to encourage them to look beyond a temporary job and make sure they took full advantage of the English programs, and to think about a course with TAFE or university. For short-term work, however, they needed to drive a car as most unskilled jobs required an early start, but often there was no suitable bus service.

Many of the Sudanese stories were heart-wrenching with long and hair-raising journeys to escape from their attackers to safety in a bordering country. George approached me for help with the personal account he had written of his escape from Sudan's terror. I visited him at his rented home in Glynde and met his beautiful wife and three children. He grew up in a village in Southern Sudan, as a child of the Dinka tribe. In 1992, at the age of seven, he began his primary schooling under a big mango tree. Then the Arab militia, known as Muraheel, attacked and destroyed his village, including his school. His father was killed by the Sudan Army Force (SAF) while on his way to Ethiopia to join the Sudan People's Liberation Army (SPLA).

In June 1996 when George was 12, he was captured by the SPLA and recruited for five years as a child soldier. They trained many young boys like him for 180 days on how to handle a gun at the frontline and how to kill the enemy. They did it for the sake of their country, to free South Sudanese from the Arab terror regime of the north — their mission. They believed that the SPLA had no choice but to recruit young boys into the army. In April 2001, while he was at a child soldier headquarters, he and 30 other child soldiers, because of the hopelessness of their situation, decided to escape from the army and walk to Uganda in East Africa for their safety and protection, and to continue their education.

They walked for more than 400 kilometres across Southern Sudan to Uganda. They had little food to eat, no clean water to drink and no medicine for treatment. Eleven of the boys died on the way. Those who made it to the border stayed there for two weeks until an officer arrived to take them across illegally at nighttime. Of these boys George was the only one to go to Australia; some of them were still in the camp and some had returned to the Sudanese Army.

At the Glenside Hosptital I searched for Shafiq, but came across Joseph instead pitting his wits against a computer game. 'How are you?' I asked.

'All right,' he said without looking up from his computer. Engrossed, he tried a few more manoeuvres to restore a building block pattern. It failed.

'Where is Shafiq?' I asked.

He looked up and said, 'He is probably in the unit.'

'Where is the unit?'

'I'll take you there.'

We stopped by a canteen and Joseph insisted on buying me an icecream. 'I should be the one buying the icecream,' I said.

'No, no, it's my pleasure.'

We reached the unit, but there was no sign of Shafiq.

And that's when Joseph's story unfolded.

Joseph had been fighting the Muslims as part of the Christian militia, also called Phalange, in Lebanon. 'I killed; otherwise, I would be killed,' he said. 'Killing was necessary and then peace. My father and brother were killed by the Palestinians while in Jewish occupied land. The rest of our family fled to Lebanon.

'In September 1982, our unit received an order to kill the refugees — the Palestinians who had escaped to Lebanon — in Sabra and Chatila. We went to Sabra and started killing the men. The truth, they never talk about the truth,' Joseph said, pointing to the TV.

Joseph brought out his documents of the case proceedings. I read the words 'crimes against humanity'.

'If I had not obeyed orders,' he said, 'I would have been shot.'

More than 800 Palestinians were killed. The Israeli defence minister, Ariel Sharon, allowed it to happen. No intervention.

After that horrific account, I met Shafiq who let me know he had, after nearly seven years in detention, secured his temporary protection visa. He seemed in fine spirits although he was diffident about going into the outside world again. He had become institutionalised and felt safe. 'I will make the change slowly,' he said.

Nearby the Glenside Hospital was the Arkaba Motel in the suburb of Fullarton, and there I met up with Abdul, an Afghani, who had been in detention for five years. I hadn't seen him for a year. His wife had been out of detention for three years looking after the children, but DIMIA could not let Abdul go out on a TPV because of his suspect background with undesirable militants. Four boisterious boys and two tiny girls took over the living room. 'The boys fight a lot,' Abdul said. Every day, Abdul's wife would take the boys to Woodville Primary School, care for the baby girls and drive 45 minutes over to Fullarton to see Abdul in motel detention. A couple of security guards remained in the same room as them. It cost hundreds of thousands of dollars a year for this special kind of detention, but no one seemed to mind. Other than his wife, no one had called in to see Abdul — he was one of the forgotten ones. The guards were on 12-hour shifts; they were friendly but bored.

In the same motel I met Ali, a Kurd, from Turkey plus two more guards. Poor Ali was a sad case with trying to commit suicide at Baxter. He went on hunger strikes when they threatened to deport him back to Turkey. Ali made excellent coffee and we chatted about the absurdity of his situation. He liked jigsaw puzzles so I said I would find him one — at least 1,000 pieces. Poor chap!

On meeting those who had been detainees for a long-term, I realised they were in no fit state to work once they had gained a temporary protection visa. From being traumatised in their own country they were further traumatised with the detention system. The medical findings showed that the rates of mental illness — post-traumatic stress disorder, depression, anxiety — were very high among people from immigration detention. It meant ongoing treatment by mental health professionals.

Chapter 23

Around the World

I WAS TEACHING ENGLISH TO migrants at Modbury TAFE in Adelaide when asked whether I would be interested in teaching English to a group of middle school Chinese teachers of English who had come to Adelaide as part of an international exchange program. Never one to miss an opportunity I welcomed the invitation.

Ten promising English teachers had been selected as the first group from Harbin to engage in a three-month course, commencing from 23 October 2002. It was designed to improve their English and cultural awareness of life in Australia.

As one of the group's English teachers I realised later that the door to China opened further to reveal China's present and past, largely through the eyes of the teachers and their parents, and friends in Harbin. I could never have imagined the journey I had begun with my first lesson introducing them to Australians and their peculiar ways.

It was easier to remember their English names: Harry, Tony, Jennifer, Cynthia, Connie, Misty, Alpha, Victoria, Amy and Catherine. My first real contact with the group was not until two weeks after they had arrived when I would have them for a full day. The head of the international exchange institute, Margot, left it up to me to teach what I thought would be suitable. I decided to focus on listening and speaking skills through using Australian documentaries about life in Australia, wildlife and the environment, and raising topical issues.

Speaking slowly I introduced myself and where I had come from. I asked each student to state their Chinese and English names and in what school they taught in Harbin. After the introductions, and talking about what we intended to do in our classes, we watched a segment of a wildlife documentary. Most understood about 30 per cent of what was said. We played it again and went over all the difficult words, phrases and Australian idioms, writing each up on a board. Then we played the documentary again with about a 25 per cent improvement in understanding. At the end of the lesson Jennifer, Cynthia, Connie and Amy approached me, and Jennifer said, 'We really enjoyed your lesson. You are the first person in Australia we can understand.'

I realised that the Australian accent had confused them. If they had heard native speakers of English they most likely came from the UK or USA. I said, 'You'll pick up what the other teachers say, just be patient. Listen as much as you can and ask questions if you don't understand.'

Over the next few lessons we played more documentaries, news broadcasts, popular songs and movie clips to cover a range of speakers. With more scenarios I encouraged both listening and speaking skills. Soon, we were listening to and singing 'Waltzing matilda', 'Advance Australia fair' and 'I am Australian/We are Australian'. They learnt the words and sang the songs at their end-of-course concert like professional performers. I was proud of their progress.

I joined in with barbecues, dinner parties at hotels, and tours to the Barossa, the Adelaide Hills and Murray Bridge. The final day ended up with speeches and a concert with songs and a play written by the group. The play commenced:

> Tony and Misty are an Australian couple and the first
> scene opens with Misty drawing the curtains and seeing
> Asian people wandering in her garden. Tony goes out to

talk to them and says, 'G'day.' Connie, a little scared, replies, 'Oh my God!' To which Tony says, 'I'm not God. But do you need help?'

What continued was an engaging dialogue about the group's experiences in Adelaide — visits to the Botanic Gardens, Wildlife Park at Cleland in the Adelaide Hills, the Festival Centre, the Barossa Valley, Victor Harbor, China Town and Glenelg, a visit to Immanuel College, and the watching of the Christmas Pageant which enthralled them. The well-acted play ran for about 45 minutes.

The following day our four teachers and organisers gathered with the group to farewell them on a two-week bus tour to Victoria, New South Wales and Canberra before their departure to Harbin in north-east China. What we could not have foreseen was that, instead of happy faces with customary Chinese smiles, everyone sobbed at leaving us. Even Tony and Henry were tearful. I had never witnessed anything like this before with a student group. Even as they waved from the bus it seemed that their faces were drowned in sorrow rather than showing the exuberance of a forthcoming trip. I felt sad, too, that they were leaving as we had formed a strong bond of friendship. Would we ever meet again?

Well, that happened sooner than I expected with an around the world trip which included invitations from Oxford University and Brighton University, from my cousin in America, from our daughter Rachel carrying out a project in India and from the Harbin group of teachers.

I first travelled to the United States where Lorraine Whittenton, my cousin, and her friend, Irene, met me at Albany. We drove to Lenox, a prosperous looking town in Berkshire, Massachusettes with the 'fall', as they say in America, displaying a full array of tinted leaves — vivid red, gold and brown — from oak, elder, elm, and maple trees. Lorraine's large country estate styled home with shingled roof and extensive gardens seemed like a touch of paradise. The forest nearby was home to black bears, moose, racoons, chipmunks, beavers and coyotes. A black bear had recently visited their garden for spoils, and, perhaps, I would be lucky enough to catch sight of one.

We toured Bear Mountains and the towns nearby in the Berkshire Hills, but we had no luck in spotting a black bear. I would have to come again.

My great-uncle Louis, who had emigrated from Scotland to America in 1910, had been a caretaker in one of Lenox's big houses, Ventford Hall Mansion, home of well-known actress and playwright, Fanny Kemble, who opposed slavery. In the main house they had a cook, a kitchenmaid, two laundresses, a parlour maid, two chambermaids, madam's personal maid, the master's valet, and three people in the pantry. In an adjoining house were the butler, greenhouse worker and groundsman, farmer, herdsman, chauffeur and coachman. Those were the days.

The table as we saw it was set with gold plates, a silver centrepiece and coloured chrysanthemums. The visitors, who met at the house in the fall for those musical soirees and plays, were of a cultured and refined class of American society, knowing each other intimately, and enjoying being entertained in luxurious surroundings.

From Fanny Kemble's plays:

'Why, the poor of Lenox? We have no poor in Lenox.'

'A gentleman always removes his hat in my presence.'
'I'm not a gentleman, I'm the butcher.'

From her quotes which I liked:

The large and rapid fortunes by which vulgar and ignorant people become possessed of splendid houses, splendidly furnished, do not of course, give them the feelings and manners of gentle folks.

The whole gamut of good and evil is in every human
being, certain notes, from stronger original quality or
most frequent use, appearing to form the whole character;
but they are only the tones most often heard. The whole
scale is in every soul, and the notes most seldom heard
will on rare occasions make themselves audible.

The house still opened as a theatrical venu, and we were treated to
a performance of a play by Virginia Woolf.

After leaving Lorraine, I next spent two days in Chicago and
wandered around the shores of Lake Michigan, and discovered in
a natural history museum the way in which people reversed the
obnoxious water pollution from the Chicago River.

Then I flew to Edinburgh and hired a car at the airport to drive
to Merith House Hotel in the city. But I took a wrong turn and was
on my way to Glasgow instead. I managed somehow to find my
way back. Although I had driven in Edinburgh many years before,
everything had changed with so many one-way streets. With a stroke
of luck I arrived before dark and flopped into bed after booking in.
The traffic roared outside my room, but I fell asleep oblivious to
the din.

The next day I walked along Princes Street and through the
castle grounds before taking a bus to the Pentland Hills for dinner
with Elizabeth and George Munro. Elizabeth's brother, Allan
Carmichael, a close friend from school and university days had died
from heart failure; she had let me know of Allan's untimely death,
and had invited me to visit them. Over a port and a roast beef
dinner we talked a lot about Allan and school contemporaries from
Elgin. George liked to provoke and said that anyone who went to
Springfield Primary School was 'upper class' or 'snobbish', much to
Elizabeth's chagrin.

I spent a night at Craigellachie Lodge, with a welcome change
from a traditional Scottish guesthouse breakfast of fried eggs, bacon,
sausage and beans to kippers and scrambled eggs.

Then I drove on to Garmouth and Elgin where I caught up with friends. I walked along the beach from Kingston-on-the-Spey towards Lossiemouth, along the Spey River by Fochabers, through Elgin's streets and the Cooper Park, and chased up history of the Mann family in Elgin and Banff.

For Dad's sake I called into Baxters of Speyside and received a royal welcome with a personal tour of the Baxter plant, of seeing the broth being canned, the liquor additions, the jam making and beetroot bottling. Kay, Gordon Baxter's private secretary, showed off the Gordon Baxter library with memorabilia and press cuttings galore which included a meeting with the Queen, photos, letters and mementoes. Gordon had assigned Kay to put the 120-year history of Baxter's together into a book worth reading. What a challenge!

I left Elgin's bustling town for the quiet of the highlands. I made my way to Kinlochbervie on the north-west coast, and drove to Durness where I walked along Balnakeil beach — on a par with Australia's best. A wide, inviting stretch of golden sandy beach, a calm sea and blue skies seemed more typical of the coastline near Port Macquarie in New South Wales. Nearby was Smoo Cave which Liz and I had visited 35 years previously.

I drove south through hill and loch country, with the hills occasionally studded with conifers but mostly bare except for tough mountain grasses. I hiked to the lower slopes of An Teallach, passing through forest and on to a rocky road leading to a plateau, which I traversed to a path that descended to a valley and loch. I walked for three more hours admiring the highland peaks, surrounding hills with waterfalls, and with heather, deer grass, mosses and lichens all making up the highland scene — what more could I wish for?

I came across a highland souvenir shop — a treasure trove of drawings, photos and books — run by a Salvadorean lady who had looked after the shop for 25 years. From what I had heard about Salvador, she was far safer in the Scottish Highlands.

A cold chill hung in the air the next day as I hiked near Glen Torridon viewing lochs and heather on hill slopes surrounded by conical and rounded peaks. Intervening stands of Scots pines blended in with the full autumn colours of birches, elms and oaks.

I drove through through the glacial valley of Glencoe where the Clan MacDonalds suffered their loss of clansmen by the treacherous Campbells. I reached Killin, located at the western end of Loch Tay, an ideal base for exploring the Southern Highlands.

To my dismay, however, when I woke up early at the Killin B & B, I could barely see the mountains due to heavy mist. Disregarding the mist, and after a full Scottish breakfast, I left for the Ben Lawes Visitor Centre, driving slowly with headlights on. After parking the car at the centre, I climbed up through the mist towards Ben Lawes. After passing through small valleys the trail opened up to a stiff climb. I puffed and panted, weighed down by the Scottish breakfast. The mist cleared further up with a mini-Mount Everest vista of mountains all around. A surreal sight of mist below, hiding Killin and the lower glens, separated two worlds of mountain tops and valleys. I reached the top of Ben Ghlass and descended back to the visitors centre to see my car lights still on. Two fit-looking lads pushed me on my way.

I stayed the night in Leslie, Fife, with Stewart Binnie, my old school friend, and his wife Florence, and we discussed the changes going on in Scotland. According to Stewart, Scottish industry had all but gone. Farmers were trying to diversify into tourism, fishing and other cottage industries.

The following day, on 27 October 2004, I drove down to Brighton on the south coast of England to deliver my talk on refugees at the University of Brighton. Professor Richard Black introduced me, and, after I had delivered the talk and slide show, the students asked questions about the Australian refugee policy. In discussion with the students afterwards, one said, 'We liked the human touch after what we had heard from previous speakers who were more theoretical.'

A few days later, I reeled off the same talk to Oxford University students and staff, and numerous questions followed which enlivened the seminar. At dinner I continued to discuss the harshness of the Australian mandatory detention policy with Professor Graeme Rodgers. He suggested I look at their website and think about applying as a visiting scholar. I thought about maintaining an interest in the areas with which I had become involved — population movements, forced migration, agriculture, resource management and sustainable livelihoods. It was tempting, but felt that to immerse myself in full-time academia again was not on the agenda.

As part of a guided tour I visited the famous Bodleian Library and became absorbed with the old collections and the vaulted ceilings and carvings. Well worth seeing was the Convocation Hall, which once seated members of parliament and the king. I could have spent two days at exhibits and galleries of the Ashmolean Museum.

Our bus went to Blenheim Palace where Winston Churchill was born in 1874. His forebear, John Churchill, had received a gift of money from Queen Anne to build the palace in recognition of his leadership in the victory over the French in the War of Spanish Succession in 1704.

Before leaving the car at Heathrow Airport, I spent two days with Stuart Lothian, our godson, and his wife, Sarah, at New Malden. We lunched at a pub with Stuart, Sarah, and Alasdair and Pat, Stuart's parents. The satay chicken burghers went down well with a pint of Guinness. We all walked around Richmond Park where ponds teemed with wildlife, and then went back to Alasdair's place for catch ups and refreshments. The sad news three weeks later was that Alasdair, fit and healthy-looking, died suddenly of a heart attack.

On the flight to Chennai the next day, I watched a repeat of 'Yes Minister', and talked to an aid worker from London needing a six-month take-it-easy surfing spell from his community aid set-up. The plane landed at 1.30 am and I made my way by taxi to the Hotel Pandian where I caught up with my niece Mary the next morning.

Mary and I had planned to spend a week with Rachel and her friend Nikki, who were taking part in a rural health project for women. We took an auto rickshaw to the central station which was packed with Indians waiting to pile on to trains. We boarded ours for Katpadi and engaged in conversation with a young and vibrant Indian entomologist and an older man who had definite views about a whole range of subjects, including cricket, family breakdown, environmental degradation, the problem of water hyacinth in waterways and lakes, DDT and other chemicals, the disappearance of vultures and the attitude of the young today. We listened mostly for three hours and then, thankfully, we reached our station. Rachel in her Indian sari greeted us warmly.

At Katpadi, we dined with Selvar Kumar, an affable and cheery host, who was in charge of the rural health project concerned with the provision of health care services to rural women.

The next day we visited Vellore with a social welfare officer, who guided us around a 16th century fort, a temple and a museum with stone relics from the 6th century. After leaving us, we walked through the packed shopping streets, before dining on buttered chicken at Rachel's favourite restaurant, Kelaya.

Later, Rachel and Nikki panicked with last minute preparations for their final talks on their findings and recommendations to the project staff.

The presentations on the mental health problems of Indian women went well with lots of questions from about 25 staff. We then tried to cope with Selvar Kumar's overfriendliness. In the end I rode pillion on Mr Kumar's motor bike for one of the four desserts he insisted on us having.

After our goodbyes, we took a train to Kochin, where we stretched our legs around the Dutch quarter with a stop to admire murals at the Dutch Palace and to visit a Jewish synagogue. Only a few Jews remained; most had gone to Israel. We also visited the oldest church, established by the Portuguese and then renovated by the Dutch in 1789. Vaso da Gama had been buried there but his remains were later removed to Lisbon.

Carpet wall hangings and shawls were all spread out at a government tourist shop. But surprisingly there were no purchases from the three girls, despite the efforts of six salesgirls plying us with everything possible.

At the seafront we watched a snake charmer surrounded by a large number of onlookers. The snake charmer for some reason fixed his eyes on Mary who backed away as he approached her. The python wrapped around him was too much for Mary. She retreated while the onlookers laughed.

At nighttime we watched the fish being hauled in with cantilever fishing nets that were first used by the Chinese. Nearby we dined by candlelight near one of the fishing nets on prawns, squid and backwater fish.

We set off for Munna in the midst of the tea estates in the mountains with the tea-clad hills surrounding the town and with a dreamy river running through. We settled into a guesthouse for the night with Mr Aripe, the owner in his sixties, speaking impeccable English.

A tour around the countryside the next day took in the misty-topped hills, the vast tea estates, luxuriant tropical growth and even eucalyptus trees from Australia. We spotted a herd of elephants not far away on a grassy plain. Then we had further stops at boating lakes, dams, and road stalls where we sampled the local passionfruit and a kind of date fruit.

The next day we walked 10 kilometres from our guesthouse through tea estates. There was no transport as a strike with protests about the rise in fuel prices affected the whole of Kerala. We passed by cardamom trees, waterfalls, school children, villagers, tea pickers, and young college lads who caught up with me to try out their English. Mary struggled and limped along the final 3 kilometres to a village where we hailed an auto rickshaw driver who wasn't on strike. An Indian vegetarian dinner — *goli massala, tikka massala* and *paneer* revived us.

We travelled on to Kunli where we took a boat cruise through the Periya Game Park Reserve and spotted bison, sambar, monkeys, squirrels and wild boar, but no elephants or tigers as planned by our tourist guide.

Rachel and Nikki had booked a boat cruise on a rice barge for an exotic finale to our trip. We quietly chugged through a maze of backwater passages and watched the goings-on of numerous barges, small boats and villagers on the banks washing themselves and their clothes. The cuisine on board excelled with seafood, curries, chicken and numerous Kerala side dishes. On the not-so-good side, according to Rachel, who had paid top price, were the mozzies, steamy heat and cramped quarters in the rooms. However, a candlelight dinner and mozzie coils helped turn the tide. We were just getting used to our new river life when it came to an end with horn blaring and the hurly burly of road traffic.

Mary and I left Rachel and Nikki who would continue their Indian adventure with a visit to a health resort for five days of pampering. We hired a kamikaze driver back to Kochin, and on the way, as our taxi headed straight for an oncoming van, Mary piped up, 'I think I'm going to die.' Somehow, with honking horn and flashing lights, the driver found a passing gap.

We spent the last day sightseeing at Mamallapuran on the coast but the day proved a mini-disaster. The shopping was poor for Mary, and monsoon rains drenched us as we sloshed through puddles of mud and rubbish left on the streets. Mary continued shopping while I viewed rock carving sites. We met up again at a French-run restaurant, the Nautilus, where a less-than-inviting meal arrived one hour after our order.

We arrived back in Chennai to chaotic traffic scenes, punctuated with fire-crackers for the Divali festivities.

We parted the next day with Mary flying back to Adelaide and I flying to Delhi for the night. A spiced Indian meal at the Western End Hotel in Delhi set my stomach into knots.

With Delhi belly, I landed at Beijing at 8.30 pm on 14 November 2004 and chose a nearby hotel called Blue Sky. But there were no blue skies for me as I crashed with my stomach churning and diarrhoea at the run. I felt sick and weak and started shivering. With hardly any sleep during the night, I summoned my reserves of energy to pack and go on the airport bus.

As the plane took off for Harbin, my earnest prayer was that my stomach would cease churning, my diarrhoea stop, and the sickness feeling would dissipate. My prayer was answered — no mad dash to the toilet on board the plane.

Three charming teachers — Cynthia, Jenny and Connie — greeted me at Harbin airport. It was great to see them again on their turf. I settled into a spare unit, at no cost, thanks to Cynthia. We chatted about plans for the next few days. Cynthia's husband, John, bought a few supplies, green tea, and some tablets to stabilise my stomach. I soon felt that I was on the mend.

The temperature was just below zero and took my breath away, having just arrived from a sweltering week in India. My temporary flat was spacious with two large bedrooms and all mod cons — for me anyway. And a large TV!

The next day, Cynthia was on deck to show me around — her school where she taught, the city sights and her husband John's fish tanks.

We met Catherine, Amy and Alpha, for a stroll to an old Russian quarter and along the banks of the Songhua River. Ice was forming on the river at minus five degrees. A coffee house warmed us up with Irish coffee on tap.

With Misty and Tony I visited Dragon Tower, the highest building in Harbin, offering expansive views of the city.

Later, I dined with Jenny and her husband, Jack, and five of Jenny's students. Jack's mother worked hard in the kitchen while we engaged the students in English.

A school day followed with a talk to Connie's students. Then Jenny cornered me for a talk to more than 60 of her students, all crammed into one classroom.

Later in the day, I met with 30 teachers of English at Jenny's school to speak on ways in which we might teach English in Australia.

After a frank discussion following the talk, the biggest problem, I gathered, was the inability of teachers in China to move away from a set method of teaching designed to conform to a uniform curriculum, set throughout China and which had a standardised way of assessing the performance of students. An ability to complete grammatical exercises, therefore, took priority over improving listening and speaking skills. If the students performed well so did the teachers, it seemed, for their career. It would take a courageous teacher to break the cycle.

After breakfast with Connie the next day, Victoria picked me up for a visit to the Harbin history museum, which gave an insight into the major dynasties and included displays of weapons, pottery, clothing and agricultural implements.

On Saturday 20 November, Connie took me to her parents' place in the countryside near Harbin. The farm home was simply laid out with central heating and basic facilities for cooking. A walk into the cornfields followed with Connie latching on to my arm. We watched the corn stalks being loaded on to carts for firewood.

I met Harry and a friend for another museum visit in Acheng city, accompanied by Connie, Jenny, Victoria and Cynthia, to view Jin Dynasty relics. At a Chinese banquet, Harry and his friend took centre stage after drinking too much beer and liquor. The party threatened to get out of hand with raised voices as they argued, but maybe it was just the Chinese way. Later, at a farewell dinner the mood was more subdued.

With a stopover in Hong Kong on the return journey to Adelaide, I managed a sightseeing trip to the New Territories. We visited a forest monastery and Kam Tin village with a history of settlement of Chinese refugees from Jiangzi province over 1,000 years ago. From the border with China we viewed Shenzhen, a major city in Guangdong province, designated as the first of China's economic zones with a burgeoning population of over 10 million. Then we stopped at a jewellery factory and two wishing trees. Every year, as part of the Chinese New Year's festivities, tourists and locals wrote their wishes on paper tied to an orange, then threw them to hang in banyan trees, in the hope their wishes would come true.

Back in Adelaide, I found a part-time job with the Australian Refugee Association to assist refugees in their search for employment and to advise on what studies they might undertake to bolster their employment opportunities and career. I worked with Hafez, an Iranian, and Sue, the head of our threesome team. I met with mostly Sudanese refugees whose first priority was making money, as their main objective was to provide fares for their immediate relatives to join them. The market for unskilled labour was limited with employment in factories, such as poultry processing and the abattoirs. The Sudanese often needed a car to travel to work so we encouraged them to take driving lessons. Ideally, they could work and undertake a TAFE course.

Another invitation to go to Harbin arrived.

Chapter 24
Teaching in Harbin, China

AFTER A LONG DAY'S FLIGHT on 12 July 2008 from Brisbane to Singapore and then on to Beijing, a warm hug from Jennifer made up for any weariness. Jennifer's sister Flora drove me to my hotel.

On the following hot summer's day, we jostled with hundreds of others to climb the Great Wall of China with its varying-sized steps. Exhausted, sweaty but exhilarated, a steady climb revealed different views of the Wall and the surrounding hills. We arrived at one of the outlook towers to collect our certificates, while less energetic visitors took a chair ride to the fourth stop and walked from there.

Back in Beijing, Jenny, Sirgin, a friend of Jenny's as guide, and I visited the Temple of Heaven, a complex of religious buildings patronised by the emperors of the Ming and Qing dynasties for annual ceremonies of prayer to heaven for a good harvest.

Later, we wandered around the Summer Palace with its more appealing gardens, lakes and waterways — all a luxurious and outlandish retreat for royal families to rest and be entertained. A woman fainted with the heat, so we attended to her until an ambulance arrived.

After three more days soaking in the sights of Beijing, Jenny and I took separate flights to Harbin. I had plenty of time to check in and pass through the security gate. But I was stopped because of Jenny's nutrition tablets and her two bottles of red wine. After an explosive test for the tablets I returned to the check-in counter to hand in the bottles of wine. They sent me to a counter where they packed the bottles into a case. I left my passport at the counter and I only realised this when I rejoined the lane at the check-in counter. I dashed back and then tried to check in again but had to go to an oversized check-in counter with the case of wine, and then through security gates where they re-examined Jenny's tablets. What a rigmarole! Finally, I just made it as the last passenger to board the plane.

On arrival at Harbin a welcoming party overwhelmed me — Cynthia, Grace, a close friend of Jennifer's, another Grace and her daughter Angel who were keen to migrate to Australia, and Jack was there for Jenny. Angel presented me with a huge bouquet of flowers. All too much!

Cynthia and her husband John provided a place for me to stay. After a rest we dined out and then walked along the Songhua River, a tributary of the Amur River that borders Russia and North-East China. In November 2005 there was an outcry from Russia threatening to bring a lawsuit against China for allowing the river to become contaminated with benzene. The spill stretched 80 kilometres and reached the Amur River in Russia; it led to a shutdown of Harbin's water supply.

The next morning, Connie called by with her husband, Daniel, and son Chang Chang, and we sauntered along the Songhua River, meeting up with small groups singing, exercising, playing ping pong or performing Tai Chi. One group sang with patriotic fervour, all conducted by an enthusiastic elderly man.

For a 10-year-old, Chang Chang was progressing well with English, which had replaced Russian as the most important language; it provided a means to succeed on the international stage.

The welcome back party for Jenny and me was overwhelming. Harry, Tony, Victoria, Catherine, Cynthia, Connie, and Alpha treated us like royalty with constant toasts and traditional Chinese food. Punctuated by laughter we recounted stories of their time in Adelaide.

'I can work here as an English teacher,' I suggested, and everyone voiced their approval.

Harry said, 'I will contact my friend Dr Zhang Milin who is the president of the College of Materials Science and Chemical Engineering of the Harbin University of Engineering. He may have a position for you.'

The next day, Jenny, Harry and I visited Dr Milin. My resume seemed to hit the right note, with Jenny and Harry putting in supportive references about my teaching and writing. 'Just what our university needs,' Dr Milin said. 'The higher authorities have to endorse you. Leave it with me.'

I met up with Alfa, one of the teachers who had come to Adelaide, and her friend Sherry. We toured a dilapidated housing area of Dawei district. Alfa stumbled across her mother's poky little one-room and shouted, 'What a coincidence!' Sherry later pointed out the finer points of the Greek, Baroque and Ionic styles of different buildings.

We visited three churches close to each other — Catholic, Lutheran and a modern government-built church with a seating capacity for seven hundred. Who were the Christians? Later, I gathered there were at least 50,000 Christians in Harbin with a population of 10 million, if you included the outer municipal areas. The Chinese authorities preferred people to go to the government church; they clamped down on clandestine meetings.

I went to Victoria's class of mainly girls the next day and spoke about Australia and what it was like for me in Harbin. Then there was a call from Harry to go to Dr Zhang's office to sign a three-month contract from September to December. It was all on at 4,500 yuan a month plus extras and a one-way airfare. I signed, and Dr Zhang accompanied us to lunch at a flash Chinese restaurant for hot pot. 'I want to learn English,' he said, 'as I missed out on that opportunity during the Cultural Revolution.'

The next day, Grace, Jenny and I paddled on one of the scenic lakes of Sun Island Park, where the Harbin international snow sculpture is held every winter.

Later with Amy, I visited the largest Buddhist temple in the province. The gold-plated Buddha towered over us at ten metres in height. More than 500 life-sized Buddhas filled two halls alone. Incense, praying visitors and resonant chanting provided a sacred atmosphere.

My unit on the university campus was spacious and comfortable, and a ten-minute walk away from the college. The campus swarmed with students and army cadets or freshmen who had to complete a couple of weeks training — lots of marching and shouting.

On my first day, I discussed with Dr Zhang and Dr Yan the program of English teaching and the revision of scientific papers for publication. Dr Yan would advise on any problems I encountered.

Dr Fan Zhuang Jun came in with the first paper for revision — one on the preparation of nanoparticles for supercapacitors using carbon material. I waded into it.

As the papers piled up, I soon realised that it was cutting edge science, such as investigating light weight alloys for aerospace, electronic and the automobile industries, and delving into areas such as electrochemistry, graphene nanosheets and nanowires. The papers covered research into the improvement of gas sensors, supercapacitors, drug release carriers, fuel cells, waste management, and even solid rocket propellants.

A lot of the terms I had to look up — often on Google — and become familiar with before I could get to grips with the papers, and then of course to correct the English, or perhaps I should say 'Chinglish'.

On Happy Teachers Day, the students presented me with a bouquet of flowers, and Dr Zhang came in with a box of moon cake and towels. All too much and really not deserved by a new teacher.

Masters, PhD students and staff called in to the office where I worked at my computer and discussed their papers before and after the revision. Most students had a poor command of spoken English, so it was hard to communicate with them, and often I had to seek a third person to help out. Each paper took at least a day to revise and prepare for publication in an overseas journal.

At the same time I commenced English classes to postgraduate students. Listening and speaking practice had been minimal in their school days. So, with a revolutionary approach, we listened to songs from Abba and the Beatles — 'Fernando' and 'Yesterday', and then tried to sing them.

At the weekend I accompanied a group of Jenny's friends by train to Yichun, a city to the north-east of Harbin and close to the Russian border. A backdrop of forest-clad hills surrounded Yichun, and Liu Chin, our guide, led us to a wood-sculptured park bordering a river, where we admired the wood statues of birds and animals, and of famous Chinese scientists and naturalists who had lived long ago and had contributed to China's progress.

We then negotiated a boarded walk in a national forest to overlook vast stretches of Korean pine, silver birch, fir, poplar and spruce.

After a noodle lunch we went rafting down a river. While five rafts drifted downstream, the inevitable water fights kept everyone screaming.

The next day, after a Chinese salad, chewy bread and dumplings for breakfast, we relaxed at the riverside near a Buddhist temple. At lunchtime, toasts and *ganbei* or 'bottoms-up' were too much for Jenny who became tipsy.

The five-and-a-half hour trip back to Harbin by bus passed through lush green carpets of crops — corn, rice and soybean — with a narrow band of trees lining the roadside. We rolled into the bright lights of Harbin at nighttime.

The next day I went to Cynthia's school to meet the principal and present a talk about Australia to 90 students — a two-hour session with the girls asking my views on pollution, the Olympic Games, schooling in Australia, the earthquake in Sichuan, and my thoughts on China as a country.

Cynthia raised problems with the teaching and learning of students — long hours, no time for playing or other activities for children, no time for holidays, parents forced to get the best out of children to succeed, all to the detriment of the child's development.

Later, a tearful and depressed Jenny poured out her heart on her uncertain future. I tried to encourage her in further study. Her aunt Li suggested that she go to Australia or Canada to do a master's course in education.

Then on 7 August 2008, everyone geared up to watch the Olympic Games opening ceremony the following day. Meanwhile Jenny's aunt Li organised a meeting with her cousin Decheng Zhang, a professor of the College of Humanity at Harbin Normal University. Over a VVIP lunch at a most expensive hotel we talked over the opportunities for cooperation between South Australia and Heilongjiang in the travel industry.

Decheng Zhang then invited Jenny and me to a dinner reunion with his friends at a Karaoke dining place where we danced and sang. Spurred on by Decheng, a boisterous singer, I sang 'Eidelweiss', danced and gave a speech.

Lunch with aunt Li and Jenny the next day in a restaurant featured beef hip joints and knuckles. Not my favourite — too gristly. Jenny ate every morsel and slurped up her marrow juice through a straw.

The director of the college, Dr Zhang Milin, invited me to dinner with Harry, Alfa, Victoria and Harry's classmate, but I was all set to watch the opening ceremony of the Olympic Games. Fortunately, they, too, realised the clash, so after a hastier than usual meal and toasting, we all rushed back to our respective homes to watch the opening ceremony showcasing Chinese history in grandiose style.

On the university campus I slowly adapted to Chinese college life with over 23,000 students on my doorstep. To walk around the outside of the campus grounds took an hour — it had the largest campus area of any university in the north-east of China. It was one of the most prestigious universities in China and easily spotted on Google Earth. Our five-storey apartment block housed retired teachers and other staff — more or less my age, I suspected — and foreigners like me.

I walked around the campus most mornings, setting off at about 6 am, when older people were already exercising, performing Tai Chi and even swinging on parallel bars, stretching, and playing tennis. I couldn't imagine the same in Australia where dogs usually took charge of their owners in parks and along streets, with an occasional lone jogger or walker.

At one end of the campus many shoppers headed towards street stalls set up for selling fruit and vegetables. In one area, they said, the largest library in north-east China had not long been built. Its curved-shaped end sections and park at the front made an impressive centrepiece for the campus.

Quite often, someone I met for the first time asked my age and other personal questions which Australians wouldn't ask for fear of being too forward. But it was the Chinese way and when in China do as the Chinese do.

I helped Jenny with her IELTS (International English Language Testing) preparation. Her mother-in-law cooked a curried chicken and I was about to cut a pear in half for dessert.

'No, you can't have half of this pear,' said Jenny. 'It will bring bad luck.' That was my first introduction to a superstitious mindset for many in China.

At the weekend I visited Connie's place in the country to see her parents at a village not far out of Harbin. On the menu were fish, pork, vegetables and Harbin beer. Only Connie spoke English, but I added a few Chinese phrases at the appropriate time like *hao chi* (delicious) and *chi bao le* (I have eaten enough). We walked through the fields at the back of the house to see the ripened corn, cabbages and spinach. From December to May it was too cold for farming so Connie's father relaxed with beer-drinking friends.

Through Connie, I asked her father, 'How did the family come to Harbin?'

He said: 'My great-grandparents came to Harbin village from Henan province — they were farmers, but there were too many people in the province. My great-grandfather was handsome and healthy with three sons and got married after he went to Harbin. He settled down and leased some land from a landlord to grow watermelons and corn. Under the People's Republic of China the land belonged to the country. He employed people for farming, became richer and bought a house.

'My grandfather was not very tall. He had a sharp mind and took charge of the family. He had two sons and three daughters — all lived together in a big house. They had three horses, a big yard and everyone worked together on the farm. My father continued to farm the land and handed it on to me.'

For the next weekend I joined Cynthia and her daughter Dor Dor, Victoria and her son, and a group of about 20 others on a bus heading to a mountainous area to climb Xiang Lu. After a cramped ride and non-stop chatting, we set off to climb, but it was slow progress, in single file mostly, as about one thousand other hikers had joined us. Never had I seen so many on one walk. Children clambered onto rocks chasing each other while adults plodded upward.

The vivid autumn colours made all the hard effort worthwhile. We stopped for a picnic below the final climb to the summit. On the way down we waited a long time for our turn to cross on a swinging bridge over a chasm.

Exhausted, we reached our bus and everyone slept on the way back except for Cynthia who chatted non-stop.

Amy and Jenny arrived at my unit in the evening — two cooks didn't spoil the broth this time, but jibed as they blamed each other or the utensils.

Dining out happened almost every day. I enjoyed Peking duck at a restaurant with Cynthia, Jenny, and Grace and her daughter Angel, whom I rechristened Ruby after Linda's daughter. Jenny and Grace argued over who was the most beautiful — an unbelievable carry-on in a first-class restaurant. The waiter made sure my glass was topped up with Harbin beer.

Cynthia and I then spent more than two hours at the Jewish synagogue recapturing the heady days of Jewish life in Harbin during the 1920s and 1930s. The displays covered a fascinating account of Jewish life in Harbin from 1900 to about 1950. Harbin was a fishing village until 1898 when the Russians were granted a concession to build the Chinese Eastern Railway as part of the Trans-Siberian railway. Russians poured into Harbin, along with Jews often escaping from pogroms in Russia in those days of turbulent upheaval, which included the slaughter of many Jews in about 1905 and, later, the persecution of Jews following the Russian revolution in 1917.

White Russians, too, sought haven in Harbin, and both Jews and Russians made significant contributions to the multiethnic way of life. Chinese farmers also migrated northwards from Shandong and Hebei provinces, as Heilongjiang province was relatively underpopulated by comparison with the rest of China. Many farmers later moved from the rural areas of the province to Harbin and started businesses.

In contrast to Russia, the Jews in China lived in harmony with the Chinese and were respected for their way of life and business dealings. Even to this day some of the older folk in Harbin recall how smart the Jews were in their business enterprises. For the younger set, I was not so sure that they fully appreciated their Jewish past. Three English teachers said that they had never visited the Jewish museum but were happy to accompany me — an eye-opener for them. No Jews lived in Harbin today, though. The last Jew died in 1985.

Accompanied by a pianist and violinist, we dined at Hotel Modern. Dor Dor surprised us with her gargantuan appetite. Formerly, as the Moderne, the hotel provided a venue for theatre and concerts. Completed in 1913, the founding Russian owner, Kaspe, suffered the loss of his son Semen in 1933. Pianist Semen Kaspe, aged 24, had planned to give a series of concerts but was kidnapped. His father could not afford to pay the ransom and his son was killed three months later.

On a visit to Victoria and Misty's school I gave a two-hour session on teaching English to about 25 female teachers of English. The only male English teacher, I learned, had opted out of the meeting. I found it hard to believe that a number of teachers had never talked to a native English-speaker.

After realising that education had always played a key part in Chinese society, I learnt about the folk tale of a girl who wanted to be educated, but the only way was to pretend to be a boy. She fell in love with a fellow student and they spent most of their time together. He was not aware she was a girl. The girl dropped hints after three years. Eventually she devised a plan to say that she had a pretty younger sister who would make him happy. The boy fell for her, but marriages were arranged so she didn't have a chance. He died and she visited his tomb and made a wish about being a butterfly. The tomb opened up and they flew off together as butterflies.

From a popular folk tale to a Chinese wedding that Dr Zhang suggested we attend at Daqing. Dr Li joined us and we set off at 6 am through the streets of Harbin towards the bridge to the north side and on to Daqing, a distance of 160 kilometres. Along the way corn fields had been newly harvested and a few farm labourers were picking up corn cobs that were left by the harvesters. Grassy areas intermeshed with corn fields to provide grazing for sheep, goats and cattle. Birch trees and conifers lined the highway. At Daqing we joined the wedding party for the bride.

Two hundred people had gathered in the function room and sat at dining tables awaiting the ceremony. Men at a couple of neighbouring tables were playing cards while the noise level in the hall had reached ear-piercing proportions.

The wedding celebrant welcomed everyone, including me as a special guest, at which point the video recorder operator swung towards me to record this strange specimen from Australia. After a simple ceremony, food arrived on platters — too many, so they stacked up on each other. So much food and so much left behind for the cleaners to parcel out to non-VIPs. I had my first taste of thinly sliced pig's ear and chicken stomach. The bride and bridegroom came around to each table. Dr Li had primed me with a *zhu ni xingfu* (I wish you happiness), which seemed to get the right response.

After the wedding celebration, we drove to the wetlands where we braved the rain and cold wind for a boardwalk to one of the vantage points for viewing the red-crowned crane, one of the rarest species of cranes. No luck though on this occasion. Huge stretches of common reed covered much of the wetland area. The reed was harvested once a year and sold to the paper mills. On the way back to our car we met a fisherman with a half bucket full of live cockroaches that he was going to sell to a restaurant. If he couldn't sell them, he would fry them for himself. Was I interested in buying them? Definitely not!

We retreated to our hotel room and warmed up before a sumptuous Mongolian hotpot. A Mongolian lady and her Chinese husband joined us. We toasted Mongolian style — *Maroochi gar,* as I remember. We had individual hotpots, and these were topped up with slices of lamb, mushrooms, black fungus, vegetables, tofu squares and sweet potato.

The second part of the wedding ceremony took place at a country village — home of the groom's parents. On the way we passed through wetland areas and drove over an uneven man-made brick road — in appearance like a miniature Wall of China.

The wedding ushers herded us into a tent for about 100 guests — the first of five sittings for 500 guests in total. The master of ceremonies cracked a few jokes which had everyone laughing. But no one interpreted so I missed out. The dishes of fish, meat and vegetables arrived, and Dr Zhang coerced me into having *baijiu* for the toasting. After, the bride and groom greeted us, table by table, and then retired for the photo session. Soon a request — could I join the newlyweds for a photo. Of course. I thanked them and sat between them.

Outside, pigs wandered everywhere, and the second of the four remaining dining groups lined up to enter the tent.

The next day, we visited the oil fields surrounding Daqing. One hundred thousand people were engaged in the largest oilfield in China with 60,000 wells. All over the flat countryside oil machines drilled for the precious oil and gas.

Back in Harbin, Jenny was ready for the IELTS exam at Heilongjiang University. 'I am scared. I am going to die. What happens if I fail?' asked Jenny. I tried to encourage her.

Jenny didn't sleep and was a bundle of nerves before taking the various reading, listening speakling and writing exercises. She felt she had performed below the required standard. 'If you have,' I said, 'I am going to give up as a teacher of English.'

After the exam, Jenny finally appeared but looked as her world had caved in. The interviewer offered no encouragement with her blank-looking face. No eye contact, she said. And then there were sobs and the release of pent-up emotions as we went to her mother and father's unit. Jenny's mother had prepared a spread of steamed fish, crisp pork, Chinese salad, beans and boiled squash, spiced prawns, mushroom soup, lettuce, tofu and cucumber spices and another pork dish. And first class green tea from Tia Guaning (Fujian province). Overwhelmed! If Jenny failed her test, I might disappear.

Jenny's father had graduated at Chang Chun University in 1970 in engineering and worked in a tractor company for many years before joining a pharmaceutical company as an engineering designer. He was eager to show me photos of his first visit abroad, soon after the door had opened for Chinese to travel under Mao's successor, Deng Xiaoping.

His great-grandfather had come from Shandong as a farmer and settled in Oolong. His grandfather became a landlord and was not well liked; he moved to Harbin.

Times were very hard during the famine but no one lost their life in Harbin, which was better off than other cities. Rations were strict and shared. In the country it was a different story. Power struggles and strikes added to their woes.

Just before I left to return to Adelaide, Jenny rang to say she had gained a score of 7.0, enough for her to apply for a master's course in education in Australia. We both felt happy and relieved.

Chapter 25

Return to Harbin

Two years after my first visit to Harbin I returned for another spell of teaching and to help out with the publication of scientific papers.

Dr Zhang and his colleagues, Professor Han, Professor Wang and Professor Peng, welcomed me with a banquet and lots of toasting. Cynthia kindly acted as the official interpreter.

In the office, another welcoming party of research students and staff overwhelmed me, including Dr Zhang's wife, with a bouquet of flowers and speeches to let me know that most of the papers I had revised on the previous visit were published in international journals.

Professor Yan and his wife Xue came into the office, and we chatted about their new baby boy and how naughty he was. We lunched at the campus canteen with hundreds of students, and I selected *doufu* or bean curd, potato strips, and *jiezi* or eggplant, and rice.

At my office I read a paper dealing with supercapacitors derived from graphene nanosheets for energy storage, before giving a talk to students about the pitfalls of writing a scientific paper in English.

The research paper on supercapacitors later appeared in the *Chemistry of Materials* with eleven Chinese authors and one Australian author — me. This happened with a number of papers before I put a dampener on having my name as part of the Chinese line up. Most of the authors, including me, had nothing to do with the research, but it was Chinese protocol to include the director and others of standing in the college. Because the Chinese research authorities had my email from these publications, I received invitations at the rate of about one a week to attend Chinese conferences.

On Teachers Day, ten students crowded into the office to present two bouquets of flowers – roses, crysanthemums, lilies — and a basket of oranges, pomegranates, dragon fruit, rockmelon, black and white grapes, and the largest mango I had ever seen. Their kindness blew me away. Yan had to run me back in his newly purchased car to my apartment as I couldn't have carried the flowers and the fruit. I wondered what they did for Mother's Day or Father's Day.

At the weekend Cynthia and I took a ferry to the north side to meet her parents. Cynthia's father talked about the new development in their district — an extensive building program with parks and amenities for the future. Farmers had become rich with the government buying their land for development; some had received more than a million yuan. In the remote parts of the province the government had encouraged people to settle as farmers with free land and financial assistance.

Cynthia's grandfather had walked from Lioning province in 1930 to Heilongjiang province, a distance of more than 1,000 kilometres. 'How did he come?' I asked.

'He carried his goods with the help of a pole and baskets supported on his shoulders,' Cynthia's father said. 'He was very poor at the time and had no horses. He became a farmer after making some money in Harbin, and then lived in the wilderness, growing corn, soybean and wheat, as well as fishing and hunting wild animals. The environment was very clean, not like now. He was happy and later he went to Harbin to become a justice secretary for the party.'

Cynthia's father worked in the personnel department in charge of new party members. During the Cultural Revolution he was in middle school when it closed for two years.

'What did you do when the school closed?' I asked.

'I went back to the countryside for farm work in a collective,' he said. 'Our family was very poor at that time, and I didn't go back to school when it reopened. I spent three years doing farm work and then became a teacher in middle school from 1972 to 1982. I attended night lessons and studied politics, history and Chinese. I graduated from teachers college and in 1969 I joined the party; I was very excited and in a formal ceremony swore allegiance to the national flag.

'I saw Mao in Beijing — briefly, because his car passed quickly. I cried a lot when I saw him. Mao was very brave as he walked among the people without guards in 1966. At that time everyone was loyal to the party and there was no need to lock the doors. In the Cultural Revolution, Mao had a bad impression of powerful cadres and asked students to fight against the leaders. But Mao shouldn't have been so cruel. He couldn't control the outcome. Mao wanted the teachers to be practical and not act according to the book. "Farmers, workers and soldiers should go back to the fields," he said.

'The economy closed and China became an isolated country — Mao thought it could develop on its own. The Cultural Revolution was a mistake — its aim was good but the way wrong. The young people thought it was fun to fight against heaven [authority]; earth was for the people. We must not bow down to any bad things. Life was very poor, but we were not afraid of hard work. We were very excited — we could conquer nature and tried to reform bad things. We were very hardworking.'

'What about the famine?' I asked.

'The famine occurred from 1959 to 1961, but fewer people suffered from the famine in Heilongjiang province compared to other provinces. People moved north from the south, soldiers became farmers and developed Xingjiang and Heilongjiang provinces. More land was opened up. Now Koreans rent our farmland for up to 70 years and even own factories.'

'What was life like under Japanese occupation?'

'During the Japanese occupation, the Japanese forced people to build road banks; if they refused, they were killed. Coal, wood, other resources and food, went to Japan. My grandfather helped build a road. The Japanese killed themselves at the end of the war, and some children became Japanese orphans. The children were given to Chinese, and, after growing up, they went back to Japan. Young people know little about the Japanese, but the older ones can't forgive. Most of my generation hate the Japanese.'

We ended the talk on a solemn note — I would find out more about the Japanese occupation.

I thanked Cynthia's father for telling me about his past. We then walked through the Heilongijiang Institute of Technology grounds and garden areas, passing by a lotus pond.

Cynthia and I took the ferry back to the south side as it grew dark. The new moon gleamed over the Songhua River with a high-rise skyline silhouetted in the background. We dined at a noisy restaurant on dumplings and Chinese salad in Daowei District, the oldest part of Harbin.

I started to absorb a few customs into my daily life, like toasting staff members at a dinner in a restaurant and talking loud enough at meal time so as to be heard. There was no such thing as a quiet dinner as everyone raised their voices — it was the Chinese way. Some of the restaurants I visited were virtual shouting matches, and the acoustics didn't help. On special occasions an exclusive room for your party was much more preferable with the improved service and not having to compete with diners at nearby tables.

Harbin thrived with its ten million people. Traffic jams, though, were common as more people could afford to buy cars. There were no rules as far as I could work out. No quarter given. The amazing thing was that cars moved from lane to lane without flashing indicators and bulldozed their way from side streets into main stream traffic. It worked until the law of averages took over. Weight was might and cars reigned over pedestrians if you crossed the street. Safety didn't apply on pedestrian crossings when the lights turned green. It was eyes everywhere and prepare for the unexpected, as it was common for a driver to go over the crossing in front of you.

A standing custom was that if you helped someone, that person would usually offer something in return, as a token of appreciation. That often meant for me after finalising the revision of a paper an invitation to lunch or dinner. How could I refuse?

The siren rang one Saturday as a student came in for his lesson and he explained the reason: 'The Japanese invaded Harbin on this day in 1931 and took control of Heilongjiang, Jilin and Liaoning provinces.'

On that day, Amy, Cynthia and I visited the Japanese war museum which depicted the horrific acts carried out by the Japanese of Unit 731 when they occupied Harbin from 1931 until the end of the Second World War. As we walked up to the entrance, a young woman came out, looking very distressed. Later I understood why, as the display rooms and the buildings all around showed how Japanese used their captives, mostly aged 30 to 40, in barbaric germ warfare experiments.

The Chinese had gone to great lengths to preserve the war museum so its people would never forget what the Japanese had done to them during this time. It was no wonder that people I met, especially the older set, would not have anything to do with the Japanese.

Shiro Ishii, the commander of military Unit 731 even received accolades — praised by the people and media with an award for his medical research findings on returning to Japan. The whole experience, like Tuol Sleng Genocide Museum in Phnom Penh, portrayed unbelievable cruelty and hard-to-fathom depths of depravity.

On a happier note, the autumn weather was still pleasant and warm in the middle of the day, but winter was fast approaching, and it wouldn't be long before the Songhua River would be frozen over.

As the Mooncake Festival drew near I might have wallowed in a lonely unit wishing I were somewhere else. But Jenny and Amy came to the rescue, and we celebrated the festival with Jenny's husband, Jack, and his mother-in-law, dining on steamed fish, cauliflower, beans, pork slices, Chinese vegetables and rice, accompanied by Harbin beer. Jack and I watched a rodeo show from America on TV and a game of billiards from the UK.

Later, Amy introduced me to a young student, Richard, his English name, with a mixed Russian – Chinese background. Richard had become acquainted with his Russian side and culture through his grandfather, who had come with his well-educated father and mother from St Petersburg. His grandfather was 23 at the time and had graduated at St Petersburg University with an engineering degree. In 1969 they migrated to Harbin because of commercial interests and weren't affected by the Cultural Revolution.

Some of Richard's Russian forebears had blue rounded eyes and light skin, but Richard reckoned he received a raw deal from his genetic background with smaller brown eyes, darker skin and wiry hair. 'My aunts were the lucky dogs,' he said. 'They had blue eyes, a paler skin and lighter-coloured Russian hair.'

'Did your grandfather marry a girl from Harbin?' I asked.

'He married a Chinese girl from Acheng, a town near Harbin. She was of noble birth and a descendant of the Manchu minority. As a Manchu she was typically reserved. By chance, they met at a party and she, at 18, was attracted by his handsome looks. She did not complete her education at university and married him instead. However, after marrying she became disinterested in his Russian background and they often quarrelled. He was even scared of her hot temper. She was kindhearted but couldn't control herself. She sometimes spoke ill of his Russian background. My grandfather's Chinese wife couldn't stand anything to do with Russia. Their marriage was very difficult, but it survived.'

'Did your grandfather keep in touch with people he knew in Russia?'

'Yes, my grandfather did keep in touch with relatives in Russia and often went back to visit them. But my grandmother stayed at home. Relatives would visit them in Harbin for music and dancing, and drinking of vodka, Chinese wine and beer. My grandfather would play the accordion while singing Russian songs in a yodelling fashion, which no one understood, but we knew instantly they were of Russian origin. Grandfather liked opera and listening to Russian composers like Tchaikovsky, and he would swim in the Songhua River in winter when the temperature fell below zero.'

Richard, a gifted student, spoke Russian, English and some French and Hungarian. He had been to England on a study tour and the experience had given him confidence in speaking English. In addition, he travelled to Russia to visit relatives and had absorbed part of his Russian heritage. At this point he offered me a mildly alcoholic drink, *gewasa*, made from fermented bread. The taste was not quite up to Harbin beer standard but passable. I could buy the drink in the supermarket at Qiulin if I wanted.

Richard continued:

'My grandfather was amazed that the Chinese hardly ate bread, preferring a round large dough-like roll for breakfast. The Russians, on the other hand loved their bread, black or white, and bakeries sprang up in Harbin to principally serve the Russian public with *leeba/chaleeba*. Other missing items in the Harbin diet were spicy Russian sausage, *gabasa*, and of course coffee and vodka. My grandfather drank every day and loved the Harbin beer as well as the vodka and Chinese wine. The beer was first brought to Harbin by the Russians in 1900, and the Jews, seeing a profitable enterprise, established breweries. He grew his own vegetables, a common part of Russian rural life. The vegetables would be salted and stored.'

'I gather Russian was an important second language in those days,' I suggested.

'Yes, but the Russian language in schools has given way to English; it has been relegated to specialist courses at university. Twenty years ago, Chinese spoke fluent Russian but not now. Because of Harbin's proximity to Russia, trade and commerce continue to be important, and so there is still a place for interpreters and business Chinese to speak Russian in the north-east of China. Many Russians today come to Harbin for short periods of time — usually for business interests, sightseeing or for stocking up on goods which are much cheaper on the Chinese side. But the Chinese have closed their borders to immigrants from Russia.'

'What about your great-grandfather?' I asked.

'I don't know a lot about him, but he was an interpreter for the Japanese at the time of Manchuria's occupation by them. He witnessed some unpleasant sights like 40 bodies of killed Chinese.'

'Your forebears have passed through an extraordinary time involving both Russia and China, and the Japanese occupation,' I said. 'Your story gives a valuable insight into that period of history.'

After a few more words together, I thanked Richard and wished him the best in his studies. I realised with Richard's story how enriching mixed backgrounds of forebears can be.

From the 200 thousand Russians who lived in Harbin during the early part of its development, only a handful of descendants remained.

Connie and her friend called around for me and we drove to her parents' place on the farm. We joined a pre-wedding get-together for lunch and then toured the farm to assess the crops of corn and vegetables — carrots, cabbages, turnips — and coriander. Xue, 13-years-old, looked after me and not afraid to try out his English at any opportunity. His favourite sport was basketball and he loved pop and hip-hop music.

In the evening I shared a hot pot meal with Dr Li and his friends. The hot pot was divided into two — a spicy Sichuan mixture and a soy milk mixture. Bean curd, thin slices of meat, mushrooms, lettuce, kelp and noodles were added to the hot pot. We drank Snow beer instead of the usual Harbin beer.

We had three days of official holiday but had to make up for them by working at the weekend — an unbelievable Chinese custom. I made a token gesture of conforming to the rule and then quietly disappeared.

On 29 September 2010, I received an invitation to a dinner hosted by the Governor of Heilongjiang province to celebrate the 61st anniversary of China's republic. All the foreigners and a sprinkling of locals assembled at the Shangri-La Hotel — one of the finest in Harbin. The dining hall featured ten large chandeliers ringing a central chandelier of about two metres in width. I enjoyed a chit chat with Jia, Lili her English name, and her mother over a spread of prawns, bamboo shoots, spare ribs in sweet-sour sauce, Chinese vegetables, beef cuts, mushrooms, chicken and duck. And all accompanied by the Great Wall of China Cabernet Sauvignon — almost passable by Barossa standards. Svetlana, from St Petersburg and I chatted as best we could in French. She had bypassed English for French at university.

Looking like a model with a trim hairdo and wearing a trendy white jacket, Jenny introduced me to her uncle Chengchao Liu, Richard his English name, who spoke perfect English and had taught English at Harbin Engineering University for ten years. He was born in 1951 and lived in a Russian-style timber framed home, in a housing complex for four families. He migrated to Canada in 1991 where he started his own café business in Toronto.

Richard had never met his grandparents who had come from Shandong province to settle outside Harbin as farmers. As a landlord, his grandfather was dispossessed of his land after 1949 — it was parcelled up for the poorer people. His grandparents died young, and his parents went to school in Harbin where they faced hard times during the Cultural Revolution and the famine. China's economic development had rocketed ahead following Mao's death, but the political side remained stagnant with little progress towards a democracy, according to Richard.

'Before 1979, living conditions were very poor with no running water,' Richard said. 'At the end of the block was a fountain and they carried the water with two buckets and a pole twice a day. There was a hole in the ground for a toilet; the toilet waste was taken away as fertiliser for farming land. They burned wood and coal. Two brothers and one sister and his parents lived in a 20-square metre room with a small bathroom. The heat from the stove went through the wall. They had radio but no TV, and no telephone until the 1990s. Farmers brought in vegetables and fruit to sell at a street market. Fish came from the coastal areas such as Dalian. As an accountant my father earned from 60 to 100 yuan per month.'

'How did the Cultural Revolution affect you?' I asked.

'Well, that depended on family history. If rich, they put a sign on you. It was a class struggle. The Communist Party originated from the lower class; it started from nothing and overthrew the rich class. In 1959, the anti-rightist movement encouraged people to criticise the Communist Party, but it backfired. Their jobs were taken and they were sent to the rural areas or put in prison.

'Party members were honoured and had power to succeed, to survive or become a leader. But a lot of problems existed. People didn't make enough money; health and education were not given enough attention; there was a heavy tax for companies; and buying a house was difficult. Even in the 1990s it was not possible to buy a car or own your home. There was no social system and not much welfare.'

'But nowadays it has changed,' I said.

'Yes, the Chinese government is the richest in the world,' said Richard. 'Most people are happy but satisfaction level is not high. Human rights are taken for granted; government officials decide the outcome. It is the only political system; you put a message on the internet and you will be in trouble. Protests occur, but whoever has money has power, such as building developers. Houses are removed, but people can't do anything.

'They appointed Deng Xiaoping who appointed Jiang Zemin and then Hu Jintao — it is tightly controlled and not going to get better. Just feed the people while everywhere bribery exists and government officials make money from people and the system. The government now spends a lot on things like the Olympic Games but not enough on welfare, or to improve housing by controlling prices, which are out of control.'

'Surely, there are improvements for people now, though, compared to times past,' I suggested.

'Before the Cultural Revolution the system was not as corrupt as it is now. In the 1950s and early 60s the officials served rather than took money. In those days the whole country was poor and no one thought of making money — most cadres worked with the people.

'The higher the economic development the higher the political development. We have a big difference between poor and rich. Making money has become an important goal. Government officials make money and have more power and more power means more money.

'In the Cultural Revolution schools closed — I went to a rural area for redirection. In the 1966 June 1 Manifesto, I was in second year middle school in Harbin when classes were stopped. We all took part in the revolution, followed Mao and put papers on walls, challenged the system, turned against teachers — they were targets. We also forced landlords to kneel on the ground while we beat them. Some teachers were put to death; the principals were targeted the most. My principal jumped from a building — it happened a lot. Mao had made himself God. All started from a power struggle.

'Grandfather was classed as a landlord; everyone had a personal file, a record of family background. Your background became a big issue. Everyone asked "What family background are you?" On your arm could be written 'Red Guard' in Mao's handwriting. Because my grandfather was a landlord I was a 'black class' and couldn't be a revolutionary. I felt inferior. The poorer the better for the student. When talking about the person talk about class struggle.'

'What about your schooling?'

'For the first few months with no school everyone was happy. We changed names because some had a feudal meaning. We paraded with signs. "Long live the Cultural Revolution." "Long live Chairman Mao.", "Turn over the old system". In Harbin, fights between groups were common. We used guns; even tanks came into the streets. To see Mao, we went to Beijing by train with students packed onto luggage racks even. Mao flashed past in his car. We were excited and thought he was God.

'I never went back to classes. I played with my classmates and even went to school, but there was no class. After one year, I asked myself "What's next?" In 1968 I went to a rural area, 1,000 kilometres away and close to inner Mongolia. We were on a village farm, where 30 of us lived together. We only went home once a year. We weeded, planted and harvested wheat, 12 hours a day. I taught myself carpentry and built furniture for the home. In 1977, after the Cultural Revolution, the university entrance exam was restored and most students went back to the city. I studied hard and became a teacher of English at the Harbin Shipbuilding Engineering Institute.'

'You have done well, despite your setback in education,' I commented.

'Well, I had to make up for lost time but I was highly motivated.'

A lunch followed our chat, with steamed fish, Chinese vegetables, prawns, beans and two kinds of tofu, and, of course, Harbin beer.

I let Richard know I had received a request from Myra, a Russian Jew in Adelaide, to search for the gravesite of a Jewish relative who had been buried in the Jewish Cemetery on the outskirts of Harbin. 'I can help you find the site,' Richard said.

The next day, Richard introduced me to his friend, Ocean, who was only too happy to drive me there. Ocean ran a successful building business; he had adopted his English name from reading a travel magazine.

We located the cemetery, with 593 gravestones engraved in Russian and Yiddish, in a tranquil setting. The gravestones were scattered haphazardly among trees and undergrowth. We searched for about an hour before Ocean secured the help of a Chinese historian and genealogist who was researching the history of Harbin's Jewish people. She knew of David Binder, Myra's relative, and with the help of a map she located the gravesite. We took photos to pass on to Myra and her family. David and his wife, Pasha, had moved to Harbin from Hailar in 1937. The Japanese had burnt their property while David's brother, Boris, lost his farm in a severe bombardment by the Japanese, and was later beheaded in 1945. Boris's wife, Chaya, and two sons were left homeless and forced to move to Harbin.

Ocean and his wife, Aroma, then treated us all to a seafood lunch at a Russian-built restaurant by the Songhua River. In a Russian ambience, with photos of Russians in Harbin, and Russian memorabilia, it wasn't too hard to imagine life in Moscow of the Orient, as Harbin was known.

After, we walked through the Botanic Gardens which had something for everyone — flowers in full bloom, autumn colours, an amusement park, fun area, including a gong that you could sound for one kuai a hit, small lakes, cute bridges, towers, a carriage to take you back a few years, a heaven-sent toilet, avenues of pines and other conifers, silver birch, larch, oak and maple trees, and, the most beautiful of all, lots of brides — some in traditional white and others in turquoise gowns. They posed for photos in all kinds of settings; one couple perched on a heart-shaped seat in the middle of a decorative wall.

On Sunday, I sauntered along Central Street, Zhong Yang Dajie, and then took a side street and braved a pedestrian crossing before landing safely in the grounds of the Russian Orthodox Church, Saint Sophie. Inside, photos all around the walls depicted life in early times with a special emphasis on the Russian contribution in establishing the Chinese Eastern Railway link.

The next day and the last day of the holidays, mild autumn weather encouraged Cynthia and me to meander through Qunli district, an ultra modern development and housing area for thousands of people, who lived in 25-storey high apartment blocks, and enjoyed facilities, such as park areas and newly formed wetlands. Cynthia had bought a home there for 1.4 million yuan — about $280,000. She would move into her new apartment in two years' time. The grand scale and complex of Qunli opened as a showpiece of modern city development. An imposing statue of Wan Yan Liang, a Mongol warlord astride his horse and ready to conquer, overlooked the whole complex. A brutal man like his father, Wan Yan Liang conquered the northern part of China in 1150 and usurped the emperor's throne. Nearby the statue, a Mongolian yurt and historical displays depicted the Jin dynasty of that era.

On another weekend, a hike in the hills at Hong Tou proved a photographer's paradise with so many colours of autumn leaves — yellow, brown, magenta, rose, green, and every combination in between. Our group met at the Overseas Chinese Hotel where we boarded a bus for our two-hour trip through the countryside laden with harvested corn fields. Workers picked through the crop for corn missed by the harvester.

After parking alongside about 60 other buses and hundreds of cars, we wended our way up to the mountain tops, a patchwork of multicolours sparkling in the morning sun. We jostled for space along the paths with more than two thousand hikers. Victoria's daughter sang exquisitely for us and all the hikers in earshot. At one stage a photographer grabbed me for photos with his daughter. Where would those photos end up? I wondered. A photographer's paradise, though, with every new scene like an autumn wonderland.

We picnicked near the top with fish, lettuce and rice, cucumber, pumpkin and meat slices, chicken wings and goose meat. Most of us were foot weary on reaching the bus and slept for our trip home.

I settled down for a relaxing day at home, and then Connie rang at 10 am and suggested I come around for a meal. I said that I would walk along the Songhua River to her place. I took the bus to Zhong Yang Dajie and walked the 1.4 kilometres of cobblestone to the Flood Memorial Tower in Stalin Park, which commemorated the battle against the floods in 1957. The cobblestone road ran for another 2 kilometres alongside the Songhua River. On the way I stopped to watch kite fliers, bubble blowers, ice hockey players on roller skates, card playing groups, old style dancers, singing groups and musicians. Arriving at Connie's place, Daniel was busy filling an urn with small red grapes ready for two months of fermentation with icing sugar. The yeast would come from the grapes themselves.

We all went by car to Connie's parents' farm for dinner. At the small farm house in the village, about an hour's drive out of Harbin, we joined Connie's father in the fields and watched him and two women workers cut the tops off white turnips. Nearby a truck carried newly harvested corn, grown in rich black soil and fertilised with organic residues. The corn was laid out on the roofs of farm buildings or homes before being marketed. With the rapidly approaching winter and with at least four months of Siberian ice and snow on the ground there was little else the farmer could do but close up his farm and wait for the thaw. He relaxed, played cards, Chinese chess and mahjong, visited friends and kept warm.

Dinner servings of a local fish and tiny shrimps, fried eggs, Chinese salad and potatoes, went down well with Harbin beer. Connie asked me to say grace as her mother and father had become Christians two years before and they enjoyed meeting every week for fellowship with a local group of Christians in a nearby village. Connie's mother proudly showed me her Bible donated by the International Bible Society. On the way back, Connie talked about how important their Christian faith had become for them.

Some of the houses I saw in the village farm area had solar power heaters. The Chinese were well into dealing with climate change and had made great strides in some heavily polluted cities. They still had a long way to go as they relied on coal, about 70 percent, for supplying their energy requirements. A disturbing statistic was that over 2,500 miners died in one year in coal mines and the authorities had suggested that the managers go down into the mines along with the miners. I was sure they would find a way around that.

Lili rang and we met at a Russian tea house to savour Russian tea, cookies and bread in a quaint room with an old Russian piano in one corner, a fireplace and photos of Russian scenes long ago in Harbin, and lots of Russian memorabilia.

Lili, whom I had met at the Governor's party for foreigners, was the coordinator with the International Exchange College at the North Eastern University. Lili didn't fit the Harbin persona with her free-spirited and relaxed attitude, and with an upbringing and education in Finland as well as in Shenyang.

She was not afraid to tell the truth about China as she saw it. Her English, learnt in Finland with an American accent, was fluent.

Lili had applied for a PhD scholarship to go to a Finnish university to work on bamboo for pandas. Having been in Finland until her middle school years she had a more Western outlook on life — independent with strong views about the way Chinese were going or had gone.

'I have a Finnish boyfriend,' she said, 'but I am not going to have an expensive Chinese style wedding. A Chinese wedding can last two or more days with a huge expense for food and having a lot of guests. The wedding is very much a parent-controlled event as the parents invite most of the guests and spare no expense to impress. Strangely enough many want the wedding to be held in a church — no stigma. Even if there was no association with a church or Christianity, the minister obliged. Sometimes it's like a factory where the couple have half an hour before the next couple arrive.'

'Is this all part of Western influence?' I asked.

'Yes, it's hitting the south more but slowly working its way north. But our Chinese culture doesn't allow for much freedom of expression and creativity. Parents try to control the career pathway of their children. The expectation of a fine job is just too much for some as they wait for the right one to come along. This is unrealistic and they should take up any job to start their career. But no, the job is not right for a number of reasons and some wait for a long time for the 'right' job to appear. They can get work, but the job is not good enough for them.'

'How about the Chinese parents? Do they have much influence on their one child to succeed?'

'They put tremendous pressure on their child to go to the best university and do well. A lot of bribery goes on, especially with rich parents who have poor to average students. Parents put pressure on teachers to perform and can bolster their child's chances to succeed by giving money to the right people. They try to control the career pathway of their children.'

'What about politics?'

'No one talks about politics; it's a no-go area of conversation,' Lili said. 'The education system is all about passing tests; the importance of learning and finding out goes by the board unless it is directly related to passing tests.'

'And learning English?'

'Very few learn to speak as they have no chance to practise. It's a crazy system which operates to favour the rich and powerful. Competition is fierce for few places and kids often study for twelve hours or more a day — no chance to play or act like normal kids.'

Lili was determined not to fall into the Chinese mould. Her parents had no influence on her job or any arrangement concerning her marriage.

Victoria, Cynthia and Catherine joined me for dinner the next day, and we all kept our jackets on because of the cold, even in the restaurant. Victoria wanted to buy a car — the trend for young professionals all over Harbin. We dined on chicken wings, Sichuan spicy meat and vegetables, eggplant and mushrooms.

An icy cold day and the likelihood of snow followed. When would they turn on the central heating? I thought.

I met with Dr Youxhio Okamoto from Japan. who was in charge of polymer research at the college. Invited to his farewell dinner, I savoured for the first time authentic Japanese cuisine with sushi, raw salmon, raw tuna and vegetable salad all delicately spiced with mustard and sauce. We sat around a table placed onto the floor for our discomfort, well not quite as we were able to place our legs into a sunken base. At our table sat a hotch potch of speakers: two spoke fluent Japanese, a Communist Party leader spoke Russian, Dr Zhang tried to speak everything, Dr Li translated into English for me and into Chinese for everyone else, and another scientist did his best to speak English; the toasting with sake, Japanese rice wine, encouraged everyone to speak. I had intended to ask Dr Okamoto in private how he felt about what happened during the Japanese occupation, but the occasion didn't arise — perhaps, it was better that way.

The next day, I felt queasy but just managed to give an English class on 'Results and Discussion points' as well as play 'G'day' by Slim Dusty and 'Click go the shears'. I also threw in the Lindy Chamberlain story with photos of dingoes and Uluru.

I spent the morning revising a paper on waste water treatment in China — every sentence needed improvement. I persevered and finally the conclusion appeared — a most welcome sight. In the afternoon, I sampled different Chinese teas at a tea house. The Chinese had over centuries perfected the art of making so many different kinds of tea, all with different flavors — more that 1,500 kinds. So a group of eight of us watched them being made by a professional tea maker before tasting. They included Oolong tea, Qimen Hong Cha (a black tea), Shoumei (a white tea), Chun Mee (a green tea), Jun shan Yin Zhen (a yellow tea) and Jasmine tea. Tea was much more popular than coffee, especially for people who wished to relax, chat and listen to music.

Jenny's uncle, Decheng Zhang, introduced me to Hugues and Jeanne Gaalon, who had been in Harbin for four years as innovators in an education program for special needs of young children. Financed by themselves from what they earned in China, they had produced educational material especially for children suffering from epilepsy and other impairments. Also they had given a counselling education service for children who had suffered in the Sichuan earthquake.

'How do you find the education system here?' I asked.

'The education system is very tightly controlled. Creativity and social emotional skills are limited,' Hugues replied. 'The primary school children go wild if let off the reins. We need a proper balance with discipline and giving freedom. But there is no fun in growing up — everything is geared to passing exams. Weekdays, evenings and weekends are full.'

'How does this affect their performance?'

'Well, shame is a big factor — especially with mistakes or performing poorly. Tests and exams all reflect proper answers as given by the teacher. The way of learning emphasises memory. No room for creativity.'

'How about the influence from Western culture now that there is much more interchange of ideas through the internet and other sources?'

'The influence of the West is creeping in, especially in the south with drugs and heavy music but not so much in the north. Japan is more seduced by the West at this stage. The advantages of the present system are that people have respect for each other, for older people, for teachers and parents. Even though they lack freedom it is easier to control and keep order. Even for our children it is easier here with less influence of harms that modern Western society can bring, but it is difficult to make friends and socialise because of differences in maturity and outlook. Young people are very open to faith issues and want to ask questions. They just need the opportunity.'

After our time together I caught a taxi back to the university campus. It was the first week of November and an icy cold evening. The snow and icy patches on the roads made it difficult to walk with confidence.

The next day I lost the key to my unit in the snow; it wouldn't be found for four months until the snow and ice had melted. I found someone who spoke to the building manager who came over and gave me the master key. I then had to walk down to the market place and find a key cutter. After a lot of searching in wrong places I finally found one. I called the building manager and in broken Mandarin I told him I had a spare key and could he come and pick the master key up.

Later, I went to Cynthia's street in Hesong district and dined at a nearby restaurant on *jiaozi* (Chinese dumpling), Chinese cabbage and eggplant. A phone call from Jun, a student at Harbin University of Engineering, invited me to dinner with his family. Oh no! I was full but had to accept, so I raced back home in a taxi for a quick change and up to Hong Kong Hotel where I met Jun, his sister, father and mother, and his uncle and aunt. The hotel spread was magnificent — steamed fish, chicken, beef, vegetables, noodles and all washed down with Harbin beer with lots of repetitious toasting – 'I am very glad to meet you' several times from Jun's uncle.

Jun explained his course in shipbuilding at the University of Harbin Engineering which would later include two years at Strathclyde University in Scotland. I had taught Jun a few lessons and so his family responded in gratitude.

Jun's father ran me back, stopping on the way to buy a supply of bananas, apples and grapes to keep me going until it was time to return to Adelaide.

Before leaving China, I flew to Shanghai to visit the Shanghai Jewish Refugees Museum. Shanghai had accepted about 18,000 Jewish refugees fleeing the Holocaust in Europe. I was keen to know what had happened to the Jews under the Japanese occupation. I found out what David Kranzler, a Holocaust historian, called the 'Miracle of Shanghai' where Jews and Chinese lived in relative harmony and most survived. I spent time wandering through the Exhibition Hall displaying 'Memories of Shanghai'.

I couldn't leave Shanghai without strolling along the famous waterfront, the Bund, on the bank of the Huangpu River.

The next day I joined a Chinese tourist group and travelled by bus to Zhuijiajiao, a traditional village on the outskirts of Shanghai. We walked alongside canals, over arched stone bridges, and on streets paved with stone, and through homes dating back to the Ming and Qing dynasties.

Again, the only Westerner, I joined another Chinese group to Suzhou the next day. We wandered through its famous gardens, parks and courtyards, taking in the pride of its heritage.

On the last day I travelled with Helen, a friend of Ocean's, to Nanjing by train travelling at 300 kilometres an hour. At the Nanjing Memorial Hall, hundreds of young Chinese people lined up to visit the museum, which was dedicated to the memory of 300,000 victims who lost their lives during the Nanjing Massacre in 1937. The graphic displays depicted the terrible atrocities perpetrated by the Japanese Army; many of the victims were innocent civilians. The evidence even came from the diaries of Japanese soldiers. While the Memorial Hall reminded us all of the horrors of war, the downside for Chinese, I felt, was that they might not find it easy to forgive, and, worse still, hatred of the Japanese would be passed on from generation to generation. Helen herself would never have known the extent of the atrocities committed by the Japanese had she not gone to the museum.

Chapter 26

Writing memoirs and miscarriages of justice

JUDE AQUILINA, A POET AND office worker at the South Australian Writers Centre, suggested that I assist people who phoned or called in to the centre with their stories. New to the game of appraisal, I simply read the stories as a reader would and then re-read them with a mind on structure, ease of reading, style and errors. The stories I read over the next seven years were mostly memoirs and they never ceased to amaze me, covering traumatic experiences, disease, adventure, crime, abuse, violence and war. For me, each story was an enriching experience; in a small way, I had entered into another person's life.

Leonie gave an intimate and detailed account of her heart surgery involving aortic stenosis and titled her story as *Rusted out* — an appealing title, I thought. The story engaged hospital staff, family and friends. She included attractive illustrations in her publication, showing a light-hearted touch to a serious operation which turned out well for her.

Beth searched deep within herself for inner strength and resolve to meet the challenges that confronted her as a migrant to Australia. A 'baptism of fire' described her first day's encounter with the Australian bush — a bumpy ride along a dirt track, over potholes and corrugations, and with her uncle's utility breaking down. The bumpy track continued through her teens and into her mid-twenties with her work experiences, illnesses that left her debilitated, her marriage at 17 to Spence, a binge drinker, and her bringing up of her three children on her own in desperate circumstances. What Beth described about the Coorong captured the bare essentials of existence more reminiscent of the early pioneers. Barely surviving in its harsh yet raw beauty, Beth came to an ultimate decision concerning her marriage to Spence and their three sons. She showed remarkable tenacity and resilience, as described in her book *Until they were older*.

In Jenny's story, she suffered from her parents' strict control of her life, all stemming from Nazi times. The Hitler Youth organisation, formed by the Nazi Party, indoctrinated German youth with an ideology of racial and national superiority. The organisation began in 1926, and, by 1939 at the outbreak of the Second World War, membership was compulsory. The youth movement demanded absolute obedience to Hitler and the Nazi Party. Dissent was not tolerated and punished severely. Jenny's parents could not let go of their past and forced her to part with her child out of wedlock to the New South Wales Community Services.

Kevern in *The life of Fred* recounted his experiences while growing up in the Port Adelaide area, showing enlivened glimpses of the past with colourful characters, humour and anecdotes. His book appealed to readers with nostalgia for the 1930s and 1940s and to those who wanted to know more about life during the Great Depression and the Second World War.

Max invited me to attend his 90th birthday and launch his book on farm life in the Barossa and his Second World War experiences. He had several harrowing experiences and one narrow escape when his unit fought the Japanese in New Guinea.

Robert wrote about his encounters with locals at his ports of call on an around the world yachting adventure.

Gerard, a Frenchman, wrote about his time as a conscripted soldier in the French Army fighting the Algerians toward the end of the French–Algerian War.

Phoebe was born in Holland and grew up under the domination of a much older sister. She experienced the Second World War as an 8-year-old. Later, she became a teacher, married and migrated to Australia. Her life in Australia took many twists and turns, as told in *Phoebe*.

Ruth wrote an account of her turbulent time in Africa with her husband Peter, in *Uncertain winds*. After leaving their happy life in Kenya, they continually searched for a place to settle where Peter could live out his dream as a farmer, but any success they achieved was followed by disaster, as once-peaceful countries were shattered by wars, and the family, facing ruin and danger, was forced to move.

In one story, *Brutalised*, I spent a lot of time going over Warrens' account of his growing-up in Queensland institutions. In one institution he described how he and other boys were forced by the superintendent to strip naked and then lashed with a length of thick, hard leather across their bare backs, leaving them bleeding profusely. I could hardly believe the suffering Warren and others went through in those times. Jude and I had the privilege of launching Warren's book in August 2015 to a packed gathering at South Seas Books in Port Elliot.

On a much lighter side, Roger Trevor wrote of his time as Santa Claus for twelve years in Myers. I launched his book at the café where he worked in the city.

Jude rang me up one day to suggest I meet with Kent Lines who had written two large volumes of a biographical novel based on his life experiences of growing up as an orphan, then as a wartime sniper in Vietnam, and, finally, as an agent for Mossad in Israel and the CIA. 'Yes, I would,' I said, in anticipation of a spy thriller.

When we met at the Writers Centre, Kent didn't seem like he could hurt anyone with his mild-mannered and engaging way of talking about his stories. He had spent years writing them, but his health had deteriorated as a result of injuries in Vietnam, to the point that he needed help to complete his story.

Kent was somewhat of a recluse and lived alone in a city apartment. He found difficulty in talking about painful aspects of his life and, perhaps, found it easier to write about those experiences.

On our third meeting, Kent could barely walk back to his apartment which was only 200 metres from the Writers Centre. He suffered from a degenerative brain function that was normally associated with boxing. His doctors could do nothing for him.

With pressure from other work I let Kent know that I could not undertake the editing and re-structuring required to complete his stories. He was very disappointed as he felt that I understood his background and was the best person to help him.

Two months later, Jude rang to tell me the sad news that Kent had passed away. With regret, I realised that he had not fulfilled his last aim in life, so I re-read his stories to select and reduce what he had written to about 80,000 words. I cut and paste, inserted connecting parts and wrote the ending. My time in Israel helped with this.

Custom Book Publications accepted the manuscript for publication with the title of *Jericho man* and a front cover design of former prime minister Golda Meir in a sniper's scope sight. Most of the story is based on Kent's experiences in an orphanage in America, his time at university, in Vietnam, and with the CIA and Mossad in Israel.

If true, Kent played a key part in preventing Israel using nuclear-armed Jericho missiles. Golda Meir, the prime minister of Israel, showed strong leadership when Syrian and Egyptian military forces launched a surprise attack on the unprepared Israeli forces, on the holiest day of the Jewish year, Yom Kippur, on 6 October 1973. With Israel's survival at stake, Golda Meir tried desperately to expedite American military aid. At the same time, she authorised Israeli Defence Forces to go on alert with nuclear-armed Jericho missiles — the ultimate option. Enter Kent Lines.

Miscarriages of justice

Edward Splatt rang me after first contacting the South Australian Writer s Centre and asked if I would I be interested in writing up his story. Like most people who had lived in Adelaide during the late 1970s and early 80s, my memory had dimmed to recall the Splatt case, which had featured so prominently in the media, along with the Lindy Chamberlain story.

Edward Splatt was charged with the murder of Mrs Simper, a 77-year-old Adelaide woman who had been badly beaten, sexually assaulted and strangled in her bedroom.

The case was complex, dealing with paint, metal particles, various types of fibres, wood, foam spicules, birdseed and sugar found in her room, all of which were linked to Splatt, a spray painter in an engineering workshop opposite Mrs Simper's house. It was a rare case in that the only evidence leading to the identification of the accused was the scientific evidence.

Splatt was convicted of the murder in 1978. His appeals were unsuccessful. However, Stewart Cockburn, a journalist with the Adelaide nespaper, *The Advertiser*, became convinced of the unsatisfactory basis of the prosecution case. He ran a campaign in *The Advertiser* for two years before the government agreed to a Royal Commission. Splatt's conviction was subsequently overturned in 1984 and he was paid $300,000 by way of compensation. He had spent six-and-a-half years in prison.

I visited Splatt in his Cheltenham home after agreeing to look at his account of what had happened. In a dark-lit room full of memorabilia, I sat down with two Maltese Shih Tzus yapping at my feet. Yvonne, Splatt's wife, took the dogs away, and with no preliminaries, Splatt said, 'It's all here,' as he handed me the 540 fullscap pages he had written about his case. I glanced over the neatly handwritten account, before I said, 'Are you happy for me to take them away and photocopy them?'

'Of course, write the story. It's all there. Anything you need to know, I'll be here.' Splatt looked at me with an intensity that seemed to cry out for justice. I left with the promise I would see him again soon.

I was hooked after reading Edward Splatt's own account, mostly written in prison. At our subsequent meetings, I was amazed how well he could recall dates, times, names and places relating to every detail of his trial and imprisonment.

An embittered man, he had become obsessed with his case and the need to find closure. I wasn't sure if a book could do that. I gradually got to know Yvonne, who had endured all of her husband's pain and anguish over the miscarriage of justice, which was only fully exposed by the Royal Commission. All she wanted was to let go of the past, but that was not possible with Splatt's continual reminders of what had happened. He vented his feelings towards the police, the chief forensic investigator and the forensic scientists who had misled the jury in the presentation of their evidence.

It was never in Splatt's mind to accept his sentence passively, as advised by his lawyer, Jack Elliott, who had exhausted all legal avenues. Nothing swayed him from proving that he and his family were innocent of all associations with the murder of Mrs Simper. Splatt's continual writing had commanded respect among fellow prisoners and guards, as well as the public who gradually became aware of his efforts to clear himself. Why would a man persist year after year to proclaim his innocence, especially through his immense writing efforts?

While a set of coincidences—'the united force of all the circumstances'—worked against Splatt, another set worked for him. Through his own determined efforts he made contact with Stewart Cockburn, the one person he believed might speak out on his behalf. Cockburn had been a respected investigative journalist with *The Advertiser*; he believed in Splatt's innocence and used his skills to galvanise public opinion and, in turn, the government into responding with a Royal Commission. But for Cockburn's efforts,

Splatt could have easily languished in gaol for the rest of his natural life, given his worsening health.

Edward Splatt, in my mind, epitomised the tenacious character of an Australian battler against the odds. His constant letter writing, his prodigious note-taking and his sketching had consumed his daily life in prison and stood out as a 'tour de force' of all time for an Australian prisoner.

I had to write the story, drawing on Splatt's account, the trial transcripts, scientific and legal reports, newspaper articles and the Royal Commission. I interspersed the writing with his own description of the time he spent in prison. It seemed to hang together, but I would not know for sure until it was reviewed. My scientific background helped as I tried to be as objective as possible in distilling the essential elements of the case down to a level for the average reader.

I completed the Splatt story in 2008 and titled the book *Flawed forensics: the Splatt case and Stewart Cockburn*. Graham Archer, presenter of Channel 7's *Today Tonight Adelaide*, launched the book at the SA Writers Centre to a packed atrium.

At the same time another high profile South Australian case was drawing public interest through media coverage. Henry Keogh had already served 13 years of his 25 year non-parole sentence in prison for drowning his fiancée in a bath. The primary evidence came from a forensic pathologist whose competence had been brought into question over the way he conducted the post-mortem examination.

I attended a court session in which the state medical board launched misconduct proceedings against Adelaide's chief forensic pathologist who had given pseudo-scientific evidence, according to three eminent scientists, for the prosecution at Henry Keogh's murder trial. The district court, however, did not reach a finding of unprofessional conduct against the pathologist.

After the court session I made my way across Adelaide's Victoria Square. David Szach, who had been sent to jail for murder of a lawyer, caught up with me at the traffic lights. 'I can't believe it,' he said. 'There should be a judicial inquiry to investigate all the cases in which the psychologist has given evidence in court.'

'Yes, but it is going to be an uphill battle to achieve that now after his clearance of any wrongdoing,' I replied.

'*They should not have released me*,' David said, changing the subject. 'I should have served my life sentence.'

Knowing that a life sentence meant at least 20 years, I had to agree. How could David Szach have been released after serving only 14 years of a life sentence? I thought.

With no strong backing from the media, no overwhelming plea from the public for justice, and no overruling physical or mental condition which might have persuaded the state governor to act mercifully, what had prompted the government of South Australia to act in such an unprecedented way?

David had good reason to be fired up. The same pathologist, whose professional conduct had been questioned in the Keogh case, had given damning evidence at his trial which had influenced the jury to find David guilty of the murder of prominent Adelaide lawyer Derrance Stevenson.

'Could you look at my case and write it up, just as you have done for Splatt?' he asked.

'I'm not sure, David.' I sounded evasive with the thought of having to investigate another case so soon.

David and I talked briefly on a grassy knoll separating two busy lanes of traffic that skirted Victoria Square. Then we adjourned to a nearby café where David spilled out details of his conviction. What he said reeled me in to delve deeper into his case.

In the next few weeks I ploughed through the trial transcripts, the grounds for appeal, and the reports by forensic scientists investigating the evidence presented by the pathologist.

David and Derrance, the lawyer he was convicted of killing, were homosexual lovers. They had lived together at Derrance's home and office premises on Greenhill Road in Adelaide for more than three years. Derrance had been free to engage in homosexual activities, thanks to Don Dunstan, former premier of South Australia. As premier for most of the 1970s, Dunstan had pioneered a new period of enlightenment and tolerance, with decriminalisation of homosexuality, the introduction of equal rights for women and the recognition of Aboriginal land rights.

'A lover's tiff that went out of control,' the media raised as a likely motive, but there was no evidence to suggest anything untoward in their relationship. David and Derrance had spent an amicable afternoon with two associates of Derrance on the day before Derrance was murdered.

The day after Derrance's murder, Tuesday 5 June 1979, Derrance's secretary received two calls from clients to inform her that Derrance had not appeared in court. She became concerned about his whereabouts and at 11 am she received a call from David in Coober Pedy.

'Is Derrance there?'

'No, he's not, David,' the secretary said.

'Could you please leave a message on his desk? Would you tell him I have arrived safely and I'm just about to go and do what he asked?'

Following the secretary's concern about the whereabouts of Derrance, three police officers arrived at Derrance's premises by 3.30 pm and began searching, but it was not until 5 pm that an officer tried to open the freezer. The lid would not budge and on closer inspection it had been tightly sealed with glue. With force the officers prised it open and gazed at a body in a partially undressed state with the head wrapped in two plastic bags.

The key witness for the Crown prosecution was the forensic pathologist who estimated time of death from 4.45 to 8.45 pm. Unknown to David's defence team, the pathologist had used a cooling formula that was not applicable to estimate the time of death.

The pathologist also stated with confidence that the maximum amount of time that the body would have been out of the freezer was no more than one hour. But in reality he had no way of accurately determining the time between the shooting and when the body was placed in the freezer.

The Crown, therefore, linked David to the crime when he was alone with Derrance. This allowed sufficient time, an hour if necessary, for Derrance's body to be placed in the freezer. David was identified by a witness as the man coming out of Derrance's place at 6.40 pm — the ID was later shown to be unreliable. These two factors underpinned the prosecutor's case to the jury.

Based on the discrediting of the pathologist's evidence by two eminent scientists and a lack of credibility in the witness testimony, a clear basis opened up for David to lodge an appeal. The flaws alone, proving the evidence at the trial to be non-probative, should have been enough to set the conviction aside, even if there were other evidence of apparent guilt.

But the law didn't allow for a new appeal, despite fresh and compelling evidence.

David, a mild-mannered person, not given to flights of anger or cursing, had persisted in his efforts for more than 35 years to clear his name. He had sought help from forensic scientists, lawyers, a former Adelaide University professor of law, and the media, and had submitted two petitions to the Governor of South Australia.

'You never applied for parole?' I asked him at one of our meetings.

'No, I refused because I did not commit the crime. If I had applied for parole, it would have meant I was guilty,' he said.

'Well, how were you released? Surely, the only way is to apply for parole, admit guilt and show remorse?'

'You are right. That is the only way. I should not have been released. I became an embarrassment and a liability. They tried to silence me.'

The case of David Szach, I concluded, was a serious case of miscarriage of justice. The foundation on which the case was based — the sighting of Szach coming out of the house, having supposedly committed the crime, and the pathologist's evidence — was flawed. Improper police procedures used in the identification of Szach by an eye witness, combined with the pathologist's evidence based on unsound scientific principles, significantly contributed to the flawed evidence and to the miscarriage of justice. More disturbingly, it appeared that evidence had been manipulated to support a preconceived view for the Crown's case. Evidence strongly suggested that it was a premeditated murder, carried out at a later time than specified by the Crown, and carefully planned to implicate Szach — a set-up.

In *Body in the freezer: the case of David Szach*, published in October 2015, the spotlight fell on the police, forensic and judicial systems, as well as Adelaide's murky past in the 1970s and 1980s.

On a positive note, under a new law passed in 2013 by the South Australian parliament, for the right of appeal with fresh and compelling evidence, David Szach hoped to have his case reviewed.

For me, writing had opened the door to people's lives in a way I could never have imagined. Helping to write their stories and see them in print made all the effort worthwhile.

Chapter 27

Darwin

ON SATURDAY, 17 JUNE 2006, Liz and I geared up to drive to Darwin in Rachel's Hyundai Tucson. I tried to contemplate a 3,000 kilometre trip through the centre of Australia and a two-and-a-half month stay away from our Gawler home.

We pursued a leisurely pace up to Port Augusta, stopping at Stone Hut for a crusty, mouth-watering, wood-oven baked pastie — Cornish, of course. And armed with Anzac biscuits we motored on to Wilmington, through Horrocks Pass, and on to the main road to Port Augusta, where we went for a brisk walk in the chilly evening air to the old bridge over the gulf before settling down.

The next morning we left Port Augusta at the start of the Stuart Highway that went all the way to Darwin, covering a vast area of arid lands through Central Australia to the tropical Top End, as it is called. The highway was named after explorer John Stuart, a Scotsman, who in 1862 was the first European to go across Australia from south to north. We soaked in the early morning light on saltbush country as we journeyed north, with a stop for coffee at the Heritage Centre.

I thought I would check out the mothballed detention centre at Woomera. That was a big mistake. After taking a couple of photos of the five-metre high main gate and the one-metre high coiled razor wire between the inner and outer fences, a car rolled up and a burly, angry-looking man hopped out. 'Can't you read?' he said.

'No, I didn't read any signs.'

The man looked as though he would go into a fit and said, 'The video camera has already passed a photo on to the Commonwealth Police in Canberra and you are in deep trouble.' He tried to grab my camera, but I held on to it. I should have asked for some ID, but it didn't occur to me at the time. We left.

At Coober Pedy we met up with pleasant caravaners — a welcome change, and motored on to Cadney Homestead for the night.

We crossed the border the next day with oranges, lemons and apples. We spotted a fruit quarantine sign advising us to ditch our fruit. Well, we ate four apples and four oranges and gave the rest to an Aboriginal mother.

Just before Alice Springs we followed the Ross Highway to Emily's Gap — an unusual chunk cut out of a MacDonnell Range outcrop east of Alice. We walked through the gap where a large number of students were sketching the brown-red, angular rock formations towering above them. Aboriginal drawings of three caterpillars symbolised the dream time heritage of the Arrernte people.

At Alice Springs we walked for an hour along the Todd River where groups of Aboriginals had camped or were just sitting in small clusters in the dry river bed. The local Aboriginals, we learned, resented rural Aboriginals coming in and damaging the environment.

As we moved out of Alice Springs the 'red centre' turned a deep reddish-brown, with shrubs, a variety of grasses, spinifex and ephemerals, and small trees on either side of the Stuart Highway.

Then we motored on to Wycliffe Wells, the UFO capital of Australia where numerous sightings of UFOs have been made. A couple of green men welcomed us to the hotel. 'Aliens don't exist,' Liz said. 'In fact, it's sacrilege to suggest any visitation at all.'

'Liz, I said, 'with so many sightings of UFOs around the world it wouldn't surprise me if one or two of those were genuine.' We agreed to differ.

We stopped to admire the Devil's Marbles, a collection of huge, red and rounded granite boulders that started out many millions of years ago with molten rock reaching the surface.

At Tennant Creek, further on, we walked through the town, where Aboriginal children frolicked in an Arts and Crafts centre while older ones sat on the walkways or careered up and down the street in beat-up cars. We met up with a policeman who said he was running a territory about the size of England.

At Renner Springs the next day, we met an Israeli who said, he was stuck in the bush and trying to save money. '*Mazal tov*,' I said, and wished him the best.

At Elliot for another break we greeted more Aboriginals; the roadhouses seemed like a magnet for them.

Daly Waters pub was the next stop with lots of outback characters inside and outside the pub. And paraphernalia everywhere with photos, ribbons, trophies, mugs, stickers and signs.

At Larimah we stopped for a shaded lunch followed by a light beer at a homely pub with sqawking parrots in aviaries, a green python and lots of memorabilia. A pink panther sign outside added to the pub's charm and offbeat character.

We drove on to Katherine, passing rocky outcrops, water holes, rivers and denser vegetation. An evening buffet, a free bottle of Wolf Blass Shiraz and grilled barramundi awaited us at the All Seasons Motel.

Our Katherine Gorge walk took us to a vantage point well above the river to view the gorge and open tropical woodland. The climb exhausted Liz. Another kilometre and I would have had to carry her back to the car.

The following day we arrived in Darwin to house-sit for Louis, Juglio and their three children. The deal was to look after their house while they were away on holiday. And to look after their pets — feed a white mouse, Maisy, with birdseed; Alice, a blue tongue lizard that loves a cuddle, and feed every second day with cat food; Aldo, a small python — just leave alone (no problems); Daisy and Pip, the turtles — feed every night by hand a food block chopped into small bits, and have a supply of bandaids handy; fish (no names) in kitchen tank, a goldfish tank and the bird bath — just a pinch of dried fish for each and top up with water. And Rosie, the Staffordshire Terrier — she needs a walk every day, water, dog food, a chop when we go out and cuddles. Some family!

We met up with our daughter Rachel and George Roussos, an electrical engineer with his business in Darwin. At the Sailing Club they seemed a happy pair, enjoying each other's company. With three bottles of white wine how could we not enjoy the fish dinner, the sun setting over the sea, the warm balmy night air and convivial company?

Talk about being thrown in at the deep end. With two weddings for Andrew and Linda to attend, we had to devise an ad hoc plan for minding Jackson and Ruby until bedtime. With playing trains, hide and seek, hide the hat, dancing and jigging, swimming in the pool and bedtime stories we nearly made it.

After all that, Jackson pooed his pants. Ruby screamed her heart out on being settled down and vomited over Liz. We let Ruby stay up for three hours and sheer exhaustion won in the end. At least she showed interest in the World Cup Soccer in between wandering around the house. At midnight we were all in and crawled away for our first night of house sitting.

The next day — recovery day — was topped off with a prawn-cooked dinner accompanied by unwooded Chardonnay at George's place. George and I discussed Alexander the Great's journey to India and whether the Kalash people in Northern Pakistan were direct descendants of Alexander's men. And how did Alexander die — malaria or from poisoning?

I walked along the coastal strip near Fanny Bay and met Jack who was at least ninety. 'When it goes below 21 degrees I put on seven layers, it's that cold,' he said.

'I wouldn't want it to be any hotter,' I said.

'What are you? Some kind of Eskimo. Where are you from?'

'Scotland originally, but now living near Adelaide. Anything below 21 degrees is a bonus for me.'

While we talked, a police car pulled up to investigate an Aboriginal chap sprawled out on the grass nearby. Two officers stepped out and one prodded the man and said, 'Eddie, wake up.' Eventually he did after more prodding.

'Can't understand why the Aborigines don't have more 'go' in them,' said Jack. 'They succumb so easily to drink, go on the dole and sniff petrol.'

We talked a little more about the Aboriginal problems in Darwin before Jack shuffled away. His gaunt frame and failing eyesight didn't deter his early morning amble. We met up a few more times on our walks.

We had a full day with the children, and Jackson disobeyed orders not to swim in his clothes. Too late to stop him, so the shoes, top, socks and pants all came off. He went home in the nude. We chided him and he chanted, 'Grandad and Granny not nice to me.' Ruby, however, was an angel this time and loved the playground with swings and slides. Later, at the family's backyard swimming pool Ruby slipped off the deep end and sank to the bottom. I grabbed her under the armpits and lifted her up. She gasped and spluttered but was all right. I realised how easy it was for children to drown or near-drown even in the presence of adults. Swimming pool-related accidents were common in Australia for toddlers and young children.

Another full day and I was determined to tire out Jackson with a chasing game, cycling, dancing, swimming and racing. And Thomas the train game — 'you be Harry, Grandad. I'll be Thomas and Ruby is Percy,' said Jackson. At eight o'clock his eyes grew heavy and with a thumb in his mouth he barely uttered any protest as we stopped a video mid-stream. I picked Jackson up and popped him into bed. He was asleep as soon as his head hit the pillow. I was exhausted — the price had been too high.

With time off, Liz and I walked around to East Point and viewed the old gun emplacements, and the anchor for the five-kilometre boom which stretched across the bay to deter submarines during the Second World War. We inspected the command towers, the signal tower and anti-aircraft sites. Mangrove thickets jutted out to sea, and inlets and outcrops of rocks provided attractive venues for strollers, fisher folk and fossickers.

We all spent a day at Litchfield National Park, but the Buley rock pool wasn't conducive to swimming or bathing as there were too many tourists and the rocks were too slippery. We trekked to Tolmer Falls, exhausting for me with piggy-backing Jackson and carrying Ruby. At Wangi Falls we delighted in a cool swim while admiring the plunging falls. Nearby, thousands of flying foxes had taken up residence.

On the first day of July, Liz and I set off on a short West Australian adventure. We arrived near dusk at Springvale Homestead. A wedding reception was in full swing with music, and later a firework display. Loud bangs punctuated our sleep. Of course, it was fireworks night for the whole of the Northern Territory.

The next day we drove along the Victorian Highway for nearly 300 kilometres to arrive at Timber Creek. We passed charred tree trunks on our left and a more intact open woodland with tall grasses on our right — the road had acted as a firebreak.

At Joe Creek we braved a one-and-a-half hour hike up to the base of the escarpment which continued on through Livistonia palm trees, white currant bushes and leafy ferns, as well as spiny spinifex. We gazed all around at the red rocky escarpment and the lush green hillside vegetation. We had left the hectic world behind and entered a forgotten paradise — even for Aboriginals, who had revelled in their dreaming land and bushland ways before white man came.

Further on, at Policeman's Lookout we took in a magnificent sunset over Victoria River. A couple of grey nomads had parked nearby for a few days so we yarned for a while before returning to

Timber Creek Motel in the fading light. We nearly hit a kangaroo on the red dust road leading out of Policeman's Lookout.

We continued on the Victoria Highway, stopping at Cockatoo Lagoon in Keep National Park, where we sighted a black-necked stork and a couple of brolgas. Lilies bloomed on the lagoon and a flock of geese had parked on the limbs of a dead tree. We walked on the rocky fringe of the lagoon, keeping an eye open for salties.

As we neared Kununurra we detoured on a road to Lake Argyle and the Ord River Dam, taking in magnificent views of the stark red rocky outcrops and lush tree-dotted hillsides of paper bark, grey box, woolly butt, baobab and palms. We picnicked by a shady tree bordering the Ord River and close to the gushing outlet of a four-metre diameter conduit through the dam wall.

We rested overnight at picturesque Kona Lakeside Tourist Park with our cabin fronting the palm-fringed lake.

The next day we stopped at Parry's Lagoons, a wetland feast with every kind of waterfowl you could imagine — egrets, cormorants, spoonbills, ducks, magpie geese, coots, brolgas, herons, ibis, darters — all savouring, it seemed, the calm suffusion of lagoon ambience. No salties, thank goodness.

On our way to Wyndham, we viewed from a lookout King River and four other rivers meandering their way through the extensive mud flats to Cambridge Gulf. The town itself had seen better days and could easily do with a make-over. But, maybe its dilapidated buildings and beat-up port facilities added a character of its own.

We picnicked at King River and watched the spell-binding sunset over Lake Kununurra before returning to our campsite.

The next day we toured the Ord River irrigation area with sugar cane production in full swing, along with mangoes. Indian sandalwood held promise for the future. Also, melons, chickpeas, maize, cotton, bananas and vegetable crops thrived on clay or river loam soil. The Ord River scheme covered about 54,000 square kilometres, with an irrigated area of over 14,000 square kilometres. The Heliothis moth had caused a problem with the cotton but was being tackled with a natural insect repellent. Fruit fly could be a problem and cane toads were on the march from the east to invade the area. The pastoral stations produced live cattle for Indonesia, Malaysia and the Philippines.

At Hidden Valley, our next stop, we viewed a mini-Bungle Bungles with rocky beehive outcrops of sandstone. Interpretive displays showed how the sand blew in 360 million years ago and had hardened into layers before weathering into their beehive shapes.

On the way back to Katherine and Darwin we passed road trains, a lone cyclist, Aboriginals in beat-up cars, flocks of cockatoos and galahs, Brahman cross cattle, kangaroos and baobab trees. At our overnight stay in Katherine, I watched the World Cup soccer semi-final between Portugal and France. It was hard to imagine that a lapse of concentration — or over-eagerness on the part of a Portuguese player — gave France the winning score with a penalty goal.

Back in Darwin, Jade arrived on 9 August 2006 — a beautiful brown-haired, chubby-cheeked girl for Linda and Andrew. She slept soundly in hospital, barely opening her eyes, and was the apple of everyone's eye.

After more days of baby-sitting and child minding, and walks along the coast at Casuarina Beach and at Lee Point, we set off back to Gawler via Kakadu National Park. With an overnight stay at Cooinda we joined the sunrise cruise on the Alligator River. From Pluto to Rambo, and at least a dozen other crocodiles, our guide kept up a running commentary. 'There are three things the crocs fear,' he said. 'First, other crocs, especially male ones that could attack or even kill; second, the extent of the dry and wet seasons for their eggs to survive. If it is too dry the eggs dry out too much, if too wet they could be washed away; and third, Steve Irwin, the crocodile man.' The joke about Steve Irwin would not have been made had our guide known that the well-known crocodile adventurer would be killed by a sting ray three days later.

On the river, we caught sight of all kinds of birds — egrets, darters, white bellied sea eagles, ducks, magpie geese, the Jesus bird which walked on water, pelicans, spoonbills and kingfishers. We came across a large piece of dead wood and the guide said the wood was known as 'dead dog wood' as it did not have any bark. How many times had he told that line?

We stopped at Mataranka Homestead for the night and managed a quick swim in the thermal pool before dark.

We retraced our steps along the Stuart Highway and at Coober Pedy we stayed at an underground motel for the night. A sandstorm howled all night through a hole in the rock ventilators. Next morning we wandered through the Desert Cave to view the history and development of opal mining before setting off on the last stretch to home.

Andrew and Linda's wedding (1994)

Ralph Mann with father Adam (my great-grandfather)
and sister Mary (photo taken in Banff, Scotland,
shortly before Ralph was killed in action in France, 1917)

My father and mother, Tom and Anne,
celebrating an anniversary

Sister Mandy with 2-year-old Jackson

A Greek wedding for George and Rachel

Jackson, Ruby and Jade (Linda and Andrew's children)

Iraklis, Eva, Ruby, Linda and Jade at Cleland
Conservation Park, Adelaide

Autumn delight with Eva (Rachel and George's daughter)

Rachel and son Iraklis

Tom and Liz

Chapter 28

Family and a few extras

THREE DAYS AFTER OUR TAX consultant declared we were living on the edge of a financial precipice, and that I should find full-time work again, Linda rang in the evening of 7 October 2005, and said, 'Our house has burnt down.'

'You're joking!' I said, trying to gather my senses into reality, as I knew Linda never joked in that way.

'It's true. There's nothing left. We are all right — safe.'

'Thank goodness,' I said, still trying to take in the enormity of what she had said.

Apparently, something had set off an explosion in Andrew's shed which caused a fireball to race through the house. Linda wrenched Jackson, aged three, and Ruby, aged one, who had just begun to walk, from their beds. They retreated to the back garden and watched the inferno. The police and fire brigade arrived.

Neighbours rallied around and helped. A friend offered a room for the night. Rachel and George arrived to console Linda and Andrew. The next day they searched through charred remains and retrieved a few items of kitchenware, but all the clothes were sooted and soaked with the water doused onto them.

Their plight went on the *Northern Territory News*. Friends and neighbours continued to help, and they found accommodation for two weeks in an apartment. We all had to remind ourselves that everyone was safe, and the tragedy paled into insignificance with the recent tragedies abroad of famine in Niger, killings in Dafur, Sudan, the Bali bombings and the earthquake and loss of more than 30,000 lives in Pakistan. The tsunami and the Florida hurricane also destroyed many homes.

Linda, with her amazing resilience, and having already suffered the loss of her car and belongings with the Katherine flood, faced what lay ahead in building up their home again with a positive do-attitude. Andrew lost two vehicles in the fire, as well as one in the Katherine flood and another trying to cross a flooded river in the Northern Territory outback.

While Linda and Andrew tried to pick up their lives again, I applied, at an almost scrapheap-age of 64, for work.

Job applications and getting police clearance should not be too hard for a minor activist, I thought. I applied for positions of a trainer in amenity horticulture and of academic skills adviser at the Australian National University. I held off for the cellar hand at a local winery. But another thought: I could become a speech writer for George W Bush. I had a practice run:

> We are fighting the enemy of the American people — a tough enemy that won't respond to reason and fair play. But these terrorists are up against a tougher adversary. We, the American people, will take the fight right up to them. They will find out just how determined and resolute the American people are. We are not about to give in. We will never bow to their evil ways and intentions.

> We are at war. We are fighting for true freedom, true democracy — American democracy, American freedom. Everyone has a right to that kind of freedom. We know we are on the right path. Look at our record. We will not be put off by the threats and activities of terrorists who would oppose us.

> Although we went into Iraq for the wrong reason we
> have a right to be there now, to bring about our type of
> democracy, our way of life, and our kind of stability for
> the Iraqi people. And we will stay for as long as it takes
> to do the job. We don't have a timetable. A timetable
> will give the enemy the advantage they need. We could
> be there for a hundred years but we will do the job that
> has to be done.
> I thank you all.

Anyway, I had no luck at the jobs for which I had applied, age most likely being the main barrier. And I didn't apply to be a speech writer for George Bush. I continued as a voluntary worker with the Gawler Visitor Information Centre, mostly advising tourists where to go in the Barossa Valley. I also had a spell with the Gawler Voluntary Resource Centre, a new umbrella-type of organisation which serviced the needs of all voluntary organisations in the Gawler region. Mike Rann, the premier, opened the centre. We chatted briefly about the important role of voluntary organisations.

On 19 October 2005, I thought about Frank, my brother, who had died 40 years before. He would have loved the Australian outback, fishing, shooting and just being in the open. The mystery of his disappearance off the passenger liner *Australis* in the Mediterranean Sea remained. Mandy thought that he had fought with one of the passengers and was knocked overboard in the early hours of the morning. No one came forward. No sighting. Just despair for Mum, Dad and Mandy on the rest of their sea voyage to Sydney. Knowing Frank's mental state, and what he had already gone through with treatment in mental institutes, he might well have taken his life. Ending up in a mental institution in Australia wasn't for Frank, a person who loved wide open spaces.

With the lack of progress in money-making jobs or ventures, I consoled myself that worldliness was a blight of the Western world, and for us the great Australian blight. All nations gravitated towards it, a dominating Western culture coupled with a globalised lack of identity and uniqueness.

It seems strange that we are masters of our own destiny — most of us — but succumb to elemental and persuasive forces governing our way of life. Subtle brainwashing, consumerism, living each day for material gain and the comfortable nest egg at the retiring end of life. What happened to free thinking minds? And challenges? Challenges to flow against the tide of humanity in discovering an eternal sense of being, values, truths, qualities, and a destiny that transcends our transitory state.

I often think about Ralph Mann, my great-uncle, who had set off from Banff in Scotland for a new life in Australia in 1910. He sailed on the *Otway* of the Orient Line and took up residence in Kent Town, Adelaide, working initially as a carpenter. He joined the South Australian Police Force in March 1913, earning eight shillings a day as a recruit and for his first case in court gave evidence against a shopkeeper in Hindley Street charged with sly grog selling. The shopkeeper had unwittingly poured two glasses of Walker's whisky for Ralph and another police recruit.

In court, Mr Smith for the defence proceeded to put a series of questions to Ralph for the purpose of testing his credibility. Noticing his peculiar accent, Mr Smith asked:

> Where were you in England? — I was never there. [An insulting question]
> Not with that rich accent? — No.
> Where were you? — In Scotland.
> What were you there? — A carpenter, and then I joined the police force.

Despite the defence lawyer's gruelling attack on Ralph as a credible witness he had been unable to show that the evidence of the police recruits was untrue and the defendant was ordered to pay ten pounds in costs (*The Advertiser*, 1913).

After a brief spell as a police officer, Ralph, aged 27, joined the 10th Infantry Battalion at Oaklands recruitment centre in Adelaide on 29 December 1914. He embarked on *HMAT Honorata* from Adelaide on 20 April 1915 for Gallipoli, where he suffered shrapnel wounds to his foot and thigh in August 1915 and was transferred to a general hospital in Ghezireh, Egypt. After recovery he was transferred to the 50th Battalion in February 1916.

In the spring of 1917, the First Anzac Corps planned to attack the Hindenburg Line and move towards the village of Bullecourt in northern France. The Hindenburg Line was the last and strongest of the German Army's defence and consisted of three well-defended trench systems, established in the winter of 1916–1917 on the Western Front from Arras to Laffaux. Ralph was part of the 13th Brigade that attacked Noreuil, a heavily defended outpost village, north-east of Bapaume. He suffered fatal wounds to the chest on the day of attack, 2 April 1917. Ralph was buried at the Bapaume Australian Cemetery. The battle for Bullecourt cost 10,000 Australian casualties.

Dr Roger Freeman compiled a memorial history of the 50th Battalion, *Hurcombe's hungry half hundred*. As well as excellent descriptions of the battles, he included a large number of photos and extracts from letters and diary notes of soldiers. He came across a photo of Ralph and his sister Mary, and my great-grandfather Adam, taken while Ralph was on leave in Scotland. With no letters passed on by Ralph, this was a welcome finding. But more important in memory of Ralph was to realise we could claim the Gallipoli medallion.

On a serendipitous note, the photo of Ralph that Dr Freeman passed on, showed him with a distinctive nose, a distinguishing feature which enabled me identify him with confidence on the front row of his battalion, from an enlarged photo displayed on a pillar at the entrance to Adelaide's Torrens Parade Ground from Victoria Drive.

I think of Ralph and the sacrifice he made as a young settler. I wonder, too, if we had exchanged places, would I have joined up as a volunteer when war broke up. From the accounts I had read, young men could not wait to fight the enemy. Moral pressure would have been a great influence.

There was also a sense of adventure, a strong sense of affiliation with the British Empire and pride in King and country. The poster of Lord Kitchener with his finger pointing at the viewer saying 'Your country needs you' was a powerful persuader.

Perhaps I would have succumbed and joined, but in the hindsight of later years I would not have gone to war. Knowing of the folly in going to Gallipoli and the senseless loss of life and the futility of a protracted trench war, who, in their right mind, would go to war? But that is not playing the game since we are all caught up in our own web of deception at the time, that war is honourable, patriotic and fulfilling with regard to a glorious outcome. And, of course, the sense of achievement and status on returning home.

The First World War seemed by all accounts a senseless one, its justification debated often by historians. In contrast, the Second World War appeared to have much greater moral justification with the invasion of first Poland, and then other European countries by Germany. Irrespective of the justication, we fall far short as Christians, or as a Christian nation, to Jesus Christ's teaching and commitment to non-violence. The battle for peace by peacemakers, like Mahatma Gandhi and Len Reid, will continue to be a long and hard fought one.

The TV news provided our daily dose of Iraq bombings and the Israeli–Palestine conflict. What would the headline news be without the support of these countries? On one news broadcast the Iranian president came up with a novel idea by stating, 'We are going to wipe Israel off the face of the world.' But that was a one off. Iraq would be back on the number one spot the next day.

With regard to Israel, I continued to follow its progress but became disillusioned with Israeli efforts to establish peace and to promote a homeland for those who had been evicted from their homes in Israel's territory. About 150 settlements in the West Bank accounted for more than 600,000 settlers. The settlements were in violation of the Fourth Geneva Convention, which stated that an occupying power shall not deport or transfer parts of its own civilian population into the territory it occupies.

With the increase of Israeli settlements on land that was not allocated to them under the agreement for a Jewish home, and the violent and reactive stance against Palestinian extremism, there seemed no hope for either a one-state or two-state solution. The two-state solution had become even less likely with the growing number of Israelis taking up residence in formerly owned Palestinian land.

For a while it seemed as though the Americans had gone into hibernation, but with the loss of more than 2,000 US military servicemen, they began to realise the extent of Bush's folly. The casualty figures and the devastation from hurricanes stirred up people's slumbering state. Questions were asked about the slow, disorganised response to these catastrophes and to the rising casualties and cost of the Iraq War.

Back on home ground, our 38th anniversary on 28 October 2005 arrived with Liz never losing her charm, grace and her loving ways. We celebrated with a blustery walk along the beach from Grange jetty to Sempahore jetty.

Rachel, our daughter, gave me a pep talk about earning and saving money for retirement, and staying in our own home as long as possible. I taunted her by saying that we would all go to the Greek Islands in June. 'No way,' she responded, 'Mr Never-travel-again.'

A week later, Rachel seemed sure about a life with George, but her interests would be curtailed like travelling plans for a 6-month adventure with her friend Nikki to Asian countries which included Mongolia, Thailand, Vietnam and India. I dared not say 'yes' or 'no' for a life with George; she had to make up her own mind. She gave me some advice, though, when I must have bemoaned my financial situation. She reminded me of all our blessings — a house, two lovely daughters, a lovely wife, career, travel to many countries, friends, fitness and health. 'You have been very blessed by God,' she said. 'Never mind the money factor.' A daughter's wisdom.

Five months before my official retirement started I split my week into three: volunteering at the Gawler Visitor Information Centre, the Gawler Volunteer Resource Centre, and refugee visitation through the Australian Refugee Centre.

On 7 November 2005, it was visitation day, but I stayed at home with a cold; anyway, I couldn't compete with Donald Rumsfield. Neither could the town council workers who had to close shop. And the traffic was all diverted from the cavalcade route. Like a knight in shining armour he pranced through our streets. The war protesters were out in force, thronging the steps of Parliament House. Rumsfield would not have taken any notice — he had the hide of a rhinoceros, after what he had fouled up in Iraq. An inane comment came from foreign minister Alexander Downer: 'He's good for Adelaide: it will showcase Adelaide.' The headlines could have been the next day: 'Spokesperson for weapons of mass deception comes to Adelaide.'

Two weeks later, Dad celebrated his 89th birthday on 20 November. I wasn't sure how Dad survived to eighty-nine. He had been through shell shock from the Second World War, suffered from depression, anxiety attacks, fear of the unknown, especially death, and a host of medical complaints — angina, diabetes, giddiness, being prone to falling (not a medical condition but could lead to one), insomnia, sickness during the night, heartburn and digestive disorders. I wished Dad all the best for his 90th year.

Later, George and Rachel discussed the possibility of a life together. In furthering his cause, he said, 'I'm intelligent, a good business manager ... and I'm humble too.' Rachel could not suppress her laughter. She always saw the funny side with her Monty Python sense of humour. She decided.

Rachel had always wanted a simple low-cost wedding and she would have had her way if the wedding had been held in Adelaide. George's sister, Anna, caught wind of the Adelaide venue and said she couldn't attend because she would be flying to Adelaide when she had just given birth to twins. So Rachel and George conceded to having the wedding in Darwin.

The next snag was the Greek monk who imposed a number of conditions for the marriage in Darwin. His uncompromising attitude offended Rachel. 'No trouble,' said George. 'We can easily fly up a Greek priest we know from Adelaide.' Fortunately, the Greek monk in Darwin didn't object and the wedding ceremony could take place in the Greek Orthodox Church.

George, his family of four sisters and two brothers, and extended family of more than 150, attended the wedding. The original family had come out from the Greek island of Kalymnos in the late 1950s. Many of the Kalymnians were sponge divers living a harsh sea existence for several months of the year. The Kalymnians had suffered from the hands of the Ottoman Empire and then from the Italians, Germans, and even the British.

With an engineering degree from Adelaide University, George had his own construction company based in Darwin. His father, Iricles, had been in the building trade since coming to Darwin. George's mother, Irene, confided that there had been a number of girls in George's life, each keen to settle down with him. 'George was not interested in any of them until Rachel appeared on the scene,' she said. From our point of view Rachel and George seemed well-matched with George having a friendly, easy-going manner, as well as being a hard worker in his building business.

The celebrations started two days before the wedding with a bed-warming party. The bed was freshly made with new linen. Women sang traditional Greek songs after scattering petals, rice and money on the bed. The men sat outside on the patio drinking ouzo.

On the eve of the wedding, George's friends held a buck's party. Andrew, Linda's husband, organised the sound system and some music. He kept tight control over his sound equipment, but things got out of hand when one of George's brothers tried to play his own music. When Andrew refused to let him near the console, he punched Andrew on the head. Andrew fell to the ground. He then staggered to his feet, gathered all his sound gear and stormed out of the house leaving everyone music-less.

On the day of the wedding Rachel looked stunning in her ivory wedding dress and George looked stunned after the night before. A pre-gathering at a honeymoon villa with a tropical garden and crystal waterfalls was the best part of the wedding for Rachel and her friends. Lots of cheer and champagne flowed.

We arrived in a chauffer-driven limousine at the Greek Orthodox Church. As we briefly assembled at the church entrance I handed over Rachel to George. The couple then walked slowly down the aisle while the guests followed (the opposite to our custom). The Greek priest, Father Con, in a flowing black robe and outer white vestment that encircled his enormous girth and flopped at his feet, welcomed everyone as we took our place. Rachel, George, Linda and George's aunt and uncle stood for the next hour with their backs to us and facing Father Con as he conducted the wedding ceremony. We understood very little, as it was mostly in Greek. For us it was a ritualised, impersonalised and incomprehensible service. For light entertainment there was the swapping of halos and a three-times walk around a table.

Father Con chanted from time to time. To Rachel it sounded like a Gregorian chant and she couldn't help laughing as she recalled her zany Gregorian chanting sessions with me at home. Father Con noticed her amusement and acknowledged her hilarity with frequent smiles, none of which fitted in with the solemnity of the traditional Greek occasion. I wondered what was going on with this mirth swapping — it didn't make sense until Rachel explained it to us later.

After the wedding there were lots of shaking of hands — probably about 150 times as the guests lined up to wish Rachel and George the best and to congratulate the parents and parents-in-law.

Then after all the photos we headed to Pee Wee's restaurant, a popular nighttime venue with an idyllic coastal outlook for watching the sunset over Darwin Harbour.

We enjoyed the lavish finger food followed by barramundi and fillet steak, and accompanied by red and white wine. At our table were George's mother and father, and Maria, his sister. Nearby at the bridal table were a lively Rachel and Linda, a stoned-looking George and the best man. The five-tiered ivory wedding cake stood close to one end of the bridal table. George could have easily knocked it over with his 'Leaning Tower of Pisa' state.

There was no master of ceremonies — George had forgotten to arrange one or had not thought it important. So there were no speeches at this stage.

After dinner, Rachel and George took to the dance floor for the bridal waltz and then invited others to join in. Liz and I danced, and most of Rachel's friends, but the Greek side declined to dance to Rachel's selection of music. A little later, with Greek music, most joined in. But, unfortunately, the power unit packed in — blowing up from a combination of high volume intensity and a covering that had been mysteriously placed over it. For the second time in two days, Andrew was annoyed, but he kept his cool and promised to return with another unit as soon as possible.

In the interlude of no music, Rachel, George and I gave speeches and that seemed to have a calming effect. I said how loving Rachel was and that she often came home to stay with us. The only problem was that she brought everything home with her, including a two-metre long piece of driftwood that she had picked up from the beach. Rachel found beauty in the most unusual of things and strangest of people. I stopped short of making any analogy with George.

After the speeches Andrew arrived back with a new power unit to play Greek music. This was really what saved the reception. Without Greek dancing there could be no celebration. Long live Zorba! Somehow we all kept our cool till midnight when the limousine arrived to signal the end of all festivities. Rachel remarked that it had been the most stressful day of her life.

That was my first experience of a Greek wedding. 'A colourful and eventful day! And some upsets,' I remarked to Father Con who had been at the reception.

'That's life,' he said as he shrugged his shoulders.

While George and Rachel set off to Tasmania for their honeymoon, Andrew and wee Jackson invited me to go on a fishing trip in Darwin Harbour. As we passed close to Mandorah on Cox Peninsula, Andrew dropped anchor to check his fishing gear. The boat pitched and heaved too much for my stomach. One of Andrew's mates suggested I look at the horizon, but that didn't work, so I jumped overboard — I was passed caring about stinging box jellyfish, sharks and crocs. We were near land and I made my way back to Darwin by a ferry.

Neighbours

Back in Gawler we caught up with our neighbours who were of the same vintage. Kay, next door, walks with Liz each day. I walk in Dead Man's Pass Reserve, opposite our home, and meet up with local walkers and their dogs.

Who was the dead man? The name of the reserve came from a man who died in the pass in 1839. Colonel William Light, South Australia's first surveyor-general, who surveyed Adelaide and Gawler, came across the dead man in the hollow of a tree, having known of his demise from a previous party that met the man before he passed away. No one knew who he was — a runaway sailor, perhaps, or even a bushranger. In memory of him, I wrote the following poem:

> As misty vapours waft the air
> and dewy blades of dawn
> drip forth their pearly sheen,
> raucous calls ring out
> from atop majestic boughs

The Pass awakens
to autumnal scent,
kookaburra laughter gives way
to dulcet sounds of warblers soft
in orchestral suite

With well-trod paths of tarnished red,
and mallee stems of lacquered brown
look down from slopes on lofty gums,
some gnarled and bare, yet some
so flush with foliage flare,
guard the dense rush watercourse

Flowering gums host humming bees
and parrots search for titbits rare,
willy wagtails create a stir
and magpies strut and shrill the air,
a friendly call, and frisky dogs
race round and round in playful yelp
while owners meet in carefree watch

This peaceful scene dreams on and on
when once there was no hope for one
who passed this way in summer heat
and faded from this earth to toil
his soul rests now to savour all
in Dead Man's Pass.

Kay and Allan Evans are our next door neighbours. Allan had fought with the British forces in Malaya against the communist insurgents in the 1960s and suffered post-war trauma.

Wayne Clarke, our other next door neighbour, had fought in the Vietnam War, which impacted adversely on him and his wife, Margaret, and family. He campaigned for full recognition of Vietnam veterans for their sacrifice and bravery.

We had neighbours, too, who suffered from manic depression or bipolar disorder. One reminded me of my brother, Frank. I worried about his mental health and that he might take his life. The right kind of help seemed to be lacking for those who suffered from serious mental health issues. Suicide had become a major health problem in Australia with about 8 to 10 suicides every day, more common than motor vehicle accidents as a cause of death for Australian men.

I wondered if it was the same for Aboriginal communities. In the *Weekend Australian*, with an article entitled 'Worse than Somalia for remote blacks', it certainly appeared that way with the findings of a senior bureaucrat who had spent the past year in the Mutitjulu community in Central Australia. Passive welfare fuelled the worst. No other group, it seemed, in the Australian community rivalled the desperation and plight of the Aboriginal people. The health of a nation did not depend only upon the mental and physical health of individuals in the community but also on the bonding contribution, support and linking together of one another to create purposeful lives and livelihoods. Promoting our community health and even our spiritual well-being — that was the challenge. How do we bring the depressed back into society through capacity building?

In the not-so-lucky Australia, we learned that in any one year, around one million Australian adults have depression, half a million have bipolar and over two million suffer from anxiety.

Dad and Mandy

Every few months I would fly to Brisbane and see Dad, and Mandy who was still part-time nursing in an aged care home. When Dad was fit enough we walked around the bays near Wynnum, not far from Nazareth House — the Catholic residential care facility that looked after him.

Then at the age of 92, Dad died on 12 May 2009. Mandy watched him slowly decline in health — it was remarkable that he had lived so long, given his medical history and his battle with depression. How much could be attributed to the Second World War, we didn't know, but it seemed like a major part. Dad was the last surviving member of the 6th Battalion of the Seaforth Highlanders. Gordon Baxter of Baxters of Speyside always regarded Dad not only as a successful salesman and export manager but also as a loyal friend. I felt sad for Dad that he could not find a way through his depression.

Mandy and I have kept in regular contact with each other since Dad died. She has battled through the debilitating effects of hepatitis B, contracted while she was a nursing sister at Ernabella aboriginal community. Leaving her demanding role in a Brisbane aged care home, she became a foot reflexologist. I have valued her sisterly friendship, although she has put me in my place from time to time. Her sense of humour has always put a lighter tone on serious matters.

Jumping forward

In April 2014, we visited friends, Joan and Vern, in Whitianga, on the eastern side of the Coromandel Peninsular in the North Island of New Zealand, staying a few days at their bed and breakfast holiday home. We discovered that Captain Cook had come there to observe the transit of Mercury in 1769 — commemorated by a cairn at Cook's Beach which told his story.

Then at Mercury Bay at Whitianga we found out that HMS *Buffalo*, the first ship bringing settlers to South Australia in 1836, had sunk in 1840. Artefacts from the ship were on display at a local museum. We also stayed with friends Sonia and Reg, in Tauranga; they had moved from Gawler to this popular town, in the Bay of

Plenty on the east coast. Reg was adamant that living expenses there were far cheaper for retirement than in Australia.

I spent May 2014 at the Harbin University of Engineering in north-east China helping out again with the editing of scientific papers written in Chinglish. Over seven years of assistance I would have edited more than 400 papers.

Coming up to 75, Liz and I are in full demand as grandparents supporting Rachel with Eva and Iraklis, and Linda with Jackson, Ruby and Jade, as they are both struggling mostly on their own to raise the children while their husbands, George and Andrew, work in their construction and electronics businesses in Darwin.

Rachel is doing her utmost for Iraklis (5) to help with his sensory issues. Rachel's Eva (8) has highs and lows with being bright and bubbly one moment and in the dumps the next. She's quite a performer on stage and a real drama queen at times.

Linda seems able to meet any challenge ahead with an indomitable spirit. Jackson (13) is a fine, sensitive lad and loves go karting and making films — could be the start of a career. Ruby (11) is a dreamer and cries on your shoulders from time to time, especially with maths problems. She loves her dolls, bunnies, dancing and writing. Jade (9) Irish-steps everywhere, even in the kitchen. She performed very well in Irish dancing for her age group at a national competition in Sydney. Her lithesome body flits over the dance floor like a fairy.

Liz is holding up very well despite her medical conditions of osteoporosis and osteoarthritis. She loves her roses and herb garden. Her brother, Jonathan, who did not fare well growing up in a boys institution, is planning to marry a Balinese woman. Perhaps we will take part in the Balinese wedding.

We try to keep up with friends in Adelaide and further afield. From time to time I go bushwalking in the Barossa Ranges and the Adelaide Hills.

With more than 50 years in Australia, the most treasured time has been with Liz, who has not lost any of her love, warmth and friendliness from when we first met nearly 49 years ago.

On 30 April 2016, with the close of these memoirs, I celebrated my 75th birthday — 52 years out of Scotland. I took Ruby to her roller skating class in the morning. With the poise of a professional she moved gracefully around the floor. Back at our place she wanted to play 'school' in which I was the student and she the teacher, or principal if I didn't perform. With the aid of a whiteboard she outlined my tasks for the day — no let off for a birthday. And no time off for recess if I spoke out of turn. 'Although you are 75, you still have a lot to learn,' she said. What a teacher in the making!

Later, Linda arrived with Jade, who had achieved a second overall placing in an Adelaide Irish dancing competition. Jackson joined in, too, for the birthday party, which was topped off with a marble cake and Persian love cake, courtesy of Liz and assistant chef, Ruby. After, we gathered at the piano for a singalong of our favourites. A perfect birthday! Rachel, George, Eva and Iraklis were on a weekend beachside holiday so we would catch up for a mini-celebration later.

Chapter 29

On reflection

I HAVE BEEN VERY FORTUNATE to meet all kinds of people, of different backgrounds, ethnicities and religious persuasions. People help shape who we are, and over the years I have realised how important they have been in my life. I am very thankful to my family and people I have met on my way. I value especially my Scottish education, with the encouragement of Ms Stewart in primary school to help lay a foundation that would allow me to go to Aberdeen University, and to work in Australia and other parts of the world.

I believe we are all on a spiritual journey — one of faith more than sight. If we choose, we can respond to the light we receive. We can also reflect that light and become like lighthouses. Or we can stray from that light, but, ultimately, we cannot sidestep our creative destiny. We can never opt out of our creation because God created us. Life remains with us always even when we leave the physical body. So, we can always choose light or darkness. The purpose of punishment, I believe, will always be remedial.

For me, Jesus Christ offers a way for God to meet us as we are, and not to earn our way. Being and becoming are more important than doing and accomplishing in this sense. With the right attitude and faith — the working of a spiritual force — we open up a free pathway to God's power.

I am very thankful for the gift of life. For me, it's amazing to realise that we have this gift, to appreciate the wonder of creation, to be a part of that creation, to search out and discover, to realize our identity and recreate ourselves, to share and help others along their journey, all in a moment of time, it seems, of earth's lifetime of a few billion years.

Dare we go through life and ignore the signposts altogether? Most people have enough twists and turns in their lives to allow them to ask a few pertinent questions about the true essence of life and what might be an appropriate response. Following the right signpost can lead to a discovery of our spiritual destiny — a plan for each person according to their make-up and peculiar part to play in the scheme of things.

Dare we learn from our circumstances and yield to our spiritual nature to explore the truth for our lives — a plan unfolding and expressing God's love? And dare we let faith — the key to life — grow as we expose ourselves to challenges? In God, I believe, we realise our being, our place and our destiny. We become the person we are meant to be in a rich and fulfilling way.

Looking back, I could never have planned my life's journey, and all the opportunities that opened up, for which I am thankful to God. Australia has been good to me in opening up an agricultural career. That led to going to developing countries, often war-torn ones. I landed on the front line with the fight against drugs, met with those who struggled to eke out a living and survive, worked with refugees in desperate plight, and known those in Australia who have struggled against post-war trauma, depression and mental illness, as well as friends who committed suicide. To share with people in these different types of hardship and trauma puts a focus on life, I found, that cuts to the core of our existence.

On a global level, I believe we must climb down from our rapacious perch and seek a simpler, interconnected and sustainable lifestyle. Over-exploitation of resources, the gap between the rich and poor, population pressures, the refugee crisis, pollution of the environment, the powerful and the powerless, and climate change will all meet headlong to bring people together; otherwise, we fall as one. The survival of the human race is at stake.

With warring conflicts threatening to destabilise our world, we need to find a way to peace, to emphasise sharing, compassion and coexisting responsibly with one another and nature, and, ideally, to embrace a spiritual dynamism of love rather than hate.

To quote Burns:

> For a' that, an' a that,
> It's coming yet for a that,
> That Man to Man, the world o'er,
> Shall brothers be for a' that.

Maybe one day, when all the world can make music together, like Dr Sarmast's Music School in Afghanistan, the world will be a different place; to hear the music of life rather than the drum beat of war.

Printed in the United States
By Bookmasters